Responding to Conflict in Africa

Responding to Conflict in Africa

The United Nations and Regional Organizations

Edited by

Jane Boulden

palgrave
macmillan

RESPONDING TO CONFLICT IN AFRICA

First published in 2013 by
PALGRAVE MACMILLAN®
in the United States—a division of St. Martin's Press LLC,
175 Fifth Avenue, New York, NY 10010.

Where this book is distributed in the UK, Europe and the rest of the world, this is by Palgrave Macmillan, a division of Macmillan Publishers Limited, registered in England, company number 785998, of Houndmills, Basingstoke, Hampshire RG21 6XS.

Palgrave Macmillan is the global academic imprint of the above companies and has companies and representatives throughout the world.

ISBN: 978–1–137–27199–0 (paperback)

ISBN: 978–1–137–27200–3 (hardcover)

Library of Congress Cataloging-in-Publication Data is available from the Library of Congress.

A catalogue record of the book is available from the British Library.

Design by Newgen Imaging Systems (P) Ltd., Chennai, India.

First edition: May 2013

10 9 8 7 6 5 4 3 2 1

Contents

Illustrations

Figures

Tables

Maps

Acknowledgments

First, I would like to express my deep thanks to the authors represented in this volume. Singly and together they have provided very strong contributions to this book and to the field of study as a whole. I am grateful for their willingness to be part of the project and their patience with the process that got us to the final product.

Most of the authors were able to present the early drafts of their chapters at a workshop made possible through the generous funding of the Social Sciences and Humanities Research Council (SSHRC). I am grateful to the Queen's University Centre for International and Defence Policy in Kingston Ontario, and particularly Professor Kim Nossal and Maureen Bartram. I am grateful for their support on this and other projects. Thanks are also due to a number of other experts in the field who came to the workshop, some of them from great distances, to provide feedback on the initial drafts and the project as a whole.

Alayna Jay played a crucial role in helping with the final editing process. Dr. Andrea Charron made the whole thing possible through her enthusiasm, organizational prowess, and friendship.

Finally, a special vote of thanks is due to Chris Chappell and Sarah Whalen at Palgrave Macmillan. Sarah was consistently patient and supportive at times when alternative reactions would have been entirely justified. Chris pushed past my initial reluctance to consider this project and prompted me to give the idea serious consideration with the resulting product that is before you now.

Introduction

Jane Boulden

This is effectively the second edition of *Dealing with Conflict in Africa: The United Nations and Regional Organizations*, published in 2003. The word "effectively" is used because the subject in question has undergone a remarkable change in the ten years since the first publication. What began as a revised and updated version of the original quickly became quite a different book. That said, readers will find some of the same authors and some chapters that carry cases forward the earlier edition. They will also find a number of new case studies, reflecting the wide range of new activity in this area. As an author and editor, this is both good news and bad news. The good news is that the depth and scope of the new activity along with the addition of another ten years of experience provide an opportunity for greater analytical depth. The bad news is that this means that conflict in Africa continues to persist as a significant challenge for actors at every level.

The purpose of this book, as with the first, is to examine the issues and experiences associated with the increased level of activity between the United Nations (UN) and regional organizations in carrying out international peace and security tasks and to do so with a particular focus on Africa.

Why study this issue? After the end of the Cold War and in the wake of the successful UN-sponsored military campaign to liberate Kuwait from Iraq, the UN Security Council asked the Secretary-General to provide it with a report outlining the ways in which the UN might deal with international peace and security issues in the new environment created by those two events. The result, *An Agenda for Peace*, put forward a number of proposals for new and resuscitated mechanisms for dealing with conflict. Among them was a suggestion that UN draw on the support of regional organizations as a way of spreading the burden of UN efforts to deal with conflict. The Secretary-General argued that greater cooperation with regional organizations could help lighten the burden of the Security Council as it sought to deal with the numerous conflicts now on its agenda, while also strengthening and democratizing UN efforts to deal with conflict.[1] Regional organizations were also perceived to offer certain advantages in carrying out regional conflict-management tasks. As they are of the region, regional organizations bring strong background knowledge and existing personal and professional contacts to the process, permitting an ease of access and an ability to exert pressure that may not be available to the UN. For that reason, their involvement may seem less intrusive and be more welcome than that of the UN. And, because they are the first to be affected by

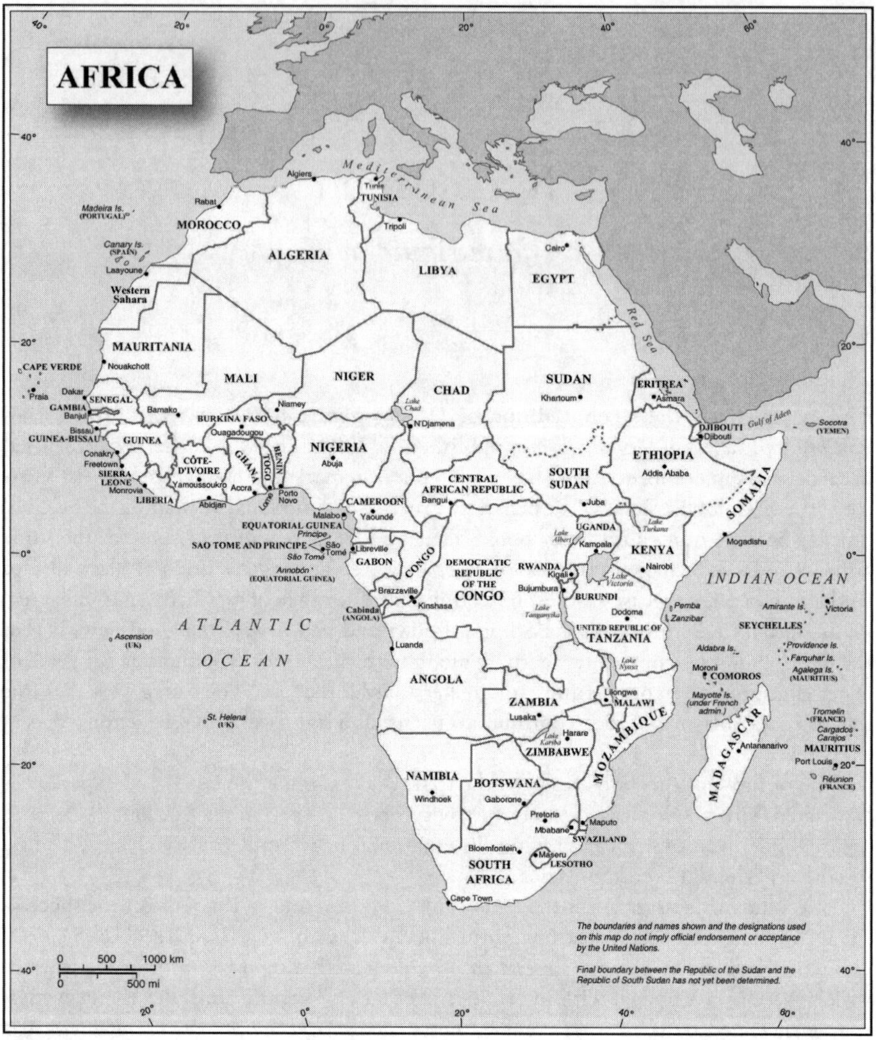

Source: Map No 4045 Rev 7, United Nations, Department of Field Support, Cartographic Section, November 2011

the conflict in question, they are more likely to generate the political will necessary to take immediate measures to deal with the conflict.

The Secretary-General's proposal received general support but little in the way of thorough analysis before it was put into practice in various ways in both Europe and Africa, drawing regional organizations into largely undefined relationships with the UN in the midst of difficult and contentious efforts to deal with serious conflicts within their regions. Since then, the international community has acquired considerable and varied experience in regional–global cooperation in conflict-response environments. The wealth of activity in this area, in turn, has generated a wide range of research on these issues. The resulting literature falls into various categories. Case study–centered work tends to be focused on the experiences of regional organizations, or the UN, or on conflict in Africa. This is a rich set of sources, many of which are referenced in the case study chapters. Another group examines the question of UN–regional cooperation in peacekeeping[2] but it is rare that it is based on a wide range of in-depth case studies.[3] Similarly, there is an increasing body of work focused on regional organizations in Africa but as with the literature on UN–regional cooperation, this area of work tends to focus on specific issues or cases.[4] This book is offered in an effort to fill that gap and to record and analyze the developments of the ten years since the earlier edition.

Why focus on Africa? First, because Africa is the region in which the assumptions and ideas associated with cooperative efforts between regional organizations and the UN have been most tested. Even while *An Agenda for Peace* was being written, the Economic Community of West African States (ECOWAS) was engaging in its first intervention in Liberia. ECOWAS went on to be significantly involved in a number of regional conflicts and has become the most experienced regional conflict-response actor on the continent and arguably beyond. Other regional organizations in Africa have followed their lead and become involved in conflicts on a number of occasions and in a number of different ways. These developments have been joined by the arrival of the African Union (AU) with a new and expansive mandate for international peace and security activity. There is, therefore, some significant experience to draw on here. Since that experience involves more than one regional organization, differing relationships with the UN, and different types of conflicts, the African case studies have the potential to generate conclusions based on a comparative assessment. In addition, for those advocating a greater role for regional organizations in international peace and security, Africa is the region that has been held out as the one with the most to gain from such a development. The argument is that involving regional organizations in conflict management provides an opportunity for local actors to have greater input into the conflict-management process—an "African solutions for African problems" approach—and to strengthen themselves in the process. An examination of the actual experience of these joint endeavors, therefore, will provide an opportunity to test these assumptions.

Second, the nature of the UN's experience in Africa has had an enduring and significant impact on the way in which the UN has dealt with conflict generally in the post–Cold War period. The impact of the UN's withdrawal from Somalia, followed by its failure in Rwanda has been considerable. An awareness of the high price of failure has affected many aspects of UN operations since and has been one of the main reasons behind various efforts to rethink the way in which the UN deals with international peace and security. The impact of Somalia and Rwanda was also evident in the ways in which Western states have responded to conflict generally. Here, in contrast to the UN, we can trace a pattern of general retrenchment on the part of Western states.

The third reason for the focus on Africa is that the UN's efforts to deal with conflict in Africa continue to generate mixed results at best. Failures and as yet unfinished efforts far outweigh success stories. Africa continues to struggle with long-standing, intractable conflicts whose continuation is a testament to the international community's inability to deal adequately with these situations. By anybody's count, the African continent is the source of the majority of the world's ongoing conflict. The imperative to develop and strengthen the international community's ability to deal with conflict more appropriately and efficiently is justified on this basis alone.

As with the first edition, the book's focus is on the context and nature of UN–regional organization interaction in Africa. To that end, the book examines three interrelated aspects of the issue: what has been said and done at the institutional level on these issues at the UN, what has been said and done by African regional organizations, and what has happened in practice in African conflict situations that have involved both regional organizations and the UN. While the case study authors were directed to ensure that they covered these three elements, they were not bound to a specific format. There are four case studies that are covered in both editions. The chapters in this edition of the book tell the whole story of the case but provide more detail and analysis on what has occurred since the last book was published. Readers interested in those cases are encouraged to read the chapters from both editions together. Whether revised and updated from the earlier edition or new in this volume, in order to trace the three themes of analysis the case studies provide a rich and deep accounting of the conflicts themselves. In addition to the UN–regional story, therefore, the case studies represent a stand-alone contribution to the case study literature associated with conflict in Africa.

The idea of the book is to engage in a comparison of the theory and the rhetoric with the practice, the actual experience on the ground. Such an assessment will help address a number of related questions that fall roughly into three categories. What can we learn, first about the role of regional organizations in conflict situations, second about the role of the UN, and third, on the basis of the first two, what do we learn about the nature of the relationship between regional organizations and the UN based on the African experience?

By way of establishing the broader theoretical and practical context in which the case studies are situated, the first section of the book deals with overall themes and institutions. My own chapter lays out what has been occurring at the institutional level at the UN by providing an overview of the Security Council debate on Africa and on the idea of greater cooperation with regional organizations. The purpose here is to document as well as analyze the UN approach, with a view to establishing the rhetorical markers against which actions taken can be measured. Chapters 2 and 3 examine the institutional developments and experiences of African regional organizations. The AU was newly created when the first edition went to press. Chapter 2's exclusive focus on its role is an indication of the extent to which the changed organization and mandate has made the AU a critical player in a very short period of time. In chapter 4, Andrea Charron examines the ways in which institutions, both UN and regional, have made new use of sanctions as a tool in their response to conflict, giving new insights into the ways in which regional organizations are taking the lead on some normative issues.

The second section of the book contains nine case studies. The case study choice was derived from a list of all African conflict situations from which those with both UN and regional organization involvement were chosen. The basic requirement for inclusion in the book was that both the UN and regional organizations were involved in the response to the conflict in a reasonably significant way. This generated a spectrum of cases ranging from the obvious choices (Darfur and Côte d'Ivoire, for example) to the less obvious choices, such as Chad and the Central African Republic (CAR). Within that group, the extent of regional and UN involvement varies across cases ranging from major operations over lengthy periods of time to more distant and sporadic involvement.

Similarly, regional actions vary from ad hoc regional efforts, as in Burundi, to sustained intensive institutional involvement as in the West African cases. The arrival of the AU on the scene means that in a number of cases, there are at least two regional actors on the scene, adding a new level of complexity, and sometimes complication, to the regional–global equation.

A valid concern is the extent to which these case studies will provide a solid enough foundation for useful comparison. Though often treated otherwise, African conflicts are widely varied, the international community's response to them also varies, and regional organizations within Africa differ considerably in their raison d'etre and their capabilities. As with any investigative enterprise, there are inherent difficulties here. The case studies do not fit into tidy packages that present themselves for direct comparison. Regions and conflicts do not exist in isolation; they overlap and interconnect. Regional organizations differ considerably in their mandates, capabilities, and area of application. Indeed, an agreed definition of what constitutes a regional organization remains elusive.[5] In part, this is a function of the difficulties inherent in defining what constitutes a region, a problem amply demonstrated by the African situation. The AU involves all African states except Morocco and for all intents and purposes it is a "regional" organization. The literature in this field often refers to other regional institutional entities in Africa as subregional organizations, although this term is primarily a geographical distinction based on the existence of a continental organization in the form of the AU rather than a term that indicates any major functional distinction between regional and subregional organizations.

The framers of the UN Charter quite deliberately chose to avoid defining regional organizations in the Charter because of fears that such a definition would restrict inclusion and would lend itself to politically motivated interpretations as to what organizations qualified as such for the purposes of the Charter.[6] Instead, the Charter refers simply to regional agencies or arrangements without defining the terms any further. Such terminology seems much better suited to the African experience than the term regional organization, as its comprehensiveness leaves open the possibility of ad hoc regional arrangements while still including more established institutional arrangements such as ECOWAS and the AU. Nonetheless, the Security Council and the Secretariat have moved to the use of "regional organization" as a blanket term for the wide range of regional actors now working on issues of international peace and security. This book follows that format. Any effort to define regional organization runs up against issues relating to the purpose, the degree of institutionalization, and the nature of decision making in these organizations. While such factors are important determinants in analyzing the role of regional organizations, they are not critical in determining whether or not a given organization warrants examination for the purposes of this study. As the focus in this book is on the roles and relationships of regional entities, a functionally oriented approach is taken. Regional organizations are considered to be multistate geographically synchronous institutional entities that have played or are playing a role in conflict situations in Africa.

In order to fully understand the nature and implications of regional organization and UN involvement, the case studies provide considerable background and discussion of the events and decisions made in the conflicts in question. The case studies reflect the nature of the conflicts they address in that they should not be read in isolation. The chapters on Darfur and South Sudan should be read together and are fundamentally connected to the chapter on CAR and Chad. The Burundi and Democratic Republic of Congo chapters link to one another as do all of the West African cases. In dealing with conflict-related analyses, there are inevitably a number of major themes that play a role and there is no shortage of them here. The impact of colonialism and decolonization, attitudes about sovereignty and statehood, attitudes of Western states toward Africa, the role of ethnicity, and the internal political dynamics of the conflicts are all touched on in the case studies in various ways. This is not, however, a book about the sources of conflict in Africa or the desirability (or undesirability) of international intervention in those conflicts. The focus remains fixed on the involvement of the UN and regional organizations, their interaction (or lack thereof), their individual and joint impact on the conflict, and what this tells us about their relationship and the practice of regional and international conflict management in Africa. In combination, the chapters paint a picture of intensive and sustained activity at the institutional and regional levels. This is itself remarkable. It was only twenty years ago that *An Agenda for Peace* raised the idea as one of a list of possibilities for new ways in which the UN might operate as it moved into the post–Cold War period.

What Does UN–Regional Cooperation Look Like?

In 1997, the UN Secretary-General spoke of a "new consensus that the primary responsibility for the solution of Africa's problems rests with Africans themselves." He suggested that "in place of interventionism" that consensus "promises a mature relationship based on mutual support and trust."[7] We are not there yet.

The practice of regional and UN actors in dealing with conflict (not just in Africa) remains ad hoc and reactive. Although it has been discussed as an objective, there is no formal structuring of the relationship and no allocation of roles, beyond the basic framework outlined in Chapter VIII of the UN Charter. Some general patterns, however, are discernible in the chapters that follow.

One of the assumed advantages of regional actors is that they are of the region and thus bring particular knowledge and connections to the table that may facilitate the conflict-resolution process. On the other hand, since they are of the region, the idea that they are devoid of political agendas relating to the outcome of the conflict is questionable. Yet, one of the unaddressed and unanswered questions implicit in the idea of UN–regional cooperation is the extent to which a certain level of impartiality or at least political distance is assumed or hoped for on the part of regional actors responding to conflict in their region. An assumption of no political distance has a number of implications for the politics of the process especially given the wide latitude of action available to regional organizations in the early stages of the conflict. Alternatively, an assumption that regional organizations will act with at least some political distance raises the question as to whether and how those on the receiving end perceive the position of the regional organization. This relates, in particular, to the practice of re-hatting troops on the ground from regional to UN missions. To what extent does this nuance factor into the thinking of parties to the conflict?

Regional actors have become regular first responders when it comes to conflict in Africa. As established in the first edition of this book, regional actors will move to fill the vacuum when other international actors do not respond to conflict. They do this regardless of whether they have an institutional mandate to do so and regardless of whether they have UN Security Council approval for operations that involve the use of force. When no one else is willing to step forward, regional actors advocate for help, provide mediation, put troops on the ground, and generally keep the process moving. They can be, as Gilbert Khadiagala tells us, "organized, persistent and patient." This means that regional organizations bear the brunt of the response burden militarily and politically.

As chapter 1 indicates, the idea of burden sharing was present in the early post–Cold War period when the idea of greater cooperation with regional organizations first gained traction. It continues to permeate the UN–regional relationship, as does the perception that burden sharing is really about burden shifting. This perception is compounded by the image of Western states prioritizing their commitments elsewhere and maintaining a risk adverse approach to conflict in Africa that took hold in the aftermath of the failed responses to Somalia and Rwanda in the early 1990s.

There are two compelling reasons why this matters. First, in relying on regional organizations to act as first responders, the UN may be contributing to prolonging the conflict. Given the lower levels of capacity available to African regional actors, they may be unable to impact the conflict in a decisive way, thus lengthening the time before some kind of agreement can be achieved and a UN response can be generated. This is not to imply that all conflicts should or could be resolved in the first instance by a military solution. However, it is possible that in some cases a stronger demonstration of or use of military capability might bring parties to the negotiating table sooner rather than later. If the Security Council's pattern of waiting for some form of peace or ceasefire agreement before authorizing a response is an effort to avoid involvement in a militarily imposed end to the violence, it begs the question as to why regional actors are better placed, politically or militarily, to do so.

Second, if the question of burden sharing is, at its base, about allocating a finite pool of conflict response resources, the idea that regions should take on a heavier load in their own region could eventually lead to regional disengagement from the relationship. If a region is carrying the bulk of the conflict-response burden on its own, why bother with the global level? Why engage in a partnership activity when it only applies to the burden of implementation and does not translate into any degree of ownership of the political process? In combination with the willingness of the Council to accept a wide latitude of regional military action without a Security Council mandate, especially when the region is in the first-responder mode, this could create a push toward greater disengagement in the partnership arrangement.

Does It Work?

When it works, regional–UN cooperation works well and in a variety of ways. For example, one actor can hand tasks off to the other when more or different pressure is needed on the parties to the conflict, when a task better suited to the other is required, or when one of the actors compromises its legitimacy in the process. However, the presence of multiple actors with multiple agendas sometimes undermines the prospects for progress and it certainly provides actors seeking to obstruct the process with multiple entry points to that objective. The existence of multiple actors also creates opportunities for forum shopping as a way to buy time or a better situation.

Whether at the regional or the UN level, it is the case that key actors in key positions can act as critical catalysts for both action and nonaction. These key actors fall into two categories: former colonial powers and hegemons, and Security Council members. The latter category includes the permanent members and also African nonpermanent members on the Council. There are a number of examples where African states on the Council had an impact on whether and how action was authorized. In 1990, a proposal to establish a peacekeeping force in response to the conflict in Liberia was rejected by the three sitting African states on the Council at the time. More recently, the tension between Nigeria and South Africa on the response to Cote d'Ivoire crisis contributed to a delay in Council decision making on a response to the crisis. Former colonial powers continue to play a role in a variety of ways in these situations such as the United Kingdom's rescue of the UN mission in Sierra Leone, and France's role in convincing Chad to accept UN forces and in the various stages of the Côte d'Ivoire crisis. Hegemonic powers from inside and outside the region can also have an impact on the course of events. The United States played an advocacy role in Darfur but was more hesitant in the early stages of the Liberian conflict. South Africa played an extremely positive role in Burundi, and Nigeria's role in the various West African crises is mixed. While the focus of this book is on regional–UN interaction, the impact of actors playing a role outside of those groupings, even while they play a role inside them means that not only are there multiple actors in this picture, but many of those actors are playing multiple roles.

Notes

1. The Secretary-General argued: "Regional organizations participating in complementary efforts with the United Nations in joint undertakings would encourage States outside the region to act supportively. And should the Security Council choose specifically to authorize a regional arrangement or organization to take the lead in addressing a crisis within its region, it could serve to lend the weight of the United Nations to the validity of the regional effort. Carried forward in the spirit of the Charter, and as envisioned in Chapter VIII, the approach outlined here could strengthen a general sense that democratization is being encouraged at all levels in the task of maintaining international peace and security, it being essential to continue to recognize that the primary responsibility will continue to reside in the Security Council." *An Agenda for Peace*, United Nations, June 1992, par. 65.
2. For a recent example, see Hikaru Yamashita, "Peacekeeping cooperation between the United Nations and regional organisations," *Review of International Studies* 38 (2012).
3. For an excellent study of UN peacekeeping operations in Africa, see Adekeye Adebajo, *UN Peacekeeping in Africa from the Suez Crisis to the Sudan Conflicts* (Boulder: Lynne Rienner, 2011).

4. As examples, see Emmanuel Fanta, "The Capacity of African Regional Organisations in Peace and Security," ERD Workshop: Transforming Political Structures: Security Institutions and Regional Integration Mechanisms, Florence 16–17 April 2009; Suyash Paliwal, "The Primacy of Regional Organizations in International Peacekeeping: The African Example," *Virginia Journal of International Law* 51 (2010); Marten Zwanenburg, "Regional Organisations and the Maintenance of International Peace and Security: Three Recent Regional African Peace Operations," *Journal of Conflict & Security Law* 11 (2006); Rosemary Durward, "Security Council Authorization for Regional Peace Operations: A Critical Analysis," *International Peacekeeping* 13 (2006).
5. For background on this debate, as well as on the debate about regionalism generally, see Louise Fawcett and Andrew Hurrell, eds., *Regionalism in World Politics, Regional Organization and International Order* (Oxford: Oxford University Press, 1995) and David A. Lake and Patrick M. Morgan, eds., *Regional Orders, Building Security in a New World* (University Park, PA: Pennsylvania State University Press, 1997).
6. For more on the background to Chapter VIII in the United Nations Charter, see Ruth B. Russell, *A History of the United Nations Charter* (Washington, DC: Brookings, 1958).
7. S/PV.3819, 26 September 1997, 5.

Part I

The UN and African Regional Organizations

Chapter 1

The United Nations Security Council and Conflict in Africa

Jane Boulden

Introduction

Two distinct and linked trends are evident in post–Cold War Security Council politics. The first is a drive, from inside and outside the Council, toward greater cooperation and interaction with regional actors and organizations in dealing with international peace and security. The second is a steady increase, with a few ebbs and flows, in Council discussion, debate, and actions on conflict in Africa. Africa is the source of some of the United Nations' (UN) most devastating experiences and most precious triumphs. That backdrop is the foundation of all of the analyses in this book. It is also the backdrop for this chapter, which focuses specifically on Security Council thinking and practice at the thematic level on the role of regional organizations and on conflict in Africa generally.

While the Security Council is the starting point, any examination of its activities involves other actors in the UN system. This is very much the case when it comes to these issues. The Security Council does not work in isolation, especially not on these issues. As the chapter indicates, the Secretary-General and the Secretariat play a vital role in providing information, moving Council thinking forward, and generating new ideas. Their work also links to that of the General Assembly and a wide range of ad hoc groups and panels established by UN actors to work on specific issues. Council activity is only one part of an extensive web of activity on regional and African issues but it provides the threads on which the rest of the activity rests.

The purpose of this chapter is not to establish a detailed outline of all of the various ideas and proposals that make their way to and through Council deliberations on conflict in Africa and cooperation with regional organizations. Rather, the goal is to outline and evaluate Security Council debate and actions in order to determine the trends in the Council's thinking on these questions as general or thematic issues. The chapter is thus intended as a complement to the case studies in the second section of the volume. In the first edition of this book, *Dealing with Conflict in Africa*, the overarching question addressed in this chapter was whether and how increased attention to cooperation with regional organizations might establish itself as a trend in Security Council work. Ten years later, the question is not whether that trend has taken hold—that is now clearly evident. The question is what the nature of that trend and the speed of its entrenchment mean for the Council, for the ways in which conflict in Africa is and should be addressed, and for global–regional relations more generally.

The first section of the chapter will outline and discuss in broad terms the practice of the Security Council in dealing with African conflict situations. The second section of the chapter will examine the debate that has occurred within the Security Council on this issue as part of a general increase in attention to thematic or general issues on the part of the Security Council in the post–Cold War period. It covers the linked but separate themes of conflict in Africa and greater cooperation in the UN–regional organization relationship. In the first edition of this book, one of the goals of this chapter was to determine if and in what way the Security Council was turning to regional organizations to deal with conflict in Africa. The answer then was yes. The ten years since then have not only confirmed this trend but have seen it substantially increase in just about every way. As a result, the discussion covered in this chapter reveals the Council working to manage the nature of the relationship while simultaneously being driven by external developments, such as the creation of the African Union (AU), and events on the ground, including the significantly increased level of activity on the part of regional organizations in response to conflict situations, especially in Africa.

UN Operations in Africa

General Characteristics

As of October 2012, of the sixty-seven total Security Council–authorized peace support operations,[1] thirty-one, or 46 percent, have occurred in Africa. Taking into account the fact that some conflict situations have been the subject of multiple operations, the thirty-one UN peace support operations carried out in Africa have addressed 16 conflict situations.[2] These figures correspond with other measures of Security Council attention to conflict in Africa. An analysis of Security Council meetings since 1994, outlined in Figure 1.1, shows that the percentage of Council meetings focused on African issues varies from a low of 29 percent in 1990 to a high of 56 percent in 2011, with a rough average of 45 percent over time.

Security Council resolutions tell a similar story, depicted graphically in Figure 1.2. From 1989 to 2011, the number of Security Council resolutions dealing with conflict issues in Africa has ranged from a low of 0.5 percent in the years 1990 and 1991 to a high of 66 percent in 2011, with a rough average of 50 percent over time.

Of all of the sixty-seven UN operations in Africa, only one operation occurred during the Cold War. This was not for a lack of situations that could have used a UN response, but is an indication of the degree to which both Africa and the UN Security Council

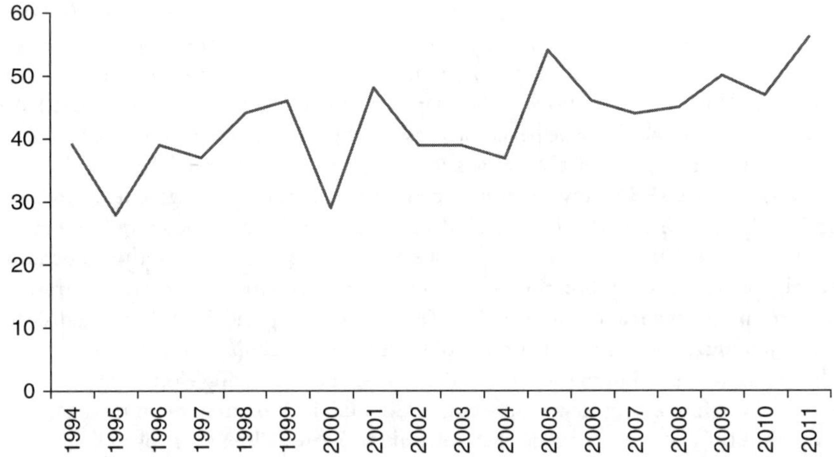

Figure 1.1 Security Council Meetings on African Conflict Issues as a Percentage of Total Meetings

Figure 1.2 Security Council Resolutions on African Conflict Issues as a Percentage of Total Resolution Numbers

were permeated by the effects of the Cold War. The exception to the UN's abstinence from Africa during the Cold War was the first UN operation in the Congo from 1960 to 1964. The Congo was one of the few places in Africa at that time that, until independence, remained outside of the Cold War struggle for influence in Africa. This fact contributed to the Soviet and US willingness to accept a UN operation there, if only as a way of buying time to ensure that the other side did not get a foothold there first.

While almost thirty years separate United Nations Force in the Congo (ONUC) from all of the later UN operations in Africa, the overall characteristics of the operation and the situation it sought to address are remarkably consistent with the operations that came later. With few exceptions, UN operations in Africa have been associated with tasks related to some form of peace or ceasefire agreement.[3] The agreement is often but not always the result of UN efforts to facilitate a peaceful resolution to the crisis. As a consequence, UN involvement may be part and parcel of the agreement itself or it may be requested after an agreement has been achieved to help facilitate implementation. Because of their association with peace and ceasefire agreements, these operations generally include any combination of the following tasks: monitoring the withdrawal of troops from a given area; monitoring a ceasefire; overseeing and implementing disarmament, demobilization, and reintegration of forces; the protection of civilian populations, including refugees or internally displaced peoples; and overseeing elections.

One of the interesting trends in Security Council decision making in the post–Cold War period is the extent to which the Council has been willing to invoke Chapter VII. As Patrik Johansson establishes, there is a definite trend upward in the Council's use of Chapter VII after the Cold War.[4] The Council's response to Africa makes up a large share of that trend. Of the thirty-four conflict situations addressed by the Council between 1946 and 2008 using Chapter VII of the Charter, seventeen, or half, are African.[5] This is in keeping with the general trends in Security Council responses to conflict in Africa described in the foregoing, indicating that the Council's use of Chapter VII in Africa fits with the general pattern of its increased use in the post–Cold War period and does not indicate any greater propensity to use Chapter VII in Africa over other regions.

Background to UN–Regional Organization Relationships

The framework for the relationship between regional organizations and the UN is found in Chapter VIII of the UN Charter. Chapter VIII outlines a system that provides for regional arrangements to settle disputes before submitting them to the Security Council. Regional entities are, however, required to keep the Security Council fully informed of activities "undertaken or in contemplation" relating to international peace and security. For its part, the Security Council may use regional arrangements for enforcement action "where appropriate" but "no enforcement action shall be taken under regional arrangements...without the authorization of the Security Council" (Article 53). Together, these articles suggest quite an active and cooperative relationship between regional arrangements and the UN. In practice, however, until the end of the Cold War, virtually no formal activity took place under Chapter VIII auspices.[6]

The idea of greater cooperation between regional organizations and the UN was revived by the UN Secretary-General's report, *An Agenda for Peace*, in 1992. *An Agenda for Peace* placed emphasis on the idea that regional organizations might be used to support UN peace efforts across the spectrum of operations from preventive diplomacy to post-conflict peace-building. The Secretary-General indicated that using regional organizations would not take away from the Council's "primary" responsibility in dealing with international peace and security, "but regional action as a matter of decentralization, delegation and cooperation with UN efforts could not only lighten the burden of the Council but also contribute to a deeper sense of participation, consensus and democratization in international affairs."[7]

In theory, the model of cooperation with regional organizations sees the Security Council authorizing an operation and then, either as part of that authorization or in a separate decision, asking a regional arrangement to undertake the authorized tasks. This theoretical model is based on the primacy of the UN Charter provisions and the role of the Security Council as the only entity with the power to authorize the use of force. In practice, events have rarely followed this sequence.

Two years prior to the appearance of *An Agenda for Peace*, an African regional organization had already taken the initiative in conflict management. In August 1990, the Economic Community of West African States (ECOWAS) established the ECOWAS monitoring group (ECOMOG) in response to the crisis in Liberia. Later that month, on 24 August 1990, ECOMOG was deployed in Liberia and began a sustained military operation there. ECOMOG was engaged in serious and ongoing hostilities in Liberia, and was effectively an intervention force. The UN's own portrayal of events euphemistically says that the UN supported the ECOWAS efforts to end the civil war, even though the operation did not have Security Council authorization and it was five months before the Security Council voiced an opinion on the matter, and then only in the form of a Presidential Statement giving general support to ECOWAS' efforts.[8] It was more than two years after ECOMOG was deployed in Liberia before the Security Council passed a resolution dealing with the Liberian conflict. The resolution placed an arms embargo against Liberia and authorized the appointment of a special representative of the Secretary-General.[9] Although the Security Council notes the request and the invitation by ECOWAS for the UN to send observers, no action was taken. It was another year, not until after the signing of a formal peace agreement, before the UN Security Council authorized the establishment of a peacekeeping mission.[10]

The Council's response to other regional interventions in the same time period demonstrated a similar pattern. In response to regional interventions in Sierra Leone and CAR, the Security Council took an initial "no comment" approach to the situation. When it finally did deal with the conflicts it chose to keep its distance, giving vocal support to the existing regional efforts and taking very limited initial steps itself. Such a policy provided tremendous freedom to the regional groups involved. The Security Council imposed no constraints on their actions and did not formally (or even informally) disapprove of the fact that their initial actions were taken without the authorization of a Security Council mandate.

The lack of attention and fuss accorded to the fact that these military interventions have occurred without Security Council authorization stands in sharp contrast to the international debate that accompanied the non–Security Council–authorized North Atlantic Treaty Organization (NATO) intervention in Kosovo later that decade. And even in the debate about NATO actions in Kosovo, the African experiences were not raised as precedents. This disparity in levels of attention and concern about the legality of regional actions has continued over time and coincides with a disparity in resource commitments that combine to create perceptions of double standards in Council decision making.

A clear division of labor has emerged between developed states and developing states, with the former primarily deployed in non–blue helmeted (mostly UN authorized) coalition operations, while the latter undertake the bulk of the peacekeeping burden. This indicates that African states bear the brunt of the conflict–response burden at both the regional and international levels. As of August 2012, for example, Ethiopia (fourth), Nigeria (fifth), Egypt (seventh), Rwanda (sixth), and Ghana (tenth) constituted five of the top ten contributing states to UN operations.[11] The bulk of Ethiopia's troops are deployed in the two operations in Sudan while the bulk of Nigerian troops are in Darfur and Liberia.[12] When it comes to burden sharing, therefore, the international community asks a great deal of these states, many of whom are struggling to meet the basic needs of their own populations. The five African states who are among the top 10 contributors to UN operations all rank in the bottom third of the 2011 Human Development Index with Egypt at 113, Ethiopia at 174, Ghana at 135, Nigeria at 156, and Rwanda at 166.[13]

Security Council Debate and Actions

The Security Council's focus on the problems associated with conflict in Africa as a general or thematic issue begins roughly in 1995. In response to two requests for action,[14] on 1 November 1995, the Secretary-General responded with a report on "Improving preparedness for conflict prevention and peace-keeping in Africa."[15] The Secretary-General noted that the lack of personnel, financial, and other resources posed real difficulties in UN operations in Africa, but that "these difficulties are not confined to operations in Africa."[16] In this context, much of the Secretary-General's report focused on how African peacekeeping capabilities could be improved within the context of the general efforts to improve UN peacekeeping capabilities. Accordingly, the Secretary-General's report discusses at length how African member states could make use of stand-by arrangements for peacekeeping troop contributions, UN training efforts, and general UN attempts to ameliorate preparation and coordination of peacekeeping planning and implementation. In terms of specific proposals to strengthen the Organization of African Unity (OAU), the Secretary-General proposed that a UN liaison officer be placed at OAU headquarters, that a staff exchange program be established between the two organizations, and that the UN provide assistance to the OAU in establishing a situation room and provide the OAU with information about peacekeeping training in which other states can participate.[17] In contrast to the debates and proposals in later years, the Secretary-General's report continuously places the issue of improving African preparedness in these areas within the overall context of the UN's own efforts. This is in keeping with the context of UN peacekeeping at the time, in which the organization was struggling to deal with the first years of the post–Cold War jump in peacekeeping operations.

In September 1997, the Security Council met at the level of Foreign Ministers to discuss ways of addressing and preventing conflict in Africa. Almost every speaker supported recent actions by the OAU to play a greater role in dealing with conflict in the region and the broader idea of encouraging greater involvement of regional and subregional organizations in the process generally. In each case, however, emphasis was also placed on ensuring that such actions took place within the context of the UN Charter. In his remarks to the Council, the Secretary-General suggested that there was now a consensus that the solution of Africa's problems lay with Africans themselves and that this determination, in turn, required a reevaluation of the role of the international community in support of Africa. "In place of interventionism it promised a mature relationship based on mutual support and trust."[18]

The Presidential Statement issued as a result of the meeting placed emphasis on the important contributions that could be and were being made by subregional organizations in Africa and supported efforts to strengthen the capacity of regional groups to contribute to peacekeeping operations "including in Africa, in accordance with the Charter of the United Nations." Concluding that "the challenges in Africa demand a more comprehensive response" the Security Council requested the Secretary-General to prepare and submit recommendations on ways to prevent and address conflict in Africa and to establish a foundation for peace there.[19]

This is the process that begins a shift in Security Council focus from looking at the issue of how to deal with conflict in Africa as part of the broader question of how the UN responds to conflict to dealing with Africa as a particular region that needs special attention. In his 1998 report to the Security Council, the Secretary-General provides an indication of why that should be so. He stated that the situation in Africa represents a particular problem for the international community, one that extends beyond the traditional question of defending states to become "a matter of defending humanity itself." He argues further that the African situation represents failure at a number of levels.

> By not averting these colossal human tragedies, African leaders have failed the peoples of Africa; the international community has failed them; the United Nations has failed them. We have failed them by not adequately addressing the causes of conflict; by not doing enough to ensure peace; and by our repeated inability to create the conditions for sustainable development.[20]

The Secretary-General's report is remarkable in that it is quite forthright about the state of the relationship between the international community and Africa and the impact this is having. The Secretary-General speaks of the international community's reluctance to assume the costs of involvement in Africa and even of "paralysis" of action. "This reluctance seems to go well beyond the lessons that Somalia offers, and it has had a particularly harsh impact upon Africa."[21] The consequences work in both directions. According to the Secretary-General, not only has the international community pulled back from Africa but this has also generated a commensurate retrenchment on the part of African states "to marginalize the United Nations from further political involvement in the region's affairs."[22]

The Secretary-General states that the support of regional and subregional initiatives is "both necessary and desirable."[23]

> Such support is necessary because the United Nations lacks the capacity, resources and expertise to address all problems that may arise in Africa. It is desirable because wherever possible the international community should strive to complement rather than supplant African efforts to resolve Africa's problems.[24]

The Secretary-General conditioned his support of the greater use and support of regional organizations, however, demonstrating his sense that while there were advantages to be gained by such a move there were also some serious potential pitfalls. In particular, he voiced concern about the implications of authorizing the use of force by coalitions of states. Perhaps, reflecting the experiences in Liberia, Somalia, and even the Persian Gulf, the Secretary-General noted that the Security Council needed to improve its ability to monitor such activities to ensure that the mandate was being fulfilled as authorized. In fact, the Secretary-General's discussion of this issue is heavily couched with concern that the shift toward greater devolution of tasks would bring with it greater distance in terms of the lines authority. Thus, the Secretary-General says: "We should not, however, draw the conclusion that such responsibilities can henceforth be delegated solely to regional organizations, either in Africa or elsewhere. Delegation does not represent a panacea for the difficult problems facing peacekeeping."[25] With respect to the question of strengthening the capacity of African organizations to undertake peacekeeping, he warns: "These efforts are not in any way intended to relieve the broader international community of its collective obligations under the Charter of the United Nations."[26]

The Secretary-General then went on to sound a general warning, while at the same time bringing the question of Africa back into the wider realm of the UN's ability and determination to act generally.

> Failure to act in the face of serious threats to peace and human lives in Africa threatens the credibility and legitimacy of the United Nations not only in the area of peace and security but also in its other areas of work. Moreover, wide disparities in the international community's commitment to preventing or containing conflicts in different regions impede the ability of the United Nations to promote a stable and just international order anywhere.[27]

Security Council Response

This sequence of Secretary-General reports was the beginning of a flurry of activity on the part of the Council. Resolution 1170 passed in May 1998, a month after the Secretary-General's report, set in motion two streams of activity. The first was a commitment to biennial meetings at the Foreign Minister level to assess progress in the promotion of peace and security in Africa. The second was the creation of an ad hoc Working Group to review the recommendations in the Secretary-General's report and establish a framework for their implementation. The working group established six subgroups to cover specific issues: the effectiveness of arms embargoes, strengthening African peacekeeping capabilities; regional cooperation; an international mechanism for maintaining security and neutrality of refugee camps; arms flows; and enhancing the Security Council's ability to monitor activities it authorizes. In combination, the subgroup activity led to the Council passing four resolutions and two Presidential Statements.[28] There was little that was earth-shatterlingly new in these resolutions or statements beyond general support for a process directed at strengthening the way the organization deals with conflict in Africa. They called for small-scale steps that would mark improvements or consolidation of existing measures or decisions. In these decisions, the Security Council did a lot in the way of encouraging and urging others, particularly the Secretary-General to take various actions. However, there was nothing in the way of innovative change or of any form of support of the process beyond the resolutions and statements.

After the submission of the Secretary-General's progress report in September 1999,[29] the Security Council held two days of debate. By now, the international response to the crisis in Kosovo, in particular NATO's moves toward organizing a bombing campaign, was having an impact on the UN generally. In his speech to the Security Council, the Secretary-General sounded a warning about the implications of the activity and decisions surrounding the Kosovo crisis, noting that if the UN is to retain its credibility, the international community's commitment to dealing with conflict "must be applied fairly and consistently irrespective of region or nation."[30] This was a theme that was echoed repeatedly in the two days of deliberations on the Secretary-General's progress report. In particular, Nigeria pointed out that the international community was spending US$1.50 per day per refugee in Kosovo, while in Rwanda and Sierra Leone, the amount spent was 11 cents per day.[31] A second and related concern expressed by a number of African speakers was that the Security Council would turn to the use of regional organizations as a way of abdicating its responsibility for dealing with conflict. In the context of the time, this concern seemed to reflect a sense that the possibility of NATO taking action in Kosovo would encourage a general handing off of activity to regional organizations by the Security Council.

By December, when the Security Council held an open debate on the situation in Africa, these themes were being voiced with more determination and concern. The looming crisis in Kosovo and the apparent determination of NATO to respond with force, even in the absence of a Security Council mandate, accentuated the disparity in the international community's responses to crises in Europe and those in Africa. Speakers from African states expressed a high level of frustration about this disparity. They argued that in spite of the level of debate and rhetoric in recent years, Africa was increasingly being left to fend for itself while considerable resources and efforts were being made in other regions. Many said that what was needed was not further debate but action and commitment. Referring to the Security Council's attitudes, the representative from Gambia spoke of a "policy of neglect" and the Brazilian representative spoke of a "distant and cautious" attitude that was haunted by the "ghosts of failure" and a feeling of "chronic impotence."[32]

More diplomatically, the Secretary-General focused on the question of a lack of adequate resources. He asked the Security Council to consider urgently how regional operations could be more fairly and efficiently financed and suggested that it was not fair to expect Africans to engage more fully in peacekeeping tasks without assistance. This concern was echoed by the Canadian representative who indicated that the devolution of responsibility for dealing with a number of conflict-related issues had occurred with little regard for whether or not the regional arrangements had the capacity to carry out these tasks. In the Canadian view, the UN's own mechanisms needed to be strengthened and improved. The challenge, therefore, was not to create new mechanisms but to ensure that the existing ones worked properly.[33]

In January 2002, Mauritius organized what was a spirited and lengthy debate under the general heading of "the situation in Africa." In an effort to generate more focused and concrete results than had been achieved so far, Mauritius submitted a specific set of guidelines for orienting the discussion.[34] The resulting Security Council debate generated a Presidential Statement, which, inter alia, created an Ad Hoc Working Group on Conflict Prevention and Resolution in Africa.[35] Once convened, the Ad Hoc Working

Group established a very specific program of work[36] and was initially very active. On the question of greater cooperation with regional organizations, the working group's first set of recommendations focused on cooperation with the AU.[37] The overall theme of the recommendations is a push toward maximizing joint activities between the Security Council and the newly created AU. They include proposals for greater information-sharing, regular joint briefings, close consultation before and after Security Council missions in Africa, and the possibility of joint envoys and joint missions.[38]

The organization experienced a particularly low point in 2003 as the US-led invasion of Iraq proceeded without a Security Council mandate. A Mexican-led Security Council debate on the relationship between the Security Council and regional organizations took place in April 2003 in the shadow of those events. Speakers reiterated earlier themes including the desirability of greater cooperation while emphasizing the need to ensure Security Council primacy.[39] Questions of regional organization capability and greater specifics about the exact role such organizations can play in specific situations are more evident here than in earlier debates. Along those lines, a Romanian-sponsored debate the following year focused specifically on UN–regional organization cooperation in stabilization processes.[40]

In a rare meeting outside of UN headquarters, the Security Council convened in Nairobi in November 2004 en route to a mission in Central Africa.[41] In addition to providing support and recognition to the nascent AU, especially the recently created AU Peace and Security Council (PSC), the meeting generated a Presidential Statement that affirmed the desirability of greater cooperation between the two organizations and to that end called on the Secretary-General to explore new means of cooperation.[42]

Over the course of the next couple of years, reports and processes external to the Council affirm and move forward the idea of greater cooperation with regional organizations, especially in Africa. In December 2004, the Secretary-General's High Level Panel (HLP), established to propose new ways forward for the organization in the aftermath of Iraq, published its report. On the question of the role of regional organizations, the HLP's starting point is that the "Security Council has not made the most of the potential advantages of working with regional and subregional organizations."[43] The HLP goes on to recommend, inter alia, that "consultation and cooperation between the UN and regional organizations should be expanded and could be formalized in an agreement, covering such issues as meetings of the heads of the organizations, more frequent exchange of information and early warning, co-training of civilian and military personnel, and exchange of personnel within peace operations."[44]

A few months later, the Secretary-General's report *In Larger Freedom*,[45] a five-year progress report on the Millennium Declaration, also picked up the theme, proposing some specific ideas on the question of the capacity of the AU and the possibility of formalizing cooperative arrangements with regional organizations. As with his initial reports on these issues, the Secretary-General placed the question of greater cooperation with regional organizations in the broader context of improving the UN's own ability to engage in peacekeeping operations.

> United Nations capacity should not be developed in competition with the admirable efforts now being made by many regional organizations but in cooperation with them... I believe the time is now ripe for a decisive move forward: the establishment of an interlocking

> system of peacekeeping capacities that will enable the United Nations to work with relevant regional organizations in predictable and reliable partnerships.[46]

The Secretary-General also weighed in on the question of coordination, saying that he intended "to introduce memoranda of understanding between the United Nations and individual organizations, governing the sharing of information, expertise and resources, as appropriate in each case."[47]

On the question of capacity-building, the Secretary-General called on states to "pay particular attention" to the need for a ten-year capacity-building plan for the AU. Weighing in on a contentious issue, the Secretary-General gave support to the idea that peacekeeping budget rules should be amended so that "in exceptional circumstances" assessed contributions could be used to finance Security Council–authorized regional operations or "multi-pillar operations."[48] For its part, in the 2005 World Summit outcome document, the General Assembly affirmed the desirability of the now widely articulated goal of greater cooperation, including through formalized agreements, and gave support to the idea of a ten-year capacity-building plan for the AU.[49]

In the midst of this activity, the Security Council moved forward on these issues in the form of two resolutions. The first,[50] an outcome of a summit-level meeting of the Security Council in September 2005, was a declaration on the Council's role in conflict prevention, especially in Africa. In addition to establishing a Council commitment to strengthen UN conflict-prevention capacity in a variety of ways, the resolution affirmed (again) the importance of regional approaches and the need to strengthen UN–regional cooperation and communication in that context. The second resolution was a product of a second Romanian-led debate. The debate and subsequent resolution[51] demonstrated an increased effort to establish an actual framework for UN–regional cooperation and to determine what specific roles regional actors could play in what types of situations. In opening the debate, the Romanian Permanent Representative noted that "creating the right complementarity and subsidiarity between the United Nations and regional action would . . . generate a considerable pool of resources assigned to peace that would ultimately lead to the ability of the international community to effectively and promptly address every tension, every threat, every open conflict and every fragile situation in the aftermath of conflict."[52]

Without challenging the goal outlined by the Romanian Permanent Representative, in speaking at the same meeting, the Secretary-General cautioned that the process must "reinforce a collective approach to security. The UN partnerships with regional organizations must provide the means to meet, rather than to avoid, our responsibility under the Charter to provide an effective international response to violent conflict wherever it occurs."[53] Resolution 1631 outlined a number of ways in which regional organizations might contribute to international peace and security including developing an ability to deploy forces rapidly in support of UN peacekeeping operations, in addressing the illicit trade in small arms, counterterrorism efforts, and conflict prevention. The resolution also asked the Secretary-General to prepare a report on the opportunities and challenges to UN–regional cooperation and to explore the possibility of framework agreements that could frame such cooperation in peacekeeping operations.[54]

The Secretary-General's subsequent report, issued in July 2006, provides a detailed summary of the evolution of the UN–regional relationship to that point, and an update as to the status of the various recommendations contained in Resolution 1631. The Secretary-General summarized the opportunities at hand as being in the establishment of a "more effective partnership...based on a clear division of labour that reflects the comparative advantage of each organization."[55] While the challenges "are the clarification of the identity and role of each member in this partnership and a programme of action for capacity-building to ensure more equal ability among United Nations regional and other partners."[56] As the Secretary-General's report indicates, when taken as a whole, outside the particularities of specific cases and past practices, the question of how to clarify roles and ensure consistency in capacity is a considerable and complex undertaking. There are questions of definition (what constitutes a region, and a subregion, as well as how to address overlap and gaps between them), questions of how to deal with the differing nature and levels of formality of the constitutions of regional organizations, and questions about the legal implications any formal relationship will have. Even if and when those challenges can be overcome, there remains the question of capacity. As the Secretary-General points out, without a resolution of the "vast discrepancy in the capacities of regional and other organizations," the idea of partnership will not progress far. Nonetheless, the Secretary-General does see the possibility of "a fully fledged and truly effective mechanism for global-regional cooperation."[57] To that end, he recommends that the Security Council recognize the guidelines that have already been agreed in various resolutions and Presidential Statements and that regional organizations interested in moving toward a formal partnership agreement inform the Secretary-General in writing.[58]

The Secretary-General's report marked the beginning of a new pace in Security Council activity on these issues. In the two years between the Secretary-General's report and his next one, the Council held three debates,[59] undertook a mission to Africa, which included a meeting with the AU PSC, and reengaged with the conflict prevention agenda.[60] The March 2007 debate, initiated by South Africa, who was on the Council for the first time in the country's history, resulted in a Presidential Statement. The statement recognized the "growing contribution" being made by the AU and invited further collaboration between the Council and the AU PSC as a way of building their capacity to undertake "rapid and appropriate responses to emerging situations."[61] The statement also asked the Secretary-General to report on specific proposals for further cooperation with regional organizations, and the promotion of deepening cooperation with the AU PSC.[62] A few months later, in June 2007, as part of a mission to Africa, the Council and the AU PSC held their first joint meeting and issued a joint communiqué outlining their commitment to develop a "stronger and more structured relationship," to hold annual joint meetings, and to move forward on the issue of capacity-building.[63]

In response to a March 2007 Council request for further specific proposals on cooperation,[64] the Secretary-General issued another report in April 2008.[65] Reiterating the proposals in his previous report, the Secretary-General offers further suggestions for cooperation on a variety of issues ranging from disarmament and conflict prevention to human rights and humanitarian action. On the broader division of responsibilities between the UN and regional actors, the Secretary-General continued to sound some warning bells while remaining positive about the overall direction of the UN–regional relationship. He notes that while the terminology of "partnership" has become common parlance, the potential for misunderstanding about its meaning remains high and the need for a clear delineation of responsibilities is also high, thus reinforcing the need to replace the ad hoc, improvised system currently in place with more consistent, reliable arrangements.[66]

These kinds of recommendations are symbolic of a step-by-step evolutionary acceptance of the desirability, and in some ways inevitability, of a more serious, formal UN–regional relationship. The language of the Secretary-General in this report makes that evident. "With the increase in the interface and synergies between the UN and regional organizations, particularly the AU, there appears to be recognition that regionalism as a component of multilateralism is necessary and feasible. There is now the possibility of a *shared* role for maintaining international peace and security."[67]

The question of capacity is consistently present in Security Council deliberations of this time. On the particularly contentious issue of funding, the Secretary-General proposed the creation of an AU–UN panel to consider how to move toward predictable and sustainable funding for regional organizations undertaking UN-authorized peace operations.[68] This proposal was endorsed by the Security Council in Resolution 1809.[69] The panel was chaired by the former Prime Minister of Italy, Romano Prodi (the report is thus often referred to as the Prodi report), and issued its report in December 2008.[70] The report is exhaustive in its coverage of the issues surrounding the question of greater financial support for UN-mandated AU peacekeeping operations. As backdrop, the panel notes that the context contains "a growing anomalous and undesirable trend in which organizations lacking the necessary capabilities have been left to bear the brunt in terms of providing the international community's initial response, while others more capable have not engaged. This inversion of responsibility is generating a trend of benign neglect in which interests rather than capabilities prevail."[71]

On the specific question of financing, the panel separates the issue of longer-term capacity-building from support for specific peacekeeping operations. It proposes the creation of a multi-donor trust fund under African ownership to build African peacekeeping capacity over time. With respect to the funding of UN-authorized peacekeeping operations, the panel emphasized that

> the key is to reinforce [Security Council] primacy while encouraging maximum flexibility at the regional level. The panel recommends the use of United Nations-assessed contributions on a case-by-case basis to support United Nations Security Council-authorized African Union peacekeeping operations for a period up to six months. Initially, at least, this support should mainly be provided in kind... The panel believes such an arrangement could benefit both the United Nations and the African Union, where the African Union, exercising its ability to respond quickly, would be providing an initial response to a longer-term United Nations commitment.[72]

The Prodi panel report was an important step in moving forward the financing debate. It carried with it, however, an accompanying emphasis on the need for the AU to develop its own plan for long-term capacity-building. This message, in broader terms, can be found consistently in Security Council debates and Presidential Statements that precede and follow the panel's report, where the Council notes that regional organizations have the responsibility to secure resources for their organizations. The panel's report prompted the Council to ask the Secretary-General for an analysis of the recommendations,[73] which the Council then took under advisement.[74]

In January 2010, with China in the chair, the Security Council returned to the broader questions of cooperation and partnership with little substantive outcome beyond affirming the need for closer cooperation.[75] In July 2010, at the request of the General Assembly, the Secretary-General returned to one of the starting points of this whole process, the question of the "causes of conflict and the promotion of durable peace and sustainable development in Africa,"[76] by providing a review of progress in the ten years since the 1998 report. The Secretary-General's assessment was generally positive. Pointing to significant economic growth, "more institutional progress than any other region in the world," and "remarkable improvement in the overall security landscape,"[77] the report goes on to assert that "Africa is on the move."[78] One of the most striking aspects in this report is the extent to which the way forward is clearly tied to state capacity. This theme runs through the entire report and is made explicit in the section on new challenges and opportunities. Here the Secretary-General states that "opportunities for peace and development in Africa will depend on the strength of African states to perform their roles effectively."[79] His first recommendation under the category of conflict response is that the "international community, in partnership with Africa, should prioritize strengthening the capacity of the state, including local governments."[80] The report marks an interesting shift in thinking on the question of capacity, making an implicit assumption explicit by recognizing that regional organization capacity-building can only go so far without capacity-building at the state level.

By 2012, the significance of world events was filtering into the ongoing discussion of UN–regional partnerships, especially with respect to the AU. During 2011, the world witnessed the Arab Spring and the UN-authorized action in Libya. The Libyan case is a particularly testing one for the UN–regional relationship because two of the regional organizations involved, the League of Arab States and the AU, disagreed on how to proceed. In January 2012, the Security Council engaged in another debate on the question of UN–regional organization cooperation, with South Africa, now in its second term as a nonpermanent member, as chair, and President Jacob Zuma present in that role. While in many ways the debate reflected past practices and included the usual support for greater cooperation, the tenor of the debate was new. In his opening statement, President Zuma noted that the proposed AU political road map for Libya "would have assisted in resolving the political conflict in that country" and that it "was completely ignored in favor of the bombing of Libya by NATO forces."[81] On that basis, he emphasized the need for greater political coherence and a common vision between the AU and the UN. "The views of the African Union must be listened to if we are to strengthen our relationship and prevent further conflict."[82]

Indicating that challenges to the UN–AU relationship must be confronted "forthrightly," US Ambassador Susan Rice stated that "cooperation cannot be on the basis that the regional organization independently decides the policy and that United Nations Member States simply bless it and pay for it. There can be no blank check, either politically or financially."[83] And on the issue of AU–Security Council consultations, she was also candid, noting that they "have not, thus far, been altogether productive or satisfactory. If they cannot be improved, they risk being jettisoned by one side or the other as not useful or worse."[84] The resolution resulting from the meeting pulled together the now long list of issues under the heading of UN–regional organization cooperation. Reflecting the statements made in the debate, the resolution also calls for improved interaction between the Security Council and the AU PSC, to work toward achieving more effective annual meetings.[85] Speaking after the meeting, the permanent representative for the United Kingdom stated for the record that the United Kingdom had concerns about ambiguity in the language surrounding the commitment for improved interaction between the two bodies, focusing in particular on the idea of coordination, implying that the language in the resolution may imply equivalence between the two bodies. In the ambassador's words,

> We do not believe that cooperation, however welcome in principle, should come at the expense either of the Security Council's primacy... or its practical capacity to respond speedily and effectively to any threat to international peace and security... In particular, the text refers in paragraph 6 to coordination between the Security Council and the African Union Peace and Security Council. In those instances where we consider coordination to be appropriate, it can occur only in the context of the primacy of the Security Council regarding the maintenance of international peace and security.[86]

Conclusion

The debates, reports, and actions discussed in this overview reveal a number of consistent patterns and assumptions. The first is the virtually unquestioned assumption that greater cooperation with regional organizations is inherently good. There are variations on this theme ranging from a whole-hearted embrace of cooperation to those who see its advantages but are cautious about its implications, but overall, the debate indicates widespread acceptance of such cooperation as an achievable and desirable goal. The idea that regional actors have intrinsic advantages in conflict situations also remains a strong assumption with little sustained or serious consideration of the potential negative aspects of the closeness of regional actors to the conflict in question.

All this has been occurring in a discourse whose overarching theme is cooperation and partnership, accompanied by subthemes of shared responsibility, a division of labor, complementary capacities, and comparative advantages. Steady progress has been made in establishing greater cooperation between the UN and regional organizations in day-to-day practical terms. Council calls for greater information-sharing, liaison, and joint UN–regional work have been gradually but steadily put into practice.[87] In July 2006, the Security Council formally adopted a commitment to expand consultation and cooperation with regional organizations, including invitations to private and public Security Council meetings "when appropriate."[88]

Establishing the organizing principles of partnership in a formally agreed framework on the basis of a shared strategic vision remains a challenge. The very fact that this idea is accepted as a desirable goal is itself a sign of how far the Council has come in its thinking. In the course of the deliberations covered here, a number of people indicated that continuing with an ad hoc process is unsustainable.[89] However, there are good reasons why the ad hoc approach may be sustained for some time. As the Secretary-General indicated, a formally agreed framework is a major undertaking. Perhaps more compellingly, while an agreed framework provides a structural base for interaction, it can also constrain flexibility and freedom of action for both groups.

The idea of partnership is inextricably linked to questions of capacity. A division of labor among partners will not provide much value added if one of the partners is incapable of fulfilling the role. The need to deal with the question of regional organization capacity in Africa was recognized in the very first Secretary-General reports and Security Council debates. A wide range of measures, not covered in this chapter, have been discussed and developed since those early days.[90] The very fact of the need for capacity-building, however, returns us to the issue of burden sharing. That was one of the rationales for the *An Agenda for Peace* proposal for greater cooperation with regional organizations. The idea of burden sharing seems fundamentally incompatible with the idea of capacity-building. While the Council discourse has changed from burden sharing to partnership, the basic goal is the same—joint efforts to deal with a shared problem. This raises a key question. Is the idea of partnership a way to empower regional actors through a process of burden sharing? Or, is it a process of burden shifting and devolution under the cover of cooperation and African solutions for African problems?

As outlined earlier and as the chapters that follow indicate, the Council's conflict-related activity in Africa is significant and sustained. The same can now be said for regional organizations whose evolution as conflict-response actors borders on the revolutionary. Yet, as was the case when the first edition of this book was published, even in the context of thematic debates, the Security Council remains reactive and is often two steps behind its actual practice. In this sense, this chapter reveals a Council whose approach is at best an effort to manage the implications of an ever-changing context and at worst veering toward after-the-fact damage limitation. Any time practice outpaces the development of agreed principles of cooperation and action, there are inherent dangers. For the Council, there are at least two potential dangers. The first is the impact on its primacy as the international actor with the ability to decide issues of international peace and security, especially those relating to the use of force. The second linked danger is the potential for gradual erosion in the Council's credibility and legitimacy, not just in Africa.

In this respect, the remarkable nature of the AU's development and stated goals are indicative of the ways in which those dangers can gather. In the last ten years, the AU has emerged as an important player in UN–regional efforts to deal with conflict in Africa. Since its arrival on the scene, the AU has also sought to claim a role as an equal partner with the Security Council. In many respects, it has succeeded. The AU role and many of its actions are the subject of approving Council statements and resolutions. Annual joint meetings between the AU PSC and the Security Council affirm the image of equality, and of the AU as the preeminent regional actor on the African stage. However, it is one thing to be equal partners in a cooperative relationship and another to be equal actors with exclusive spheres of responsibility. This goes back to an early Secretary-General warning about the implications of allowing and encouraging greater independence of action for regional organizations. It is not evident that the AU's goal is to supersede the Security Council on conflict issues but it is not beyond the realm of possibility that the pursuit of partnership and reliance on the AU and other African regional organizations for much of the heavy lifting on the African conflict scene may lead us there eventually, intentionally, or otherwise. Recently, the situation was made more complicated by the Council's decision to listen to a regional voice other than the

AU when it authorized the use of force in Libya.[91] However, that fact speaks even more strongly of the need for the Council to exercise its leadership role and to (re-)claim its territory if it wants to be in a position to respond effectively to conflict in Africa with or without regional partnerships.

Notes

1. The total figure comes from the United Nations. http://www.un.org/en/peacekeeping/operations/. This does not include Security Council–authorized coalition operations such as the US-led operation in Somalia (Unified Task Force [UNITAF]) in 1992–1993 or the North Atlantic Treaty Organization–led operation in Libya in 2011.
2. This is based on a rough categorization. Some multiple missions are the result of new mandates, while in other cases, there has been a significant gap in time between missions. The list of cases with more than one UN operation is as follows: Angola, Burundi, Central African Republic, Chad, Cote d'Ivoire, DRC, Egypt, Eritrea/Ethiopia, Liberia, Mozambique, Namibia, Rwanda/Uganda, Sierra Leone, Somalia, Sudan (including Darfur and South Sudan), and Western Sahara.
3. Instances in which the UN Security Council authorized an operation in Africa in the absence of a peace agreement include the first UN operation in the Congo in 1960–1964, the three UN-authorized operations in Somalia in the early 1990s, and the UN Observer Mission in Sierra Leone (UNOMSIL). All of these operations were contentious and difficult, with the UN eventually withdrawing completely from Somalia, and withdrawing most of its personnel from Sierra Leone when rebels overran the capital city. A different example not involving a peace agreement is the UNASOG operation, which monitored troop withdrawals ordered by the International Court of Justice.
4. Patrik Johansson, "The humdrum use of ultimate authority: defining and analysing Chapter VII resolutions," *Nordic Journal of International Law* 78 (2009): 328. Of a total of 477 Chapter VII resolutions, 456 were passed in the post–Cold War period.
5. Johansson, "The Humdrum Use of Ultimate Authority," Appendix 1.
6. For a good overview of how Chapter VIII was developed in the early stages of the debate and negotiations on the formation of the United Nations Charter, see Ruth B. Russell, *A History of the United Nations Charter, The Role of the United States 1940–1945* (Washington, DC: Brookings, 1958), pp. 107–108, 398–399, 472–474.
7. *An Agenda for Peace*, S/24111, 17 June 1992, para. 64.
8. S/22133, 22 January 1991.
9. Security Council Resolution 788, 19 November 1992.
10. The peacekeeping mission was the United Nations Observer Mission in Liberia (UNOMIL). Security Council Resolution 866, 22 September 1993.
11. United Nations, "Ranking of Military and Police Contributions to UN Operations," 31 August 2012. http://www.un.org/en/peacekeeping/resources/statistics/contributors.shtml. Accessed 14 September 2012.
12. United Nations, "UN Mission's Contributions by Country," 31 August 2012. http://www.un.org/en/peacekeeping/resources/statistics/contributors.shtml. Accessed 14 September 2012.
13. Human Development Report 2011, "Sustainability and Equity: A Better Future for All," http://hdr.undp.org/en/statistics/.
14. In 1995, the Secretary-General received two requests to deal specifically with the question of greater cooperation and support of regional organizations in Africa. The first request, from the Security Council, asked the Secretary-General to consider ways of improving practical

cooperation and coordination between the UN and regional organizations, with particular attention to the needs of the OAU. S/PRST/1995/9, 22 February 1995. The second request, a few months later, came from the Special Committee on Peacekeeping Operations. The Committee asked the Secretary-General to examine and develop proposals that had been made to improve the UN's ability to respond rapidly to emergency situations in Africa, especially through cooperation with the OAU. A/50/230, 22 June 1995.

15. A/50/711-S/1995/911, 1 November 1995.
16. Ibid., para. 16.
17. Ibid., para. 40.
18. S/PV.3819, 25 September 1997.
19. S/PRST/1997/46, 25 September 1997.
20. The causes of conflict and the promotion of durable peace and sustainable development in Africa, Report of the Secretary-General, A/52/871-S/1998/318, 13 April 1998, para. 5.
21. Ibid., para. 29.
22. Ibid.
23. Ibid., para. 41.
24. Ibid.
25. Ibid., para. 44.
26. Ibid., para. 45.
27. Ibid., para. 46.
28. S/PRST/1998/28, 16 September 1998; Security Council Resolution 1196, 16 September 1998; Security Council Resolution 1197, 18 September 1998; Security Council Resolution 1208, 19 November 1998; Security Council Resolution 1209, 19 November 1998; S/PRST/1998/35, 30 November 1998.
29. S/1999/1008, 25 September 1999.
30. "Secretary-General Highlights Positive Changes in Africa," SG/SM/7153AFR/177, 29 September 1999.
31. SC/6736, 30 September 1999.
32. SC/6771, 15 December 1999.
33. SC/6671, 15 December 1999.
34. S/PV.4460, 29 January 2002; S/PV.4460 Resumption 1, 29 January 2002; S/PV.4460 Resumption 2, 30 January 2002; S/PV.4465, 31 January 2002. For the guidelines, see S/2002/46, 11 January 2002.
35. S/PRST/2002/2, 31 January 2002.
36. See the briefing given to the Security Council by the Group's Chairman. SC/7406, 22 May 2002.
37. S/2002/979, 30 August 2002.
38. Ibid.
39. S/PV.4739, 11 April 2003.
40. S/PV.5007, 20 July 2004. The debate was guided by a "non-paper" submitted by Romania. S/2005/546, 8 July 2004. The debate resulted in a Presidential Statement, PRST/2004/27, 20 July 2004.
41. S/PV.5084, 19 November 2004.
42. PRST/2005/44, 19 November 2004.
43. "A More Secure World: Our Shared Responsibility," Report of the Secretary-General's High-level Panel on Threats, Challenges and Change, A/59/565, 2 December 2004, 14.
44. Ibid., 71.
45. A/59/2005, 21 March 2005.
46. Ibid., 31.
47. Ibid., 52. In addition, he voiced his intention to invite regional organizations to participate in meetings of UN coordinating bodies when issues of particular interest to them are discussed.

48. Ibid.
49. A/60/L.1, 15 September 2005.
50. S/RES/1625, 14 September 2005.
51. S/RES/1631, 17 October 2005.
52. S/PV.5282, 16 October 2005, 3.
53. Ibid., 5.
54. S/RES/1631, 17 October 2005.
55. A/61/204-S/2006/590, 28 July 2006, 1.
56. Ibid., 2.
57. Ibid., 19.
58. Ibid., 21.
59. S/PV.5529, 20 September 2006; S/PV.5649, 28 March 2007; S/PV.5649 (Resumption 1), 28 March 2007.
60. S/2007/421, 11 July 2007. For the conflict prevention activity, see S/PRST/2007/31, 28 August 2007; S/2007/783, 2 January 2008; S/2008/18, 14 January 2008.
61. S/PRST/2007/7, 28 March 2007.
62. Ibid.
63. Annex II, S/2007/421, 11 July 2007, pp. 29–30. As of 2012, the two bodies have held six joint meetings.
64. S/PRST/2007/7, 28 March 2007.
65. S/2008/186, 7 April 2008.
66. Ibid., 6–7.
67. Ibid., 7. Emphasis mine.
68. Ibid., 22.
69. S/RES/1809, 17 April 2008.
70. A/63/666-S/2008/813, 31 December 2008.
71. Ibid., 7.
72. Ibid., 18.
73. S/PRST/2009/3, 18 March 2009.
74. S/PRST/2009/26, 26 October 2009. The Secretary-General's report is A/64/359-S/2009/470, 18 September 2009.
75. S/PV.6257, 13 January 2010; S/PRST/2010/1, 13 January 2010.
76. A/65/152-S/2010/526, 20 July 2010.
77. A/65/152-S/2010/526, 20 July 2010, 5.
78. Ibid., 24.
79. Ibid., 25.
80. Ibid., 28. [This focus is maintained in the update report the following year, which hones in on particular issue areas as areas in need of particular attention. On the economic side, these are youth, education, and unemployment, while on the conflict side, the focus is on the connection between conflict and natural resources.]
81. S/PV.6702, 12 January 2012, 3.
82. Ibid.
83. Ibid., 15.
84. Ibid.
85. S/RES/2033, 12 January 2012.
86. S/PV.6702 Resumption 1, 12 January 2012, 10.
87. For more on this, see the various reports available from Security Council Report. www.securitycouncilreport.org. For a briefing on the United Nations Office to the African Union, see S/ PV.6[illegible]1, 21 June 2011.
88. S/2006/507, para. 30.

89. See, for example, the statement by the Minister of Foreign Affairs from South Africa, S/PV.5649, 28 March 2007.
90. A good overview is provided in Security Council Report, "Update Report no. 2, Briefing on Support for AU Peacekeeping," 16 June 2011.
91. Paul D. Williams, "Briefing, The Road to Humanitarian War in Libya," *Global Responsibility to Protect* 3 (2011): 248–259.

Chapter 2

The African Union

Thomas Kwasi Tieku

Introduction

This chapter examines the African Union (AU) peace and security institutions. It shows that they are among the most ambitious and novel continent-wide security governance mechanisms to emerge in the world since the end of the Cold War. They are drawn from collectivist security ideas, the Responsibility to Protect (R2P) framework and the human security paradigm. Some of them are informed by lessons learned from the practice of vertical postwar reconstruction exercises. The AU peace and security ideas are codified in the Constitutive Act of the AU, and outlined in detail in the Protocol Relating to the Establishment of the Peace and Security Council (PSC protocol) of the AU, in the African Non-Aggression and Common Defence and Security Pact, and in the Post Conflict Reconstruction and Development Policy (postwar reconstruction policy).[1] They are managed by a fifteen-member PSC, which has turned the AU into a major peace and security decision maker. Indeed, the work of the PSC has placed the AU in a position where it increasingly shares with the United Nations (UN) the responsibility of maintaining peace and security in Africa. The power- and burden-sharing arrangement between the AU and the UN goes beyond the UN Charter's paternalistic attitude to regional organizations. The absence of a legal cover in the UN Charter for the role that the AU is playing in the arena of peace and security is creating a number of frictions between the pan-African organization and the UN Security Council (UNSC).

I advance the aforementioned claims in four sections. The first sets a context for the analysis, noting that, contrary to popular account, the AU is actually three institutions. It is intergovernmental and supranational, and it has what I call *out-insider* features. The second section examines the four pillars of the continental African peace and security regime. The third section looks at the institutional structures on which the pillars stand. Finally, the last section examines the challenges the AU faces in its efforts to promote the African regional security innovations.

AU Institutions

Contrary to popular discourse, the AU is not a single organization. Rather, it consists of three organizations.[2] The first AU is intergovernmental in nature, comprising the governments of fifty-three states and Western Sahara.[3] The intergovernmental elements of the Pan-African organization include the Assembly of Heads of State and Government (Assembly), the Executive Council (Council), the Permanent Representative Committee (PRC), the PSC, and the Pan-African Parliament (PAP). Others are the Economic, Social and Cultural Council (ECOSOCC); the Court of Justice; the Specialized Technical Committees (STPs);[4] and the financial institutions.[5] The AU is headed by a chairperson who must be a sitting head of state. The second AU is supranational in design. It is represented by the AU Commission and the approximately 617 international civil servants who work in its various units. The third AU consists of the *out-insiders*, or the actors Ramesh Thakur and Thomas Weiss have described, in reference to the UN context, as the "outside-insiders."[6] They comprise African regional economic communities, nongovernmental organizations (NGOs), think tanks, academics, consultants, experts, independent commissions, and other groups of people who may or may not be formal members of the organization but who play central roles in shaping the ideas, practices, directions, priorities, and policies of the AU. Interactions between the first and third AU are mediated by the second AU.

The three AUs emerged on 26 May 2001 as part of a shift in the focus of the pan-African project.[7] Pan-Africanism as practiced within the institutional context of the Organization of African Unity (OAU) focused primarily on legitimizing and institutionalizing statehood in Africa. Protection of states and governing regimes in Africa became its referent. As part of the efforts to protect and consolidate the African state, the Charter of the OAU committed African governments to a treaty that contained some of the "purest statements [defending] juridical sovereignty ever to be embodied in any international organization."[8] The Charter also put in place only institutions, rules, and administrative mechanisms that strengthened sovereign prerogatives and the territorial integrity of African states. African leaders' strong support for the norm of territorial integrity of states compelled the OAU to remain silent on issues that might have tempted the Pan-African organization to pronounce on domestic state matters. The resolution of internal wars, like other domestic African problems, was naively considered to be outside the remit of the OAU. The OAU leadership did not deem it necessary to create a robust and institutionalized mechanism to deal with peace and security matters. The Pan-African organization, however, became directly involved in the resolution of disputes that arose out of border demarcations and the territorial claims of African states, and it also tried unsuccessfully to diffuse tension that resulted from ideological differences among African governments during the Cold War.[9]

Background

The outbreak of many internal wars in African states immediately following on the heels of the Cold War, which threatened the state system the OAU had contributed to building, compelled the OAU leadership to establish the Mechanism for Conflict Prevention, Management, and Resolution (MCMR). The mechanism, as the name suggests, was supposed to anticipate and prevent potential conflicts in Africa, resolve full-blown conflicts, and help rebuild states emerging from war, among other things.[10]

African governments that had questionable governance records, however, exploited the principle of noninterference in the OAU Charter to prevent the MCMR from working effectively. They feared that the OAU's involvement in internal African wars might open the gate for powerful non-African states to intervene in their internal affairs. As the then chairperson of the OAU, Algerian President Bouteflika, pointed out, "[s]overeignty is the last frontier we have in an increasingly unequal world."[11] There were also concerns that OAU involvement in internal African wars might encourage the UN to subcontract responsibility for the maintenance of peace in Africa to the Pan-African organization.[12] Even worse, some of the powerful African governments feared that the OAU's involvement in internal African wars would provide excuses for the Security Council to marginalize African peace and security matters. The relatively rich African states worried that they would be made to pay the cost of making and keeping peace in Africa. The preceding concerns compelled the leadership of the OAU to focus the work of the MCMR on mediation and soft conflict resolution matters. As Sam B. Ibok, the then director of the Department of Peace and Security, put it:

> Even though the OAU and its Charter came into existence as a continental framework for the promotion of the African collective will to ensure collective security and collective development, we have been unable in over thirty years to craft comprehensive security architecture to drive the peace and security agenda of the Continent. This is in spite of the establishment in Cairo in 1993 of a Continental Mechanism for Conflict Prevention, Management and Resolution.[13]

The creation of the AU was an opportunity for African governments to create innovative regional security institutions that would place African regional organizations at the centre of conflict resolution, while still keeping the UN engaged in African peace and security issues and preventing powerful non-African states from intervening in the internal affairs of African states. African leaders developed the Constitutive Act of the AU and the PSC protocol in large part to address these challenges.[14] The two agreements and their accompanying policy instruments carved out a distinctive continental peace and security governance niche for the AU.[15] The AU peace and security toolbox draws insights from collectivist security doctrines, the R2P paradigm, the human security framework, and vertical peace-building doctrines.

AU Peace and Security Pillars

The first pillar of African security architecture is the collectivist security paradigm.[16] This security model is based on the way conflict is often resolved in collectivist societies. Like the collectivist social system, in which members of the in-group are collectively responsible for the maintenance of the internal peace and harmony of the group, the new Pan-African peace and security architecture seeks to make every member of the AU responsible for the maintenance of peace and security in Africa. Similar to the collectivist entities that loathe any interference in their affairs by a member of an out-group, a number of rules and norms, including the powerful Pan-African solidarity norm, have been developed to protect African states from foreign military interventions. The strong support for Sudanese President Omar el Bashir and the AU's vociferous opposition to the NATO's (North Atlantic Treaty Organization) 2011 military intervention in Libya are all representative of the collectivist security idea.

The Constitutive Act and the peace and security protocol are replete with clauses that seek to protect African states from military intervention by non-African states while leaving room for African states to intervene collectively in each others' internal affairs with or without the consent of the target country. The intervention can take different forms, including mediation, as in the case of Kenya in 2008; suspension from participation in activities of African international organizations, as in the case of Mauritania in 2008; rebuke and suspension of AU membership, as in the case of Cote d'Ivoire in 2011; economic sanctions, as in the Malian case in 2012; and, as a last resort, military intervention, as in the case of Comoros Island in 2007. Conditions for military intervention are detailed in Article 4(h) of the Constitutive Act of the AU. It gives the AU the right to intervene in the internal affairs of a member state in order to "prevent war crimes, genocide and crimes against humanity." This threshold condition provided by the AU, as Maxi Schoeman pointed out, "goes 'beyond' the provision made for intervention in the internal affairs of a country in the UN Charter."[17] The AU has actually set thresholds for military intervention lower than those outlined in the legal code of any continental organization.[18] The article was introduced in order to protect ordinary people in Africa from abusive governments.[19] The specification of war crimes, genocide, and crimes against humanity as grounds for intervention has created a clear set of criteria by which the Union can decide to intervene in a state for human security purposes.[20]

Article 4(h), together with Article 4(i), which states that every African has the "right to live in peace," made it possible for the AU leadership to develop the second pillar of the new peace and security architecture. These articles opened the legal and political avenues by which the AU leadership could draw on ideas in the report on the "Conference on Security, Stability, Development, and Co-operation in Africa" (CSSDCA), and expand the definition of security from traditional state security concerns to include the economic, political, and social security of the individual, the family, and the society.[21] In a memorandum of understanding (MOU) adopted by the Assembly in July 2002 in Durban in South Africa, the AU not only accepted the expansion of the definition of security to embrace "all aspects of society," but also agreed to demand certain standards of behaviour from every government in Africa in the interest of common humanity.[22] The definition of security as a multidimensional phenomenon surpassing military considerations informed the drafting of the AU Non-Aggression and Common Defence Pact that was adopted in January 2005 in Abuja in Nigeria.[23] Human security language articulated in the MOU also shaped key AU governance instruments, such as the African Charter on Democracy, Elections and Governance that came into force on 15 February 2012.

The mainstreaming of human security in the AU, a process considered by African policy makers as a major step in the emergence of R2P at the global level, allowed

African leaders to frame Pan-African peace and security in R2P terms.[24] The clearest articulation of R2P as a pillar of AU peace and security is found in the *Ezulwini* Consensus, in which AU member states endorsed R2P.[25] The *Ezulwini* Consensus is a major AU reference document that outlines common African positions on UN reforms contained in the 2004 Report of the UN Panel on Threats, Challenges and Change in 2004.[26] It was adopted in 2005 and submitted to the 2005 World Summit meeting. The *Ezulwini* Consensus reiterated the three pillars of R2P, namely, the responsibility of states to protect their citizens; the responsibility of the international community to help states protect their citizens; and the responsibility of the international community to protect citizens of states that are unable or unwilling to protect their citizens. There are, however, three important caveats in the *Ezulwini* Consensus that showed a slightly different understanding of R2P than the conventional view outlined in either the report of The International Commission on Intervention and State Sovereignty (ICISS) or the 2005 World Summit Outcome document.[27]

First, the *Ezulwini* Consensus sought to shift to regional organizations the power to decide when, where, and how to intervene, contrary to the argument put forth by the original R2P report. The *Ezulwini* document argued that "the General Assembly and the Security Council are often far from the scenes of conflicts and may not be in a position to undertake effectively a proper appreciation of the nature and development of conflict situations." The collective wisdom of members of the AU is that regional organizations are the institutions best placed to make the appropriate assessment, and should be "empowered to take actions in this regard." Second, the *Ezulwini* delinked R2P from regime change, noting that even though "it is important to reiterate the obligation of states to protect their citizens, this should not be used as a pretext to undermine the sovereignty, independence and territorial integrity of states." Third, though the *Ezulwini* Consensus and the original R2P report converged on the idea that intervention by regional organizations "should be with the approval of the Security Council," an interesting and subtle qualification was inserted into the *Ezulwini* Consensus that effectively makes it possible for regional organizations to seek the Security Council's approval after interventions. The *Ezulwini* Consensus also indicated that the UN should "assume responsibility for financing such operations." The language used here in the document is meant to encourage the UN to take ownership for keeping peace imposed by regional organizations. This regional-led peacekeeping strategy was employed by the Economic Community of West African States (ECOWAS) in Liberia and Sierra Leone, and the AU copied it when it intervened in Burundi, Sudan, and Somalia.

This subtle effort to confine the UN to the role of paymaster general while making the AU PSC the main decision maker on peace and security issues in Africa is forcefully stated in a communiqué issued by the AU PSC prior to the January 2012 Security Council debate on AU–UN cooperation.[28] The move to regionalize peace and security decisions has angered some powerful members of the UNSC. As US Ambassador Susan Rice put it during the January 2012 Security Council debate on AU–UN cooperation, UN–regional organization "cooperation cannot be on the basis that the regional organization independently decides the policy and United Nations member states simply bless it and pay for it. There can be no blank check, politically or financially."[29] Her opening remarks went to yet greater lengths to indicate that the UN is not, and should not be made, "subordinate to other bodies or to regional groups, schedules or capacities." The strong concerns expressed by key P5 members, that the AU is trying to rewrite Chapter VIII of the UN Charter, induced the Security Council members to insert Chapter VIII language into Resolution 2033,[30] which was adopted after the debate. Resolution 2033 requires that regional and subregional organizations keep the Security Council fully informed before they undertake major peace and security operations in their regions.

The fourth pillar of Pan-African peace and security is contained in the AU policy on postwar reconstruction adopted by the AU Executive Council at its meeting in Banjul in 2006.[31] The policy is based on vertical postwar reconstruction ideas, in the sense that it is a top-down initiative designed to help local actors negotiate with foreign peace-builders, enhance local ownership and leadership, and improve coordination and peace-building processes, and it puts the AU Commission in a good position to engage with donors on peace-building issues. AU member states moved to define boundaries, ideas, processes, and institutions of postwar reconstruction because they think that peace-building is "a political rather than a technical process." They think that the peace-building blueprints being used in different parts of Africa are "borrowed from outside Africa," are grounded in civilizing logic, and are based on the assumption that external actors, rather than local people, know exactly what is needed to rebuild African states emerging from war.

The AU leadership believes, perhaps naively, that the postwar reconstruction policy can empower local Africans to bargain effectively with external actors. They claim that too often current foreign peace-builders engage in what can be called *consulformations*; that is, a series of talks on an already-finalized plan in order to make it appear as if stakeholders and, in particular, those who will be affected by the plan contributed to its development. The Executive Council is of the view that African citizens in postwar societies are seldom consulted, in the true sense of the word, on peace-building projects. The consensus position is therefore meant to offer local actors options and a context within which to engage with external interveners to develop what Roland Paris and Timothy Sisk call a "peace-building contract."[32] To counter civil society accusations that its state-building ideas are equally based on a top-down approach, the AU Commission adopted fairly consultative processes in developing the postwar reconstruction policy. Those processes included a Brainstorming Retreat for members of the PSC and the PRC, held on 2 and 5 September 2005 in Durban, South Africa; a Technical Experts Meeting of AU members, held on 7 and 8 February 2006 in Addis Ababa, Ethiopia; an AU and Civil Society Dialogue, held from 5 to 7 April 2006 in Abuja, Nigeria; a Validation Workshop for the AU Commission, held on 31 May 2006 in Addis Ababa; and, finally, a Governmental Experts Meeting held on 8 and 9 June 2006 in Addis Ababa. In September 2006, the AU Commission discussed with civil society groups the best ways to promote the postwar policy. The AU leadership believes that these processes gave a broad spectrum of Africans the chance not only to shape peace-building ideas in Africa, but to stop dumping foreign ideas on Africans.

The postwar policy is designed to discourage peace-builders from trying to "civilize" citizens of postwar states by directing the peace-builders' attention to local needs and encouraging them to respect local cultures. Leading figures at the AU Commission think current peace-building projects carry too many residual traces of the civilizing missions and projects of the eighteenth and nineteenth centuries.[33] They claim that current peace-building projects are driven by a civilizing mission, because they try to replicate representative government in the form of the presidential or parliamentary systems of government (read democratization) that exist in donor states, replace traditional and customary rules with formal written laws similar to those in donor states (read promotion of the rule of law), and spread values and ideas held by external interveners and their donors (read promotion of good governance). The projects also attempt to stimulate local people's taste for merchandised goods produced in donor countries (read economic reforms). The AU leadership thinks that while these may be well intentioned, they are likely to have disastrous long-term impacts on postwar societies. The AU Commission attached to the postwar reconstruction policy a "flexible template" to help peace-builders move beyond civilizing goals to "pave the way for growth and regeneration in countries and regions emerging from conflict."

The template is also designed to dissuade peace-builders from prioritizing some aspects of the reconstruction processes at the expense of others. A major complaint from civil society groups during AU–civil society consultations on postwar reconstruction was that many donors and practitioners tended to favor aspects of reconstruction that would generate publicity and media attention to the exclusion of other important, but less visible, areas. Often the aspects that are neglected—such as psychological healing, the retraining of former combatants, and the creation of sustainable jobs—are precisely those that are most needed by the people recovering from the war. The AU wanted to end the discriminatory practices by producing a menu of tasks essential for peace-builders to accomplish in war-ravaged African countries. Given the AU's complaints that current peace-building ideas are borrowed from outside of Africa, it is ironic that the template draws heavily from liberal capitalist democratic principles, such as the rule of law. Indeed, the democratic ideals they listed appear identical to the conventional liberal peace-building exercises the policy seeks to replace. Perhaps, these ideas somehow lose their civilizing significance when they are articulated by African elites. The hypocrisy notwithstanding, the policy could minimize the potential for conflicts over the political objectives of postwar reconstruction in the African context.

The postwar reconstruction policy provided benchmarks for measuring successes and failures of peace-building. Given the attraction of human security discourses in AU circles, it was perhaps to be expected when the then chairperson of the AU Commission claimed that every postwar peace-building process in Africa must strive to free the so-called ordinary Africans from "want and fear."[34] On the question of freeing people from want, the AU expects peace-building to create the conditions in which people affected by war can improve their living conditions; to meet basic needs, such as for health, education, and food; and to enhance their capacity to realize their potential. On freeing people from fear, the AU borrowed ideas from conventional disarmament, demobilization, and reintegration (DDR) programs. Thus, at the end of the postwar reconstruction, the AU expects peace-builders to complete the demanding task of establishing conditions for social, political, economic, and physical transformation of affected areas, societies, and states.

The postwar reconstruction policy attempted to address the obvious question of how African these ideas are, as the document reads like a poorly attributed paper or even a plagiarized review of peace-building literature. The template and the broader policy documents claimed that the state-building ideas are not African ideas per se, but that they can be adapted and embedded in certain principles to suit local African conditions. The AU has consequently developed six principles, namely, African leadership, national and local ownership, inclusiveness, equity and nondiscrimination, and cooperation and cohesion, as well as capacity-building for sustainability to guide peace-building exercises. Although many of these principles lack specificity, the AU leadership hopes that the principles of national and local ownership will empower local actors to domesticate peace-building projects and to exercise oversight in the reconstruction processes. The AU Commission thinks local Africans will use the ideas to set the terms of peace-building engagements with external actors.

AU members recognize that peace-building can easily be used to reconstruct the identities of people in societies emerging from war. The principles of African leadership are meant to help Africans determine the content of peace-building projects. Rather than turning war-torn societies into photocopies of outside cultures, AU members hope that national bureaucrats and local authorities will use the template to design, assess, implement, monitor, and evaluate peace-building projects in such a way that they reinforce core local identities and values. The AU is acutely aware that it is not enough to make Africans take leadership positions. It is equally vital that ordinary Africans get involved, in order to ensure local acceptance of peace-building projects. The principles of inclusiveness, equity, and nondiscrimination, with their emphasis on equitable distribution of power, wealth, and organic links between peace-builders and the local population, are designed to ensure that ordinary people are involved in reconstruction exercises.

Coordination and cooperation are problems of legendary severity in the current aid system, and peace-building projects that depend heavily on donor support carry this baggage as well. The principles of cooperation and coherence are meant to promote synergy among different peace-building activities, encourage genuine partnership among actors involved in reconstruction, and promote donor cooperation and coordination. As a pan-African organization, the AU would ideally like Africans based in Africa to manage every aspect of peace-building projects, but it knows that the expertise is unavailable. It developed the principles of capacity-building for sustainability to encourage peace-builders and donors to prioritize capacity-building of locals so that the local people will make the necessary efforts to consolidate and sustain peace-building projects.

AU members are acutely aware that intermediaries can sometimes be spoilers in peace-building processes.[35] Intermediaries such as peace-building consultants, NGOs, and donors are not necessarily altruistic, however morally superior the outlook they project. Intermediaries are quick to tell those who will listen that their main goal is to help war-torn states resolve the root causes of conflicts; but in practice, few have pursued this objective in any meaningful way.[36] It is not uncommon to find intermediaries putting their interests above those of the people they are supposed to be helping. The AU's aim is to minimize the incentive for self-seeking donors to turn the peace-building exercises into a lucrative industry. The benchmarks and principles are meant to discourage intermediaries from treating their work as mere jobs or careers.

Although AU peace-building ideas are general and imprecise, and at times contradictory and incoherent, their drafters made an excellent move by establishing linkages between the postwar reconstruction ideas and extant AU policies. The security elements were thus embedded in human security ideas outlined in the African Non-aggression and Common Defence and Security Pact. The political governance element draws extensively from the AU Declaration on Political, Economic, and Corporate Governance of 2002, which contains the textbook conception of political governance. The drafters of the postwar reconstruction policy thus attempted to prevent illegal seizure of power in countries emerging from war by drawing on the 1999 OAU Declaration against unconstitutional change of governments in Africa. The clear definition of unconstitutional change of government in the declaration—as the replacement of a democratically elected government through a military coup d'état, mercenary intervention, or armed rebellion, or as the refusal by an incumbent government to relinquish power to the winning party after free, fair, and regular elections—together with the mechanical way in which the anti-coup principles in the Declaration have been applied, has provided an effective mechanism with which to close a loophole in the current peace-building system. The current system has no means, except the court of public opinion, to prevent unconstitutional changes of governments during a state-building period.

The postwar reconstruction policy seeks to prevent war-torn states from sliding into electoral dictatorship. It is easy for postwar societies to practice electoral politics, or at least to hold an election with international support. However, consolidation of postwar democracies has become one of the most difficult activities of peace-building exercises. Governments that emerge from postwar electoral processes often try to use legal means to undermine democratic institutions. The recent history of Africa is replete with examples, and studies also show that authoritarian tendencies have crept into the administrations of a number of ostensibly democractic postwar states.[37] Ethiopia, Sierra Leone, Uganda, and Rwanda, for example, have all become casualties of democratic backsliding. To deal with the problem, the postwar reconstruction commits the AU to defending and protecting African democracies by linking peace-building exercises to the African Charter on Democracy, Elections, and Governance (the African Democratic Charter), which entered into force on 15 February 2012.[38]

The AU seeks to introduce a third-party oversight into peace-building processes in order to deal with the current system, which has no institutional mechanisms for either international or African peace-builders to render accounts of their performance on key aspects of their work. AU members want to make the AU Commission the overarching institution to which peace-builders and postwar societies can submit reports that show how they are performing in key areas, such as democratization. That development would be a major corrective to the current system, which is based on the belief that international pressure will be enough to nurture critical projects, such as democracy, once elections are organized and elected leaders take office in war-ravaged states. Without a third-party obligation, it has become too easy for elected leaders to use legal and constitutional means to erode democratic gains, as the cases of Burundi and Rwanda show. The AU instrument introduces third-party oversight by empowering the AU Commission to monitor progress made by postwar states in areas such as good governance, respect for the rule of law, consolidation of peace agreements, disarmament and reintegration of former combatants, and return of refugees and internally displaced persons.

Finally, the postwar reconstruction policy tries to offer institutional mechanisms for parties in postwar societies to resolve electoral disputes. Electoral disputes are major challenges in countries emerging from war, and the current postwar reconstruction system has few institutionalized mechanisms to resolve disagreements over electoral results. The policy links reconstruction to other rules, regulations, and norms that the AU has developed to minimize postelection disputes. These include requiring member states to inform the AU Commission of any scheduled elections and to invite the AU Electoral Assistant Unit to send an electoral observer mission and to give detailed rules for elections in member states. The AU Commission has the power to conduct election monitoring without the express consent of member states. The AU Commission's ability to monitor elections has thus been enhanced, as clever governments often use the "by invitation only" prerogative to negotiate the terms of the observation mission. This prerogative has been used by incumbent governments in places such as Latin America to issue an invitation so close to an election that it gives the observers little time to prepare.[39] Other governments have used the "by invitation" principle to negotiate for a sympathetic mission, to limit access to electoral institutions and to shape the election observation mission to their liking. African governments would seek to mainstream and globalize these ideas if a new Agenda for Peace were to be discussed and adopted in 2012.

Decision-making Structure

AU peace and security ideas are promoted by an organizational structure headed by the PSC.[40] The PSC, established to make swift, timely, and efficient decisions relating to all peace and security issues in Africa, is composed of ten members who are elected for a two-year term, and five members who are elected to serve for three years. There is no permanent or veto-wielding member. Membership is merit based, though every effort is made to ensure regional balance in the allocation of seats. So far, the two-year term and three-term seats have been distributed equally among the five subregions of Africa. The AU Commission acts as the administrative unit of AU peace and security architecture, while a Military Staff Committee composed of senior military officers from various African military establishments offers the necessary technical advice to the civilians managing the AU peace and security system. The PSC agenda is set by a chairperson, a position rotated among PSC members on a monthly basis. Decisions of the PSC are binding and do not require approval by heads of state to take effect. The binding nature of PSC decisions, together with its democratic character and the seriousness of its deliberations, has made the PSC the AU organ with the highest profile.[41]

The other members of the AU peace and security organizational structure are The Panel of the Wise, the Early Warning System (EWS), the Peace Fund (PF), and the African Standby Force (ASF). The Panel of the Wise comprises five highly respected African personalities who have made outstanding contributions to the cause of peace and security in Africa. They are selected by the Chairperson of the Commission on the basis of competence and regional representation to serve for a renewal three-year term. The Continental EWS consists of an observation and monitoring centre known as "the Situation Room," located at the AU headquarters in Addis Ababa. The Situation Room is supposed to be linked to similar structures at the subregional levels. The feed from the regional mechanisms, together with independent data collected by the Situation Room at the AU headquarters, is supposed to help the PSC get accurate and timely information about potential trouble spots on the African continent. The PF is made up of roughly 6 percent of AU annual assessed contributions, voluntary contributions from African states, and donation from external partners. As of the time of writing, over 90 percent of contributions to the PF came from external actors, primarily the European Union (EU) and the United States. The ASF has multidisciplinary contingents of civilian and military brigades assembled at each of the five subregions of Africa. When fully operational, the ASF will be able to deploy within thirty days, and stay in combat theater for up to ninety days. As of the end of April 2012, only West Africa and East Africa had established the nucleus and policy basis for a regional brigade.

Capacity Issues

AU peace and security ideas and institutions are among the most ambitious; they make many regional organizations and even the UN look conservative, at least on paper. However, many of the ideas are difficult to operationalize, and even harder to implement. They emphasize structural conflict prevention and resolution issues such as institutionalization of rule of law, separation of powers, respect for human rights, and consolidation of democracies in Africa. Nevertheless, as Darren Hawkins tells us, the definitions of these concepts are "not entirely open ended," and they mean different things to different people. Certainly Algeria, Egypt, Libya, and Nigeria—four of the five countries that, together, contribute 75 percent of the AU's operational budget—do not share the AU's interpretation of these concepts. Algeria and Egypt are strong believers in the OAU's definition of democracy, which includes a key provision that every state in Africa has "the right . . . to determine . . . the system of democracy on the basis of their socio-cultural values."[42] Algeria, in particular, has often called on African leaders to institutionalize this culturally determined version of democracy. The problem is that the OAU conception of democracy disables many of the structural conflict prevention and resolution mechanisms, such as protection of political rights and civil liberties embedded in liberal democracies. It is hard to see how the AU Commission can effectively monitor and implement the structural conflict prevention measures if the big four do not particularly like them. The other major player in the AU system, South Africa, has not shown the political will to stand up to the other four on these issues.

One wonders whether the AU, which is an undemocratic institution, has the legitimacy to implement a policy that has democratic governance at its core. Not only are the AU bureaucrats, the members of the Council of Ministers, and the civil societies groups who developed these security ideas unelected officials, they also developed the policy without normal legislative deliberation. It could be argued that they bypassed the challenging processes of persuasion and consensus-seeking that characterizes legislative deliberation and the formal lawmaking process. This casts serious doubt on the AU's legitimacy in promoting a peace and security system, with a liberal democratic agenda. As Jed Rubenfeld of Yale Law School tells us, international organizations such as the AU are "everything but democratic," and lack the "process of popular deliberation and consent," and it is possible that it is too much to ask an undemocratic institution to promote positive peace.[43] It is also unclear whether ordinary people in conflict zones will see the AU as a legitimately peace-promoting institution, given its remoteness from ordinary Africans. Studies conducted elsewhere in the world suggest that the AU will find it hard to gain acceptance among ordinary Africans.

Robert Dahl says that multilateral institutions generally struggle to gain acceptance among ordinary people because of their bureaucratic character, their separation from domestic democratic institutions, and the lack of participation by ordinary citizens in their decision making.[44] Public law scholar Jeremy Rabkin thinks it is the elite-driven agendas and lack of explicit democratic delegation and direct popular accountability that make it difficult for multilateral institutions to acquire the popular perception of legitimacy.[45]

Perhaps, the absence of that popular perception in the case of the AU in part accounts for the weak monitoring and reporting mechanism in the institutions. The AU Commission will rely on self-reporting to determine members' compliance with the peace and security measures. There is no external evaluation of members' compliance built into the system, nor do they have peer-review mechanisms. The AU Commission also lacks the mandate to inspect new African governments to ensure that the country accepts the peace and security norms and standards before the government is allowed to take its AU seat. Most studies show that it is through the process of monitoring new members that regional organizations such as the EU are able to force states to comply fully with their values and policies.[46] The neglect is, perhaps, unsurprising, given that bureaucrats have little say in the entry of new members into the AU, and given that all states in Africa are automatic members of the institution unless either they opt out of it or the AU Assembly refuses their application. The AU Commission does not even have the mandate to engage in routine monitoring of African states. This is in stark contrast to the EU system, where the Commission often does detailed, and partially public, monitoring of member states. Besides the obvious limitations of that approach, it is unlikely that many African states will file a detailed compliance report, as they have been complaining about report fatigue.[47]

The disarmament, demobilization, and integration ideas in the postwar reconstruction policy are superficially laudable; but as the UN, which has more resources and experience than the AU, discovered in places like Burundi, Cote d'Ivoire, and Sierra Leone, DDR is a complex process and many DDR programs stall or are only partly implemented. Both NATO and the United States have found it difficult to implement the DDR mandate in their respective missions in Afghanistan and Iraq. Can the AU succeed in areas where better-resourced organizations and even the presumed remaining superpowers have failed?

It also appears that the capacity to implement postwar ideas simply does not exist in many states in Africa, even if the political will does exist at the highest level of government. As Richard Gueli points out, the majority of states in Africa are:

> [L]argely oblivious of the quality and quantity of their engineering and construction industries. In fact, not only is the AU unclear on how to rebuild Africa, it also lacks African "statebuilders," and this imbalance is forcing it either to rely on foreigners to do the job, thus perpetuating the problem of African dependency, or to turn to military solutions, which tend to fail.[48]

The African states that have the capacity to assist in the reconstruction are reluctant to play the lead role. South Africa, which led the AU effort to reconstruct Burundi in 2003, has been reluctant to do so again. The AU requested that it lead the process of reconstructing South Sudan, but studies show that South Africa has "done precious little."[49] Given the cost of reconstructing postwar states—the best estimates suggest proper reconstruction costs between US$1.5 billion and US$15 billion a year, with completion taking on average five years—it is perhaps unsurprising that South Africa's effort has amounted to a mere drop of water rather than the needed ocean.[50]

The peace and security instruments are too complex for the AU Commission's Department of Political Affairs (DPA) and Department of Peace and Security (DPS), which have the unenviable task of implementing them. Both departments have serious capacity problems. The current structure of the AU Commission allows the DPA to recruit nine full-time professionals, of whom four are required to work on conflict- and peace-related issues, such as refugees and internally displaced persons. As of the time of writing, at least two of the nine were not at post. The rigid interpretation of the Maputo decision on the structure of the AU Commission meant that the DPA could not prioritize hiring of conflict specialists until the Commission had received a mandate from African leaders to do so. There is no indication that African governments will entertain any request to expand the DPA in the immediate future, as they have worked hard throughout the past four summits to reduce the operational costs of the AU Commission. The workload of the professionals is three times that of professionals who work for other major international organizations. Unlike most departments in international organizations, such as the UN and the EU, the DPA has no desk officers, and cannot afford to let any of the full-time professionals pay exclusive attention to a single member state of the AU. The capacity problems have forced the DPA to rely on consultants who bring another set of problems. The reliance on consultants makes it difficult for the DPA to build institutional memory.

The DPS has a staff complement three times that of the DPA. Yet, the general consensus in the literature is that it "is under-staffed and many more personnel and operational tools are needed to handle the increasing volume, complexity of work, and frequency of PSC meetings."[51] More troubling is the fact that the department has been suffering from a high turnover, with many of its most competent officials continuously being poached by other international organizations, such as the UN and the African Development Bank. The DPS in particular, and the AU in general, have become training grounds for the UN. The lure of bigger pay and less work has led some of the ardent Pan-Africanists and senior professional staff at the DPS to abandon the AU for the UN.[52] It has become an open secret that many people in the AU aspire to move to the more lucrative, even if low-ranked, positions in the UN.

The other problem with both departments is that they are generally perceived as elitist institutions whose activities are often inaccessible to ordinary Africans, particularly the younger ones. Only those with lofty titles do have meaningful access to them. However, the more active peace-builders in Africa are younger, energetic people who lack the kinds of titles that will encourage DPA and DPS officials to invite them to meetings, let alone work with them. Given the DPA and DPS top-down approach to issues, one wonders how they will be able to reach ordinary citizens to empower them to take ownership of peace-building.

Both departments have serious financial challenges, with the DPA in the more difficult position. Its activities are funded mainly through the extremely unreliable annual contributions made by AU member states. African governments have carried on with the terrible habit of serially defaulting on the payment of annual contributions. While the situation is not as bad as in the OAU era, far too many governments in Africa are happy just to accept a free ride. On average, less than 50 percent of statutory contributions are paid on time every year. Even in better times, such as in 2005, the AU was able to collect just 57 percent, representing US$36 million out of the US$63 million of assessed contributions. This money was supposed to cover the 2005 budget of around US$158 million, representing US$63 million for operations and US$95 million for programs.[53] The statutory contributions paid in that year could not even cover the US$63 million operating budget. The AU sought to change the situation in 2005 by developing a new funding formula that has compelled five African states—Algeria, Egypt, Libya, Nigeria, and South Africa—to contribute 66 percent of the AU's operational budget.[54] As AU Commissioner for Economic Affairs, Maxwell Mkwezalamba, pointed out, the new funding formula is unsustainable.[55] The shift to the "ability-to-pay system" has moved the AU out of the realm of solidarity politics, a core value and a unique feature of Pan-Africanism, into the area of *realpolitik*. There is a fear that the five states will use their financial contributions to control the AU peace and security agenda in a way similar to the one in which the permanent members control the work of the UNSC.

Conclusion

This chapter demonstrates that the AU has developed novel regional peace and security institutions for the African continent during the past decade. They make many regional organizations and even the UN look conservative. Unlike other continental organizations, the AU has redefined the sovereignty of its member states. The new conception of sovereignty allows the AU to intervene in the internal affairs of a member state with or without the consent of the target country. The organization has exercised this new power in different ways in countries such as Comoros Island, Cote d'Ivoire, Mali, Mauritania, and Kenya. The understanding of sovereignty by AU members is based on the collectivist view, in which group membership trumps almost everything. Similarly, the AU has accepted major elements of R2P. Indeed, many governments in Africa consider the creation of AU peace and security institutions to be a critical juncture in the development and conceptualization of R2P principles at the global level. The acceptance of R2P ideas by the AU opened the gate for the organization to develop the full spectrum of new peacemaking measures. The latest of these is post-conflict reconstruction policy, which seeks to enhance peace-building contracts, local leadership and ownership of peace-building programs, coordination and management of donors, and accountability and legitimacy of peace-building exercises; it is also meant to prevent postelectoral violence and democratic backsliding in states emerging from war.

In practical terms, the AU is sharing with the UN the primary responsibility for the maintenance of peace and security in Africa. It wants a new legal language and institutional basis to replace the UN Charter's paternalistic attitude toward regional organizations. Specifically, the AU wants powers and legal backing, first, to seek the Security Council's approval for peacemaking activities, including military intervention, after the fact; second, to seek to commit the Security Council to deploying peacekeepers after the

AU's military intervention; and finally, to seek to commit the UN to pay for the bulk of its peacemaking activities.

The innovative and elaborate nature of the AU peace and security architecture raises an obvious question: does the AU have the financial and institutional capacity to implement these praiseworthy ideas? This chapter indicated that African leaders seem to have bitten off more than the AU Commission can chew. It is unclear how the AU will be able to raise the billions of dollars it will take to translate the elaborate plans and strategies into reality, given that since its creation it has struggled to collect even 60 percent of the US$63 million of assessed contributions from member states. The new peace and security regime came without any additional institutional support for the overburdened AU Commission. Both the DPA and the DPS, neither of which has the required staff or expertise to carry out its original mandate, have been asked to assume the role of the implementing agency in AU peace and security architecture.

It seems unavoidable that resources and capacity challenges will oblige the AU Commission to leave key peacemaking measures on the shelf to gather dust, but senior AU officials are unwilling to use the institutional and financial challenges of the Commission as an excuse to do nothing. They claim that the AU is a master of improvisation, and is the most experienced international organization when it comes to doing things on a tight budget and with limited capacity. The AU Commission, in its own unique way of doing things, will somehow find a path to implement many of the peace and security measures.

Notes

1. African Union, *The Constitutive Act* (Addis Ababa, 2001); African Union, *Political, Economic, and Corporate Governance* (Addis Ababa, 2006); African Union, *The Common African Defence and Security Policy, African Union Commission* (Addis Ababa, 2007).
2. For a similar conceptualization of the United Nations Organization, see Inis L. Claude, Jr., *Swords into Plowshares: The Problems and Prospects of International Organization* (New York: Random House, 1956); Inis L. Claude, Jr., "Peace and Security: Prospective Roles for the Two United Nations," *Global Governance* 2:3 (1996): 289–298; Ramesh Thakur and Thomas G. Weiss, "United Nations 'Policy': An Argument with Three Illustrations," *International Studies Perspectives* 10:1 (2009): 18–35.
3. Western Sahara is a member of the AU, but its statehood is in dispute. Morocco sees it as part of its territory.
4. These are: the Committee on Rural Economy and Agricultural Matters; the Committee on Monetary and Financial Affairs; the Committee on Trade, Customs and Immigration Matters; the Committee on Industry, Science and Technology, Energy, Natural Resources and the Environment; the Committee on Transport, Communications and Tourism; the Committee on Health, Labour and Social Affairs; and the Committee on Education, Culture and Human Resources.
5. The African Central Bank, the African Monetary Fund and the African Investment Bank.
6. Thakur and Weiss, United Nations Policy.
7. This section draws on Thomas Tieku, "Explaining the Clash and Accommodation of Interests of Major Actors in the Creation of the African Union," *African Affairs* 103 (2004): 249–267. 26 May 2001 is recognized as the official date on which the AU came

into existence, because it was the date of the entry into force of the Constitutive Act of the AU. It was exactly 30 days after the deposit of the instrument of ratification by two-thirds of the member states of the AU, as provided for in Article 28 of the Constitutive Act.

8. Clapham Clapham, *Africa and the International System: The Politics of State Survival* (Cambridge: Cambridge University Press, 1996).
9. James Jonah, "The OAU: Peace Keeping and Conflict Resolution," in *The Organization of African Unity after Thirty Years*, ed. Yassin El-Ayouty (Westport: Praeger, 1994), p. 9; Sam Amoo, "Role of the OAU: Past, Present and Future," in *Making War and Waging Peace: Foreign Intervention in Africa*, ed. David R. Smock (Washington, DC: United States Institute of Peace, 1993).
10. Richard Jackson, "The Dangers of Regionalising International Conflict Management: The African Experience," *Political Science* 52:1 (2000): 41–60; Eric Berman, "African Regional Organizations' Peace Operations: Developments and Challenge," *African Security Review* 11:4 (2002): 32–44.
11. Kristiana Powell and Thomas Kwasi Tieku, "The African Union and the Responsibility to Protect: Towards a Protection Regime for Africa?" *International Insights* 20:1&2 (2005): 215–235; Adonia Ayebare, "Regional Perspectives on Sovereignty and Intervention," *Discussion Paper* (Maputo, ICISS Round Table, 2001).
12. Monde Muyangwa and Margaret A. Vogt, An Assessment of the OAU Mechanism for Conflict Prevention, Management and Resolution, 1993–2000 (2002).
13. Sam Ibok, "The OAU Mechanism for Conflict Prevention, Management and Resolution" (Addis Ababa: OAU, 1999), p. 4.
14. The Constitutive Act came into force on 26 May 2001, while the peace and security protocol became operational on 26 December 2003.
15. The analogy of AU peace and security as toolbox was first used by Mark Malan.
16. This section draws on Thomas Kwasi Tieku, "A Pan-African View of A 'New' Agenda for Peace," *International Journal* 67:2 (2012): 373–389.
17. Maxi Schoeman, "The African Union after the Durban 2002 Summit," Occasion Paper, Centre of African Studies University of Copenhagen, February 2003.
18. Thomas G. Weiss, "The Sunset of Humanitarian Intervention? The Responsibility to Protect in a Unipolar Era," *Security Dialogue* 35:2 (2004): 135–153.
19. Mark Malan, *New Tools in the Box? Towards a Standby Force for the African Union* (Johannesburg: Institute of Security Studies, 2002); Jackie Cilliers and Kathryn Sturman, "The Right Intervention: Enforcement Challenges for the African Union," *African Security Review* 11:3 (2002): 28–39. Article 4(h) has been amended to include intervention to "restore peace and stability" and in response to "a serious threat to legitimate order." African Union, Protocol on Amendments to the Constitutive Act of the African Union, July 2003.
20. Powell and Tieku, "The African Union and the Responsibility to Protect."
21. Olusengun Obasanjo and Felix G. N. Mosha, eds., *Africa Rise to the Challenge: Conference Report on the Kampala Forum* (Abeokuta/New York: Africa Leadership Forum, 1992); Tieku, "Explaining the Clash and Accommodation," 2004.
22. Tieku Tieku, "Pan-Africanization of Human Security," in *Handbook of Human Security*, ed. Taylor Owen and Mary Martin (London: Routledge, 2012).
23. Omar A. Touray, "The Common African Defence and Security Policy," *African Affairs* 104:417 (2005): 635–656.
24. Jide Martyns Okeke, "African Union and the Challenges of Implementing 'Responsibility to Protect' in Africa," XIIIth CODESRIA (General Assembly, 2011).
25. African Union, The Common African Position on the Proposed Reform of the United Nations: The Ezulwini Consensus, Ext/EX.CL/2 (VII), 7–8 March 2005; African Union, Report on the elaboration of a framework document on Post Conflict Reconstruction and Development (PCRD), EX.CL/274 (IX), 25–26 June 2006.

26. United Nations, "A More Secure World: Our Shared Responsibility," Report of the High-level Panel on Threats, Challenges and Change (2004).
27. A/RES/60/1, 24 October 2005.
28. African Union, Communiqué, Peace and Security council 306th Meeting Addis Ababa, Ethiopia, PSC/PR/COMM(CCCVII), 5 January 2012.
29. United Nations, S/PV.6702, 12 January 2012.
30. United Nations, S/RES/2033, 12 January 2012.
31. African Union, Report on the elaboration of a framework document, 2006.
32. Roland Paris and Timothy D. Sisk, eds., *The Dilemmas of Statebuilding: Confronting the Contradictions of Post-war Peace Operations* (New York: Routledge, 2009).
33. Interview by author, Addis Ababa, 24 February 2012.
34. Jean Ping, "Opening Remarks by the AUC Chairperson H.E. Dr Jean Ping on the occasion of the First Annual US-African Union High Level Meeting" (Washington, DC, 21 April 2010).
35. Desirée Nilsson and Mimmi Söderberg Kovacs, "Revising an Elusive Concept: A Review of the Debate on Spoilers in Peace Processes," *International Studies Review* 13:4 (2011): 606–626; John Stephen Stedman, "Spoiler Problems in Peace Processes," *International Security* 22 (1997): 5–53.
36. W. Bruce Dayton and Louis Kriesberg, *Conflict Transformation and Peace Building: Moving from Violence to Sustainable Peace* (New York: Routledge, 2009).
37. Michael Bratton, Robert Mattes, and Emmanual Gyimah-Boadi, eds., *Public Opinion, Democracy, and Market Reform in Africa* (Cambridge: Cambridge University Press, 2005).
38. On the African Charter on Democracy, Elections, and Governance, see Solomon T. Ebobrah, *The African Charter on Democracy, Elections and Governance: A New Dawn for the Enthronement of Legitimate Governance in Africa?* (London: Open Society Institute, 2007).
39. Thomas Legler and Thomas Tieku, "What Difference Can a Path Make? Regional Regimes for Democracy Promotion and Defense in the Americas and Africa," *Democratization* 18:3 (2010): 465–491.
40. For detailed examination of the PSC, see Paul Williams, "The Peace and Security Council of the African Union: Evaluating an Embryonic International Institution," *Journal of Modern African Studies* 47:4 (2009): 603–626.
41. Ibid.
42. Organization of Africa Unity, Report of the Secretary General to the Fifty-second Ordinary Session of Council of Ministers (Addis Ababa, 1990).
43. Jed Rubenfeld, "Unilateralism and Constitutionalism," *New York University Law Review* 79:6 (2004): 1971–2028.
44. Robert A. Dahl, "Can International Organizations Be Democratic?" in *Democracy's Edges*, ed I. Shapiro and C. Hacker-Cordon (Cambridge: Cambridge University Press, 1999), pp. 19–36.
45. A. Jeremy Rabkin, *Why Sovereignty Matters* (Washington, DC: American Enterprise Institute Press, 1998); A. Jeremy Rabkin, *Law without Nations? Why Constitutional Government Requires Sovereign States* (Princeton, NJ: Princeton University Press, 2005).
46. Darren Hawkins, "Protecting Democracy in Europe and the Americas," *International Organization* 62 (Summer 2009): 373–403.
47. Wafula Okumu and Anneli Botha, *Understanding Terrorism in Africa: In Search for an African Voice* (Pretoria: Institute for Security Studies, 2007).
48. Richard Gueli "South Africa: A Future Research Agenda for Post-conflict Reconstruction," *African Security Review* 17:1 (2008): 84.
49. Ibid., 84, 83–98.
50. James F. Dobbins, "America's Role in Nation-Building: From Germany to Iraq," *Survival* 45:4 (2003): 87–110; James F. Dobbins "The UN's Role in Nation-Building: From the Belgian Congo to Iraq," *Survival* 46:4 (2004): 81–102.

51. Rodrigo Tavares, *Regional Security: The Capacity of International Organizations* (London and New York: Routledge, 2010), p. 24.
52. Prominent DPS figures who have moved from the AU to the UN include former Commissioner for Peace and Security, and one-time number two person in the Pan-African organization, Said Djinit, former head of Conflict Management Division Sam Ibok, and former information analyst Musifiky Mwanasali.
53. High Level Panel of the Audit of the African Union, *Audit of the African Union* (2007).
54. African Union, The Financial Year for the African Union, 2012 Doc.EX.CL/721 (XXI), African Union, Addis Ababa (2012).
55. Maxwell Mkwezalamba, Statement on the Occasion of the Opening of the Meeting of Governmental Experts on Alternative Sources of Financing the African Union, African Union, Addis Ababa (2006).

Chapter 3

The Peace and Security Architecture of African Subregional Organizations

Anthoni van Nieuwkerk

Introduction

Recent years have seen an upswing in the economic fortunes of many African states. Based on a rush of new discoveries of natural resources, in particular gas and oil, it appears as if the continent might have the means to be resilient in the face of a prolonged Western economic downturn. Despite the much-hyped African economic boom, most African countries feature low on the United Nations Development Programme's Human Development Index (HDI).[1] The fifteen countries ranked lowest are all in sub-Saharan Africa. Among the thirty countries ranked at the bottom, only Afghanistan and Haiti are outside the region. Not surprisingly, an African security analyst noted, "Africa will in the short to medium term continue to experience violent conflicts which tend to be complicated and give rise to complex emergency situations."[2]

There is indeed ongoing interest in whether the African Union (AU) and its associated Regional Economic Communities (RECs) are able to pour oil on the troubled waters of Africa—the eastern parts of the Democratic Republic of the Congo (DRC), or the northern parts of Mali in particular. Turmoil elsewhere on the continent, including in western Africa, the greater horn of Africa, and the Indian Ocean island states, requires ongoing high-level attention. For some observers, the Libyan implosion and humiliating death of Muammar Qaddafi serves as an illustration of the inability of the AU to manage, never mind resolve, conflict.

Indeed, old and new security challenges act as powerful reminders and drivers for the upkeep and, where necessary, refinement of the African peace and security architecture. The basic approach has been under construction for several years now. It includes an intervention force based on subregional military and civilian standby arrangements and supported by a range of conflict-management tools such as early warning, a panel of the wise, and a peace fund. The track record of its deployments so far tells another story, and casts doubt on the viability of the idea of subregional security structures based on the

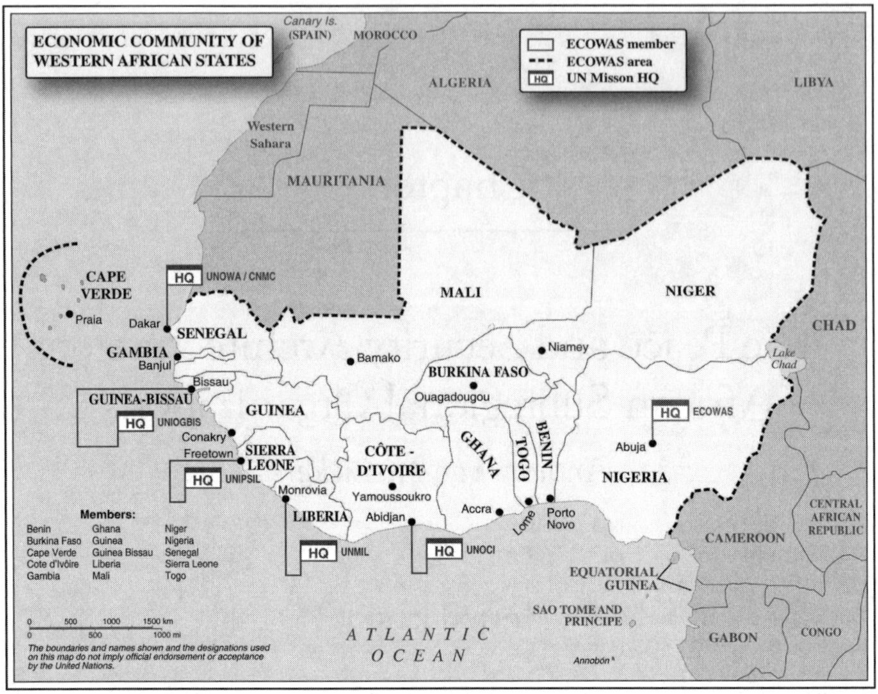

Source: Map No 4350 Rev 2, United Nations, Department of Field Support, Cartographic Section, August 2012

RECs working in tandem with the parent body—the AU—to arrest or reduce violent behavior or manage natural disasters.

This chapter will explore the AU's crisis management arrangements, commonly known as the African Peace and Security Architecture (APSA), as well as the structure and performance of three key RECs: the East African Community (EAC), the Economic Community of West African States (ECOWAS), and the Southern African Development Community (SADC). The chapter will conclude with an overall assessment of the relationship between the AU and the United Nations (UN), and between the AU and its RECs.

The chapter begins, however, with an exploration of the broader influences upon African peace and security activities—in particular, with the key national and international factors that exert an influence on Africa's ability to make and keep the peace.

Contextual Factors Influencing African Peacemaking and Peacekeeping

African Policy-Making Behavior

African decision makers are not fully in charge of their countries' destinies. As argued by Gilbert Khadiagala and Terrence Lyons in their path-breaking 2001 text, entitled

African Foreign Policies: Power and Process, a number of "severe constraints" impinge on the freedom of African decision makers.[3] These include, first, the need to consolidate power and meet socioeconomic demands at home; second, the fact that external actors have considerable influence over most aspects of African life. This influence is partly why anticolonial attitudes and opposition to external intrusion has formed, and continues to form, significant aspects of Africa's foreign and security policy behavior.

Indeed, African foreign and security policy at the beginning of the twenty-first century is still dominated by overarching constraints on the survival of weak states. The imperatives of state survival force elites to use foreign policy to garner political and economic resources from the external environment. Whether made singly or collectively, foreign and security policy reflects the continual attempts by elites to manage threats to domestic security and insulate their decision making from untoward external manipulation. I agree with Khadiagala and Lyons that contemporary African elites—many of whom subscribe to the "great man" theory of leadership—are preoccupied with political stability, legitimacy, and economic security issues whose importance seems to increase rather than diminish.

International Interests

Globally, I discern three key trends with the potential to shape and alter Africa's strategic environment. These are the emergence of a recalibrated American strategic approach to Africa; the weakening European global position due to the Eurozone crisis; and the growing presence of China in Africa.

US Strategy

Current US strategy toward sub-Saharan Africa is captured in President Obama's June 2012 Presidential Policy Directive, which declares:

> The United States will partner with sub-Saharan African countries to pursue the following...objectives: (1) strengthen democratic institutions; (2) spur economic growth, trade, and investment; (3) advance peace and security; and (4) promote opportunity and development.[4]

Three issues drive US policy on Africa: commercial interests, security interests, and democracy promotion.[5] Heightened US interest in Africa is, in part, a result of recent dramatic changes in the continent, such as rapid economic growth and improved governance, which have made Africa a much better place to do business. In addition, since many African countries are sources of natural resources like oil and gas, the United States may turn to Africa to supplement its energy needs in the future. The perceived threat posed by terrorist groups such as *al-Shabab* in East Africa shapes the American security view of Kenya and Uganda. At the same time, African nations hope to get more support from the United States in dealing with the crisis in Somalia. Reconstruction of Somalia is a critical step for the eradication of security threats in the region. Similarly, African nations are keen to garner support from the United States in addressing the violence in and around DRC, which has the potential to destabilize neighboring nations. Finally, the United States seeks to encourage African leaders to strengthen democracy, protect human rights, and increase transparency in the continent. Transparency and accountability are common themes in Secretary of State Hilary Clinton's meetings with African leaders.

European Interests

Following the Arab Spring, African migration became a source of concern for Europeans. Migration, however, is only one issue of importance between Europe and Africa. Trade, energy, climate change, democratic governance, and human rights are among the joint concerns for these regions bound together by history, culture, and geography. Indeed, that Europe and Africa share a common future cannot be ignored.

From 2007 on, the Joint Africa–EU Strategy has provided a long-term framework for relations between the AU and the European Union (EU) that is based on equality and shared interests. However, the track record of the partnership is mixed. The Strategy has highlighted differences between the two regions on fundamental issues such as civil society's participation in political processes, the role of the media in promoting democratic accountability and contributing to regime change, and the deep cleavage over international justice (the International Criminal Court being one of the most contentious issues on the table).

African decision makers perceive a diminishing enthusiasm in their European partners. In their view, the EU is quick to pledge support but does not always keep its commitments. They also question the concrete deliverables of the Strategy and find that it is hard to sell at home. Civil society, for its part, criticizes it for being too state-centric and top-down and for failing to inform African citizens about its objectives.

The Joint Africa–EU Strategy is presently "in hibernation," as research by the Open Society Foundation terms it.[6] Partners on both sides are at pains to disguise their disappointment. It was set up as a move by the regions from a donor–recipient relationship to one of equals. However, the paradigm shift, intended to fundamentally alter European and African relations, has not really taken place and it is doubtful whether the partnership can help move it forward.

Chinese Interests

The 5th Forum for China Africa Cooperation (FOCAC) was held in Beijing in July 2012. The Forum, established in October 2000, constitutes a platform for African and Chinese policy makers to enhance China's relations with African countries. As pointed out by the Centre for Chinese Studies in Stellenbosch, FOCAC is a continuity of China's central government's political agenda toward Africa, which seeks to solidify economic, political, and diplomatic ties.[7]

Since 2000, China's "go out" policy has boosted investment and trade in Africa through Chinese State-Owned Enterprises (SOEs) that operate in the continent. Such an agenda has been heavily structured via government ministries and financial institutions to boost trade, investments, and aid.

The "go global" policy has driven Chinese investment overseas in search of new markets. In 2011, trade between China and Africa reached US$160 billion, and investments totaled more than US$13 billion. China today is a major trading partner with Africa. More than 2,000 Chinese companies (SOEs, joint ventures, private and small- and medium-sized enterprises) have established business in Africa. FOCAC has played its role to facilitate these business relations.[8]

While China has a clear Africa approach, Africa has a structural disadvantage and cannot present one detailed agenda vis-à-vis Beijing. It needs to take control of its economic development path. As enshrined in the New Partnership for Africa's Development (NEPAD), transparency, corruption, and governance issues need to be addressed to ensure public service delivery to people. This should also be the key agenda for FOCAC. From Africa's side, the cooperation and partnership with China should benefit people who mostly remain disadvantaged in their livelihoods. In Sino-African economic cooperation (trade, investments, and aid), the lack of transparency, corruption, and doubtful governance performance has been denounced by civil society.

The AU Peace and Security Architecture

Having sketched the broader context and identified key factors and trends with the potential to influence African peace and security decision making, I will now turn to Africa itself. First, I will examine the continental peace and security architecture as a backdrop to the analysis of the status of the AU's RECs.

The Organization of African Unity (OAU) was established in 1963 to protect African unity and independence. The end of the Cold War period from the late 1980s onward introduced significant global and continental changes and, as a consequence, between 2001 and 2002, the OAU transformed into the AU. The objective of the new organization is to accelerate continental political and economic cooperation and integration; its leadership adopted the NEPAD as the AU's key developmental program.

The peace and security regime of the AU can be seen as a normative and policy framework.[9] Thomas Tieku makes that argument in his chapter for this volume. From this perspective, the so-called APSA rests on three pillars: socioeconomic justice, human rights and democracy, and peace and security in its narrow sense. Various legal and policy instruments underpin this framework, including the AU Constitutive Act, the AU Protocol on the Establishment of the Peace and Security Council (PSC Protocol), and the Common African Defence and Security Policy (CADSP). This structure is built on the assumption that the continent's regional mechanisms (RMs) (i.e., the seven RECs) have a key responsibility for promoting peace, security, and stability in Africa.

The Constitutive Act (CA) of the AU of 2000 is the Union's founding document or constitution. It is a visionary document, but it is also tempered by practical considerations. Its preamble recognizes the quest for continental unity and collective action and the fact that conflicts in Africa impede development. It also recognizes that peace, security, and stability are prerequisites for the implementation of the development and integration agenda. According to the CA, the peace and security objectives of the AU shall be to defend the sovereignty, territorial integrity, and independence of its member states; to promote peace, security, and stability in the continent; and to coordinate and harmonize policies between existing and future RECs. Principles of the CA include the establishment of a common defence policy for the continent, peaceful resolution of conflicts through means decided upon by the assembly, prohibition of the use of force or threat thereof, noninterference by any member state in the internal affairs of another, the right of the AU to intervene in a member state "in respect of grave circumstances, namely war crimes, genocide and crimes against humanity" (Article 4h), the right of member states to request intervention from the AU in order to restore peace and security, and condemnation and rejection of (i) terrorism and subversion and (ii) unconstitutional changes of governments.

The functions of the assembly, which is the supreme organ of the Union, are to determine the common policies of the AU; to receive, consider, and make decisions on reports and recommendations from the other organs of the AU; to monitor the implementation of policies and decisions of the AU and ensure compliance by all member states; and to give directives to the Executive Council on the management of conflicts, war, and other emergency situations and the restoration of peace. The AU's Executive Council is composed of the ministers of foreign affairs and meets at least twice a year in ordinary sessions. The Commission of the Union is its secretariat and is composed of a chairperson, a deputy, and commissioners. As the section on the PSC later makes clear, the chairperson and commissioner in charge of peace and security play an important role in conflict prevention and resolution.

Key Security Structures

The AU did not immediately decide on the nature of a new security organ. In 2001, its Assembly incorporated the Central Organ of the OAU Mechanism for Conflict Prevention, Management and Resolution. After a restructuring exercise, it adopted the Protocol Relating to the Establishment of the Peace and Security Council (the Protocol) in 2002.

As far as conflict prevention and resolution are concerned, other structures also play a key role. The Department of Political Affairs has remained a core department in the OAU/AU since its inception in 1963. The mandate of the department is to contribute to the emergence of an open political environment, within and among African countries, as well as at the international level. It attempts to play a prominent role in promoting, facilitating, coordinating, and encouraging democratic principles and the rule of law, respect of human rights, the participation of civil society in the development process of the continent, and the achievement of durable solutions for addressing humanitarian crises.

The above-mentioned Protocol, which entered into force in December 2003, established a PSC within the AU as a standing decision-making organ for the prevention, management, and resolution of conflicts. The objectives of the PSC are to promote peace, security, and stability in Africa; to anticipate and prevent conflicts (which includes promoting democratic governance), peace-building, and post-conflict reconstruction activities; and to prevent and combat international terrorism. The structure and institutional mechanisms comprising the PSC are outlined in Thomas Tieku's chapter of this volume.

The chairperson of the AU Commission plays a key conflict-management role in the affairs of the APSA. Similar to the UN Secretary General, they are responsible for bringing issues to the attention of the PSC, the Panel of the Wise, or other relevant parties, and for ensuring implementation and follow-up action. The commissioner in charge of peace and security (and responsible for the affairs of the PSC) supports the chairperson. At the time of writing, the AU had elected Madame Nkosazana Dlamini-Zuma (a previous South African minister of foreign and home affairs) to the post of chairperson of the AU Commission for a term of five years, starting in 2012.

The establishment of an African Standby Force (ASF) is aimed at enabling the PSC to perform its responsibilities regarding the deployment of peace support missions and intervention pursuant to Article 4h and 4j of the Union's CA. As one commentator noted, "Clearly, the ASF is one of the most critical elements of the APSA that will enable the AU to deliver on its promise of intervention to protect people in grave circumstances and to provide a prompt and robust response to manage and resolve African crises."[10] The ASF provides for five subregional standby arrangements, each up to brigade size (3,000 to 4,000 troops), which provides the AU with a combined standby capacity of 15,000 to 20,000 troops; between 300 and 500 military observers who are trained and ready to deploy on fourteen days' notice; a police standby capacity of at least 240 individual officers and two company strength police units (gendarmerie), which should enable the AU to staff two complex peace operations with a police component each; and finally a centrally managed roster of civilian specialists in mission administration; human rights; humanitarian assistance; governance; and disarmament, demobilization and repatriation, reintegration and resettlement (DDRRR).

The ASF design was developed on the basis of six possible mission scenarios: (1) military advice to a political mission, (2) AU observer mission co-deployment with a UN peacekeeping mission, (3) a stand-alone AU observer mission, (4) a traditional peacekeeping or preventative deployment mission, (5) complex multidimensional peace operations, and (6) peace enforcement or what the ASF Framework document refers to as intervention missions.[11]

The ASF recommended a two-phase implementation process. The first phase was aimed at developing the capacity to manage scenarios 1 to 3 by mid-2005. The second phase was aimed at developing the capability to manage the remaining scenarios by 2010. As of mid-2012, it is clear that the Standby Force, despite enormous policy development accompanied by several operational exercises, is not yet ready to assume the responsibilities envisaged for it under the six mission scenarios described earlier (although it might arguably currently deploy under scenarios 1 to 3).

The PSC is also required to assist with post-conflict peace-building activities. Article 14 of the Protocol speaks to the consolidation of negotiated peace agreements, the establishment of conditions of sociopolitical and economic reconstruction of society and state, the implementation of DDRRR programs, and assistance to vulnerable persons and groups in society. The PSC is furthermore required, in Article 15 of the Protocol, to take an active part in coordinating and conducting humanitarian action in cases of conflict or natural disaster. This translates into an expectation that the PSC shall develop its own capacity to undertake such actions, and further, that the ASF will not only be adequately equipped to undertake humanitarian activities in its mission areas, but that it will also facilitate the activities of humanitarian agencies.

The PSC anticipates a close working relationship with Africa's regional organizations. Although the Protocol talks in Article 16 of "Regional Mechanisms for Conflict Prevention, Management and Resolution," a definition or list is not provided. RMs can be assumed to be similar to the organizations defined in the Protocol as RECs. The seven RECs identified by the AU in the Protocol are the Arab Maghreb Union (AMU), the Common Market of East and Southern Africa (COMESA), the Community of Sahelo-Saharan States (CEN-SAD), the Economic Community of Central African States (ECCAS), the ECOWAS, the Inter-Governmental Authority for Development (IGAD), and the SADC.

At least four RECs—COMESA, ECOWAS, IGAD, and SADC—have evolved operational security management functions. The other RECs appear to have underdeveloped, dormant, or weak security functions. The EAC appears not to enjoy official recognition as an REC in the Protocol. The AU's common defense and security policy (CADSP), however, includes the EAC in its list of regional instruments and mechanisms.

Further complicating the picture is the fact that the AU has adopted the OAU's definition of Africa's five regions: North, Southern, East, West, and Central—but at the same time also talks of intergovernmental organizations (such as the EAC) that overlap these five regions. Confusingly, the AU Commission's 2004 Strategic Plan also identifies regional integration communities (RICs). There is therefore a significant amount of overlap among geographic regions, RECs, RICs, and RMs. The DRC, for example, is a member of ECCAS, SADC, COMESA, and the Economic Community of the Great Lakes Region (CEPGL). This state of affairs has led to confusion regarding the roles of regional organizations and, although AU documents mention rationalization, much more needs to be done in order to ensure the effective operationalization of the security architecture of the continent.

Assessment

Africa's peace and security architecture is viewed as "evolving" and analysts are cautious and even skeptical of its "strong and robust" character. The APSA faces a number of challenges.[12] First, although the AU Commission has risen as a new actor, it is not free of the influence of member states, which retain the ultimate decision-making power at the level of the AU through its General Assembly. Member states also enjoy considerable latitude in providing standby peacekeeping troops to subregional brigades. Second, collective behavior on the basis of agreed norms is often compromised by members (e.g., Sudan and Zimbabwe) who openly pursue "self-help" strategies and who exert considerable leverage at several levels. Third, the institutionalization of APSA has revealed serious capacity deficits. Many members of the AU do not meet their financial obligations, thus increasing the AU's dependence on donors and raising issues of sustainability and ownership. Additionally, conflict escalation (especially in the Horn, central and north Africa) has increased the demands on the organization.

Some analysts, such as Thomas Tieku in this volume, interpret the activities of the APSA as evidence of an emerging continental application of the Responsibility to Protect (R2P) principles—prevention, reaction, and rebuilding.[13] Reflecting this approach, the building blocks of the APSA include the AU Commission, PSC, Continental Early Warning System, ASF, Panel of the Wise, and Peace Fund. However, one finds a familiar lament in analyses of the APSA: lack of political will, coordination, and financing. Kristiana Powell argues that

> [t]he experience of AMIB and AMIS (African peacekeeping in Burundi and Sudan respectively) demonstrate that the AU requires extensive financial, logistical and political support from the international community in order to fulfill its commitments to peace and security, including the protection of civilians. An examination of donor commitments...also raises critical questions of how to appropriately sequence immediate relief and recovery activities, and longer-term strategies to reduce poverty and build a sustainable peace.[14]

Eki Omorogbe similarly concurs that the AU does not live up the ideal of "African solutions for African problems."[15] Throughout its missions to date, the AU has encountered resource challenges that undermine its efforts. The partial success of the AU has been contingent upon the financial goodwill of Western countries, particularly the EU. However, such support is not obligatory, and it has become apparent that it can be unreliable, with pledges not always honored, and payments sometimes slow.

In Omorogbe's view, the question of AU missions being funded to a greater extent by its own members, including through compulsory contributions, clearly needs to be addressed. However, it would be preferable for the UN to use its own assessed contributions to fund AU action mandated by the UN Security Council. In Omorogbe's assessment, unless there is a change to the funding regime, complex peacekeeping challenges will give rise to the conundrum seen in the case of Somalia, where the African regional organizations are unable to act, but the UN is unwilling to do so. (For more on this, see Paul D. Williams's chapter on Somalia in this volume.)

APSA faces particular operational challenges as it seeks to consolidate its policy frameworks and implementation strategies. A recent formal assessment of the operationalization of the APSA identifies a range of obstacles still to be overcome.[16] Significant findings of the assessment include the following:

- Except for the ASF and early warning system, there appeared to be limited coordination between the APSA components.[17]
- The APSA architecture did not adequately cover all existing and emerging security challenges.
- There appeared to be a vertical "disconnect" between the AU's PSC and similar organs in the RECs.
- The horizontal interface between RECs, also known as RMs, was equally limited.
- The operationalization of the APSA has been largely dependent on external partner support. However, some RECs (such as ECOWAS) have put in place their own resource mobilization strategy.
- The issue of sustainability became even more pronounced when the AU or the RECs/RMs deployed a peace operation. The AU's peacekeeping experiences in Darfur, and its current experience in Somalia, have demonstrated the risks of being heavily dependent on external support.
- There was consensus among the RECs/RMs that the AU was currently not playing its coordinating role effectively due in part to the human resource constraints at the AU Commission.

The future of the APSA will depend largely on a strong and effective AU, in concert with members and RECs. Some analysts downplay the role of "dominant powers" (Nigeria and South Africa) in favor of what they call institutionalized behavior, which is achieved when all members *internalize* the principles, norms, and rules that underpin the APSA.[18] This latter political process of "cognition" and "learning" suggests a rather slow evolutionary trajectory, and it is unclear, in light of the aforementioned challenges, how Africa will manage in the interim.

I will now turn to an analysis of Africa's key subregional organizations concerned with peace and security.

The EAC

The members of the EAC—Kenya, Tanzania, Uganda, Rwanda, and Burundi—face serious challenges relating to peace and security. In a sense, the EAC is surrounded by conflict complexes. Toward the east, it faces the Horn of Africa, in the north, Sudan and South Sudan, and toward the west, the troubled provinces of the DRC. In the Indian Ocean, the issue of piracy demands attention. As a fairly new subregional political and economic integration project (it collapsed in 1977 and was restarted in 2000), the EAC's peace and security architecture is in an embryonic state of development. It is for this reason that little research exists regarding its performance as a peace and security actor. Later, I sketch the emerging architecture. The Treaty for the Establishment of the EAC recognizes peace and security as prerequisites for the success of the region's integration process. A strategy for pursuing cooperation in peace and security matters was agreed to by the EAC in 2006.[19]

By 2009, the EAC had put in place an institutional framework by establishing various Sectoral Councils and Committees to give direction and policy guidance for cooperation in several key areas.[20] These included:

(a) Sectoral Council on Cooperation in Defence;
(b) Sectoral Council on Inter State Security;
(c) Sectoral Council on Foreign Policy Coordination;
(d) Joint Sectoral Councils on Defence, Inter State Security and Foreign Policy Coordination.

In January 2012, an EAC joint meeting of the three sectoral councils on Cooperation in Defense, Inter-state Security, and Foreign Policy Coordination adopted the Protocol on Peace and Security as well as the EAC Conflict Prevention, Management and Resolution Mechanism.[21]

The EAC Peace and Security Protocol identifies, among others, at least twenty objectives for fostering regional peace and security. These include combating terrorism and piracy, peace support operations, prevention of genocide, disaster management and crisis response, management of refugees, control of proliferation of small arms and light weapons, and combating transnational and cross-border crimes. Others include addressing and combating cattle rustling, training programs for security personnel, dispute settlement, and regional and international cooperation in peace and security matters.

Other issues also considered at the joint meeting include the progress on the development of the EAC Early Warning Mechanism and the Eastern and Southern Africa/ Indian Ocean Maritime Security Strategy and Action Plan, which has been designed to help combat piracy in the Indian Ocean. The strategy was developed collectively by the EAC, the Intergovernmental Authority on Development (IGAD), the Common Market for Eastern and Southern Africa (COMESA), and Indian Ocean Commission in 2010.

The ECOWAS

ECOWAS was originally established in 1975 as an economic integration union, but has since developed "the most elaborate conflict prevention, management and resolution mechanism in Africa."[22] In the following, I provide an overview of the key features of the ECOWAS peace and security architecture.

It is worth recounting the story of the events that forced ECOWAS to develop robust peace and security mechanisms. The Liberian crisis, which started in 1989, was the critical event in ECOWAS' transition into participating in security activities. Faced with human suffering and international disengagement from African conflicts on an unprecedented scale, and with no institutions to respond to the conflict, ECOWAS devised ad hoc security mechanisms to address the crisis. In May 1990, ECOWAS established a Standing Mediation Committee (SMC) charged with the responsibility of finding a peaceful resolution to the conflict. Following weeks of unproductive talks with various faction leaders in 1990, the SMC took the bold step of establishing and deploying the ECOWAS Ceasefire Monitoring Group (ECOMOG) amid bitter opposition from then rebel leader Charles Taylor and some West African leaders. In neighboring Sierra Leone, ECOMOG was able to reinstate the ousted president Kabbah and act as the de facto army in the absence of a national army. In 1998, this ad hoc subregional peacekeeping force intervened to restore peace in Guinea Bissau following a revolt in the national army. In December 2002, ECOWAS sent its peacekeepers to the Cote d'Ivoire, and in August 2003, a peacekeeping mission was deployed in Liberia for a second time, following the relapse of that country into violent conflict. (For more on these cases, see the appropriate chapters in this volume.)

The problems encountered and lessons learned by the various ECOWAS peacekeeping operations led to the initiation of a process meant to improve its future performance. The revised ECOWAS Treaty of 1993 represents the first serious effort in this regard In recognition of the relationship among human rights, good governance, and conflicts in the subregion, in 1991, ECOWAS agreed on the Declaration of Political Principles, which committed member states to respect human rights, democracy, and the rule of law. This was followed in 2001 by the adoption of the Protocol on Good Governance, which addresses the perceived root causes of conflict such as corruption and bad governance. The most important security protocol adopted so far is the Mechanism for Conflict Prevention, Management, Resolution, Peacekeeping and Security (ECOWAS

Security Mechanism) signed in December 1999. The mechanism establishes a number of institutions and strategies, including the Mediation and Security Council (MSC), an early warning system, a standby force, and a Conflict Prevention Framework. These are described in more detail in the following.

The MSC is comprised of heads of state and government, ministers of foreign affairs, and ambassadors, and makes decisions relating to matters of peace and security and the deployment of peacekeeping troops. Membership is on a rotational basis and comprises nine states elected for a two-year period with no permanent seats. A Committee of Ambassadors facilitates the work of the Council, and a Defence and Security Commission made up of defense chiefs and technical experts assists with planning and recommendations.

ECOWAS has also established an early warning system comprising a regional observation network and observatories. These observatories are to undertake risk mapping, observation, and analysis of social, economic, and political situations in the region with the potential to degenerate into conflict. However, aspects of this system have come in for criticism, such as their lack of capacity and coordination, and the placement of an observatory in Burkina Faso, where the concern is that its operations might be compromised by an interfering government.[23]

In 2004, ECOWAS renamed ECOMOG as the ECOWAS Standby Force (ESF), to cover its participation in conflict prevention, humanitarian intervention, enforcement, peace-building, and reduction of organized crime. The ESF forms part of the ASF. It has implemented training programs, organized military exercises, and designated logistics depots in Sierra Leone and Mali.

Finally, in order to manage West Africa's elaborate peace and security architecture, ECOWAS has developed the ECOWAS Conflict Prevention Framework (ECPF). This is a comprehensive framework document that addresses a key shortcoming of earlier security mechanisms, namely the failure to coordinate various departments and institutions within ECOWAS and its member states tasked with peace and security programming. Ironically, however, this policy framework has also been criticized for its inability to specify roles and action plans.[24]

Assessment

ECOWAS has intervened in conflicts in Liberia, Sierra Leone, Guinea Bissau, and Cote d'Ivoire, undertaking tasks ranging from safeguarding civilians to implementing peace-building programs. It has achieved mixed results in these interventions, and failure in the case of Guinea Bissau. Its interventions have been plagued by problems including poor financing and logistics, a lack of political consensus, and an absence of peacekeeping and humanitarian strategic thinking.[25] In addition, francophone West Africa remains suspicious of Nigerian hegemonic ambitions, and maintains strong ties with former colonial master France for defense and security purposes. This is a troublesome relationship, considering how the Côte d'Ivoire crisis was managed. However, many writers and analysts balance these concerns against the ongoing efforts to institutionalize peace and security response mechanisms and to promote good governance and development in the subregion.[26]

At the time of writing, it was unclear whether ECOWAS would be able to overcome a range of obstacles in deploying a peacemaking and peacekeeping force in Mali, tentatively called the standby Force Mission in Mali, in order to both restore law and order following a coup d'état and to protect regional security, given the alarming presence of the Touareg-led insurgents. Obstacles include an elusive consensus among key regional players as well as members of the UN Security Council, the need to manage the influence of foreign powers such as France and the United States, the question of funding, and the issue of capacity and staying power. However, the most pressing issue is the question of what the purpose and "end state" of such an intervention ought to be.

I will now turn to Southern Africa, the SADC, its institutional makeup and decision-making style, and the issues it faces.

The SADC

The overarching aim of SADC is to promote economic integration in order to "improve the quality of life of the peoples of the region."[27] SADC's genesis reflects this priority. When the Southern African Development Coordinating Conference (SADCC) was formed in 1980, it adopted the slogan "Southern Africa—towards economic liberation." "Liberation" was seen as a necessary condition for improvements in the quality of life in Africa. The current SADC vision is one of "a common future, a future within a regional community that will ensure economic well-being, improvement of the standards of living and quality of life, freedom and social justice and peace and security for the peoples of Southern Africa."[28]

Regional cooperation in the 1980s, even if informal and limited, succeeded in realizing a number of regional development projects, mainly in the infrastructure and food security sectors. The activities of the Frontline States alliance, in its quest to eradicate colonial rule and apartheid in southern Africa, brought about a sense of regional identity and briefly promoted a shared political vision. The SADCC was transformed into SADC in 1992, reflecting the changing regional—and external—environment. Newly democratic South Africa joined SADC in 1994, raising hopes for accelerated economic integration, but in 1998, a major regional war erupted, involving the DRC and a number of other SADC (and non-SADC) states and an attempted coup destabilized the small country of Lesotho. At that time, SADC's security structures were unresolved: the Organ on Politics, Defence, and Security Cooperation, although chaired by Zimbabwe President Robert Mugabe, was not yet formally made part of the SADC structures. So SADC played a controversial role in the attempt to resolve these crises.

In 2001, an extraordinary SADC Summit approved the proposed recommendations for far-reaching changes in SADC's institutional structure for executing its 1992 mandate. These included changes in SADC's governing structures at the regional and national levels, but most importantly a plan for the centralization of the twenty-one sector coordinating units and commissions located in twelve of its member countries. These units were brought together in four clusters in a strengthened SADC Secretariat in Gaborone, Botswana.[29]

At the August 2001 Council of Ministers Meeting and Summit in Blantyre, these changes in SADC structures were further consolidated by amendments to the SADC Treaty. Additionally, the Summit signed a Protocol on Politics, Defence and Security Co-operation that provided for an Organ on Politics, Defence and Security Co-operation under the SADC Summit.[30] The Organ has its own set of regional structures and mechanisms for policy formulation and implementation.

The Summit is the supreme policy-making institution of SADC. It is led by a Troika system consisting of the Chairperson, Incoming Chairperson, and the Outgoing Chairperson. It meets twice a year. The first meeting takes place before 31 March each year and primarily focuses on regional economic development matters and the SADC Programme of Action. The second meeting takes place in August/September and is dedicated to political matters. Decisions are made by consensus and are intended to be binding.

The Organ on Politics, Defence and Security also operates on a Troika basis. The Troika members are selected by the Summit from among its members, with the stipulation that the Chairperson of the Organ Troika cannot at the same time have the Chair of the Summit (neither can a member simultaneously belong to both Troikas).

The Protocol also provides for an elaborate structure of the Organ. Under the Chair and the Troika, there is a Ministerial Committee comprised of the SADC ministers responsible for foreign affairs, defense, public security, and state security. It operates much like the SADC Council of Ministers and has a partly overlapping membership.

The Inter-State Politics and Diplomacy Committee (ISPDC) comprises the ministers responsible for foreign affairs. It shall perform such functions as may be necessary to achieve the objectives of the Organ relating to politics and diplomacy. It may establish such substructure as it deems necessary.[31]

The Inter-State Defence and Security Committee (ISDSC) comprises ministers responsible for defense, public security, and state security. It is an established committee formed more than twenty years ago by the Frontline States (it began as the Defence Staff Committee, and became the ISDSC when South Africa joined in 1994). It has a fairly elaborate substructure, especially the Defence subcommittee and a range of sub-subcommittees on functional areas of cooperation.[32]

The Organ is supported by the Directorate for Politics, Defence and Security Affairs based at the SADC Secretariat in Gaborone. It functions under the overall supervision of the SADC Executive Secretary and is headed by a Director for Politics, Defence and Security. The Directorate's tasks relate to politics, defense, and security issues as defined in the Treaty, Protocol, and the Strategic Integrated Plan for the Organ (SIPO). It focuses primarily on strategic planning and policy analysis and development, the monitoring and evaluation of the implementation of Organ decisions, and the provision of administrative backup to the Organ. It also supervises the activities of the SADC Regional Peacekeeping Training Centre based in Harare and as of last year oversees the activities of the Southern African Regional Police Chiefs Co-ordinating Organisation.

The Organ's activities are guided by a business plan called the SIPO. A revised SIPO supersedes the original SIPO, adopted in 2004 for a five-year period.[33] SIPO II is structured around five sectors: politics and diplomacy, defense, state security (intelligence), public security, and police. The policy guide provides an analysis of each sector, followed by a number of objectives to be achieved by member states and/or the Community as a whole. All the objectives are accompanied by detailed strategies, activities, and expected outcomes. Given that the SIPO II document is yet to be released to the public, I refrain from discussing its content in detail.

The SADC Standby Force (SSF) is another key to SADC's foreign and security approach and decision making. It is to operate in harmony with the APSA of the AU, and its functions, envisaged in Article 13 of the PSC Protocol of the AU, include:

a. observation and monitoring missions;
b. other types of peace support missions;
c. intervention in a Member State in respect of grave circumstances or at the request of a Member State in order to restore peace and security, in accordance with Article 4(h) and (j) of the CA;
d. preventive deployment in order to prevent (i) a dispute or a conflict from escalating, (ii) an ongoing violent conflict from spreading to neighboring areas or States, and (iii) the resurgence of violence after parties to a conflict have reached an agreement.;
e. peace-building, including post-conflict disarmament and demobilization;
f. humanitarian assistance to alleviate the suffering of civilian population in conflict areas and support efforts to address major natural disasters; and
g. any other functions as may be mandated by the PSC or the Assembly.[34]

A cursory glance at the range of tasks associated with the SSF begs the question as to its state of preparedness and perhaps more deeply to what extent the fifteen member states of the SADC are able to provide the SSF with capacity it needs to be fully operational. It is yet to be deployed to undertake a peacemaking, peacekeeping, or recovery mission (one can hardly envisage a war-fighting intervention), and therefore how robust the decision making around its deployment will be is unknown.

Assessment

This analysis of SADC political and security cooperation suggests a developmental path from informal and ad hoc to formal, rules-based governance.[35] This is in line with those who noted that SADC provides an "evolving, institutionalised, rules-based forum within which the members meet regularly to discuss and argue about political and security issues."[36] It appears that this level of institutional evolution is necessary before common foreign policy approaches or positions can be formulated and implemented.

The SADC leadership appears rhetorically committed to full integration in both the socioeconomic and security arenas (and to the eventual merging of the two into one, human security agenda). The practice reveals the maintenance of a stable (but not always efficient) institution, used by members to behave in a disaggregated manner, driven by the overriding demands of national interest and sovereignty.[37]

Regarding crisis management and mediation efforts, SADC has benefited from valuable lessons in policy coordination relating to four crises: Lesotho, DRC, Zimbabwe, and Madagascar. In the case of the DRC, although SADC was divided in its initial responses, it propelled the search for a comprehensive solution to the crisis, and the same could be said for its role in the 1998 crisis in Lesotho. Regarding the Zimbabwe crisis, SADC engaged in an intricate diplomatic game vis-à-vis the West, which led to incremental engagement. Overcoming the clamor for sanctions was decisive in establishing a regional position on an intraregional problem, a feat that required significant coordination of interests and positions. While differences occurred within SADC over the Zimbabwe crisis, they were not sufficient to torpedo what became the regional consensus on a negotiated settlement (meaning the so-called Global Political Agreement or GPA of 2008). Regarding Madagascar, the SADC mediation from 2009 onward is another instance of attempts to develop collective approaches to an unconstitutional change of government. These attempts were not without problems (especially sharp divisions among SADC Organ Troika members at the time regarding a possible military deployment) as well as complicated mediation efforts, if not false starts. At the time of writing, the crisis remained unresolved and it will continue to test SADC's ability to promote collective policies on democratization in the region. Part of this dynamic relates to unclear roles being pursued by the AU, the UN, and SADC.[38]

On the question of a common SADC foreign policy, based on a reading of themes that emerged at SADC Summits, patterns of continuity and chance in the character of the organization's external relations can be detected. The major thematic change was the end of apartheid and destabilization, which had previously required the SADCC leadership to undertake diplomatic initiatives aimed at countering this threat and request donor assistance for recovery and development purposes. When democratic South Africa joined SADC, it changed this aspect of the organization's international relations. The need to condemn South Africa or to maintain the call for sanctions fell away. The need for a harmonized and joint approach for requesting development aid from donors still persisted, of course, as did the call for assistance to Angola (including sanctions against UNITA [União Nacional para a Independência Total de Angola]). Other countries in transition (Namibia, Mozambique) also needed international support.

However, the key feature of SADC's contemporary foreign relations relates to two themes: conflict resolution, and economic and trade issues. The major shift came with the appearance, or deepening, of violent inter- and intrastate conflict. In the period under review, major wars broke out in the DRC and neighboring Great Lakes Region, and violent conflict or political tension and mismanagement became apparent in Lesotho, Zimbabwe, and Madagascar. These events have consumed SADC's recent foreign policy activities and, together with the difficulties relating to its economic integration and trade relations agenda, have come to dominate the SADC foreign and security policy agenda. Political instability in Lesotho, Zimbabwe, and Madagascar, and the war in the DRC have received detailed attention from SADC, with various peacemaking and mediation initiatives undertaken for each crisis. The management of elections in the SADC region has also received sustained attention—perhaps because of the realization that political tensions become sharply focused around election times.

Various SADC protocols contain a foreign and security policy dimension. In particular, the protocols on security (illicit drugs, corruption, firearms, politics, defense, and security cooperation) require SADC to cooperate with the international community on a range of policy issues. In general, these protocols form the foreign and security policy framework for SADC in its operations and conduct. They guide state behavior among members and, where appropriate, collective state behavior toward SADC's external environment. However, there are two problems with the view that SADC protocols guide its foreign and security policy behavior. First, few of these protocols are ratified and adopted by individual member states. Second, even if they are accepted as frameworks for behavior, SADC does not appear to actively apply protocol language and guidelines in developing responses to those international issues with a potential impact on the Community.

These findings resonate with the view that the construction of common regional foreign policies is marked by three key requirements. The first relates to focus. There are enormous problems in forging common foreign policies because of unresolved questions of defining interests and specifying targets of foreign policy. Second, the ability to advance collective foreign policies that go beyond coordination remains stunted by the adherence to sovereignty. Analysis of the common positions adopted by SADC identified two overriding areas of common focus: conflict management and resolution, and trade and economic integration. The third factor relates to coherence and the institutional capacity to coordinate regional foreign policy. A recent analysis by Kaunda shows the weaknesses of SADC as a decision-making body:

> Generally, SADC is ineffective because of its institutional weaknesses. The institutional weakness is compounded by inadequate financing of the organization's secretariat. The implementation of the RISDP [Regional Indicative Strategic Development Plan] is slow, uneven, and inconsistent. SIPO is expected to be similarly challenged by the same constraints.
>
> The RISDP and SIPO are not co-ordinated and harmonized in implementation, despite their interrelatedness and complementarities. SADC's organizational structure is not sufficiently co-ordinated, and the secretariat is politically disempowered.[39]

In order to meet the challenges of a globalizing, insecure, and unequal world, SADC needs to pay much more attention to the operationalization of its Organ Protocol requirement to "develop common foreign policy approaches on issues of mutual concern" and "advance such policy collectively in international fora." It is a task not easily achieved. The SADC collective leadership continues to be driven by the compulsion "to look after their own," and to ensure state and regime security. Whether such a collective mind-set is able to deliver on stability, growth, and development beyond elite benefit remains to be seen.

This brings us to the question of South Africa and its relationship with the region, which has been described in terms of asymmetrical interdependence.[40] Others call South Africa a regional hegemon. Hegemony refers to the extension by one state of preponderant influence or control over another state or region. This may represent at least a potential threat to the security of another. The South African postapartheid government, under successive administrations, has not deviated from the broad template set by the ruling African National Congress (ANC) and popularized by its first democratically elected president: "our foreign policy should reflect the interests of the continent of Africa."[41] However, the trouble with South Africa's relations in the southern African region and further on the continent relates to its relatively advanced levels of development and the size of its economy. Pursuing, as it must, its national interests, particularly on economic issues, the South African government's choices sometimes cause mayhem (e.g., joining the Brazil Russia India China South Africa [BRICS] alliance, lobbying for the AU Commission position) or otherwise raise expectations ("solve the crisis in Zimbabwe, or the DRC, or ..."). South Africa dominates the region in various areas of interaction, but also depends on it, as was evident in the August 2012 election of Madam Dlamini-Zuma to the chair of the AU Commission. Unequal trade and investment, the size of the economy, its infrastructure, and its military are factors that shape the relationship.

Five points follow from the discussion so far. First, severe constraints have impinged (and continue to impinge) on the freedom of African decision makers—particularly the need to consolidate power and meet socioeconomic demands at home, and the influence of external actors. This influence shaped aspects of Africa's foreign policy behavior, including that of the SADC. As Khadiagala and Lyons note, whether made singly or collectively, foreign policy reflects the continual attempts by elites to manage threats to domestic security and insulate their decision making from unwanted external manipulation. The role of personality is key: African foreign policy decision making has always been the province of leading personalities. Contemporary African elites remain preoccupied with political stability, legitimacy, and economic security, issues whose importance seems to increase rather than diminish.

Second, new decision-making institutions (AU, SADC), combined with a "flattening" of decision making relating to foreign and security policy (meaning influences from new actors such as parliaments, media, civil society, interest groups), are testing traditional decision makers' roles and ability to control the agenda and the implementation of decisions regarding peacemaking, peacekeeping, and peace-building.

Third, a fast-evolving international context is challenging the perceptual and analytical lenses of the decision makers as never before. Key trends include the prolonged economic downturn in the West, a rising and assertive East, ongoing Western concern over terror, and renewed global interest in Africa's mineral resources.

Fourth, the character of African countries' national interest is critical. Limited resources largely confine African foreign policy to regional and continental contexts. When elites articulate national interests beyond the continent, they do so to win prestige, establish a presence in the proliferating international institutions, and forge strategic alliances with other global underdogs in an effort to extract resources from dominant power blocks. African states also construct their own continental and regional institutions, of which the OAU and its successor the AU as well the RECs such as SADC are examples.

Fifth and finally, SADC provides an "evolving, institutionalized, rules-based forum within which the members meet regularly to discuss and argue about political and security issues." The SADC leadership is rhetorically committed to full integration in both the socioeconomic and security arenas (and to the eventual merging of the two into one, human security, agenda). The practice reveals the maintenance of a stable (but not always efficient) institution, used by members to behave in a disaggregated manner, driven by the overriding demands of national interest and sovereignty.

Against this background, the literature suggests dissonant strategic cultures at play.[42] On the one hand, some analysts question the SADC's commitment to a strategic culture of peace. According to these analysts, old habits die hard: "a culture of preferring and using the military instrument fades slowly. Several remnants of military practices, both psychological as well as material, depict the SADC strategic landscape."[43] In line with this thinking, Laurie Nathan has consistently argued that SADC does not have a shared political value system to enable it to act coherently.[44] In his view, SADC has had limited success in peacemaking and in its efforts to establish a common security regime.

On the other hand, Khadiagala concludes that SADC has benefited from valuable lessons in policy coordination garnered from the four crises in Lesotho, DRC, Zimbabwe, and Madagascar. He underlines the ability of SADC, through trial and error, to promote mediation and democracy promotion. For me, SADC Summitry shows that the key feature of SADC's contemporary foreign relations relates to three themes: conflict mediation and resolution, election management, and economic and trade integration issues. On the latter, Vickers notes that recent negotiations between SADC members and the EU regarding the so-called Economic Partnership Agreements have thrown up three key challenges to collective foreign policy making in SADC: the weak foundations of the region's integration agenda; the widely disparate nature of the region's economies; and long-simmering regional tensions and mistrust, partly related to perceptions of South Africa's regional hegemony.[45]

The last word belongs to the practitioners, some of whom have pointed out that SADC has not yet clarified what type of security cooperation concept it has put into place, nor the normative values and principles that underlie regional cooperation.[46] In addition, one has to understand the SADC project from the perspective of its member states' "historical frame of mind," meaning that "the wounds and scars inflicted by the forces of colonialism and oppression continue to serve as a fundamental reference that draws the SADC citizenry together around a paradigm of political cautiousness and pragmatism."[47]

Conclusion

Against this background, what assessment can one make of efforts by the AU's PSC to work with the RECs and RMs to prevent and resolve violent conflict?[48]

The AU and the UN on Peace and Security: Speaking with One Voice?

The first category of assessment on AU–REC relations relates to the relationship between the AU and the UN and how it ought to be structured. The Charter of the UN states that its prime objective is that of maintaining international peace and security (a responsibility conferred upon the Security Council of the UN). The UN also has the right to use sanctions, blockades, and military force to this end. Chapters VI and VII of the UN Charter specify in detail how and when these activities may be used. According to Chapter VIII, the UN Security Council may further use regional arrangements or agencies for enforcement action under its authority. In terms of the UN Charter, the AU or any subregional organization that intends to undertake enforcement action must therefore seek the prior authorization of the UNSC.

The preamble of the AU's PSC Protocol is "mindful" of these provisions of the UN Charter as well as the need to forge closer cooperation and partnership between the UN and AU in the promotion of peace and security in Africa. Both sides clearly recognize the responsibility of the UN in maintaining international peace and security, as well as the principle of regional assistance. The AU itself has adopted a groundbreaking intervention clause (enforcement operations in cases of genocide, war crimes, and crimes against humanity), very much in line with the R2P.[49]

However, what if the UN is unwilling or unable to authorize timely action? Is it time for the AU to take bold steps? The choice to intervene militarily is tempting but perilous for regional organizations in Africa—it could serve to further marginalize Africa while undermining the UNSC's global responsibilities for peace and security. Even if there appears to be broad acceptance of the idea of standby arrangements (multidisciplinary contingents to participate in peace missions mandated by the AU and UN) among African ambassadors and chiefs of defense staff, the reality is that African military capabilities are very limited. As argued elsewhere, should Africa be able to develop the capacity to deploy ready contingents on standby in member states, such deployments

> would probably not have the capacity to perform more than traditional Chapter Six missions (that is, peaceful settlement of disputes), provide an initial holding force prior to reinforcement by international contingents or secure a safe zone for the provision of humanitarian assistance.[50]

If the key role of the UN—slow moving as it may be—remains uncontested, then perhaps Africa needs a more modest arrangement for a standby unit to serve as a small, rapid response force to intervene at moments of extreme crisis.

This line of thinking raises the question of the need for rapid response forces when an early warning system is in place. What is the relationship between the two? Can we assume that if the PSC is actively anticipating and preventing conflicts or crises (via early warning, and by deploying AU Commissioners and members of the Panel of the Wise), then there will be less need for rapid deployment of assets—boots on the ground, so to speak?

There are additional problems with the AU's external relationships. The history of UN enforcement is problematic given the time it takes to respond adequately to crises, the nature of international politics, and the interests of key players in the international community, any of which might prevent strengthening the structures necessary for the UN to deploy fully (this includes strengthening the emerging UN–AU conflict management relationship). There is also the fact that the permanent members of the UNSC play a minimalist peacekeeping role in Africa, and the trend, worrying for some, toward the regionalization of security.

The AU and Subregional Organizations: Who Speaks for Whom?

The second category of assessment relates to the relationship between the AU and subregional organizations. There is a widely held view in Africa that the AU Commission

Chairperson has to rely on the conflict-management activities of the continent's subregional bodies for any chance of success. According to this view, the challenge for the commission and the PSC is one of coordination and harmonization at the continental level with regard to support (diplomatic and material, where possible) for regional activities. Article 16 of the PSC Protocol provides for a formal relationship between the commission and these bodies in the form of memoranda of understanding, but it is unclear, for instance, whether the memorandum of understanding between the AU PSC and SADC is operational. Article 16 also anticipates the involvement of these bodies in the establishment and functioning of the EWS and ASF. In this regard, it is important to reflect upon the ongoing debates regarding the relationship between the AU and RECs. If one assumes that the AU and ECOWAS, or the EAC or SADC, are tied together as "nested institutions," the question of mutual or reciprocal influence emerges; that is, how to understand the impact of one upon the other. The widely held view also recognizes that normative variance and resource scarcity lead to asymmetric relationships, with the potential to impact on organizational interaction and directly inhibit smooth cooperation.

The AU's standby force was recently "validated" in Exercise Amani Africa in October 2010. The exercise shows that, operationally, the regional standby arrangements (regardless of whether military- or civilian-driven) depend to a large extent on external logistical support for their deployment—a resource limitation not solved at this point by the AU, at the center. If anything, the center itself is in need of operational refinement, hence the reluctance among regional bodies to commit fully its authority. The exercise also identified problems of overlapping membership (whereby AU member states belong to more than one REC), and the vexing question of what exactly the focus of standby arrangements ought to be—conflict prevention and peace promotion, or conflict management, peacemaking, and peacekeeping? This indicates normative variance—perhaps a result of political and cultural differences between the center and the regions in interpreting the overall mandate of the APSA.

The SADC Ambassador to the AU, Joao Ndlovu, recently argued that the AU–REC relationship was problematic both in terms of membership and purpose.[51] He traced the roots of these problems back to the Abuja Treaty of 1991, which established the African Economic Community (AEC) and divided Africa into five economic cooperation regions, namely North, Central, West, East, and Southern. The ASF was supposed to be based on the same logic, and SADC's initial planning was also based on this approach. However, over time, the ASF adopted an "African geographical" configuration, which was not the same as the REC configuration. Hence, the problem of overlapping membership occurred. The "Eastern" region, for example, came to encompass three RECs: EAC, COMESA, and IGAD. Under such a situation, where would a standby arrangement be centered and controlled? To manage this "creative chaos," the region established a Regional Coordinating Mechanism known as EASTBRIGCOM, which does not coincide with an established REC. This leaves countries such as Tanzania and the Indian Ocean island states (Mauritius, Seychelles, and Madagascar) with difficult choices in terms of committing resources to peace and security arrangements and activities. This might also explain SADC's lukewarm response to those who insist it ought to pay more attention to the maritime security needs of its members from the Indian Ocean area (island states as well as sea-facing states).

In addition, Ambassador Ndlovu argued that, like that of ECOWAS, the SADC approach was militarily driven: police and civilian components were always recognized, but never figured prominently. This approach dominated the AU approach in establishing the ASF, and on this basis, SADC created its standby brigade. It was only in 2008 that SADC political leaders insisted on a wider understanding of security, whereby police and civilian participation was to be given equal status to that of the military. This resulted in a name change: the SADC Standby Brigade has now become the SSF.

What does this mean for the peace and security agenda of Africa? To what extent are the subregional approaches compatible with and supportive of the continental ASF approach? The SADC ambassador to the AU notes that the SSF is understood as part of the ASF, yet it is managed by a REC whose objective is regional economic integration. This indicates that SADC's senior decision makers are informed by a security-development paradigm (expressed in the RISDP and SIPO's conflict-preventive, human security language), while the continental ASF seems driven by those who prefer a conflict-management approach (expressed in UN-oriented peacekeeping—if not the more recent peace support operations—language).

As I suggested in the introduction to this chapter, the AU faces a range of challenges in attaining its vision of a united, peaceful, and prosperous continent. For the organization to respond adequately to the multiple and complex peace and security-related challenges it faces, it needs to refine appropriate institutional structures and adopt relevant modes of behavior; to influence the character of international support for the process; to continue to build a strong working triangular relationship involving the UN, AU, and RECs; and to implement funding strategies for the Union.

It appears that the triangular relationship among the UN, AU, and subregional organizations is far from settled, and that this has had a negative impact on the ability of Africans to effectively and efficiently pursue their critical peace and security agenda.

Notes

1. This section draws on United Nations Development Programme, *Human Development Report 2011, Sustainability and Equity: A Better Future for All*, New York, 2011.
2. Solomon A. Dersso, *The Role and Place of the African Standby Force in the African Peace and Security Architecture,* ISS Paper 209 (Pretoria: Institute of Security Studies, 2010).
3. Gilbert Khadiagala and Terrence Lyons, eds., *African Foreign Policies: Power and Process* (Boulder, London: Lynne Rienner, 2001).
4. "U.S. Strategy Toward Sub-Saharan Africa, June 2012" (Washington, DC: The White House, 2012), accessed at http://www.whitehouse.gov/sites/default/files/docs/africa_strategy_2.pdf.
5. Mwangi S. Kimenyi, "Priority Issues during Secretary Clinton's Trip to Africa," *Opinion*, Brookings, 1 August 2012.
6. Rachel Hart, "Changing Relations between Europe and Africa," *Voices*, Open Society Foundations, 15 July 2011.
7. See "Quo Vadis FOCAC? The Fifth Ministerial Meeting of the Forum on China-Africa Cooperation," *African East-Asian Affairs The China Monitor*, Issue 74—Special Edition (Centre for Chinese Studies, Stellenbosch University, 2012).
8. Quo Vadis FOCAC?, ibid.

9. Solomon Dersso, "The Adequacy of the African Peace and Security Architecture to Deal with Serious Democratic Deficits," *African Security Review* 21:3 (2012): 4–23.
10. Solomon A. Dersso, "The Role and Place of the African Standby Force within the African Peace and Security Architecture," ISS Paper 209, January 2010, 6.
11. African Union, Policy Framework for the Establishment of the African Standby Force and Military Staff Committee, EXP/ASF-MSC/2(1), 14 May 2003, 3.
12. Ulf Engel and Joao Porto, eds., *Africa's New Peace and Security Architecture: Promoting Norms, Institutionalising Solutions* (Surrey: Ashgate, 2010).
13. Pieter Brits and Michelle Nel, "Compliance with International Humanitarian Law in Africa: A Study," in *On Strategy: Strategic Theory and Contemporary African Armed Conflicts*, ed. Francois Vrey, Thomas Mandrup, and Abel Esterhuyse (Stellenbosch: Sun Media, 2010), pp. 199–220.
14. Kristiana Powell, *The AU's Emerging Peace and Security Regime: Opportunities and Challenges for Delivering on the Responsibility to Protect*, ISS Monograph 119 (Pretoria: Institute for Security Studies, 2005).
15. Eki Omorogbe, "Can the African Union Deliver Peace and Security?," *Journal of Conflict and Security Law* 16:1 (2011): 1–28.
16. The "APSA 2010 Assessment Study" was commissioned by the AU's Peace and Security Department and was subsequently adopted by the Third Meeting of the Chief Executives and Senior Officials of the AU, RECs and RMs on the Implementation of the Memorandum of Understanding on Cooperation in the Area of Peace and Security, held from 4 to 10 November 2010, Zanzibar, Tanzania.
17. The Study notes that the full operationalization of the ASF will depend on resolving the following "key challenges": the multidimensionality of the ASF, the level of coordination and cooperation between the continental and regional levels, force generation, capacity-related issues in terms of planning, procedures, standard operating procedures (SOPS), logistics, and equipment.
18. Engel and Porto, eds., *Africa's New Peace and Security Architecture*.
19. See East African Community Peace & Security, *EAC Peace & Security Strategy Overview*, http://www.eac.int/security/index.php?option=com_content&view=article&id=67&Itemid=143, last accessed 5 September 2012.
20. Address by Hon. Beatrice Kiraso, Deputy Secretary General, East African Community at the EAC Peace and Security Conference—Kampala, Uganda, 5 October 2009.
21. See http://www.modernghana.com/news/373854/1/eac-adopts-two-major-instruments-for-regional-peac.html, last accessed 5 September 2012.
22. John M. Kabia, "Regional approaches to peacebuilding: The ECOWAS peace and security architecture," paper presented at the BISA-Africa and International Studies ESRC seminar series: African Agency in International Politics, University of Birmingham, 7 April 2011, p. 19.
23. Ibid.
24. Ibid.
25. Ibid. See also Cyril Obi, "Economic Community of West African States on the Ground: Comparing Peacekeeping in Liberia, Sierra Leone, Guinea Bissau, and Cote d' Ivoire," *African Security* 2:2–3 (2009): 119–135; Ademola Adeleke, "From ECOMOG to ECOBRIG: Regionalising the Security Architecture in West Africa," in *Regions, Regional Organisations and Military Power*, ed. Thean D. Potgieter, Abel Esterhuyse, and Ian Liebenberg (Stellenbosch: African Sun Media, 208), pp. 433–452.
26. Sebastian Sperling, "ECOWAS in Crisis Mode: Strengths and Limits of Regional Security Policy in West Africa," *FES Perspective: Regional Security Policy in West Africa* (Berlin: Friedrich Ebert Foundation, 2011).

27. This section draws on Anthoni Van Nieuwkerk, "Organisational Dimensions of Security Cooperation in SADC,' in *Proceedings of the 2006 FOPRISA Annual Conference*, ed. Jonathan Mayuyuka Kaunda (Gaborone: Lightbooks, 2007).
28. Southern African Development Community, SADC Vision, 2008.
29. SADC Extra-Ordinary Summit Communiqué, Windhoek, Namibia, 31 March 2001.
30. SADC Heads of State and Government Summit Communiqué, Blantyre, Malawai, August 2001.
31. See http://www.sadc.int/english/key-documents/strategic-indicative-plan-for-the-organ/, last accessed 29 September 2012.
32. Ibid.
33. See Anthoni Van Nieuwkerk. *Towards Peace and Security in Southern Africa: A Critical Analysis of the Revised Strategic Indicative Plan for the Organ on Politics, Defence and Security Cooperation (SIPO) of the Southern African Development Community*, Africa Peace and Security Series Number 6 (Berlin: Friedrich Ebert Foundation, 2012).
34. Article 13, Protocol Relating to the Establishment of the Peace and Security Council of the African Union, July 2002.
35. Van Nieuwkerk, "Organisational Dimensions of Security Cooperation in SADC."
36. Gabriel Oosthuizen. *The Southern African Development Community: The Organisation, its Policies and Prospects* (Midrand: Institute for Global Dialogue, 2006).
37. See Gavin Cawthra, "Security Dimensions of Regional Relations and Integration," in *Proceedings of the 2009 FOPRISA Annual Conference*, ed. C. Harvey (Gaborone: Lightbooks, 2010); G. Khadiagala, "Forging Regional Foreign Policies in SADC: A Framework for Analysis," in Harvey, op. cit.; A. Van Nieuwkerk, "SADC's Common Foreign Policy," in Harvey, op. cit.; and B. Vickers, "SADC's International Trade Relations," in Harvey, op. cit.
38. Gavin Cawthra. *The Role of SADC in Managing Political Crisis and Conflict: The Cases of Madagascar and Zimbabwe.* FES Peace and Security Series (Maputo: Friedrich Ebert Foundation, 2010).
39. Jonathan Mayuyuka Kaunda, "The Effectiveness of Institutional Restructuring in SADC," in *Revisiting Regionalism in Southern Africa: Proceedings of the Fourth Southern African Forum on Trade (SAFT), Held in Pretoria, South Africa, on 3–4 September 2007*, Institute for Global Dialogue and Friedrich Ebert Foundation, 2008.
40. See Anthoni Van Nieuwkerk, "South Africa's foreign Policy: Searching for Effectiveness in a Transforming World," in *The Future of South Africa's Foreign Policy: Continuity And Change?*, ed. S. Zondi and L. Masters (Midrand: Institute of Global Dialogue, 2010).
41. Sanusha Naidu, "South Africa and Africa: Mixed Messages?" in *South Africa's Foreign Policy 1994–2004: Apartheid Past, Renaissance Future*, ed. Elizabeth Sidiropoulos (Johannesburg: South African Institute of International Affairs, 2004).
42. Strategic culture refers to a set of shared beliefs, assumptions, and modes of behavior, derived from common experiences and accepted narratives that shape collective identity and relationships to other groups, and which determine appropriate ends and means for achieving security objectives. See Anthoni Van Nieuwkerk, "The Strategic Culture of Foreign and Security Policy-Making: Examining the Southern African Development Community," unpublished conference paper.
43. Francois Vrey, "Strategic Culture of the SADC: Militarised Pathways to Security?," *African Journal on Conflict Resolution* 9:1 (2009): 63–88.
44. Laurie Nathan, "The Absence of Common Values and Failure of Common Security in Southern Africa, 1992–2003," Working Paper 50, Crisis States Research Centre (London: LSE, 2004).
45. Brendan Vickers, "SADC's International Trade Relations," in *Proceedings of the 2009 FOPRISA Annual Conference*, ed. Charles Harvey (Gaborone: Lightbooks, 2010).

46. P. Macaringue and S. Magano, "Operationalising the SIPO," in *Towards Political and Economic Integration in Southern Africa: Proceedings of the 2007 FOPRISA Annual Conference*, ed. Gavin Cawthra and Jonathan Kaunda (Gaborone: Lightbooks, 2008).
47. Joao Ndlovu, "New SADC-ICP partnership for the implementation of the SIPO," unpublished briefing note delivered at the SADC Consultative Conference of 27 April 2006 in Windhoek.
48. This assessment draws on previous research by the author. See Anthoni Van Nieuwkerk, "The Regional Roots of the African Peace and Security Architecture: Exploring Centre–Periphery Relations," *South African Journal of International Affairs* 18:2 (2011): 169–189.
49. The 2001 report of the International Commission on Intervention and State Sovereignty (ICISS) identified two threshold cases that justify humanitarian intervention: large-scale loss of life and ethnic cleansing, underway or anticipated. It prescribes four "precautionary conditions": right intention, last resort, proportional means, and reasonable prospects of success. And it recommends that the UN Security Council be the preferred decision maker.
50. J. Cilliers and K. Sturman, "The Right Intervention: Enforcement Challenges for the African Union," *African Security Review* 11:3 (2002): 28–39.
51. Personal communication with HE J. Ndlovu, December 2010.

Chapter 4

Sanctions and Africa: United Nations and Regional Responses

Andrea Charron

Introduction

Sanctions, long a tool of United Nations (UN) action, are increasingly being used by regional actors in their responses to conflict. However, while the UN applies sanctions in response to a variety of crises types (including civil wars, interstate conflicts, acts of terrorism, and nuclear proliferation), the African regional organizations (ROs) have concentrated their use of sanctions almost exclusively on states that undergo an unconstitutional change of government, most often because of a coup d'état. What accounts for this pattern and (apparent) division of labor? There are two possible hypotheses. First, regional action could be an effort to fill a void when no UN action is forthcoming, either because the UN Security Council (UNSC) is deadlocked or unwilling to address the situation or does not have the conflict on its agenda. Second, this sanctions pattern may indicate a particular type of problem that the Security Council is not pursuing and that the ROs want to address, and sanctions are a useful means to that end.

To test these hypotheses and to unpack the application of sanctions by these disparate organizations, this chapter explores the mechanisms that the UN and ROs have to impose sanctions and in what circumstances they do so. In keeping with the theme of this book, the interaction and coordination (or lack thereof) between the UN and the ROs are reviewed. The first section of the chapter sets the context; what do we know about sanctions and what are the types of conflicts facing African states that could be subject to either UN and/or African regional sanctions? The next two sections analyze the sanctions provisions and practices of the UNSC and African ROs. The last section draws some conclusions about sanctions and the two sets of organizations. While African ROs are tackling a particular type of problem with the application of sanctions (i.e., the unconstitutional change of governments), African ROs can also prompt the UNSC to apply sanctions, suggesting that both hypotheses have merit.

Setting the Context: Sanctions and Africa

Much has been written about sanctions generally and their employment by the UN and its predecessor, the League of Nations. Considerably less has been written about the application of sanctions by ROs.[1] There are two reasons for this. First, sanctions adopted by the UNSC tend to dominate academic and policy debates for a variety of reasons, but especially because of the Security Council's primary responsibility for the maintenance of international peace and security. A decision by the Council to apply or not to apply sanctions, therefore, captures the world's attention. Second, until recently, cases of regional sanctions were few in number; this is changing quickly.

Much of the sanctions literature has focused on the question of their "effectiveness" (especially UN or US sanctions),[2] and on their use in high-profile crises such as those in Iran, North Korea, and Iraq. Other themes and issues have also occupied researchers and academics, but the dilemma of how sanctions can be used to exact a change in the behaviour of a target (especially to stop nuclear proliferation) is the Holy Grail for sanctions scholars. This then means that regionally applied sanctions—which are often adopted to treat different, especially more geographically contained crises—are understudied.

Many scholars wrestle with defining sanctions because the UN Charter is permissive, providing only suggested parameters for "measures not involving the use of armed force,"[3] and suggesting examples including a "complete or partial interruption of economic relations" and of "rail, sea, air, postal, telegraphic, radio and other means of communication" and/or "the severance of diplomatic relations."[4] Sanctions, from the perspective of the UN, tend to involve the denial of a product, service, or privilege by the senders (the member states of the organization applying the measures) against a target (a state, but more and more, against individuals and entities). Examples include a ban on travel by individuals, or the seizing of government assets. The most common UN sanctions are conventional arms embargoes—sender states apply national legislation to make sure that the target in question is not provided with guns, ammunition, parts, military training, or paramilitary equipment. Travel and financial sanctions are the next most common UN sanctions. In contrast, African ROs are more prescriptive about the types of conflicts that warrant sanctions and the specific measures to be invoked. The charters and protocols of these organizations cite unpaid dues, the failure to comply with the mandate of the organization, and, most often, the unconstitutional change of government as being subject to sanctions in the form of a suspension of membership. Despite this wide variety of sanctions, all measures applied by the UN and African ROs since 1995[5] are considered "targeted" sanctions—that is, there is a denial of access to something, and this action is meant to coerce the targets but minimize deleterious humanitarian consequences for the general population.[6] Arguably, the adoption of targeted sanctions is in many ways the most revolutionary aspect of the Council's sanctions practice, and the Council's response to conflict in Africa played a large role in prompting that innovation.

When collective security-minded organizations like the UN, African Union (AU), and Economic Community of West African States (ECOWAS), or more economically focused associations like the Inter-Governmental Authority on Development (IGAD) and the Southern African Development Community (SADC), are presented with a conflict, they generally have three options. The first is to do nothing and/or wait for another organization to do something. The second is to seek pacific means of dispute settlement. The third option is to apply coercive measures up to and including the use of deadly force. Sanctions are said to be the middle way between "words and war" because they are thought to be more than just talk but not as destructive and politically charged as the application of force. They are, increasingly, the tool of choice for international organizations dealing with crises—especially in Africa, sadly plagued with many. Because of the flexible and fungible nature of sanctions (they can be applied or removed, added to or scaled back, applied to an entire state or to particular actors, and can cut off a state completely, or only selectively target areas, services, and individuals), they provide organizations with maximum flexibility.

Famines, coups, ethnically based conflicts, ideological battles, terrorism, and interstate wars represent some of the types of crises that the UN and African ROs have attempted to tackle. Civil wars and unconstitutional changes to government[7] are, by far, the most common variants of conflicts that have gripped Africa since the end of World War II, and the UN and African ROs have dedicated considerable attention and resources to them. Sub-Saharan Africa, for example, ranked as the second most conflict-ridden region in the world in 2011, with ninety-one ongoing conflicts, ranging from wars to violent crises. All but one (between Sudan and South Sudan) was of an intrastate nature.[8] In addition, Africa has witnessed hundreds of plotted, attempted, and successful unconstitutional overthrows of governments since the 1950s; thirteen of the fifteen states belonging to ECOWAS have experienced coups.[9] In 2011, there were three attempted coups d'état (strikes against the state) in ECOWAS member states Guinea, Guinea Bissau, and Niger.[10] There were two in the first half of 2012—in Mali and another in Guinea Bissau.

Given the number of conflicts in Africa, it is not surprising that it is the most sanctioned continent in the world. An analysis of all the mandatory[11] African sanctions regimes applied by the UN and African ROs since 1990 is summarized in Table 4.1. The UN has applied twenty-nine mandatory sanctions regimes since 1990,[12] seventeen of which targeted twelve African states. This means that nearly forty percent of the UN sanctions regimes target Africa.[13] If one includes the sanctions applied by the AU, ECOWAS, and other African regional groups, twenty out of fifty-five African states have been sanctioned. This means that roughly one in three African states have been subject to sanctions.[14] Clearly sanctions are the tool of choice to address crises in Africa; no other region in the world has come close to receiving this level of attention in terms of the application of sanctions.

Having set the context, the next two sections consider the UN and African ROs and their respective sanctioning activities. What mechanisms do the UN and African ROs have with which to apply sanctions? Do the organizations target the same conflicts and/or states, or different conflicts and states? Do they apply sanctions for the same reasons—or with the same objectives? Finally, do they coordinate or work together in their application of sanctions? The following sections are dedicated to trying to answer these questions.

Table 4.1 African States Sanctioned between 1990 and August 2012

Organization	UN	AU	ECOWAS	IGAD	SADC
Number of African states sanctioned	12	10	7	1	1
Number of member states	193 (53 African)	53	15	8	15
% of states sanctioned	6 (23 if Africa only)	19	47	12	7
Which states	Angola, **Côte d'Ivoire**, DRC, Eritrea, Ethiopia, **Guinea-Bissau**, Liberia, Libya, Rwanda, Sierra Leone, Somalia, Sudan	CAR, Comoros, **Côte d'Ivoire**, Guinea, **Guinea-Bissau**, Madagascar, Mali, Mauritania, Niger, Togo	**Côte d'Ivoire**, Guinea, **Guinea-Bissau**, Liberia, Mali, Niger, Sierra Leone	Eritrea	Madagascar
Most sanctioned states	Liberia (3xs), Sudan (2xs), Libya (2xs), Eritrea (2xs)	Guinea-Bissau (2xs), Mauritania (2xs)	Guinea-Bissau (2xs)		

Boldfaced states have been sanctioned by three or more organizations.
Burundi has been sanctioned by neighboring states, not by an African RO (see note 5).
The EU is not discussed, but it has applied twenty-seven sanctions regimes against twenty-one African states: Burundi, CAR, Comoros I and II, Congo/Zaire, **Côte d'Ivoire**, Djibouti, Equatorial Guinea, Ethiopia, Eritrea, Gambia, Guinea, **Guinea-Bissau I and II**, Kenya, Liberia, Malawi, Mali, Nigeria, Rwanda, Sudan I and II, Togo I and II, and Zimbabwe I, II, III.
The Arab League is not discussed, but it has sanctioned African states Egypt and Libya.

The UN and Sanctions

UNSC sanctions are more advanced and involved than of any of their regional counterparts. Despite the marked changes in the way in which the UNSC uses the sanctions tool, the drafters of the Charter would still recognize them as sanctions within the spirit of Article 41 of the UN Charter. Some things about sanctions have not changed: unanimous agreement (or acquiescence) among the permanent five (P5) is still essential, all decisions related to the application and interpretation of sanctions still rest with the UNSC, and member states and their designates, not the Council, are still responsible for applying the necessary regulations and legislation to give sanctions effect.

For the UNSC, the trigger for sanctions is a threat to or breach of international peace and security as defined in Article 39 of the Charter. In practice, the Council has included intrastate/civil wars, interstate wars, international terrorism, and proliferation activities in this category.[15] If we look more closely at the seventeen UN sanctions regimes that have targeted twelve African states since 1990 (Table 4.2), twelve addressed a civil war

Table 4.2 UN Sanctions Applied against African States since 1990

Type of Conflict	Number of Sanctions Regimes
Civil wars	12
Interstate wars	2
Terrorism	2
Coups	1
Total no. of sanctions regimes	17

of some variant: Angola, Côte d'Ivoire, the Democratic Republic of the Congo (DRC), Liberia (three times), Libya, Rwanda, Sierra Leone, Somalia, and Sudan (Darfur). Two regimes addressed interstate conflicts (between Ethiopia and Eritrea, and between Eritrea–Djibouti and Somalia). Two addressed state support of terrorism (Libya[16] and Sudan[17]). The latest, against Guinea Bissau, is the only regime to exclusively address an unconstitutional change in government.[18]

Civil wars, UN sanctions, and Africa are inextricably linked. The UNSC tends to use sanctions to deal with the *effects* of civil war (e.g., regional destabilization or increasing levels of violence) more than the *causes* of the civil war (e.g., ethnic rivalries or coups). In many cases where African civil wars were treated with UN sanctions, a peace agreement was negotiated by a RO or neighboring states backed by a UN or UN-blessed mission that was in place prior to the application of UN sanctions (especially for sanctions regimes applied in the late 1990s and 2000s). Sometimes, a peace-spoiling event prompts the Council to adopt more coercive measures, and thus the UN sanctions signal support for the previously applied regional efforts. Sanctions, usually consisting of an arms embargo followed later by travel bans and (often) financial measures, are applied. The duration of these regimes is sometimes decades long. Sanctions are renewed year after year as the Council assesses the conditions required for termination of the sanctions measures. The measures are often "tweaked" in response to events on the ground—certain sanctions may be terminated in recognition of progress in some areas, while other sanctions remain in place until all conditions are met—many of which are specified in the peace agreement in place, and often include free and fair elections.

The Council targets state and non-state actors with sanctions, although arms embargoes against the state in conflict remain the measures of choice. These are often adjusted to exempt the democratically elected governments of the day and the UN or regional missions deployed so that they may continue to receive the necessary weapons and ammunition to maintain order. The Council applies financial and travel sanctions to target members of rebel groups and/or peace spoilers (but rarely sitting heads of state). Natural resource sanctions against the illegal trade of diamonds and timber are fast becoming a common theme in UNSC responses to African conflict. The advantage of these sanctions is that they can be applied either to aid governments in gaining legitimacy and funds, and/or to cut off a potential source of illegal funds to rebels. Importantly, these measures mean that the Council has made a link between the exploitation of exportable products, especially gems, and the financing of armed conflict that may mean a greater application of these types of sanctions, especially in resource-rich Africa. The adoption of these measures has been so successful that the

Council may sanction other resources in the future, including charcoal, fish, and possibly even cattle—all lootable resources that fund the purchase of arms and ammunition that can then prolong intrastate conflicts.

Acute events like coups, while troubling and monitored by the UNSC, are not sanctioned automatically. Instead, the Council condemns the coup, recognizes the efforts of ROs, and waits for the outcome. For example, in 2012, the Security Council passed Resolution 2056 (drafted by Morocco, Togo, South Africa, and the European states)[19] condemning the military coup in Mali, but it did not impose mandatory sanctions[20] like the AU and ECOWAS did. Instead, it noted the UNSC Presidential and press statements previously made and underlined the considerable efforts of the AU and ECOWAS to restore constitutional order. The rest of the resolution concentrates on the violence, instability, human rights violations, and support to terrorist groups in the Mali and the Sahel region; this was in line with its primary responsibility for the maintenance of international peace and security. For the coups in Mauritania in 2008, Guinea in 2008, and Niger in 2009, no UN sanctions were applied (indeed there are no UNSC resolutions concerning these specific states for these years). However, the AU, ECOWAS, and/or SADC applied sanctions, and the UN, as an organization, condemned the coups and recognized regional efforts by other means, including Presidential Statements, thematic resolutions, the Secretariat and/or the Human Rights Council.

When the UNSC has sanctioned a state subject to unconstitutional changes of government (like Côte d'Ivoire in 2010), the UNSC already had sanctions in place to mitigate the impact of the wider civil war (already in the post-conflict phase when former President Gbagbo refused to step down after losing the election). There are only three cases when the UNSC has applied sanctions specifically because of a coup. They include sanctions against Haiti between 1993 and 1994, initial measures against Sierra Leone in 1997, and the latest coup in Guinea Bissau in 2012. In all three cases, UN sanctions were adopted in support of the engagement and measures undertaken by the Organization of American States, the AU, ECOWAS, and/or the Community of Portuguese Speaking Countries (CPLP) to restore constitutional order. The UN has yet to apply sanctions for a coup absent a previous response from an RO.

UN sanctions are applied in layers in response to peace-breaking events and lifted piecemeal to allow for more subtle changes to the level of coerciveness of the sanctions. For example, in the first round of sanctions against Somalia in 1992, the Council applied a general arms embargo[21] against the state to prevent conventional weapons from flooding into the country from outside sources and thus further destabilizing an already troubled state in the midst of a civil war. Focused on wars in the Balkans, Rwanda, and against terrorism, the Council let the arms embargo against Somalia languish. In 2008, reflective of its new approach to sanctions, the Council applied a second round of sanctions to address the instability in Somalia; this included a travel ban, financial asset freeze, and arms embargo against any individuals or entities who violated the general arms embargo, violated the terms of the newly signed Djibouti peace agreement and/or obstructed the flow of humanitarian assistance to Somalia.[22] In 2009, having received reports from its subsidiary bodies, including those from a panel of experts and three African ROs requesting additional measures be applied,[23] the Council adopted a third round of measures against Eritrea and against individuals and entities in Eritrea who contributed to the instability in Somalia.[24] This placed a general arms embargo on Eritrea (and banned Eritrea from exporting any arms as well) in addition to individual arms travel, and financial sanctions against those including, but not limited to, the Eritrean political and military leadership, who violate any of the sanctions and/or aid armed opposition groups bent on destabilizing the region.

UN sanctions are only as "effective" (meaning they put the desired pressure on the intended targets) as the number of member states that apply the necessary legislation to give them effect. Given, however, that many of the UN sanctions involve the denial of arms, assets, or travel privileges, it is of paramount importance that the neighboring states comply with the measures. In Africa, however, there is an enormous capabilities gap between the expectations of the UNSC and the resources of African states. Neighboring African states are often at conflict and/or the target of sanctions and lack the police or customs officials to monitor the import or export of goods, let alone contraband weapons that slip easily into the country via the largely unmonitored African borders. For example, the main airport in Monrovia, Liberia, was limited in its ability to enforce UN sanctions until an electronic passport reader that could flag listed names of targets was installed. Until then, the "hard line" of sanctions monitoring depended on an officious, but often poorly paid Liberian official: (a) to recognize the name from a list of potentially hundreds of names found on police, customs, UN, and other lists (of course trains and cars do not require this kind of passport check) and (b) not to accept a bribe to ignore the travel ban. At the same time, most of the UN targeted lists do not have passport numbers or even all of the aliases/ages of the targets (photos would be extremely helpful, but are not available). The AU and ECOWAS member states do attempt to comply, at least minimally, in the form of an obligatory letter to the Sanctions Committee indicating that they are applying the necessary measures. However, without the capacity, funds, or incentive to dedicate precious resources to what many see as a losing battle—few African countries manufacture small arms and weapons and so they can only try to tackle the enormous illicit market[25]—the "effectiveness" of sanctions is always questionable.

Does the UN experience with sanctions mirror regional efforts? Do the African ROs have similar mechanisms to apply sanctions? Are they applying them against the same conflicts as the UN?

African ROs and Sanctions

Table 4.3 provides a summary of the African regional experience with sanctions. If we look at the twenty-two sanctions regimes applied by African ROs, twelve were applied by the AU against ten member states: Central African Republic (CAR), Comoros, Côte d'Ivoire, Guinea, Guinea Bissau (2xs), Madagascar, Mali, Mauritania (2xs), Niger, and Togo. Eight were applied by ECOWAS against seven states: Côte d'Ivoire, Guinea, Guinea Bissau (2xs), Mali, Niger, Sierra Leone, and Togo. One was applied by SADC, against Madagascar, and one was applied by IGAD, against Eritrea, targeting twelve different African states. The AU and ECOWAS imposed sanctions against the same state on six occasions (against Côte d'Ivoire, Guinea, Guinea-Bissau, Malia, Niger, and Togo). Twenty-one of the twenty-two African sanctions regimes are applied to address an unconstitutional change of government. Guinea-Bissau and Côte d'Ivoire have been sanctioned by the most number of ROs (as well as by the UN and the European Union [EU]).

Table 4.3 African ROs and Sanctions since 1990

Organization	AU (53 Members)	ECOWAS (15 Members)	IGAD (8 Members)	SADC (15 Members)	Total
Number of sanctions regimes	12	8	1	1	22
Number of sanctions regimes addressing an unconstitutional change of government	12	8	0 (interference in another state)	1	21
Number of African states sanctioned	10: Guinea-Bissau (x2), Mauritania (x2)	7: Guinea-Bissau (x2)	1: Eritrea	1: Madagascar	12

Burundi was sanctioned by neighboring states for civil war and regional instability.

While the UN Charter makes a mention of measures to be applied in cases of breaches and threats to international peace and security (the primary concern of the UNSC), the African ROs have focused on responding to unconstitutional changes of government and the sanctions measures reflect this fact. Through the adoption of charters, constitutions, and protocols that call for sanctions mainly in the form of suspension of memberships, one goal of the African ROs is to promote good governance and democracy by responding to coups (military coups being the most common) in the hope of deterring future occurrences. Indeed, each organization has adopted codes that are variations of the Commonwealth of Nations[26] 1995 "democracy clause" authorizing a collective response to democratic violations including coups.[27] Therefore, rather than tackling many different types of conflicts via the application of sanctions, as the UNSC does, the AU, ECOWAS, and SADC have focused on responding to unconstitutional changes of government. Since the African ROs have not nearly the resources and machinery associated with their sanctions regimes as does the UN (especially sanctions committees and panels of experts that can aid the UNSC with decisions about targets and the most appropriate measures to apply),[28] they have relied on a denial of membership as the primary sanctions measure. Unlike the UN sanctions, which can linger for years, even decades, African regional sanctions are lifted fairly quickly after constitutional order is restored.

The Organisation of African Unity and AU

The predecessor of the AU, the Organisation of African Unity (OAU), was founded in 1963. In the early years of its history, the OAU found sanctions politically difficult to justify because of an adherence to the principles of the protection of territorial integrity and noninterference in the domestic affairs of member states.[29] Furthermore, given that there was little experience with sanctions applied by organizations (other than the failed League of Nations examples, the UN having yet to apply its first mandatory sanctions against Southern Rhodesia or South Africa), there was little appetite to experiment. Indeed, there was no provision in the OAU Charter for the application of sanctions and, according to Thomas Tieku, while the idea of sanctions was discussed at the first summit of OAU held in Cairo in July 1964 and sanctions committee was formed, the heads of state agreed not to sanction each other and the work of the committee focused primarily on apartheid South Africa. (The name of the committee became the OAU Sanctions Committee against the Apartheid Regime of South Africa in 1986.) The one area that was negotiable and subject to sanctions-like measures (including preventing representatives of recalcitrant states to speak at OAU meetings or fill OAU positions) rested with member states in arrears with their budgetary contributions.

Given, however, the number of coups facing Africa between the 1960s and 2000 (78 "successful" unconstitutional overthrows of governments between 1961 and 1997),[30] the OAU began to turn its attention to this African problem. According to Monica Juma:

> Even when it became apparent that the OAU needed to address insecurity, it was guided in its actions by the principle of "non-interference." It thus adopted mechanisms that privileged the use of soft power such as mediation and persuasion, such as the OAU's Commission of Mediation, Conciliation and Arbitration (1964) and subsequently the Conflict Prevention, Management and Resolution Mechanism (1993).[31]

One could add to this list of soft power mechanisms the myriad of declarations focused on unconstitutional changes to government, including: the *1999 Algiers Declaration on Unconstitutional Changes of Government*,[32] the *2000 Lomé Declaration for an OAU Response to Unconstitutional Changes of Government*,[33] the *2002 OAU/AU Declaration on Principles Governing Democratic Elections in Africa*, and the *2003 Protocol Relating to the Establishment of the Peace and Security Council of the African Union*. Combined, the first three documents underlined the unacceptability of coups. The fourth document, importantly, outlines the consequences of such actions, which includes the application of sanctions (under Article 7(1)g of the Protocol) and establishes a body to make the decision to apply sanctions—the Peace and Security Council (PSC).[34] One of the reasons for the change on the principle of noninterference in the domestic jurisdiction of member states is outlined in the AU's Preamble of the *Charter on Democracy, Elections and Governance*: "the unconstitutional changes of governments . . . are one of the essential causes of insecurity, instability and violent conflict in Africa" and so the member states of the AU commit to "promot[ing] the universal values and principles of democracy, good governance, human rights and the right to development."[35] Sanctions could have been applied as a consequence of many different types of instability (as is the case for the UN), but for the OAU and AU, sanctions were linked to the process of accession to power. The adoption of these protocols and provisions to apply sanctions explain, in part, the shift from the less interventionist OAU to the new, more engaged AU.

The AU's 2001 Constitutive Act outlaws coups in Articles 4m, 4p, and 30. Two articles in the Act allow for the imposition of sanctions—Articles 23 and 30. Article 23 deals with the consequences of defaults in payments and failures to comply with AU policies. Article 30 is a trigger for sanctions in the event of an unconstitutional change in government.

Article 23 reads:

1. The Assembly shall determine the appropriate sanctions to be imposed on any Member State that defaults in the payment of its contributions to the budget of the Union in the following manner: denial of the right to speak at meetings, to vote, to present candidates for any position or post within the Union or to benefit from any activity or commitments, therefrom;
2. Furthermore, any Member State that fails to comply with the decisions and policies of the Union may be subjected to other sanctions, such as the denial of transport and communications links with other Member States, and other measures of a political and economic nature to be determined by the Assembly.

Article 30 states that: Governments which shall come to power through unconstitutional means shall not be allowed to participate in the activities of the Union.

To date, Article 23 is invoked less often than Article 30. In the case of Article 23(1), many African states face continual financial hardship. The AU, for example, gave an exemption to Sierra Leone despite being in arrears in its membership payments in 2003;[36] others, however, have been subject to sanctions.[37] In the case of Article 23(2), it is the Assembly that must decide on the nature of the transgression and the sanctions measures to be applied and is yet to be invoked. The fact that a sanctioned state may apply to the *African Court of Human Rights and Justice* to question the reasons for the sanctions and the measures recommended may be deterring the invocation of Article 23(2).[38] Member states instead have been warned of transgressions and given an opportunity to comply before there is talk of sanctions.[39] Therefore, Article 30 is the main sanctions mechanism. There is debate as to whether or not suspension from activities of the organization is automatic or if a formal decision must be made (and then by whom—is it just the PSC or in consultation with the Assembly?) The myriad of charters and protocols breeds confusion; the use of the word "shall" no less than two times suggests that the consequence of sanctions is intended to be automatic. However, the suspension of the state tends to throw the baby out with the bathwater; Article 30 is intended to get at the coup participants, not the entire state. Therefore, rules of procedure have been adopted to ensure a more consistent approach to the suspension.[40] The other debate is whether or not the sanctions should be applied only to reestablish a previously democratically elected government or to reestablish any unconstitutionally changed government. The UNSC, for example, has applied sanctions to benefit "elected" governments—sanctions against the de facto Cédras regime to reinstate President-elect Aristide in Haiti being the most famous example. The AU Assembly has decided[41] not to allow perpetrators of unconstitutional changes to participate in elections held to restore constitutional order. In addition, there is a growing trend by the AU to release preemptive press statements urging parties to continue with "dialogue" in situations where a coup may be possible. For example, the PSC of the AU released such a statement on 22 April 2010 when institutional reforms planned under the new Constitution of Comoros derailed.[42]

Togo is often cited as the "cause célèbre" of the potential power of Article 30. After being suspended from the AU for a coup in 2005, Togo is now relatively stable and won an elected, nonpermanent seat in the UNSC for 2012 and 2013. In a very few cases, the AU has gone beyond suspending the state in question and has enforced individual travel/visa restrictions and some financial asset bans on coup leaders from Comoros, Guinea, Madagascar, Mali, and Mauritania, but little information is available on the impact of these measures.

In two cases, the AU recommended that the UNSC apply additional measures not already in effect. In 2009, the AU called on the Council to impose sanctions against foreign actors, both within and outside the region, especially Eritrea, which were providing support to the armed groups engaged in destabilization activities in Somalia and undermining the peace and reconciliation efforts as well as regional stability.[43] Referencing this call in its resolution, the UNSC applied sanctions against Eritrea on 23 December 2009, pursuant to Resolution 1907. Resolution 1907 imposed an arms embargo against Eritrea in addition to travel restrictions and a freeze on the assets of its political and military leaders. The measures imposed on the Eritrean government illustrate the collaboration that can potentially exist between regional and international institutions.[44] However, the AU did not apply additional measures, nor did ECOWAS or SADC (although they were supportive of the UN's efforts). Only IGAD suspended Eritrea's membership.[45]

The second case involves Côte d'Ivoire in 2010. In early December, after the second round of presidential elections were held on 28 November 2010, the AU decided to suspend the participation of Côte d'Ivoire in all its activities until the democratically elected President Outtara assumed state power. According to Bellamy and Williams, the statements of the AU (and ECOWAS) were a "critical determinant of Security Council action."[46] Indeed, they refer to ROs as the "gatekeepers" influencing how issues are framed and the range of plausible policy options available to the Security Council.[47] The actions of the AU, therefore, helped prompt the UNSC to adopt Resolution 1962 on 20 December 2010, which recognized the decision of the AU (and ECOWAS as well) and renewed the mandate of the UN Operation in Côte d'Ivoire (UNOCI) until June 2011.

Curiously, no specific mention is made of sanctions in either the Report of the UN Secretary-General on UN–AU cooperation in peace and security[48] or the resulting UNSC Resolution 2033 (2012) on cooperation between the UN and African ROs. However, the message of the need for continued but enhanced cooperation between the AU and UN on peace and security issues in Africa can certainly apply to sanctions as well.

The AU recognizes that it is inexperienced at the application of sanctions and that there are many impediments to their "effectiveness," which is why it is debating the need to create a sanctions committee of experts to advise it (similar to the UN's panel of experts system) on sanctions application.[49] Some of the challenges facing the AU include domestic and regional politics (which makes garnering the necessary support to impose sanctions difficult), weak AU leverage, limited inter-African dependency, lax borders, endemic and systematic corruption, and inadequate resources,[50] not to mention the unwritten rule of "brotherhood" among the members. However, in some respects, the AU is of the opinion that it applies sanctions in a more principled way than does the UNSC. Having deliberated at length on the *UN Report of the High-level Panel on Threats, Challenges and Change* (2004), the AU adopted a Common African Position known as "The *Ezulwini* Consensus" (2005), which focused significantly on the issue of peace and security. In it, the AU Heads of State reminded the UNSC of some of the guidelines they expected it to follow when adopting sanctions. The AU suggested that sanctions be:

> exercised in accordance with the United Nations Charter and international law. Sanctions should be considered only after all means of peaceful settlement of disputes under Chapter VI of the United Nations Charter have been exhausted and a thorough consideration undertaken of the short-term and long-term effects of such sanctions. Further, sanctions should be imposed for a specified time-frame and be based on tenable legal grounds and should be lifted as soon as the objectives are achieved. Sanctions should also be smart and targeted to mitigate their humanitarian effects. In this regard, there is need for the UN to define the objectives and guidelines for the imposition of sanctions.[51]

The AU has certainly practiced what it preaches. It has applied only targeted sanctions for a limited time and for a clear reason—the unconstitutional change of government. To what effect, however, requires more study.

ECOWAS and Sanctions

ECOWAS is one of the most successful African ROs in terms of its ability to intervene in crises impacting its fifteen members. Its influence on decisions made by the UNSC with regard to sanctions has been especially significant. ECOWAS was founded in 1975 to promote economic integration and development in West Africa. The initial ECOWAS treaty did not have a sanctions article per se. The Heads of State and Government was the main authority with the ability to make decisions on behalf of ECOWAS.[52] It applied trade sanctions against Liberia and Sierra Leone in the 1990s and was instrumental in petitioning the UNSC to follow suit.[53] Indeed, the case of Sierra Leone was the first example of the Security Council authorizing an RO to enforce its sanctions:

> Acting also under Chapter VIII of the Charter of the United Nations, [the UNSC] authorizes ECOWAS, cooperating with the democratically-elected Government of Sierra Leone, to ensure strict implementation of the provisions of this resolution relating to the supply of petroleum and petroleum products, and arms and related matériel of all types, including, where necessary and in conformity with applicable international standards, by halting inward maritime shipping in order to inspect and verify their cargoes and destinations, and calls upon all States to cooperate with ECOWAS in this regard.[54]

In practice, the monitoring and enforcement of the UN sanctions by ECOWAS was poorly done, but the precedent had been set. It is now considered routine for the UNSC to authorize UN and regional missions to report on and/or enforce UN sanctions—especially its arms embargoes.[55]

ECOWAS, like the OAU and AU, found that unconstitutional changes of government were very unsettling for the region, making the pursuit of economic integration difficult. As the existing ECOWAS treaties and protocols had no provisions for the suspension of a member state impacted by coups, ECOWAS needed an automatic mechanism with which to respond to the unconstitutional changes to government that had plagued thirteen of its fifteen member states.[56] To this end, in 2001, member states of ECOWAS agreed to a new protocol, based on a revised regional vision, focusing on the promotion and enforcement of democratic principles. The new protocol not only outlined the importance of separating the powers of government, it also set out clear consequences in the event of an "abrupt end to democracy."[57] The protocol outlawed many of the tactics used in recent coups, including changing a state's election laws six months prior to an election, and stipulated that free, fair, and transparent elections are the only acceptable means of accession to power.

Article 45 of the ECOWAS Protocol on Democracy and Good Governance (supplement to the protocol relating to the Mechanism for Conflict Prevention, Management, Resolution, Peacekeeping and Security, 1999) is reminiscent of the Article 30 of the AU's Constitutive Act (2000):

1. In the event that democracy is abruptly brought to an end by any means or where there is massive violation of Human Rights in a Member State, ECOWAS may impose sanctions on the State concerned.
2. The sanctions which shall be decided by the Authority, may take the following forms, in increasing order of severity:
   - Refusal to support the candidates presented by the Member State concerned for elective posts in international organizations;
   - Refusal to organize ECOWAS meetings in the Member State concerned; and/or
   - Suspension of the Member State concerned from all ECOWAS decision-making bodies.
   - During the period of the suspension the Member State shall be obliged to pay its dues for the period.
3. During the period of suspension, ECOWAS shall continue to monitor, encourage, and support the efforts being made by the suspended Member State to return to normalcy and constitutional order.
4. On the recommendation of the Mediation and Security Council, a decision may be taken at the appropriate time to proceed as stipulated in Article 45 of the Protocol of 10th December 1999.[58]

Under Article 45, according to Frederick Cowell, the only sanctions ECOWAS can directly impose are limited political sanctions relating to individual states' membership of ECOWAS, such as suspension from ECOWAS meetings. Other sanctions are contingent upon member states agreeing at the heads of government level.[59]

The focus on good governance and Article 45 was the impetus behind the condemnation by ECOWAS of the coup attempts in Togo (2005) and Guinea Bissau (2008 and 2009) and the coup in Guinea (2008). Guinea's first free and fair elections were only held in 2010. According to Sebastien Sperling: "Given the fragile nature of, and deficits in, democracy in almost all the member states, the unanimity and resoluteness with which ECOWAS has condemned and applied sanctions for the most recent violations of the regional protocols is remarkable."[60] Guinea, Niger, and Côte d'Ivoire were all suspended from membership and ECOWAS mediators were sent to Guinea-Bissau after its coup in 2008. Mali and Guinea-Bissau are the latest cases (2012) to be sanctioned based on the Protocol for Democracy and Good Governance. The member states insisted that the military juntas in Niger and Guinea relinquish power to democratically legitimated governments. In the case of Côte d'Ivoire, ECOWAS recognized the challenger, Ouattara, as the winner of the presidential election sixteen days sooner than the UNSC[61] condemned incumbent Gbagbo's coup and requested he leave office.

ECOWAS, like the AU, also struggles with conflicting political will, inadequate funding, and poor logistics,[62] which makes the decision to apply more ambitious or additional sanctions beyond the simple suspension of membership found in Article 45 difficult. Furthermore, there remain glaring examples of impunity. For example, President Blaise Compaoré, who came to power by way of a military coup, has been ruling Burkina Faso since 1987. He has secured another term of office (because of a controversial interpretation of the constitution), but there has been very little reaction by ECOWAS. (Ironically, he was ECOWAS' mediator in Guinea and Côte d'Ivoire). This suggests that the focus of ECOWAS is on the holding of elections, not the quality of campaigns or governance of the states.

Other ROs and Sanctions

Most of the other African organizations—including the New Partnership for Africa's Development (NEPAD), the Common Market for Eastern and Southern Africa (COMESA), Economic Community of Central African States (ECCAS), and the largest, the African Economic Community (AEC)[63]—are primarily trade and developmentally focused organizations that have neither threatened nor applied separate sanctions measures apart from fulfillment of international obligations as constituent member states of the aforementioned sanctioning organizations. However, three have threatened and recommended that sanctions be applied by the UNSC and AU: the IGAD, the East African Community (EAC), and the SADC. Only IGAD and SADC have applied sanctions.

In 2011, IGAD (Sudan, South Sudan, Ethiopia, Djibouti, Uganda, Kenya, and Somalia), the EAC, and the state of Ethiopia recommended to the UNSC and to the AU that additional sanctions[64] be applied against Eritrea for its destabilizing activities in Somalia. The additional sanctions called for by the ROs included measures focused against Eritrea's economic and mining sector and other foreign financial sources to cripple the regime's negative activities mainly in Somalia. There is controversy as to whether or not IGAD then formally suspended Eritrea's membership. According to Eritrea, it had voluntarily suspended its membership in IGAD for four years (as per Article 22 of the 1996 Agreement to establish IGAD), returning in 2011 only to be barred from IGAD meetings, especially on the topic of Somalia.[65] Others maintain that Eritrea was suspended from IGAD and had yet to be asked to return, although there is no provision for suspension or return in the Agreement. In 2012, the council ministers of IGAD also threatened to apply sanctions against Somali parliamentarians who elected a new speaker of Parliament, Madobe Nunow, while the incumbent, Sharif Hassan Sheikh Aden, was out of the country, counter to the country's peace process and specific agreements including the Kampala Accord and Transitional Federal Charter.

SADC has fifteen members (including economic heavy weight, South Africa). The organization is dedicated to promoting sustainable and equitable economic growth and socioeconomic development, which in turn should promote peace and stability. The constitutions of all SADC member states are meant to enshrine the principles of equal opportunity and full participation of citizens in political processes—but this is theory. The goals of SADC are cooperation and the (preferably adjudicated) settlement of disputes. Article 33 of The Treaty of SADC states that sanctions may be imposed against a member state that:

1. persistently fails, without good reason, to fulfill obligations assumed under [the] Treaty;
2. implements policies which undermine the principles and objectives of SADC; or
3. is in arrears in the payment of contributions to SADC, for reasons other than those caused by natural calamity or exceptional circumstances that gravely affect its economy, and has not secured the dispensation of the Summit.

To date, only Madagascar has been subject to SADC sanctions in the form of a suspension of membership because of an unconstitutional change of government in 2009. (The AU also suspended Madagascar.) Zimbabwe, by contrast, despite an atrocious human rights record, has not been sanctioned by SADC. This prompted an editorial cartoon showing members of SADC putting "pressure" on Zimbabwean President Robert Mugabe in the form of a massage and offering him presents of oil, hot towels, and foot rubs.[66] Instead, SADC has asked that organizations like the EU lift their sanctions against Zimbabwe in order that SADC may address the Zimbabwean economic disaster that is impacting the rest of southern Africa.

SADC was recognized for its enforcement of UN sanctions against the National Union for the Total Independence of Angola (UNITA). The UN Angola Sanctions Committee and Monitoring Mechanism met frequently with SADC for its input on the enforcement and monitoring of the arms, diamond, and travel sanctions.[67] The UN Monitoring Mechanism commended SADC for creating a certificate of origin for diamonds and for its regional policy to control weapons sales and prevent illegal arms trafficking.[68]

Conclusion—African Problem, African Solution?

All UN member states (which include African states) are required to implement mandatory sanctions when the UNSC adopts them. Since the UNSC has sanctioned a lot of African states, why would African ROs sanction additional African states? There were two hypotheses:

1. because the UN has not sanctioned a state either because it is deadlocked, unwilling to address the situation, or because it has not made it onto the Council's agenda (perhaps it is too small or the UNSC requires more time to contemplate the ramifications?); and/or

2. because there is a consistent, particularly African problem that the Security Council is not pursuing but that the regional organizations want to address, and sanctions are a convenient conduit.

The first is the traditional answer, and it is commonly referenced when the UNSC fails to sanction a politically charged situation like that in Syria. The second is the African answer. For the UNSC, civil wars, interstate wars, international terrorism, and proliferation are the triggers for sanctions. Acute events, like coups and the unconstitutional changes of government, fall in the African regional in-basket. Indeed, the charters and protocols of many of the African ROs specifically include a sanctions trigger clause for coups. Referring to Table 4.3, twenty-one of the twenty-two regional sanctions regimes were imposed in response to an unconstitutional change of government. Of those twenty-two regional sanctions regimes, all involved a suspension of membership or participation of the state from the organization in question.

This means that the targets, objectives, and measures applied by African ROs are different from those of the UNSC. Given that the UNSC has the primary responsibility for international peace and security, whereas many of the ROs have a development and integration focus, it is not surprising that the sanctions regimes would vary; the mechanisms to adopt sanctions are very different and the main focus of the organizations is different. What is interesting and what is underreported in the literature is the number of occasions when the decision of an RO to either apply sanctions and/or petition the UNSC (and AU) to apply additional sanctions is met with a favourable response. This suggests that the "gatekeeper" role of ROs (i.e., the influence they have on how issues are framed and the range of plausible policy options available to the Security Council) outlined by Alex Bellamy and Paul Williams applies across many African ROs—not just the AU or ECOWAS, the main security-focused African organizations. Therefore, ROs have the ability to prompt action from the UNSC, suggesting that the first hypothesis is also in play.

However, while ROs often petition the UNSC or AU to apply additional measures, there is still work needed to strengthen the communication and working relationships of all of the organizations to in turn help enforce the sanctions when they are imposed. In some cases, coordination and cooperation have contributed to success, as in the case of SADC and the role it played to enforce UN sanctions against UNITA in Angola. In other cases, the assistance, or lack thereof, still poses a challenge to the effectiveness of UNSC sanctions. Given the renewed pledge by the UNSC to cooperate with African ROs (especially with the AU), this may be a fruitful area of cooperation.

In terms of the promotion of democracy and better governance—a common theme present in the charters and protocols of ROs—the sanctions-triggered clauses are of limited use. While the suspension of a state from the relevant organization or its activities after a coup underlines the unacceptability of unconstitutional changes of government, they do not necessarily promote good governance. The suspension is lifted after constitutional order is restored, but without an analysis of whether or not the quality of governance (e.g., separation of the powers of the government or quality of judicial decisions) is actually improved. In many cases, elections are held for elections sake. Intimidation, corruption, and changes to constitutions still allow many leaders to cling to power. In addition, the suspension of an entire state because of the actions of a few individuals may be too blunt an instrument to be an effective deterrent to would-be coup leaders.

What requires more study is why some African states, particularly Guinea-Bissau and Côte d'Ivoire, are the subject of multiple sanctions regimes. Compared with conflicts in the DRC or Somalia, for example, they are not as lethal. Is it that these states have a particularly strong advocate, such as a P5 member, on the UNSC that is pushing for sanctions? Or, conversely, is it because they have no advocates protecting them from sanctions that they are targeted more readily? And what is the true impact of these sanctions on the civilians of these states? The unintended consequences of targeted sanctions are often overlooked.

Sanctions continue to be the tool of choice for the UN and for the ROs—to what effect, however, still requires more thought.

Notes

1. This includes the African ROs discussed in this chapter: the OAU, AU, ECOWAS, SADC, and IGAD. In addition, the EU's use of sanctions has not been studied in depth despite the number of regimes it has adopted. The exception is Clara Portela's excellent book. See Clara Portela, *European Union Sanctions and Foreign Policy: When and Why Do They Work?* (London: Routledge, 2010). The EU will not be discussed in this chapter, but it has applied twenty-six sanctions regimes against twenty-two African states. Other regional organizations that have employed sanctions are: the Arab League (which suspended Egypt from its organization from 1979 to 1989, and more recently suspended Libya and Syria), the Organization of American States, and the Association of Southeast Asian Nations. However, the latter two have not sanctioned African states.
2. A list of literature that focuses specifically on the question of "effectiveness" includes: Daniel W. Drezner, "Bargaining, Enforcement and Multilateral Economic Sanctions," *International Organization* 41 (2000): 73–102; J. P. Davis Dashti-Gibson and B. Radcliff, "On the Determination of Success of Economic Sanctions: An Empirical Analysis," *American Journal of Political Science* 41 (1997): 608–18; G. C. Hufbauer, J. J. Schott, and K. A. Elliott, *Economic Sanctions Reconsidered, 2nd Edition* (Washington, DC: Institution for International Economics, 1990); R. N. Haass and M. L. O'Sullivan, *Honey and Vinegar* (Washington, DC: Brookings University Press, 2000); Lisa Martin, *Coercive Cooperation: Explaining Multilateral Economic Sanctions* (Princeton, NJ: Princeton University Press, 1992); W. Kaempfer and A. D. Lowenberg, "The Theory of International Economic Sanctions: A Public Choice Approach," *American Economic Review* 4 (1988): 786–793; Robert Pape, "Why Economic Sanctions Do Not Work," *International Security* 22:2 (Autumn, 1997): 90–136; G. Tsebelis, "Are Sanctions Effective? A Game Theoretic Analysis," *Journal of Conflict Resolution* 34 (1990): 2–28; David Baldwin, *Economic Statecraft* (Princeton, NJ: Princeton University Press, 1985).
3. United Nations Charter, Article 41.
4. Ibid.
5. In 1995, the permanent five members of the UNSC penned a non-paper on the humanitarian impact of sanctions to the President of the Security Council stating that "further collective actions in the Security Council within the context of any future sanctions regime should be directed to minimize unintended adverse side-effects of sanctions on the most vulnerable segments of targeted countries" (S/1995/300 13 April 1995). Regional organizations have followed suit.
6. The sanctions imposed against Burundi by its neighbors were comprehensive, but the sanctions were not applied by an African RO. In 1995, the seven neighboring states restricted

all goods in or out of Burundi by blockading its vital transport links. The circumstances of this case, however, remain unique. First, the military coup on 24 July 1996 finished off the last vestiges of democratic rule in a very unstable Burundi. The situation was exacerbated by the genocide in neighboring Rwanda, against which tepid measures were applied (a UN arms embargo applied after-the-fact and a small UN mission), and the seething Hutu/Tutsi enmity in both countries. Given the concern that the extreme violence could spread, the fact that the UNSC was bogged down with the Balkans, its multiple, disastrous interventions in Africa (especially Somalia and Rwanda), and the OAU's inability to coordinate a response, the neighboring states took matters into their own hands, literally and figuratively. For a full account, see Gilbert Khadiagala's excellent chapter on "Burundi" in *Dealing with Conflict in Africa: The United Nations and Regional Organizations*, ed. Jane Boulden (New York: Palgrave Macmillan, 2003), pp. 215–252.

7. The Lomé Declaration for the OAU Response to Unconstitutional Changes of Government, signed in 2000, defined several situations that constitute an unconstitutional change of government: (i) a military coup d'état against a democratically elected Government; (ii) intervention by mercenaries to replace a democratically elected Government; (iii) replacement of a democratically elected Government by armed dissident groups and rebel movements; (iv) the refusal by an incumbent government to relinquish power to the winning party after free, fair, and regular elections. Coups are defined as the "illegal seizure of power by domestic actors through unconstitutional means," *Protecting Democracy: International Responses*, ed. Morton Halperin and Mirna Galic (New York: Council on Foreign Relations, 2005), p. 2.
8. Three hundred and one intrastate conflicts were recorded for 2011. Asia and Oceana had "first place" with 124. Heidelberg Institute for International Conflict Research, *Conflict Barometer 2011* No. 20 (2012): 3–4, accessed on 28 February 2012 at http://ipsinstitute.org/wp-content/uploads/2012/02/ConflictBarometer_2011.pdf. A "civil war" is defined as "a violent conflict within a country fought by organized groups that aim to take power at the center or in a region, or to change government policies" in James D. Fearon, "Iraq's Civil War," *Foreign Affairs* 86:2 (March/April 2007): 2–15, especially 4. This definition sounds very much like the goals of a coup.
9. Senegal and Cape Verde are the exceptions.
10. In Guinea, President Alpha Condé survived an assassination attempt by a group of soldiers on 19 July 2011, while at least three people were killed when his guards fended off the assault. An attack on the military headquarters by soldiers in neighboring Guinea-Bissau on 26 December 2011 was also labeled an attempted coup d'état by the government. In 2010 in Niger, the government of President Mahamadou Issoufou arrested a group of military officers in late July, allegedly foiling an attempt to topple the new government. No sanctions were adopted as the coups were all foiled. See Heidelberg Institute for International Conflict Research, *Conflict Barometer 2011* No. 20 (2012): 6, accessed at http://ipsinstitute.org/wp-content/uploads/2012/02/ConflictBarometer_2011.pdf on 28 February 2012.
11. Meaning the membership of the organization was required, by law, to give effect to the sanctions by passing the necessary national laws and regulations. Occasionally, sanctions are voluntary or hortatory, meaning that they are recommended but states have the option to apply them or not. In addition, these do not include sanctions applied because a member state is in arrears with their fees or if recommended by the General Assembly.
12. In addition to the seventeen African regimes listed in Table 4.1: Americas = 1 (Haiti); Asia = 2 (Al Qa'ida, Taliban and Associates, and North Korea); Europe = 4 (Yugoslavia, Federal Republic of Yugoslavia I, FRY II, and Kosovo); Middle East = 5 (Iraq I, Iraq II, Iraq III, Hariri [Lebanon]). See Andrea Charron, *UN Sanctions and Conflict: Responding to Peace and Security Threats* (London, UK: Routledge, 2011) for a full analysis.

13. Of the 193 member states of the UN, fifty-four of which are African, the UN has sanctioned 23 percent or 1 in 4.5 African states since 1990.
14. This ratio increases to one in two if you include sanctions applied by the EU and the Arab League (a total of twenty- nine of fifty-four African states sanctioned).
15. Reviewing all UN mandatory sanctions regimes adopted since 1990, the UNSC has applied sanctions to address interstate conflicts (four times), intrastate conflicts (fifteen times), nuclear proliferators (three times), and sponsorship of international terrorism (four times). See Charron, 2011.
16. For Libya's involvement in the destruction of Pan American flight 103 and Union de transports aerens flight 772. S/RES/748 (1992) lifted in 2003.
17. For its involvement in the assassination attempt against former Egyptian president, Hosni Mubarak, in 1996.
18. On 12 April 2012, a military coup undermined the conclusion of a democratic electoral process in Guinea-Bissau. The UNSC adopted a Presidential Statement (S/PRST/2012/15) and *two* press statements on 12 April and 8 May before unanimously adopting S/RES/2048 on 18 May 2012, applying mandatory travel sanctions against five members of the military junta—the "Military Command." The UN sanctions against Sierra Leone were prompted by a coup but then lasted decades longer to address state and regional instability and are thus classified under the category "civil war."
19. S/2012/512 (5 July 2012).
20. The UNSC did recommend a voluntary arms embargo for the Sahel region. Later, in December 2012, the Movement of Unity and Jihad in Western Africa (MUJWA) was added to the Al-Qaida sanctions list. Therefore, Mali is not (yet) subject to mandatory UN sanctions although the terrorist group MUJWA operating in northern Mali and southern Algeria been added to a pre-existing UN sanctions regime.
21. S/RES/733 (1992).
22. S/RES/1844 (2008).
23. The AU, IGAD, and EAC.
24. S/RES/1907 (2009).
25. Matt Schroeder and Guy Lamb, "The Illicit Arms Trade in Africa: A Global Enterprise," *Africa Analyst* (2006): 69–78.
26. The majority of Commonwealth members are African states.
27. Millbrook Commonwealth Action Programme on the Harare Declaration 1995: para. B3 "Measures in Response to Violations of the Harare Principles." The 1991 Harare Principles focused on free and democratic political processes. Harare Commonwealth Declaration 1991: para. 4.
28. Magliveras (2011: 20) suggests that this is a major lacuna for the AU (and likely other regional organizations). Found at http://www.academia.edu/1103678/THE_SANCTIONING_SYSTEM_OF_THE_AFRICAN_UNION_PART_SUCCESS_PART_FAILURE (January 11, 2013). Konstanitonos D. Magliveras, "The sanctioning system of the African Union: Part success, part failure?" Revised version of a paper presented at an Expert Roundtable on "The African Union:The First Ten Years" which was organized by the Institute of Security Studies, AddisAbaba, Ethiopia, 11 – 13 October 2011.
29. See Article II and Article III (paras. 1, 2, and 3) of the OAU Charter, 1963.
30. Sekei Saungwene, "A Critical Look at the Charter on Democracy, Elections and Governance in Africa," in Open Society Institute, *African Governance Monitoring and Advocacy Project*, May 2007, and the Heidelberg Institute for International Conflict Research. *Conflict Barometer 2008. 17th Annual Conflict Analysis* (Heidelberg: Department of Political Science, University of Heidelberg).

31. *Compendium of Key Documents Relating to Peace and Security in Africa*, ed. Monica Juma (Pretoria: Pretoria University Law Press, 2006), p. 2.
32. At the OAU Assembly meeting at Algiers, Algeria, the Assembly declared that several governments that had come to power through unconstitutional means since the Harare summit should restore constitutional legality by the next annual summit in 2000. OAU Ass., Decision on Unconstitutional Changes of Government, 35th Sess., Doc. No. AHG/Dec.142 (XXXV), para. 1 (12–14 July 1999), http://www.africaunion.org/root/au/Documents/Decisions/hog/9HoGAssembly1999.pdf. These states were Comoros, Congo Brazzaville, Guinea Bissau, and Niger.
33. In the Lomé Declaration, the OAU Assembly declared: "We express our grave concern about the resurgence of coups d'état in Africa. We recognize that these developments are a threat to peace and security of the Continent and they constitute a very disturbing trend and serious set-back to the ongoing process of democratization in the Continent... We reaffirm that coups are sad and unacceptable developments in our Continent, coming at a time when our people have committed themselves to respect of the rule of law based on peoples['] will expressed through the ballot and not the bullet." Coups leaders would be given six months to restore constitutional order before a range of limited and targeted sanctions was imposed including visa denials for the members of the illegal government, restrictions in diplomatic contacts, as well as restrictions in trade with other member states.
34. The Peace and Security Council is made up of fifteen members (on the basis of equitable regional representation and rotation—not unlike the UNSC). Each member of the PSC has a vote. Like the UNSC, the PSC acts on behalf of all state members and once a decision is made by the PSC, it is binding on all members. The great difference is that there are no "vetoes"; if a decision is not reached by consensus (the preferred method), a two-thirds majority (or ten of the fifteen members) is required to agree on substantive issues, which would include the decision to apply sanctions.
35. Preamb. paras. 8 and 6 respectively.
36. Executive Council *Decision on the Report of the Sub-Committee on Contributions EX/CL/Dec. 25 (III) (July 8, 2003).* As cited in Konstantinos D. Magliveras, "The Sanctioning System of the AU: Part Success, Part Failure?" Revised version of a paper presented at an Expert Roundtable on "The African Union: The First Ten Years," which was organized by the Institute of Security Studies, Addis Ababa, Ethiopia, 11–13 October 2011, p. 7.
37. In 2001, Burundi, Cape Verde, the Comoros, Djibouti, the CAR, DRC, Gambia, Guinea-Bissau, Liberia, Mauritania, Niger, Seychelles, Sao Tome and Principe, Sierra Leone, and Uganda were stripped of voting privileges for being in arrears for more than two years.
38. Magliveras, "The Sanctioning System," p. 8.
39. Ibid., 8.
40. The adoption of Rule 37 of the Assembly as cited in Magliveras, "The Sanctioning System," p. 10, outlines a five-step process to deal with unconstitutional changes to government which is: first condemn the coup, second issue a warning, third ensure AU and international responses are similar, fourth ask the PSC to convene and make a recommendation, and finally, fifth, suspend the state from the AU.
41. Decision on the Prevention of Unconstitutional Changes of Government and Strengthening the Capacity of the AU to Manage Situations Doc. Assembly/AU/4(XVI): para. 6i) b)a (February 2, 2010).
42. PSC/PR/BR(CCXXVII), 22 April 2010.
43. S/2009/388. See also Assembly of the African Union, Decision on the Report of the Peace and Security Council on its Activities and the State of Peace and Security in Africa, Assembly/AU/Dec. 252(XIII), 13th Ordinary Session, 1–3 July 2009.

44. Mireille Affa'a Mindzie, "Intervention and Protection in African Crisis Situations: Evolution and Ethical Challenges," *Criminal Justice Ethics* 29:2 (August 2010): 174–193.
45. Although there are disagreements as to whether Eritrea was suspended from the organization or just not allowed to participate in IGAD meetings to do with Somalia. See the section on *Other Regional Organizations and Sanctions.*
46. Alex Bellamy and Paul. D. Williams, "The New Politics of Protection? Côte d'Ivoire, Libya and the Responsibility to Protect," *International Affairs* 87:4 (2011): 833.
47. Bellamy and Williams were thinking specifically about the role of regional organizations as gatekeepers for the protection of civilians; however, the same can be said of the role of African regional organizations and the UNSC's decisions to apply sanctions.
48. S/2011/805 (29 December 2011).
49. However, while the UNSC creates a separate sanctions committee and panel of expert group for each sanctions regime, the idea was that there would be one sanctions committee to advise the PSC on all AU-related sanctions.
50. Institute for Security Studies (ISS) Public Seminar Series, "Enhancing the African Union Sanctions Regime" (Addis Ababa, 28 October 2009): 5.
51. Section A: The Role of Sanctions in the Common African Position on the Proposed Reform of the United Nations: "The Ezulwini Consensus" (2005).
52. Article 7, ECOWAS Treaty (1975). In the revised ECOWAS Treaty (1993), Articles 7, 8, and 9 are pertinent. Again, sanctions are not mentioned specifically, but the Authority may make binding decisions on behalf of member states.
53. For a useful summary, see Chapter 5, "Sanctions and Regional Security: The Crisis in West Africa," in *Sanctions and the Search for Security: Challenges to UN Action*, ed. David Cortright and George A. Lopez (New York: International Peace Academy, 2002), pp. 77–92. For example, the UNSC applied an arms, petroleum products, travel, and financial sanctions against Sierra Leone largely because ECOWAS had already applied significant measures. See S/RES/1132 (1997).
54. S/RES/1132 (1997): para. 8.
55. For example, to strengthen UN sanctions against Sudan, the UNSC noted in its resolution 1945 (2010), "the enhanced cooperation and information sharing between [the hybrid UN/AU mission] UNAMID and the [UN] Panel of Experts facilitated by the Department of Peacekeeping Operations' guidelines and the decision of UNAMID to establish a focal point to facilitate information sharing with the Panel of Experts regarding the arms embargo." See S/RES/1945: preamb para. 11.
56. ECOWAS' 1981 Protocol on Mutual Assistance and Defence, for example, specifically excluded intervention in purely internal conflicts and was focused around military interventions, not sanctions.
57. Protocol A/ SP1/12/01 on Democracy and Good Governance: Supplementary to the Protocol relating to the mechanism for conflict prevention, management, resolution, peacekeeping, and security (Dakar, December 2001).
58. Referring to Article 45 of the Conflict Prevention Protocol (1999), which states: "Restoration of Political Authority: In situations where the authority of government is absent or has been seriously eroded, ECOWAS shall support processes towards the restoration of political authority. Such support may include the preparation, organization, monitoring and management of the electoral process, with the cooperation of relevant regional and international organizations. The restoration of political authority shall be undertaken at the same time as the development of respect for human rights, enhancement of the rule of law and the judiciary." The cross-referencing required to decipher the numerous protocols breeds confusion.

59. Frederick Cowell, "The Impact of the ECOWAS Protocol on Good Governance and Democracy," *African Journal of International and Comparative Law* 19:2 (2011): 331–342, especially 335.
60. Sebastian Sperling, "ECOWAS in Crisis Mode: Strengths and Limits of Regional Security in West Africa," *Perspective* Friedrich Ebert Stiftung (February 2011): 1.
61. Indeed, the UNSC noted the decision of ECOWAS to apply the provisions of Article 45 of the ECOWAS Protocol on Democracy and Good Governance relating to the imposition of sanctions against Côte d'Ivoire, including the suspension from all ECOWAS decision-making bodies until further notice, in its resolution (S/RES/1962), adopted on 20 December 2010. For an excellent summary of events, see Alex Bellamy and Paul Williams, "The New Politics of Prevention? Côte d'Ivoire, Libya and the Responsibility to Protect," *International Affairs* 87:4 (2011): 825–850.
62. Cyril Obi, "Economic Community of West African States on the Ground: Comparing Peackeeping in Liberia, Sierra Leone, Guinea Bissau and Côte d'Ivoire," *African Security* 2:3 (2009): 119–135, especially 130.
63. The eight regional blocs consisting of AU, AEC, COMESA, *Economic Community of Central African States* (ECCAS), ECOWAS, SADC, EAC, and IGAD represent the largest populations of all thirteen of the African regional blocs. (Not discussed are la Communaute Economique et Monetaire de l'Afrique Centrale [CEMAC], Southern African Customs Union (SACU), Union économique et monétaire ouest-africaine [UEMOA], Union du Maghreb arabe [UMA], and Greater Arab Free Trade Area [GAFTA]).
64. In addition to the mandatory UN arms embargo, travel ban, and asset freeze.
65. Argaw Ashi, "Eritrea Barred from IGAD Meetings," 24 August 2011. Available at http://asmarino.com/news/1155-eritrea-thrown-out-of-igad-meeting. Accessed 3 August 2012.
66. Jimmy Kaija, "SADC and Zimbabwe Sanctions: Which Way Forward?" Africa on the Blog, 14 October 2010. Available at http://www.africaontheblog.com/sadc-and-the-zimbabwe-sanctions-which-way-forward/. Accessed 31 August 2012.
67. S/RES/1295 (2000).
68. S/2001/1996: paras. 108 and 253–256. See David Cortright, Linda Gerber, and George A. Lopez, "Implementing Targeted Sanctions: The Role of International Agencies and Regional Organizations," in *International Sanctions: Between Words and Wars in the Global System*, ed. Peter Wallensteen and Carina Staibano (New York: Frank Cass, 2005), pp. 144–158.

Part II

Case Studies

Chapter 5

Burundi, 2002–2012

Gilbert M. Khadiagala

Introduction

The civil war in Burundi that began in the 1990s propelled the coalescence of regional and international engagements that remain instructive for comprehending the division of labor between the United Nations (UN) and regional institutions. This interaction has fostered more partnership and burden-sharing than competition and burden-shifting, which is unique in Africa's conflict resolution. In the mid-2000s, the transition from the African Union (AU) Mission in Burundi (AMIB) to the United Nations Operation in Burundi (ONUB) and the close collaboration in the mediation of ceasefire agreements strengthened this partnership. In my chapter in the previous edition of this book, I argued that the interplay between the international community and local actors in Burundi stemmed from collective creative efforts to find a balance between global and local responsibilities, particularly in the circumstances of divisive policy debates about the nature and extent of burden-sharing, responsibility, and resources in resolving African conflicts.[1]

This chapter focuses on a decade of events that deepened the regional–international intervention around the implementation of the Burundi peace process that was concluded in Arusha, Tanzania, in August 2000. It examines the roles of regional actors in mediating among the Burundian parties, the intervention by South African military forces to protect the returning leaders, and the role of the AMIB, ONUB, and the United Nations Integrated Office in Burundi (BINUB, Bureau Integre des Nations Unies au Burundi) forces in the military and political stabilization of Burundi. The concluding section examines Burundi's contested 2010 elections in light of the legacy of regional and international efforts to put Burundi on a stable institutional footing. This chapter contends that the UN–regional actor partnership was enabled by the fact that regional actors were organized and could set the pace and shape for engaging the UN and other external actors. Equally vital, international actors brought multiple sources of pressure and resources to bear in Burundi because the region had clear leadership that had invested considerable resources in diplomatic and political initiatives for the stabilization of Burundi. Burundi

Source: Map No 3753 Rev 6, United Nations, Department of Peacekeeping Operations, Cartographic Section, September 2004

provides a template for modes of engagements between the UN and regional actors, but there should also be recognition of the unique circumstances surrounding the case.

Mediation Efforts beyond the Peace Agreement, 2002–2006

The Arusha Agreement for Peace and Reconciliation of August 2000 that ended Burundi's civil war was the culmination a number of concerted bids by regional mediators to address the conflict that had emerged following the assassination of Hutu President Melchior Ndadaye by the Tutsi army in October 1993.[2] Burundi's neighbors organized a regional peace initiative between 1995 and 1999, under the leadership of former Tanzanian President, Julius Nyerere, to mediate the conflict; former South African President Nelson Mandela then succeeded Nyerere. When he assumed the mediation role in 1999, Mandela used the regional peace initiative to mobilize international pressure to supervise the protracted process that yielded the Arusha Agreement. Mandela's mediation marked South Africa's entry into the Burundi conflict, in a role that would significantly expand over the years. Both regional and international actors came to respect and tolerate South Africa's intervention, largely because Pretoria was emerging from years of isolation and was able to bring considerable resources to resolving the conflict.[3]

This agreement was a major breakthrough in the search for a negotiated settlement to the conflict but it faced formidable obstacles from the outset. First, while the agreement was signed between predominantly Tutsi parties allied to the government-dominated party—that is, the Union for National Progress (UPRONA, Union pour le Progrès national), led by President Pierre Buyoya—and parties affiliated to the leading Hutu rebels, the Front for Democracy in Burundi (FRODEBU, Front pour la Démocratie au Burundi), most of the key Hutu rebel movements boycotted the agreement. Thus, Hutu parties such as the Party for the Promotion of Hutus (Palipehutu-FNL, Parti pour la libération du peuple hutu-Forces nationales de libératio)—and its splinter factions, the National Council for the Defense of Democracy-Forces for the Defense of Democracy (CNDD-FDD, Conseil National pour la Defense de la Democratie-Forces pour Defense de la Democratie)—rejected the Arusha Agreement and continued fighting the government. Despite the agreement's partial nature, the regional mediators hoped to build on the limited gains in Arusha in order to gradually conclude comprehensive ceasefire agreements with the rebel groups and return the country to normalcy. Second, although the agreement called for the deployment of an international peacekeeping force, in the absence of a comprehensive ceasefire neither the AU nor the UN could deploy. Thus, as an interim arrangement, Mandela convinced the South African government to deploy the South African Protection Support Detachment (SAPSD) in October 2000, to protect exiled Hutu leaders and to participate in the post-Arusha transitional arrangements. This deployment was critical in jumpstarting the inauguration of the transitional government led by Pierre Buyoya, and later by Hutu leader Domitien Ndayizeye. With the inception of the transitional government, a measure of confidence building was injected in the peace process, allowing a remarkable return to stability.[4]

Building on the success of Mandela's mediation, and having deployed a protection force, South Africa under Deputy President Jacob Zuma took the lead in mediating comprehensive ceasefire agreements with the rebels. As in the previous Mandela initiatives, Zuma worked closely with the existing framework of the Regional Peace Initiative on Burundi (comprised primarily of Tanzania, Uganda, and the AU) in order to mobilize diplomatic efforts around the objective of stabilization.[5] In the dual roles of distant and engaged actor, South Africa marshaled its own domestic resources for a leadership role that also galvanized supportive international action in the quest for peace. Zuma's mediation (dubbed South African Facilitation), beginning in June 2002, was important for three major reasons. First, after the deployment of the SAPSD, South Africa gained considerable leverage over Burundian parties, leverage that was useful in the negotiations. Second, with the potential escalation of other mediators, it was important for South Africa to keep the mediation on track to avoid the distraction of parties. Third, in addition to its good relations with members of the regional initiative, South Africa had a broad international legitimacy that allowed it to mobilize international action around the Burundi problem. Thus, South Africa became the key interlocutor between regional and international diplomatic actions in ceasefire negotiations and in the mobilization of resources for the deployment of AMIB and United Nations Office in Burundi (UNOB).[6]

Ceasefire negotiations between the transitional government and rebel groups revealed the deep-seated fissures among the parties that the Zuma team of mediators tried to bridge. Specifically, while the government preferred agreements that would incorporate rebels into the transitional arrangements, the rebels insisted on renegotiating some of the provisions of the Arusha Agreement.[7] Despite these disagreements, the mediators achieved a major breakthrough in October and December 2002 when the government and rebels reached two ceasefire agreements. The October 2002 agreement was between the transitional government and two rebel movements—a faction of the CNDD-FDD led by Jean-Bosco Ndayikengurukiye and a faction of the FNL led by Alain Mugabarabona. The December ceasefire agreement was the most notable one, bringing Pierre Nkurunziza, with the largest wing of the CNDF-FDD, into the peace fold. Following the ceasefire agreement with Nkurunziza, Zuma continued to engage the parties in negotiations over issues such as the participation of the former armed movements in transitional institutions, disarmament and demobilization, and the creation of a new security apparatus. These negotiations culminated in the signing of the two Pretoria Protocols in October and November 2003 and in a comprehensive ceasefire between the transitional government and Nkurunziza in Dar es Salaam, Tanzania, in November 2003.[8] This ceasefire agreement helped to ease the levels of violence and was instrumental in facilitating the deployment of AMIB and ONUB forces.

Negotiations with the Palipehutu-FNL faction led by Agathon Rwasa proved more difficult. Throughout 2003, Rwasa spurned Zuma's mediation as his forces launched sustained attacks on Bujumbura and other parts of the country. Rwasa demanded direct negotiations with the transitional government in a bid to renegotiate major provisions of the Arusha Agreement, a move that would have unraveled the transitional institutions. In November 2003, a summit meeting of the regional peace initiative on Burundi asked the FNL to join the peace process in three months—otherwise it would be branded as a terrorist organization; the meeting also asked the UN to support the regional position for the purposes of coordinating of multilateral pressures.[9]

Following the November 2003 ceasefire agreement, South Africa led concerted efforts to broaden the mandate of the SAPSD into that of a fully fledged AU peacekeeping force. The notion of establishing an African mission in line with Chapter VIII of the UN Charter had first been proposed by a summit of the Great Lakes regional peace initiative on Burundi in Tanzania in December 2002, to build on the momentum of the ceasefire agreements. At the same time, the UN Security Council responded by pledging to support the deployment of the African Mission. The AU authorized the establishment of AMIB in April 2003 for an initial period of one year, subject to renewal and pending the deployment of a UN peacekeeping mission to be mandated by the UN Security Council.[10] Although it was the first fully fledged AU peace operation, AMIB was essentially a merger of the SAPD with troops from Ethiopia and Mozambique. Its mandate was to oversee the implementation of the ceasefire agreements, support disarmament and demobilization initiatives, contribute to political and economic stability, and create conditions for the establishment of a UN peacekeeping mission.

In the agreement for deployment, the troop-contributing countries were to initially sustain themselves, pending reimbursement from the AU—but with only meager resources in its peacekeeping budget, the AU expected to fund AMIB's budget from pledges and donations from Western donors. Overall, donor pledges of US$50 million fell short of the actual budget, which was estimated at about $134 million at the end of the fourteen months of AMIB. Besides, an international trust fund to assist AMIB received only US$10 million from donors. As Festus Agoaye notes,

> At both the strategic and operational levels, it is equally pertinent to note that the establishment and deployment of AMIB was affected by considerable challenges. The mission's logistical sustainment and funding was particularly problematic, owing to the lack of substantive support from within Africa, as well as from the UN and the international community to provide requisite assistance.[11]

Because of the lukewarm international response to financing AMIB, South Africa ended up providing the bulk of the funding. As Human Rights Watch noted in January 2005:

> South Africa bore most of the cost of the initial African Union peacekeeping force and has also invested substantial political resources in trying to facilitate agreements in Burundi. Its leadership has sometimes meshed poorly with that of other heads of state in the region, but all came together to provide forceful backing for the most recent advance towards a constitution.[12]

Resource constraints hampered AMIB's ability to contribute significantly to the stabilization of Burundi through effective disarmament and demobilization, but its presence was important in increasing the level of confidence among parties in the transitional institutions and generating momentum for the return to normalcy. Resource shortfalls were also fundamentally addressed by the fact that AMIB was a limited- and time-bound institution, awaiting the deployment of the UN Security Council–mandated peacekeeping mission. Addressing the Security Council in December 2003, Zuma acknowledged the contributions of the AU and regional actors but underscored the urgent need of additional resources:

> We wish to reiterate that the continued success of the Burundi peace process requires more direct United Nations involvement...We believe processes should now be put in place to look into how the United Nations can become actively and directly involved in the Burundi peace process. It is our well-considered view that conditions are now conducive for the United Nations to express its support and solidarity by taking over the African mission in Burundi, re-hatting the existing military contingent and deploying a United Nations peacekeeping operation.[13]

The Role of ONUB in Burundi, June 2004–December 2006

The transition from AMIB to ONUB on 1 June 2004 marked the convergence of regional and international efforts to stabilize Burundi. Furthermore, it reflected the continuity of regional initiatives under South African leadership in Burundi. By building on and buttressing African efforts to deal with local problems, ONUB symbolized the complementarity of UN commitments and regional efforts that Mandela had championed in his mediation. ONUB furnished a new lease of life for AMIB, overcoming AMIB's resource shortfalls, but also underlining that African security concerns had international relevance and resonance. By coming late into a long-drawn peace process, ONUB was able to learn from the lessons of previous actors and institutions and draw into ranks senior officials familiar with the peace process.[14]

During ONUB's initial deployment period of six months, AMIB's forces formed the bulk of the force. By December 2004, when the mission was extended for an additional six months, ONUB had grown to 5,000 personnel, with a total of fifty-one countries participating and with Pakistan, Kenya, Nepal, South Africa, and Ethiopia providing most of the troops and observers. The mission was headed by a Canadian, Carolyn McAskie, as Special Representative of the Secretary-General, with South African Major-General Derrick Mbuyiselo Mgwebi as the Force Commander. ONUB was authorized to carry out the following duties:

- Ensure the respect of ceasefire agreements through monitoring and investigating their violations.
- Promote the disarmament and demobilization of militias and monitor the quartering of the Burundi Armed Forces, as well as their disarmament and demobilization.
- Monitor the illegal flow of arms across Burundi's borders.
- Contribute to the creation of the necessary security conditions for the provision of humanitarian assistance, and facilitate the voluntary return of refugees and internally displaced persons.
- Contribute to the successful completion of the electoral process stipulated in the Arusha Agreement, by ensuring a secure environment for free, transparent, and peaceful elections.
- Protect civilians under threat.
- And ensure the mobility of ONUB forces in the conduct of their duties.[15]

ONUB was deployed less than five months before the 31 October 2004 deadline of the transitional period established by the Arusha Agreement. The tightness of the deadline was compounded by the fact that Burundian political parties had not made appreciable progress in drafting a new constitution that would lead to elections and so end the transitional period. Regional states, through their summits, decided to extend the date for the elections, first to April 2005 and then to August 2005, in order to permit the parties to address the outstanding issues before holding elections.[16] South Africa and regional actors remained at the helm of negotiations for a draft constitution, reflecting the need to retain the previous division of labor between the UN and regional actors. As Stephen Jackson notes, South Africa's continuing political role in the mediation arose because the mandate of UNOB

> did not explicitly mention any overt political roles for the UN. This role remained with South Africa, who had brokered the ceasefire agreement well before there was a SRSG or a mission in place. South Africa continued to play a key political role through the end of the transition, including negotiating the Pretoria agreement that broke the logjam in the formulation of the new constitution.[17]

In negotiations for the draft constitution, Zuma and the team from Uganda and Tanzania faced severe political deadlock within the transitional government over ethnic representation in future governments. The Arusha Agreement had recognized that Hutus and Tutsi would respectively have 60 percent and 40 percent representation in parliament and government, but divisions arose as to whether the parliamentary seats would be allocated to ethnic groups or ethnic political parties. Tutsi parties, afraid of losing in the polls, demanded a guaranteed quota for parties within the 40 percent seat allocation, a demand rejected by Hutu parties. Navigating around this impasse, the South African mediators suggested that the constitution could provide sufficient guarantees to minorities, but not the survival of political parties. With ONUB providing supplementary pressures during negotiations for a draft constitution in Pretoria in July and August 2004, the parties accepted the position of the mediators on power sharing.[18] The regional actors and ONUB also exerted considerable pressures on the Burundian parties to expedite the formation of an Independent National Electoral Commission (CENI, Commission Electorale Nationale Independante) and the establishment of a provincial electoral calendar by August 2004.

The breakthrough in Pretoria enabled the Burundian national assembly to adopt an interim constitution in October 2004 that provided guarantees for all communities in the post-transition institutions. In February 2005, Burundian voters overwhelmingly approved the new democratic constitution, which supported power sharing between the Hutu and Tutsi. Following the constitutional referendum, ONUB, through its electoral unit, took the leadership role in supervising five elections at the communal, legislative, senate, presidential, and village levels within a period of six months. As Jackson has noted:

> The elections were roundly understood by ONUB leadership as a key element in what the UN could provide in Burundi in 2004/2005. As a result, all available resources were employed to deliver election materials in all the provinces, to raise public awareness, and reinforce civic education. ONUB helicopters were turned over to the task of airlifting ballot boxes to remote hilltop polling stations and staff from other sections were pressed into service either at a logistical level or, just as importantly, as a visible international presence at locations where elections risked disruptions.[19]

The election of former rebel leader, Pierre Nkurunziza, as president in the elections of August 2005 formally ended the transitional process. With more than 90 percent of the vote, Nkurunziza obtained a solid mandate to consolidate peace and reach out to the FNL, which did not participate in the elections and which continued to wage war against the government. The ONUB and its regional partners expected the new government to reach out to political parties and incorporate them into an inclusive decision-making process set to address the enormous challenges of development, security, and human rights violations. However, President Nkurunziza initially used the electoral mandate to impose the CNDD-FDD positions on opposition parties that disagreed with the government. The intimidation and marginalization of opposition parties led to renewed threats of a coup d'état, the arrest of opposition politicians, and the resurgence of human rights violations. A UN Security Council report noted in March 2006 that, "the representation of political parties and their inclusion in the decision-making process remains an area of concern."[20] Under pressure from ONUB, Nkurunziza finally ended the paralysis in government and parliament by conceding to a multiparty government in November 2007, in compliance with constitutional provisions regarding party, ethnic, and gender representation, two years after the democratic elections.

From ONUB to BINUB

After his inauguration, President Nkurunziza requested the drawing down of ONUB forces, as part of regaining the sovereignty of Burundi. In June 2006, following consultations with the Burundian authorities, the UN Security Council extended ONUB's mandate until December 2006. The United Nations Integrated Office in Burundi (BINUB) replaced ONUB in January 2007, keeping its primary focus on: peace consolidation and democratic governance; security-sector reform and civilian disarmament; human rights, transitional justice, and judicial sector reforms; information and communications; and reconstruction and socioeconomic development. BINUB was initially authorized for one year, and was led by an Executive Representative of the Secretary-General.[21] Alongside BINUB, the major international actor in Burundi following the elections was the UN Peace-Building Commission, which was launched in October 2006 to mobilize resources in the post-conflict reconstruction phase with an initial monetary injection of US$35 million.[22]

During the postelection phase, the efforts of South Africa and regional actors were focused primarily on negotiating a lasting ceasefire with Rwasa's FNL. Although UNOB had attempted to launch negotiations with the FNL in July and August 2004, these talks ended when the FNL massacred 150 Congolese refugees at the Gatumba camp in Burundi in August 2004.[23] In the lead-up to the 2005 elections, Tanzania led unsuccessful initiatives to mediate a ceasefire and FNL's participation in the elections. During the election period, the FNL launched attacks in several provinces, but these attacks did not cause major disruptions to the process. In the postelection period, however, both the government and its international partners recognized the need to reengage the FNL if Burundi were to attain lasting peace and reconciliation.

Thus, in March 2006, Tanzania initiated talks in Dar es Salaam between Rwasa and the government. These negotiations proceeded in fits and starts because while the government sought only a ceasefire, the FNL wanted comprehensive negotiations on military and political questions, in a bid to revisit the Arusha Agreement. Under the

South African mediation and the regional mediation, the negotiations took place in two commissions: a military commission to address the disarmament and demobilization of the FNL and their integration into the security services; and a political commission to address issues such as provisional immunity for FNL leadership, refugee return, and the FNL's participation in national politics. The mediators achieved a major breakthrough in June 2006 when the government and the FNL signed an Agreement on Principles toward lasting Peace, Security, and Stability in the presence of South African President Thabo Mbeki and Tanzanian President Jakaya Kikwete. As part of the ceasefire agreement, the AU agreed to establish a Special Task Force to protect the FNL leadership and combatants, including their movement toward designated assembly areas.[24]

Technical negotiations continued in Dar es Salaam until September 2006, when, facing intense pressure from the regional actors (including threats to arrest its leaders), the FNL signed a Comprehensive Ceasefire Agreement and pledged to continue negotiations on the outstanding political matters. However, while the FNL subsequently participated in meetings of the Joint Verification and Monitoring Mechanism (JVMM) in the early months of 2007, there were severe differences over the implementation of a lasting ceasefire; in addition, negotiations on the outstanding political issues stalled.[25] In a bid to break the logjam, the mediators brought President Nkurunziza and Agathon Rwasa together for a private meeting in Dar es Salaam in June 2007. In addition to agreeing to reinvigorate the JVMM and exchange political prisoners, they discussed the necessity of the FNL leaders returning to Bujumbura to take part in national decisions. Nevertheless, severe differences persisted. As the South African mediator, Safety and Security Minister Charles Nqakula explained to the UN Security Council in November 2007.

> The greatest problem was that the Ceasefire Agreement did not dispel the suspicions and mistrust that had characterized the earlier negotiation process. The Government of Burundi did not believe that the Palipehutu-FNL would honor the Agreement. But, for their part, the Palipehutu-FNL were also deeply suspicious of the Government and felt that it would not deliver on its side of the Agreement.[26]

Compounding the stalemate was the deterioration in the political climate in Bujumbura, with a standoff between the government and opposition parties and severe splits within the CNDD-FNL.

After the June 2007 Dar es Salaam meeting, a major split occurred within the FNL when 2,700 dissidents, dissatisfied with the leadership's refusal to join the peace process, broke away and requested demobilization or integration into the security forces. Rwasa and other key leaders denounced the defections. BINUB and other humanitarian agencies were reluctant to accept the dissident soldiers as genuine, thereby forcing South Africa to provide them with food supplies. Charles Nqakula told the UN Security Council that South Africa's gesture was driven by the fact:

> If we had not intervened as we did, we would have allowed a situation which would catapult the country into an orgy of violence and undermine efforts to reach a durable peace in Burundi. For our part and in our humble logic, we thought that it was necessary for us to take in those people, protect them against attack and of course ensure that they themselves did not go into Burundi to commit atrocities.[27]

In July 2007, FNL representatives walked out of the JVMM, claiming that it was partial toward the government. Subsequently, the South African mediation team met with the regional actors in Pretoria in September 2007 and asked Tanzania to impose an ultimatum on FNL leadership based in Tanzania to join the peace process or face expulsion. In response, the FNL publicly rejected the mediation of Nqakula, claiming that the mediators had engineered the split in the FNL. Thus, even as the UN Security Council renewed the mandate of BINUB for one year in December 2007, there was no progress in finalizing a deal with the FNL. In renewing the mandate, the UN Security called on the "Secretary-General, including through BINUB, to play a robust role in support of the peace process, in full coordination with regional and international partners."[28]

Despite the deadlock, South African mediators convened a meeting in Cape Town of regional and international actors to discuss the Burundi peace process in February 2008. The meeting reached consensus on a common approach to support the peace process through a roadmap of sequenced steps, which it titled the "Program of Action to Take Further the Peace Process in Burundi." As part of the renewed efforts, the meeting agreed to establish a Group of Special Envoys for Burundi to support the mediators. A Political Directorate was also established in Bujumbura, comprised of representatives of countries involved in the process. These new institutions were meant to bolster the mediation and boost the pressure on the Burundian parties. The Program of Action comprised two phases: first, conclusion of the disarmament and demobilization of the FNL, following the return of the FNL to the JVMM by 1 April 2008 and the return of FNL leaders to Burundi by 1 May 2008; and second, the reintegration of FNL members into national institutions, as well as socioeconomic integration at the community level.[29] The government and the FNL endorsed the Program of Action by the end of February 2008. Despite severe skirmishes between the Burundian army and FNL rebels after the latter attacked Bujumbura and surrounding areas in April 2008, the FNL rejoined the JVMM and returned to the negotiating table at the end of April. To speed up the process, the mediators imposed a deadline of 31 December 2008 for the implementation of the Comprehensive Ceasefire Agreement; this generated the momentum for a series of talks that led to Rwasa's return to Bujumbura at the end of May 2008.[30]

Rwasa's return signaled the determination of regional actors to bring a quick end to the protracted stalemate that had engulfed the country; it also vindicated the strategy of staying the course even in the face of disappointments and the deep mistrust between Burundian parties. There was also expectation that Rwasa and President Nkurunziza could continue the face-to-face negotiations that regional actors had started in Dar es Salaam in June 2007, talks that would build mutual confidence between the two leaders and facilitate the resolution of all outstanding political and military issues. On his return, Rwasa spelled out the broad agenda that he sought to negotiate with the government: release of political prisoners, political and military integration, amendment to the constitution to permit the transformation of the FNL into a political party under its existing name, and a truth and reconciliation commission.[31]

To push for a speedy resolution of these issues, Charles Nqakula invited the Group of Special Envoys on Burundi, the government, and the FNL to a meeting in June 2008 at Magaliesberg, South Africa. This meeting underscored South Africa's continuing leadership role in the mediation process, which it played due to a combination of bilateral and multilateral pressures. Furthermore, it demonstrated that meeting the parties in South Africa was an effective way of exerting these pressures and focusing the parties on the issues at hand. In the Magaliesberg Communique, both parties committed to

- renounce violence and resolve all issues peacefully;
- respect the timelines established in the Program of Action;
- address simultaneously all the outstanding issues, including the political accommodation of the Palipehutu-FNL in national institutions;
- refrain from inflammatory actions or declarations;
- find, at the earliest possible time, a mutually acceptable solution to the question of the registration and naming of the Palipehutu-FNL as a political party; and
- spare no effort in completing all the steps outlined in the JVMM Program of Action and the Joint Operations Plan (JOP), including the demarcation and establishment of assembly areas.[32]

For their part, the Group of Special Envoys committed themselves to supporting the mediation process and the parties by

- mobilizing the international community to provide financial support for the facilitation and peace process; this would include interceding with donors about the provision of humanitarian assistance until the conclusion of the DDR process;
- supporting the transformation of the Palipehutu-FNL into a political party, including training its cadres;
- paying special attention to the reintegration aspects of the DDR process, especially regarding the Palipehutu-FNL combatants;
- promoting security-sector reforms that would facilitate the reintegration of the Palipehutu-FNL members into the national security forces; and
- considering ways of providing financial support to the government to address pressures occasioned by rising food prices.[33]

The bickering among the parties, however, reemerged in the later phase of 2008, owing to the refusal by Rwasa to change the name "Palipehutu" (meaning, "the defense of Hutus") in accordance with the constitution that outlawed ethnic parties. In addition, Rwasa submitted a memorandum stating that he would not comply with the demobilization of his forces prior to the registration of his party in the current name. He proposed to exempt the Palipehutu-FNL from having to comply with the constitution with regard to its current name until after the 2010 elections. In the face of the rising tensions, mediators and regional actors were again drawn into the conflict to help resolve the deadlock. During a confidence-building meeting in Ngozi, Burundi, in August 2008, the two parties sought to narrow their differences.[34]

After a meeting of regional states in October 2008, a ministerial delegation of South Africa, Uganda, and Tanzania delivered a hard-hitting message to the Burundian parties containing the following provisions: there would be no extension of the 31 December 2008 deadline for the engagement of regional actors in the peace process; the government would have to accommodate the FNL in national institutions, in conformity with national laws; the FNL was to immediately send its forces to assembly points for disarmament, demobilization, and reintegration; and the FNL was to eliminate the ethnic connotation in its name.[35]

The threats from the regional actors, particularly over the looming deadline, propelled the two leaders into a hasty agreement at a summit meeting of regional leaders in Bujumbura on 4 December 2008. After months of stagnation and stalemate, the summit triggered movement on the conclusion of the negotiations. The major breakthrough was the resolution of the four major questions that had threatened to scuttle the Comprehensive Ceasefire Agreement. On the issue of disarmament, demobilization, and reintegration, the FNL agreed to send its fighters to assembly points by December 2008. The summit rejected the FNL's demand that the Burundian army be disbanded. In a concession to the FNL, the government agreed to release all political prisoners, and to incorporate thirty-three FNL members into senior state positions. The participation of these leaders in government was made conditional upon the FNL changing its name, in accordance with the constitution. In January 2009, in line with the summit declaration commitments, the government released a number of FNL prisoners while the FNL made a decisive move to change its name from the Palipehutu-FNL to FNL, allowing it to register as a political party. Progress was also registered on the disarmament and demobilization front. By April 2009, most of the FNL fighters had surrendered their arms and some had been integrated in the national army. In May 2009, the government issued several decrees nominating twenty-four FNL senior officials to government positions, with Rwasa nominated as the Director General of the National Institute for Social Security.[36]

With remarkable progress made in implementing the December declarations, the South African mediator, Nqakula, ended his mandate in May 2009 and the AU Special Task Force withdrew from Burundi by March 2009. A new mechanism, the Partnership for Peace in Burundi, was established on May 2009, for six months, to replace the South African mediation framework. Comprised of representatives from the Political Directorate, the Secretariat of the International Conference on the Great Lakes Region, and BINUB, the Partnership was chaired by former South African ambassador to the UN, Dumisani Khumalo. The new body was charged with mobilizing support from regional states and the international community to assist the consolidation of peace in Burundi. Additionally, it was mandated with monitoring the peace process, contributing to an enabling environment for the period leading to the elections, and providing early warning to regional leaders.[37]

Toward the 2010 Elections: Peace Consolidation or Regression?

The regional involvement in the ceasefire negotiations built on the intricate compromise established in earlier years between the UN and local actors premised on shared responsibilities and complementarities that actors and institutions could bring to the table. Being a poor country with no strategic interests or resources, Burundi, perhaps, lent itself to the successful convergence of regional and international efforts. However, more germane to the outcome, the compromises that made success possible arose from the previous lessons about avoiding competition in navigating Burundi's fractious politics. The successful conclusion of the negotiations in December 2008 thus reinforced the advantages of the established division of labor. Now accustomed to years of regional hand-holding and supportive international prodding, the challenge to the Burundian parties was whether the gradual disengagement of regional actors would galvanize national energies into forming consensus on managing differences and stabilizing political competition.

As the risks associated with delays in the implementation of the Comprehensive Ceasefire Agreement diminished, preparation for the second post-transitional elections in 2010 emerged as the most pressing task for sustaining the gains achieved in the peace process. Since 2007, BINUB and the Peace-building Commission engagements had sought broad institutional reforms in governance, the judiciary, and the economy, to lay the foundation for peace and stability. Both institutions had also launched various initiatives to facilitate dialogue among different stakeholders, including the political factions, in order to build confidence as Burundi prepared for the second round of five successive elections. For instance, a three-year "Cadres de Dialogue" project funded by the Peace-building Commission was instrumental in bringing together parliamentarians, political parties, civil society and the media at regional forums to promote civic education, national dialogue, and reconciliation. Furthermore, BINUB had initiated programs to promote and protect human rights and strengthen civil society, all of which were geared toward contributing to the climate of political tolerance and transparency necessary for electoral competition. Similarly, justice-sector reform programs sought the consolidation of the rule of law by strengthening the independence and capacity of the judiciary.[38]

In spite of these programs, however, there were limits to the ability of international action to foster meaningful consensus in a political environment that remained partisan and deeply fragmented. The CNDD-FDD's battles with opposition politicians after the 2005 elections had resulted in almost two years of political stalemate, until a national compromise was arrived at in November 2007. However, this was only a temporary lull in the bitter conflicts both within the CNDD-FDD and across the entire opposition political spectrum. As early as September 2008, Burundian professionals had raised concerns that the 2010 elections might "return the country to violence if the international community does not pressure the government and the opposition to play fair."[39] In an attempt to influence the outcome of the elections, the CNDD-FDD resorted to curbing the opposition parties' rights to freedom of expression, association, and assembly. Throughout 2009, the human rights situation deteriorated, with an increase in restrictions on civil and political rights, and with targeted violence and intimidation carried out by authorities. The UN Secretary-General's report of June 2009 underscored the deteriorating political climate:

> Despite the...improvement in the political climate, concerns have continued to be expressed about persistent disruption in the activities of opposition parties and, in some cases, violence against their members by the police and, allegedly, by members of the national intelligence services and local officials. This situation has created a malaise among the political class and civil society activists.[40]

Equally worrisome was an upsurge of politically motivated killings and paramilitary training of the youth of the parties. In particular, the youth wing of the CNDD, the *Imbonerakure*, worked closely with police and military units to effect widespread intimidation of opposition figures.

Conflicts also coalesced around the establishment of the Independent National Electoral Commission (CENI). After polarizing and inconclusive debates, President Nkurunziza issued a decree in December 2008 that outlined the mandate of the CENI; this decree superseded the decree issued in June 2008, and subjected the CENI to executive control. In January 2009, President Nkurunziza summoned parliament to approve nominees to the CENI, but neither chamber of parliament endorsed the list of names because of the government's lack of consultation with political parties. Responding to these calls, the government consulted with parties and civil society before presenting a new list that the parliament approved in February 2009.[41] The standoff over the CENI resurfaced again in September 2009 when the Ministry of Interior announced the creation of an electoral department within the ministry, igniting opposition claims that there could be political interference in the elections. The government gave repeated assurances that the CENI would operate independently and that any conflicts related to elections would be managed through the Permanent Forum for Dialogue, a body formally established in October 2009.[42]

In May 2009, donors established a mechanism to coordinate international assistance for elections after the government requested UN support for the electoral process. As part of this process, BINUB established an electoral support program through which the CENI would benefit from technical expertise and support in the planning and implementation of electoral operations. Of the estimated $46.5 million budgeted for the elections, the government committed US$7.9 million, while the rest was funded by donors through the Peace-Building Commission and a United Nations Development Program (UNDP)-managed basket fund for donor contributions.[43] Although donors continued to reiterate the significance of transparent elections in post-conflict reconstruction, the government made further attempts to shape the framework for the elections through the manipulation of voter registration, support for dissenting elements within opposition parties, criminal charges against some opposition leaders, violation of political parties' right of assembly, and increased restriction and control of the activities of civil society. Pointing to these activities, Peter Maurer, Chair of the Peace-building Commission's country-specific configuration for Burundi warned in December 2009:

> Burundi is entering a crucial stage of peace-building. Elections will be held at all levels of government in 2010, and they will enable us to assess the progress achieved. If the elections are carried out in a free, fair, and peaceful manner and lead to universally accepted results, the peace process will be made more durable. It will then become possible to focus even further on the underlying causes of conflict and poverty. However, if the opposite happens, the peace process will be jeopardized, new wounds will be opened and the old ones will be more difficult to heal.[44]

Following the May 2010 elections for councilors in Burundi's 117 communes, in which the CNDD-FDD won 64 percent of the votes, opposition parties rejected the results, claiming that the government had massively rigged the process. Twelve of the opposition parties, including the FNL, formed a coalition—the Alliance of Democrats for Change-Ikibiri (ADC, Alliance democratique pour le changement-Ikibiri)—and announced a boycott of the presidential elections of 28 June 2010, instructing their members not to take up their seats in local councils. Rather than negotiating through the Permanent Forum for Dialogue, the government imperiled the whole electoral process by imposing severe restrictions on the freedom of movement of opposition leaders, arresting dozens of opposition activists, and banning all opposition party meetings. Opposition parties subsequently boycotted the presidential election in June, the legislative and senatorial polls in July, and the village elections in September 2010, resulting in overwhelming victories for the ruling party and the consolidation of its control over all state institutions. Major opposition leaders, including Rwasa, fled the country out of fear of prosecution.[45]

International observers from the European Union and local civil society groups pronounced that the May local election had been conducted in conformity with international norms and that the alleged irregularities had not been significant enough to reverse the will of the people. Donors also criticized the opposition's boycott of the remaining elections because they thereby forfeited the chance to obtain significant representation in the legislative branch. While they denounced the opposition's boycott, the donor governments that underwrote Burundi's peace process hardly spoke out against the government's draconian response at all. While acknowledging the government's intimidation of opposition leaders, including the FNL, the UN Secretary-General's Executive Representative in Burundi put a brave face on the outcomes:

> Despite the deep divide among political actors over the elections and the fact that a single party will dominate the political landscape in the next five years, it is remarkable that neither of those factors has led to the return of large-scale violence, as has been widely feared. I believe that the fact that confrontation has remained predominantly confined to the political realm is a testament to the maturing of the political class of Burundi, the vibrant role played by its increasingly strong and independent civil society, and above all, the population's desire for peace and development.[46]

In the wake of the 2010 elections, the newly reconstituted ONUB (the successor to the BINUB) and the Peace-Building Commission focused on initiatives aimed at promoting dialogue between the government and extra-parliamentary opposition, helping the government strengthen its key institutions, supporting efforts to enhance the capacity of the security and defense forces, and supporting Burundi's integration into the East African Community (EAC).[47] These initiatives were undertaken against the backdrop of a surge in violent incidents since the 2010 elections, amid fears that Burundi could head back into all-out conflict. Exiled leaders such as Rwasa and Leonard Nyangoma, long-time leader of FRODEBU, regrouped in the DRC and began to launch attacks in Bujumbura Rural Province. Throughout 2011, the government blamed the increasing levels of insecurity in the province on the work of bandits and common criminals, but with the increase in the scale of the killings, the government blamed them on Rwasa and Nyangoma. In a May 2012 report, Human Rights Watch documented political killings stemming from the 2010 elections—and blamed the Burundian government for most of them:

> The ruling party had a chance to foster a new beginning for Burundi following the 2010 elections. Instead we have seen the systematic targeting of former rebel combatants and members of the political opposition. Many of those who refused to succumb to pressure to join the CNDD-FDD have paid with their lives.[48]

Conclusion

The UN and regional actors made tremendous contributions to peace and stability in Burundi, motivated by the shared conviction that concerted coordination of efforts could make a difference in stemming the convulsions that threatened the Great Lakes region. Building on the relationship of close collaboration honed during the worst phase of the conflict in the 1990s, the initiatives of the last ten years consolidated a division of labor that originated in an appreciation of the comparative strength each player could muster. Events in Burundi demonstrated that the UN could fruitfully engage with African actors in conflict resolution where the African actors were organized, persistent, and patient. Additionally, South Africa's role in Burundi underscored the importance of creative African leadership in galvanizing both African initiatives and international engagement in conflict resolution. South Africa was able to play an effective leadership role in conflict resolution because it garnered the support of proximate regional states, who did not feel threatened by the intervention and who also benefited from South Africa's leverage.

Prior to the 2010 elections, African actors disengaged from Burundi because they felt that the country had made considerable progress toward building endogenous institutions that would sustain peace. Besides, after almost fifteen years of regional initiatives in Burundi, there was a sense of fatigue with the engagement. Despite this, Burundi's membership in the EAC as of 2009 has promoted a dynamic in which regional values, strictures, and practices will continue to influence national reconciliation efforts. One of the vital objectives of the UN Peacebuilding Commission has been to help Burundi integrate into East Africa by strengthening the national institutions that play a role in regional integration.[49] A peaceful and prosperous Eastern Africa affords Burundi the larger framework in which to manage some of the profound political and economic problems that have confronted it in the past. For this reason, regional integration is both an avenue for enhancing economic interaction and a conflict prevention mechanism. It is also instructive that Burundi hosts the Secretariat of the International Conference of the Great Lakes Region (ICGLR), an initiative that seeks to build peace and security in the region.

However, neither the well-intentioned efforts of the UN nor a propitious regional environment can substitute for meaningful domestic efforts in nation-building, the promotion of inclusive governance, and the equitable distribution of resources. Although external actors have helped Burundi to consolidate peace and make substantial progress after its civil war, deepening these trends will remain the responsibility of the Burundian authorities as they build a culture of democratic dialogue and ethnic amity, and pursue the demilitarization of state and society. The 2010 elections were an opportunity for Burundi to demonstrate the ability to overcome the legacies of internecine conflicts without the overweening hand of the international community. Following opposition protests about the conduct of the 2010 elections, President Nkurunziza managed to calm the political waters—however, the decisive gauge of the solidity of democratic institutions will be the 2015 elections.

Notes

1. Gilbert M. Khadiagala, "Burundi," in *Dealing with Conflict in Africa: The United Nations and Regional Organizations*, ed. Jane Boulden (New York: Palgrave, 2003), pp. 215–251. Stephen Jackson, in *The United Nations Operation in Burundi (ONUB)-Political and Strategic Lessons Learned* (New York: Conflict Prevention and Peace Forum, 2006), also concedes on page 11 that "over such a lengthy peace process, an informal, but mutually understood division of labour had emerged amongst regional and international actors."
2. For a background to the conflict, see Ahmedou Ould-Abdalla, *Burundi on the Brink: 1993–1995: A UN Special Envoy Reflects on Preventive Diplomacy* (Washington, DC: The United States Institute for Peace, 2000); Rene Lemarchand, "Consociationalism and Power Sharing in Africa: Rwanda, Burundi, and the Democratic Republic of the Congo," *African Affairs* 106:422 (2007): 1–20; and Leonce Ndikumana, "Distributional Conflict, the State, and Peace Building in Burundi," *Round Table* 94:381 (2005): 413–427.
3. For a good coverage of South African role, see Roger Southall and Kristina Bentley, *An African Peace Process: Mandela, South Africa and Burundi* (Pretoria: the Human Resources Council, 2005).
4. For this phase of the conflict, see Khadiagala, "Burundi," pp. 225–242.
5. For analysis of Zuma's mediation, see George Rautenbach and Waldermar Vrey, "South Africa's Foreign Policy in Africa: The Case of Burundi," in *The Burundi Peace Process: From Civil War to Conditional Peace*, ed. Henri Boshoff, Waldermar Vrey, and George Rautenbach (Pretoria: Institute for Security Studies, 2010), pp. 11–49; Southall and Bentley, *An African Peace Process: Mandela, South Africa and Burundi* (Pretoria: the Human Resources Council, 2005).
6. Southall and Bentley, *An African Peace Process*. See also Kristina Bentley, "The Peace Process in Burundi: Reflecting on South Africa's Role," *South African Yearbook of International Affairs* 2005 (2006): 21–28.
7. Jan van Eck, "Lessons from the Burundi Peace Process," in *Africa's Peacemakers? Lessons from South African Conflict Mediation*, ed. Kurt Shillinger (Johannesburg: Fanele, 2009), p. 172.
8. Ibid. Van Eck notes that the CNDD-FDD signed the ceasefire agreement in Pretoria because "They were under massive pressure, including threats that they would be declared terrorists by the international community if they refused," p. 172.
9. United Nations Security Council, "The Situation in Burundi," 4 December 2003, 4.
10. African Union, Communique of the Ninety First Ordinary Session of the Central Organ of the Mechanism for Conflict Prevention, Management and Resolution at Ambassadorial Level, Central Organ/MEC/AMB/Comm. (XCI), 2 April 2003.
11. Festus Agoagye, "The African Mission in Burundi: Lessons Learned from the First African Union Peacekeeping Operation," *African Security Review* 15:3 (2006): 9–15. For a comprehensive analysis of AMIB, see Henri Boshoff and Waldermar Vrey, "The African Mission

in Burundi," in Rautenbach and Vrey, "South Africa's Foreign Policy in Africa: The Case of Burundi," in *The Burundi Peace Process*, ed. Boshoff, Vrey, and Rautenbach, pp. 51–73.

12. Cited in Kristina Bentley, "The Peace Process in Burundi," 25.
13. United Nations Security Council, "The Situation in Burundi," 4 December 2003, 4.
14. Henri Boshoff, ONUB Electoral Section, and Waldemar Vrey, "The United Nations Operation in Burundi," in *The Burundi Peace Process*, ed. Boshoff, Vrey, and Rautenbach, pp. 75–116. See also Jackson, *The United Nations Operation in Burundi*, pp. 10–11.
15. United Nations, S/RES/1545, 21 May 2004.
16. Jackson, *The United Nations Operation in Burundi*, p. 19.
17. Rautenbach and Vrey, "The Implementation of South Africa's Foreign Policy in Burundi," in *The Burundi Peace Process*, ed. Boshoff, Vrey, and Rautenbach, pp. 75–116.
18. Jackson, *The United Nations Operation in Burundi*, pp. 19–20. Van Eck, "Lessons from the Burundi Process," p. 172, claims that "Zuma eventually imposed the CNDD-FDD proposal [on ethnic representation] on the Tutsi minority parties."
19. Jackson, *The United Nations Operation in Burundi*, pp. 18–19.
20. United Nations Department of Public Information, "Security Council Calls for 'Immediate Cessation of Hostilities and Human Rights Abuses' in Burundi," 23 March 2006. See also Van Eck, "Lessons from the Burundi Process," p. 172.
21. United Nations Security Council, "Resolution 1719(2006)," October 2006.
22. Shepard Forman, Gigja Sorensen, and Rahul Chandran, *A Field-Based Review of the Peacebuilding Commission in Burundi* (New York: Center for International Cooperation, January 2010), p. 3.
23. Jackson, *The United Nations Operation in Burundi*, pp. 17–18.
24. United Nations Department of Public Information, "Security Council Extends the Mandate of Burundi Operation Until 31 December, Unanimously Adopting Resolution 1692 (2006)," 30 June 2006.
25. S/2007/287, 17 May 2007.
26. United Nations, S/PV.5786, 28 November 2007.
27. United Nations, S/PV.5786, 28 November 2007, 4.
28. United Nations Department of Public Information, "Security Council Extends Integrated Office in Burundi Until 31 December 2008," 19 December 2007.
29. Boshoff, "Bringing the Peace Process in Burundi to an End," in *The Burundi Peace Process*, ed. Boshoff, Vrey, and Rautenbach, pp. 120–121.
30. S/PV.5966, 26 August 2008.
31. S/2008/745, 28 November 2008, 2.
32. Boshoff, "Bringing the Peace Process in Burundi to an End," pp. 122–123.
33. Ibid., p. 123.
34. S/2008/745, 28 November 2008, 3.
35. S/PV.6037, 11 December 2008, 3.
36. S/PV.6138, 9 June 2009, 3.
37. S/PV.6037, 11 December 2008. See also, United Nations Department of Political Affairs, "South African Facilitator Tells of 'Significant Step Forward' as Security Council Considers Situation in Burundi," 11 December 2008.
38. For analyses of these initiatives, see S/PV.6037, 11 December 2008; S/2009/270, 22 May 2009.
39. Fred Oluoch, "Burundi Worries over Poll Chaos in 2010," *The East African*, 13 September 2008. Human Rights Watch reported the arrest of more than a hundred political opponents of the CNDD-FDD between June 2008 and April 2009.
40. S/PV.6138, 9 June 2009, 4.
41. S/2009/270, 22 May 2009, 4–5. See also International Crisis Group, "Burundi: from Electoral Boycott to Political Impasse," International Crisis Group (ICG), 7 February 2011.

42. S/2009/611, 30 November 2009, 2–3.
43. S/2009/611, 3.
44. S/PV.6236, 10 December 2009, 4
45. S/PV.6439, 9 December 2010, 1–9. See also Josh Kron, "Opposition calls Election in Burundi a 'Masquerade'," *New York Times*, 30 June 2010.
46. United Nations Department of Public Information, "Burundi's Transformation to Stability Still Fragile, Reversible, Despite Progress: Secretary-General's Executive Representative Tells Security Council," 9 December 2010, 4.
47. S/PV.6538, 17 May 2011, 1–5; United Nations Department of Public Information, "International Community Should Commit to Matching Burundi's Peace Consolidation Efforts, Senior United Nations Officials Tell Security Council," 17 May 2011.
48. Human Rights Watch, *"You Will Not Have Peace While You Are Living": The Escalation of Political Violence in Burundi*. New York: Human Rights Watch, 2 May 2012.
49. United Nations Peacebuilding Commission, *Outcome of the Fifth Review of the Implementation of the Strategic Framework for Peacebuilding in Burundi* (New York: Fifth Session Burundi Configuration, 21 April 2011), p. 6.

Chapter 6

Chad and the Central African Republic

Arthur Boutellis

Introduction

A chapter on Chad and the Central African Republic (CAR) could seem out of place in this edited volume dedicated to the relationship between the United Nations (UN) and regional organizations in dealing with conflicts in Africa. The post-2003 crisis in eastern Chad and CAR, resulting from the arrival of some 200,000 Sudanese refugees across the border from Darfur, intensified in 2005. Although the African Union (AU) had in 2006 encouraged the UN and others to take certain steps to enhance security along the borders among Sudan, Chad, and CAR and protect refugees, the peacekeeping mission the UN Security Council authorized in 2007 neither resulted from nor led to effective UN–AU cooperation. Rather, the UN mission in Chad and CAR (known by its French acronym MINURCAT) and the AU regional peace initiatives evolved on two separate, albeit interdependent, tracks. The roles of the two intergovernmental organizations, and their relationship, were also largely shaped by the powerful states that supported them when they fit their national and regional interests, but undermined their work and sidelined them at other times.

Although the trend of the last decade had been toward regional organizations taking a lead role in action before the UN Security Council addressed a conflict situation,[1] this was not the case in Chad and CAR. The role of the AU in Chad and CAR contrasted sharply with the lead it had taken a few years earlier when the Darfur crisis erupted in 2003, when it mediated and subsequently deployed the African Mission in Sudan (AMIS) the following year. Although the regional organization took part in the successive Chad–Sudan agreements, it never took a lead role. Instead, it was the regional powers, and Muammar Qaddafi's Libya in particular, that led the various regional and Chadian political processes established after 2003, facilitating both the Chad–Sudan peace accords and discussions between the government of Chad and various rebel groups.

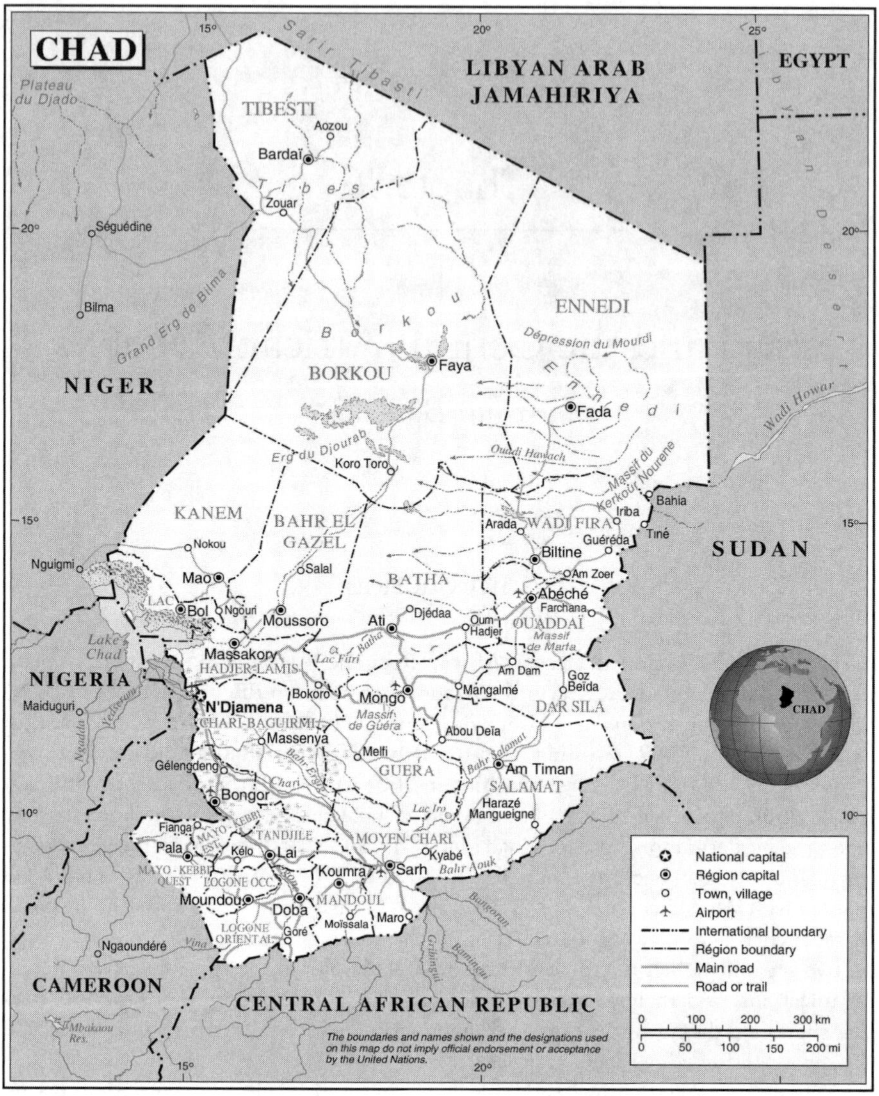

Source: Map No 3788 Rev 8, United Nations, Department of Field Support, Cartographic Section, March 2009 (Colour)

When the possibility of a peacekeeping mission in Chad and CAR emerged, the AU option was not pursued. This was true in spite of both key developments in the building of the UN–AU relationship during the same period, and the authorization of the AU/UN Hybrid Operation in Darfur (UNAMID), as well as of a UN-financed support package for the AU mission in Somalia (AMISOM) in 2007. The AU had been reluctant to get involved in what it had perceived as Chad's internal affairs, and most of its attention had been instead dedicated to Sudan, from where the crisis had emanated. Libya, and also Chad and Sudan, had long opposed any sort of international peacekeeping presence in

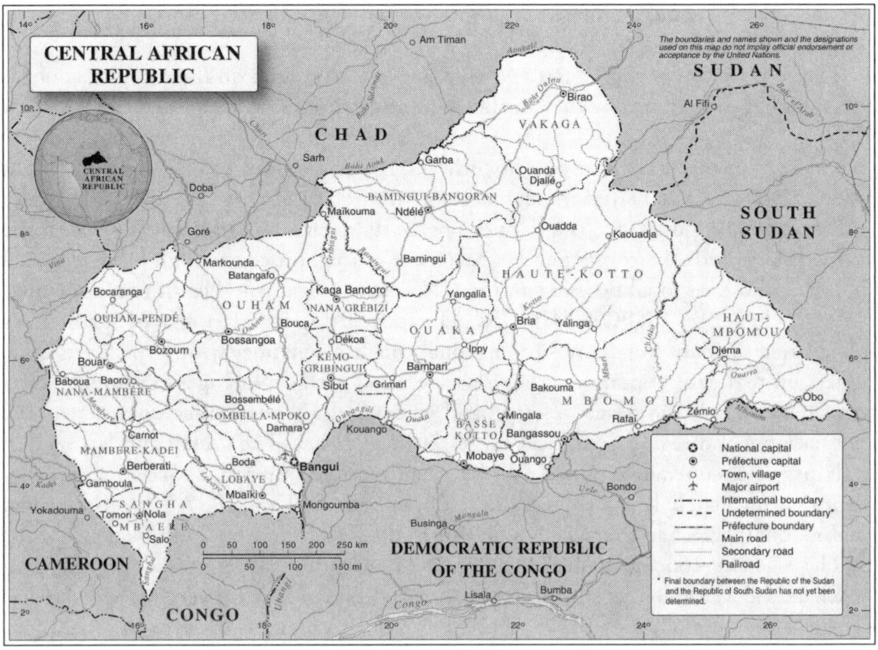

Source: Map No 4048 Rev 5, United Nations, Department of Field Support, Cartographic Section, November 2011

the region, and multiple attempts to deploy an African force to monitor the Chad–Sudan border had already failed when the idea of a UN mission started to emerge.

The UN Security Council eventually authorized the deployment of a dual international presence of a UN civilian and police operation (United Nations Mission in the Central African Republic and Chad, MINURCAT), and a European Union military force (EUFOR) on 25 September 2007.[2] This was more the result of the sudden coincidence of Chad, CAR, and Western geopolitical interests in 2007, rather than of a regional peace initiative. As a former colonial power in the region, France was eager to "multilateralize" its military presence and foreign policy in these countries. Under pressure from domestic constituencies, other actors, including the United States, supported the idea of having international forces across the Darfur border after Khartoum objected to the deployment of UN peacekeepers on its soil earlier that year. France also convinced the reluctant Chadian authorities to accept a peacekeeping mission, on the basis that it would be devoted solely to the protection of civilians (POC) in eastern Chad and northeastern CAR and would not interfere in Chadian internal affairs.

MINURCAT indeed was mandated with the primary task of protecting civilian populations and humanitarian actors, but was not given an explicit political mandate and would therefore play no role in supporting either the national Chadian or the regional Chad–Sudan political processes. This meant that the UN mission did not have the mandate to address the root causes of the conflict, whether at the national or regional level. The "regional dimension" of MINURCAT's mandate was limited to liaising and exchanging information on emerging threats to humanitarian activities with the

AU and other regional organizations, as well as with the other UN missions present in neighboring Sudan and CAR.

The first section of this chapter provides some background on the complex regional and national dimensions of the conflict that affected eastern Chad and northeastern CAR, as well as on the various peace initiatives spearheaded by regional powers. The second section discusses why and how the UN (and the European Union [EU]) got involved and the role played by regional organizations and regional powers. It argues that peacekeeping does not and cannot operate in a vacuum, and that in order to be successful, it needs the consent and engagement of the host country, and the sustained support of both regional powers and the UN Security Council. The third section analyzes the challenges EUFOR/MINURCAT faced during its initial deployment and as it later tried to adapt to national and regional conflict dynamics within the limits of its protection mandate. It points to the risks associated with deploying a mission in a context where there is "no peace to keep," and where the UN has limited control over the root national and regional political causes of the conflict. The fourth and last section explains the circumstances and *Realpolitik* that prompted the Chad–Sudan rapprochement that ultimately led to the sidelining of both the UN and the AU at a time when international focus had shifted from Darfur to the future state of South Sudan.

The chapter concludes that the perceived instrumentalization of peacekeeping in Chad and CAR by certain powers to push different but converging agendas has damaged the credibility of the peacekeeping tool. It points to some of the inadequacies of the peacekeeping tools in certain contexts, and to the risk that in the absence of a viable political strategy, they can unwittingly contribute to sustaining autocratic regimes instead of encouraging democratic governance reforms. It finally suggests that in a context where the permanent membership and legitimacy of the Security Council are increasingly questioned by other member states, and where regional organizations increasingly assert themselves, both the UN and the AU have much to gain in building an effective strategic partnership on peace and security in Africa.

Context

Regional Conflict and National Politics

In 2003–2004, the arrival of some 200,000 Sudanese refugees across the border, the establishment of rear bases by Darfurian rebel groups, and the displacement of more than 170,000 Chadian civilians as a result of growing insecurity in eastern Chad exacerbated the tensions between Chad and Sudan. At the local level, these population movements also aggravated preexisting ethnic conflicts between different tribes of farmers and herders in eastern Chad and northeastern CAR, while reinforcing cross-border intercommunity loyalties.[3]

The post-2003 crisis in Chad and the CAR, which intensified after 2005, cannot be seen in isolation from the Darfur crisis in neighboring Sudan. However, while there is no question that the conflict had a regional dimension, it should not be seen simply as a "spillover from Darfur" or "Darfurization" of eastern Chad, as it is sometimes presented. In reality, the root causes of the crisis are found at the regional, national, and local levels, with regional dynamics exacerbating the internal political and security crisis in Chad and CAR.

Chad's border with Sudan was established in 1923 by French and British colonial powers, which thought to demarcate the powerful Sultanates of Ouaddai and Darfur. However, some ethnic groups were divided by the new border, including current President Déby's own Zaghawa clan (present in eastern Chad and western Sudan, including Darfur). Under French colonial rule, his family was forced to flee to Darfur, from where Déby launched the military coup that deposed President Habré in 1990. Déby's close relationship with the Sudanese authorities explained in part his initial reluctance to become embroiled in the Darfur crisis, until his own Zaghawa clan convinced him to actively support the Darfur rebellion.

This led to a regional proxy war between Chad and Sudan, with President Déby's regime supporting the Justice and Equality Movement (JEM)—one of the main rebel movements in Darfur—while Khartoum attempted on multiple occasions to unify the Chadian rebel groups operating out of western Darfur and northeastern CAR, in order to destabilize or even overthrow the Déby regime. However, this military activity on both sides had little impact on civilians in eastern Chad. Similarly, the state of conflict that has prevailed over the last decade in CAR is due largely to internal problems related to a series of coup attempts and armed rebellions with interferences from neighboring countries.

At the national level, the start of the current Chad crisis can be dated back to 1979, which marked the end of the "southern" President Malloum's regime, the conquest of power by the northern elite and the start of a bloody era in the history of Chad. The national security forces became divided along ethnic and religious lines, and although Chad's army remains one of the largest in Africa, it still lacks unity and an integrated command structure. Different factions, including army defectors, are often recruited among a single ethnic group to confront the government in the hope of influential government positions. The successive integration of several of these armed rebel groups into the army since the 1990s has further fragmented the institution.

Although President Idriss Déby's arrival to power in 1990 opened a long period of relative stability until 2002, and despite continuous external support (from France, the United States, Libya, and Sudan until 2003), his many governments have been incapable of uniting the people of Chad or reforming political and social institutions.[4] Over the years, President Déby concentrated powers and built up a clientelist system around his Zaghawa clan, which also composes the great majority of his Presidential Guard. About one hundred members of this Guard have also been protecting CAR President François Bozizé since Chad supported his arrival to power in a 2003 coup against former CAR President Ange-Félix Patassé.

The start of oil production in 2004 increased Chad's financial resources considerably, but did not result in greater redistribution of revenues among its people. Indeed, arguing about national security imperatives, President Déby was quick to challenge the terms of the loan agreement signed with the World Bank and an oil consortium based on a Norwegian social model, where 90 percent of revenues had to go to priority sectors such as health, education, rural development, and infrastructure. Chad eventually won its battle with the World Bank, adopting a January 2006 law reversing priority sectors with 80 percent of oil revenues now going to "administration and security."[5] In 2005,

President Déby arranged for a constitutional reform that allowed him to get a third term as president in May 2006.

The Succession of National and Regional Agreements

Various parallel political processes have been established since 2003 in response to these regional and national crises. Although Libya had played a destabilizing role in Chad in the 1970s and 1980s, the proxy war between Chad and Sudan and the crises in Darfur and eastern Chad gave Muammar Qaddafi the opportunity to portray himself as a regional peacemaker, facilitating both the Chad–Sudan peace accords and discussions between the Chad governments and various rebel groups. Qaddafi's investments, largesse, and leadership role in the Community of Sahel-Saharan States (CEN-SAD)[6] bought Libya respectability and influence across the continent, which helped legitimate Qaddafi's new role as a regional peacemaker and helped him to gain prevalence on the international scene. From 2008 to 2009, Libya served a two-year term on the UN Security Council representing the Africa group, and Qaddafi was elected chairman of the fifty-three-nation AU for one year in 2009.

While the AU took part in many of the successive Chad–Sudan agreements, the regional organization never took a lead role. By contrast, when the Darfur crisis erupted in early 2003, the newly established AU, encouraged by its Western allies, quickly became involved in mediation efforts and later deployed observers with the African peacekeeping mission in Darfur (AMIS) in 2004, at a time when the UN Security Council was focused on finalizing the North-South Sudan Comprehensive Peace Agreement (CPA). However, the AU observers in both Sudan and Chad lacked the logistical means to effectively monitor the border. Although Chad had accepted that a few of the AU observers would be based on its territory, President Déby, not unlike Sudan President al-Bashir, perceived the AU as siding with rebels and supporting other Western agendas, hence leading to the "internationalization" of internal and regional issues.

The Tripoli Agreement of 8 February 2006 was Libya's most significant attempt to broker a Chad–Sudan peace deal in which President Déby and President Bashir agreed to resume relations and to end support to all rebel groups. The agreement was reached at a mini-summit that had been organized and financed by Qaddafi; it was attended by then AU chairperson Congo Brazzaville President Sassou-Nguesso.[7] This summit took place around the time the UN Security Council was considering a contingency plan for sending UN troops to take over from the AU in Darfur, and presented the opportunity for both Qaddafi and the parties to the conflict to show that the region did not need UN peacekeepers. However, while Libya intended to oversee the implementation of the agreement (including by sending its own force in support of the AU observers), it failed to do so and a 13 April 2006 rebel attack on N'Djaména led to the severing of Chad's diplomatic ties with Sudan.[8] The AU's failure to effectively monitor the border and prevent the rebel aggression on Chad only reinforced President Déby's distrust of the organization.[9]

In parallel to the regional process described earlier, Libya also helped broker the October 2007 Syrte Agreement between the government of Chad and the remaining Chadian armed groups. This included a ceasefire, amnesty, provisions for disarmament and reintegration, and appointment of rebel leaders to government posts. There, as well, implementation never followed suit, and violence erupted again soon afterward. The AU was reluctant to get involved in what it perceived as national affairs, as reflected in its February 2007 communiqué[10] condemning the attacks perpetrated by armed groups against Chad and CAR, as unacceptable attempts to take over power by force in violation of the Lomé Declaration and the Constitutional Act of the AU. In the same communiqué, the AU also urged the Chadian authorities to engage in dialogue with all of the Chadian political stakeholders, including the political and military movements, and it encouraged the Chairperson of the AU Commission and other involved actors to facilitate such a dialogue and a negotiated solution to the crisis in Chad. However, President Déby was not ready to accept an inclusive dialogue, and even insisted that Syrte would be the last agreement he would sign with the rebels.[11]

It is only after a few more failed agreements—and a major February 2008 rebel attack on N'Djaména (described later in this chapter) that almost deposed president Déby—that the AU decided to take on a greater role as mediator in the regional conflict. The AU mandated Libya's Qaddafi and Congo Brazzaville's Sassou-Nguesso as permanent mediators in the Chadian crisis, a decision that the UN Security Council officially supported.[12] It was also under an AU mandate that Senegalese President Wade negotiated the Chad–Sudan Dakar Agreement of 13 March 2008, which detailed steps to normalize relations. However, this time, the implementation of the agreement was to be supervised by a Contact Group that would meet on a monthly basis.[13] The agreement also envisaged the deployment of an African force to monitor the Chad–Sudan border, which Libya would finance and for which Senegal and Congo Brazzaville would provide troops. Sudan accused Chad of opposing such an African monitoring force, even though they had already agreed to it in the February 2006 Tripoli Agreement.[14]

It was another two years before a border-monitoring force saw the light of day. Instead, the idea of a UN peacekeeping mission in Chad and CAR started to emerge as a result of a coincidence of Chadian, Central African, and Western geopolitical interests at the end of 2007. While Libya and Sudan had long resisted the idea of an international military force in the region, Chad's President Déby and CAR's President Bozizé eventually agreed to it. At least initially, Chad regarded the peacekeepers as a friendly buffer force—partly due to the important involvement of France, Chad's ally—that could support the regime's survival at a limited cost, as long as such a UN mission would not have a political mandate.[15] Peacekeeping cannot and does not operate in a vacuum; it requires the consent of the host country and the support of both regional powers and the UN Security Council. While these conditions would eventually be realized and the mission authorized, both Chad's consent and the support by regional and Council powers would soon prove difficult to sustain once the mission was deployed.

The UN's Involvement

UN Security Council Dynamics and the Region

The UN's initial engagement in the situation in Chad and the CAR can be dated to Secretary-General Kofi Annan's 18 April 2006 briefing of the Security Council on

Sudan, during which he underlined the risk that the Darfur crisis could spill over into Chad and CAR.[16] That same day, the AU Special Envoy and Chief Mediator for the Inter-Sudanese Peace Talks, Salim Ahmed Salim, raised the regional dimensions of the conflict in a public statement to the Council. Beyond the personal amity between the former Secretary-General and Tanzanian diplomat, there was a sense of a common UN–AU position on Chad and CAR in 2006, as illustrated by the 20 September 2006 communiqué of the AU Peace and Security Council, in which the AU "encourages any steps that could be taken, including by the United Nations, to enhance security along the borders between Sudan and Chad and between Sudan and the Central African Republic, as well as ensure the protection and security of refugees in Chad."[17]

In December 2006, the UN Security Council decided to dispatch a multidisciplinary technical assessment mission to Chad and CAR. Ongoing hostilities in eastern Chad and the northeastern CAR limited the ability of the mission to visit the area. However, preliminary recommendations suggested that, should the conditions permit it in the future, a UN peacekeeping operation could be mandated to monitor the border areas while working to improve security through the facilitation of political processes, dialogue, and the POC, with available capabilities[18]—that is, a UN mission with a political mandate.

However, informal consultations on 10 January 2007 revealed profound differences of opinion within the UN Security Council. On one side, France, supported by the United States and the United Kingdom, called for the urgent deployment of a UN multidimensional presence both in Chad and CAR. On the other side, other Council members and the UN Department of Peacekeeping Operations (DPKO) cautioned that for a UN presence to be effective, a ceasefire, a political process, and the consent of the parties were required. When briefing the Council, the UN DPKO, represented by then Assistant Secretary-General Hédi Annabi, insisted that the necessary conditions for the deployment of a peacekeeping force were not present due to ongoing fighting in Chad and CAR and the lack of a political process in Chad. Annabi concluded by recalling a phrase from the "Brahimi Report"[19]: the UN Secretariat should tell the Council what it needs to know, rather than what it wants to hear.

Many in the international community also feared that such an international mission would serve to support undemocratic regimes in both Chad and CAR, and that the French were attempting to "multilateralize" their support of the Déby and Bozizé regimes. The French military was present in both Chad (under Opération Épervier) and CAR (under Opération Boali), providing training and logistical support to Chadian and Central African Armed Forces (FACA, Forces Armées Centrafricaines), and also monitoring the Sudanese border with regular surveillance flights.[20]

The Government of Sudan had just rejected the deployment of a UN peacekeeping operation in Darfur—intended as a replacement for the ill-equipped AU Force AMIS[21]—as decided in Security Council Resolution 1706 of 31 August 2006. This Sudanese objection also brought the United States and United Kingdom closer to the French proposal for an international force in eastern Chad and northeastern CAR, as a second-best alternative to a UN peacekeeping presence in Sudan.[22] The US government in particular was under pressure from nongovernmental organizations and public opinion to do something in response to what it deemed as "genocide" in Darfur.[23] Although Chad and CAR had until then been considered side-issues to Darfur by Council members, Security Council Resolution 1706 had already envisaged "the establishment of a multidimensional presence consisting of political, humanitarian, military and civilian police liaison officers in key locations in Chad, including in the internally displaced persons and refugee camps, and if necessary, in the Central African Republic."

These discussions coincided with an acceleration in the development of the UN–AU relationship, including the signing of the 16 November 2006 Joint Declaration on the enhancement of the UN–AU cooperation, known as the Ten-Year Capacity Building Programme for the AU, the authorization of the UNAMID in July 2007 and a UN-financed support package for the AMISOM, and the start of annual joint consultations between the AU Peace & Security Council and the UN Security Council. However, both the UN and AU were focused on Darfur and were reluctant to take on an additional military presence in Chad, for which it would be difficult to generate troops on short notice. Additionally, many within UN DPKO still thought that there were great risks associated with deploying a mission in a context where there is "no peace to keep," and where the UN would have limited control over the root national and regional political causes of the conflict.

Chad Consents to a European Force, with the UN, but without a Political Mandate

When the idea of a UN peacekeeping presence in Chad and CAR first emerged in 2006, it was rejected by the Chadian government and the leading regional powers, Libya and Sudan. While President Bozizé of CAR favored the idea, President Déby, much like Sudan, was concerned that the UN was trying to use Chad as a proxy for addressing the conflict in Darfur, and that the UN would want to get involved in Chadian internal politics as suggested in the December 2006 report of the Secretary-General to the Security Council.[24]

The massive humanitarian presence in eastern Chad, the many official visits (including by then-Senator Barack Obama in September 2006), and the establishment of an International Criminal Court (ICC) field office in Abéché in early 2007 all contributed to making Chad a window onto Sudan, but also further isolated Chad on the continent. While under international pressure to accept peacekeepers, Chad was concerned that accepting such an international military presence on its territory would unnecessarily increase tensions with a neighbor with which it wanted to normalize relations. President Déby felt that if it were to take this risk, such an international force should be co-deployed with the Chadian army so as to form a buffer zone against rebels.[25]

Although a 30 November 2006 visit of then French Prime Minister de Villepin to Chad convinced the Chadian president to accept the idea of an international presence in principle, many questions remained as to the nature of that presence.[26] President Déby questioned the relevance of a military force and suggested in a *Note Verbale* dated 7 November 2006 that a "international civilian force," made up of gendarmes provided by African countries and paid for by Europe or the UN, would be better adapted to protecting refugees and displaced persons, while the Chadian army would remain in charge of military matters.[27] There was a sense that CAR would welcome any international presence, but would ultimately go along with Chad's decision.

In October 2002, following a deterioration of the security situation in CAR, the Economic and Monetary Community of Central Africa had established a Multinational Force of the Central African Economic and Monetary Community (FOMUC) consisting of 380 troops from Chad, Gabon, and the Congo to contribute to the stability of the CAR and the restructuring of the Central African Armed Forces (FACA). However, the subregional force was critically under-resourced and its mandate was to expire at the end of June 2007.

The UN DPKO, which had argued that the necessary conditions for the deployment of a peacekeeping force were not fully present in Chad for the above-mentioned reasons, was also strictly opposed to deploying a UN civilian and police presence without an international military force. As France was exploring options, the idea arose of an African force as envisaged in the Tripoli Agreement. It was soon ruled out by President Déby, who cited the difficulties plaguing AMIS across the border.[28] Bad memories also remained from the first African peacekeeping force deployed in Chad in the early 1980s.

Following a second report from the Secretary-General, on 23 February 2007,[29] and President Déby's persistent refusal to allow the deployment of a UN military force, the French government put forward the idea of deploying a European Union Force (EUFOR Chad/CAR) alongside a UN civilian mission. France's sudden enthusiasm for an EU peacekeeping force resulted from the combination of its geopolitical interests in safeguarding the stability of Chad and CAR regimes, its eagerness to further the EU's role in crisis management and to test the European Security & Defense Policy (ESDP), and the "humanitarianism" of then French Foreign Affairs Minister Kouchner.[30]

France faced the hard task of convincing its European allies and the Chadian regime of the value of an EU mission in Chad and CAR. Many compromises would have to be made in the process. On the European side, resistance from Germany and the United Kingdom—wary of cost implications and suspicious of France's African agenda—would eventually lead France to commit to providing the bulk of the troops and funding for the EU mission. On the Chadian side, President Déby first conceded to the principle of a European force during Kouchner's June 2007 visit to N'Djaména.[31] He did so based only on an understanding from France (which was providing 57 percent of EUFOR troops) that the military force would only be deployed in the eastern part of the country (and not operate in areas immediately bordering Darfur), and that the co-deployed UN civilian mission would not have a political mandate. Chadian authorities also hoped that accepting a European force would bring additional international assistance—especially from the European Commission—to the country, and create favorable conditions for reconstruction and development in this region.[32]

UN Security Council Resolution 1778 was adopted on 25 September 2007. It authorized the deployment in Chad and CAR of a dual international presence of a UN civilian and police operation (MINURCAT) and a EUFOR, under Chapter VII of the Charter of the UN, for one year. The European force would consist of 3,700 troops, while the UN presence would include 300 UN police officers and 50 military liaison officers. The mandate focused on the POC, with a multidimensional presence primarily intended to "help create the security conditions conducive to a voluntary, secure and sustainable return of refugees and displaced persons."[33]

EUFOR/MINURCAT

EUFOR/MINURCAT Deploys at Height of Regional Tensions

Few will remember that the first time an African regional organization mandated a peacekeeping force was in 1981 in Chad. Then, following an initial Nigerian peacekeeping force in 1979, the AU's predecessor, the Organization of African Unity (OAU), authorized a multinational force of roughly 3,500 troops from Nigeria, Senegal, and then Zaire. This first African mission was made possible by the coincidence of Nigerian and Chadian geopolitical interests, and political pressure (and logistical backing) from France and the United States. As the mission was deployed, Senegalese peacekeepers soon found themselves caught between Chadian government forces and rebels from the Armed Forces of the North (FAN), who eventually seized control of the country. This led to the hasty departure of the African peacekeepers. Then Chadian President Oueddei had regularly criticized the OAU force for not fighting on behalf of his forces. FAN rebel leader Habre subsequently ruled Chad from 1982 until being deposed himself in 1990, by his former minister of defense and Idriss Déby.[34]

History does not repeat itself, but it came close in February 2008. The first EUFOR troops arrived on 28 January 2008, and MINURCAT civilians had to suspend their initial deployment after a coalition of Chadian rebel forces[35] arrived in N'Djaména on the morning of 2 February. The rebels had successfully crossed the entire country from the Sudanese border in only three days, and inflicted a major defeat on the Chadian army (killing its chief of staff) the day before at Massaguet, eighty kilometers outside of N'Djaména. The first few Austrian soldiers that arrived in N'Djaména as part of EUFOR found themselves trapped in the middle of the fighting as rebel forces quickly took control of most of the capital, with the exception of the heavily defended presidential palace. The survival of Déby's regime in the following days has been attributed to disagreements that arose between rebel forces when victory was in reach and the launching of Déby's attack helicopters from the airport, which was made possible by the protection provided by French Opération Épervier troops stationed there.[36]

This heightened tension between Chad and Sudan during the very onset of the EUFOR/MINURCAT mission highlighted the disconnect between the mission's limited protection and humanitarian mandate and the regional political and security dynamics. The international peacekeeping "solution" was not mandated to address the root causes of the instability in the region. The February attacks also highlighted the ulterior motive that underpinned Chadian consent to the deployment of a peacekeeping force, which it expected would serve as a buffer against rebels. They also reinforced the concerns that a predominantly French EUFOR could create some confusion and might not be perceived as neutral. This despite MINURCAT, EUFOR, and Opération Épervier operating under differing mandates.

The attacks revealed the Déby regime's weakness and its dependence on its French ally.[37] They also made Chad more willing to consent to the international presence—as long as it effectively served as a buffer, or at least had a dissuasive effect on rebel border incursions. At the same time, Chadian rebels and opposition movements became convinced that EUFOR/MINURCAT would not be a neutral humanitarian force but would instead support the French goal of protecting the regime. France had backed Déby's refusal to enter into a dialogue with rebel forces. The lack of reaction after the arrest and subsequent "disappearance" of opposition figure Ibni Oumar Mahamat Saleh in days following the February 2008 N'Djaména battle further reinforced this sentiment.[38]

The speed of the attacks did not give the UN time to foresee the possibility of a larger political transition in the case of either a ceasefire agreement between Déby and the rebels or a complete collapse of Déby's regime. Such scenarios would have probably called for a more "traditional" peacekeeping mandate, but with President Déby surviving in extremis and the rebels chased back to the Sudanese border, MINURCAT's mandate remained unchanged. The Special Representative of the Secretary-General (SRSG) for MINURCAT Victor Angelo arrived in country soon afterward, in March 2008.

The AU issued a communiqué on 2 February 2008—which the UN Security Council supported[39]—strongly condemning the rebel attacks, calling on all the countries of the region to respect the unity and territorial integrity of Chad and mandating the Libyan and Congo Brazzaville leaders to engage the Chadian parties with a view to ending the fighting and to initiate efforts aimed at seeking a lasting solution to the crisis. However, Libya's rapprochement with Paris over the Bulgarian nurses affair,[40] and its covert support to Déby during the February N'Djaména battle, compromised its credibility as an unbiased mediator. In March 2008, Chad and Sudan signed a nonaggression pact, which was broken a few weeks later when Chadian-supported JEM rebels launched a spectacular raid on Khartoum in May that many interpreted as an act of retaliation by Chad for the rebel attacks on N'Djaména three months previously.[41]

Was EUFOR/MINURCAT a Regional Solution?

The situation in Chad and CAR had initially been brought to the attention of the UN Security Council in the context of the UN peacekeeping operation in Darfur, which Khartoum later opposed. When the idea of a UN peacekeeping presence across the border from Darfur started to develop, some UN Security Council members were initially reluctant to include northeastern CAR in the mandate. France was soon able to convince them of the importance of stabilizing the Darfur–Chad–CAR tri-border region—where French forces had clashed with rebel forces in March 2007[42]—and deterring Chadian rebels from using it as a rear base.

Following the initial delay in deployment caused by the February 2008 rebel attacks, EUFOR Chad/CAR reached its initial operational capability on 15 March 2008 and its full operational strength in September of that year. With 3,700 troops deployed both in eastern Chad and the northeastern CAR city of Birao, EUFOR, in addition to being the biggest EU military operation to date,[43] can also be considered the first transborder or "regional" peacekeeping operation ever to be deployed.[44] However, while EUFOR force headquarters were in N'Djaména and the eastern Chadian town of Abéché, both the operation headquarters led by Irish Lt. General Nash and the strategic reserve of 600 troops were based in Europe. While UN staff generally viewed the EU force as a component of a larger UN-led operation, the EU planners approached the EU mission as a parallel deployment of two discrete, if complementary, missions.

Furthermore, although EUFOR/MINURCAT was effectively deployed across Chad and CAR, the absence of a political mandate—one that would support national and regional political processes—prevented it from playing a role in addressing the root, regional causes of the conflict. Paragraph 2(d) of Resolution 1778 limited the regional dimension of the mission to liaising and exchanging information on emerging threats to humanitarian activities with

> the Sudanese Government, the AU, AMIS and the AU/UN Hybrid operation in Darfur which will succeed it, the UN Peacebuilding Support Office in CAR (BONUCA), the Multinational Force of the Central African Economic and Monetary Community (FOMUC) and the Community of Sahelo-Saharan States (CEN-SAD).

In spite of the occasional courtesy visit by Bassolé, the Joint AU–UN Chief Mediator for Darfur, and the participation of MINURCAT in quarterly UN intermission regional coordination meetings (with United Nations Mission in Sudan [UNMIS], UNAMID, United Nations Organization Mission in the Democratic Republic of the Congo [MONUC], and United Nations Peace-building Office in the Central African Republic [BONUCA]), the mission did not have the mandate to discuss political issues affecting Chad at these meetings.[45]

Although EUFOR/MINURCAT deterred a resumption of mass killings and gave a sense of security, it was largely unable to fill the security vacuum left by the lack of government presence in the east.[46] Some observers argued that the mission failed to achieve its two main objectives of creating the conditions for the sustainable return of refugees and displaced persons and protecting the civilian population and humanitarian workers.[47] One of the major reasons behind this was the evolution of the situation in eastern Chad from how it was before 2005, when insecurity was primarily caused by cross-border attacks by Janjaweeds[48] and other armed groups, to how it stood in 2008, when the most important problems were common banditry and intercommunity violence, which called for a police (and justice) response rather than a military force, no matter how robust and mobile. Paradoxically, the presence of the mission may have contributed to a rise in insecurity because it allowed the presence of more humanitarian organizations, which in turn became the targets of attacks and kidnappings. EUFOR also lacked sufficient troops to deploy to all areas of insecurity.

The international force did not deter rebels from attempting another attack on N'Djaména in June 2008, and the EUFOR Irish troops stationed in the eastern town of Goz Beida did not confront rebels as they drove toward the capital. Although this was not part of the force's mandate, it led president Déby to accuse EURFOR of collaborating with rebels against government troops.[49] Yet, the rebel column was stopped shortly after this, by Sukhoi-25 fighter jets and attack helicopters newly acquired by the government of Chad from Ukraine.[50]

Alongside EUFOR, MINURCAT, lacking a political mandate, largely focused on the work of its authorized 300 UN police officers. The mission faced delays in the deployment of its personnel and in the establishment of the special UN-supported Chadian unit Détachement Intégré de Securité (DIS); this unit was charged with providing security in refugee camps, in sites with concentrations of internally displaced people (IDPs) and in key towns in neighboring areas, and it was supported by a MINURCAT Trust

Fund.[51] The training of the 850 DIS members due to be deployed in eastern Chad was not finished until February 2009 and the UN faced additional challenges in procuring DIS vehicles and construction of DIS police stations and posts.[52] Although the CAR government had expressed interest in training and logistical support for their own police force, or even the adaptation of the DIS concept to the CAR realities, MINURCAT's police involvement remained limited to Chad.

MINURCAT II's Short-Lived Attempt at Changing the Course

The transition from EUFOR/MINURCAT to MINURCAT II in March 2009 could have been an opportunity for a new UN mandate that would have recognized the direct link between security in eastern Chad and the need for a more representative and legitimate Chadian State and the normalization of Chad–Sudan relations. However, the Government of Chad's reservations about an international military presence came to the fore once again in 2008, during the protracted discussions necessary to determine the mandate, size, location, and rules of engagement of a UN force under MINURCAT II.[53] Chad ultimately consented to the UN force in a large part because it could not afford to alienate the international community at a time when tensions with Sudan were at a high.[54]

At the end of the summer of 2008, MINURCAT had actually warned that, in spite of the announced restoration of diplomatic relations between Chad and Sudan, both sides were building their military presence along the border and that there was a real risk that their proxy war could turn into a direct confrontation. In the lead up to the full takeover by MINURCAT II, SRSG Angelo tried to make the case in front of the Security Council for a more flexible interpretation of the mandate that would make the mission more effective. The SRSG noted that the absence of a political mandate sidelined the mission and it recommended that the UN, in close consultation with key regional players, be allowed to play a greater role in the Dakar Agreement implementation process, to which three Permanent 5 (P5) members (France, the United Kingdom, and the United States) were also observers. SRSG Angelo attended the 12 September 2008 Asmara meeting of the Contact Group, during which Chad and Sudan agreed to exchange ambassadors. However, a controversy arose over whether to involve UN and AU military planners on the issues related to the border-monitoring "Peace and Security Force." The next meeting took place on 15 November 2008 in N'Djaména and discussions stalled over funding that force.

The SRSG also recommended that the UN peacekeeping mission replacing EUFOR should include a number of Formed Police Units (FPUs), so that it could carry out its protection mandate more effectively by responding to the rise in banditry and criminal activity. This recommendation was favored by the government of Chad, which hoped that the mission would further invest in capacity-building efforts and increase the size of the DIS from 850 to 1,700 instead of spending over US$800 million a year on maintaining its own large but ineffective force when it was the Chadian army effectively patrolling the border area. However, the UN DPKO lacked francophone FPUs and argued that the proper role of such units was to ensure the safety and security of UN personnel through public order management[55] rather than to patrol refugee camps and IDP sites.

Security Council Resolution 1861, adopted on 14 January 2009, brought no fundamental change to the role of the UN in Chad. It did not give the mission a political mandate, either with regard to the regional political processes or in support of the organization of Chadian national elections initially scheduled for 2009 (but later postponed to 2011). Instead, it simply reiterated the mission's "role as observer with UNAMID in the Contact Group that was established under the 13 March 2008 Dakar Accord to monitor its implementation and assist, as necessary, the Governments of Chad, the Sudan and the Central African Republic to build good neighborly relations."[56] Although MINURCAT II would continue reporting on political developments in Chad and CAR, as well as regional developments, Chadian authorities regularly reminded the mission that it did not have a political mandate and advised that reporting on internal political developments be as brief as possible. The Chadian authorities also took issue with the fact that the mission employed "political affairs" officers, and with the large UN presence in N'Djaména, despite the fact that its mandate was limited to eastern Chad.[57]

Although it was rumored that the Economic Community of Central African States (ECCAS)[58] would ask the UN to include military observers along the Chadian–Sudanese border, this did not materialize in the new mandate. The main change that MINURCAT II brought was an expanded civilian component to support the government of Chad's efforts in the areas of justice and the rule of law, prison reform, human rights, and local reconciliation efforts (civil affairs). Faced with difficulties in getting the authorized strength of 5,200 troops from member states on time, it initially had to rely on the re-hatting of EUFOR troops as UN troops.

MINURCAT II would not be much more "African" than EUFOR was. Although a Senegalese General took over as Force Commander and 140 African troops were provided by Ghana and Togo, 1,877 out of the 2,085 troops that started with MINURCAT II were re-hatted from eight EUFOR contributors. This is largely explained by the short two-month delay between the adoption of Resolution 1861 authorizing MINURCAT II and the date of 15 March 2009 set by EUFOR for the transfer of authority. This was when the troop strength initially recommended to the Council by UN DPKO had ultimately been reduced in size. In spite of the United Kingdom's continued questioning of the necessity of a presence in northeastern CAR, the new MINURCAT would keep 300 troops stationed in Birao.[59]

Meanwhile, the Security Council expanded the mandate of BONUCA, the UN mission in CAR that was first established in 2000 following the conclusion of a UN peacekeeping operation,[60] to include supporting security sector reform, the rule of law, and the disarmament, demobilization, and reintegration (DDR) of ex-combatants, as well as promoting and supporting an inclusive political dialogue among the government, rebels, and opposition leaders. In January 2010, its name was converted to BINUCA to reflect the "integrated" nature of the mission, which was designed to ensure the coherence of peacebuilding support activities by the various UN entities present in CAR. Parallel to this, ECCAS deployed the Mission for the Consolidation of Peace in Central African Republic (MICOPAX) in July 2008, which succeeded the critically under-resourced FOMUC operation; it was hoped that MICOPAX would bring a greater number of regional actors into the effort to stabilize CAR. At the time of writing, MICOPAX receives funding from the EU and is composed of 500 troops and a civilian component, including 150 police officers; it also supports the DDR and political processes in CAR.[61]

MINURCAT's Withdrawal in the Context of Regional Rapprochement

Chad Withdraws Its Consent

As MINURCAT continued to struggle to generate troops and had only reached about 60 percent of its authorized strength of 5,200, the UN Secretary-General received a Note Verbale dated 15 January 2010 from the Government of Chad asking to commence negotiations to determine the "practical modalities" for withdrawal of MINURCAT. The UN was largely caught by surprise and subsequently put all new troop deployments on hold. This happened only two months after President Joseph Kabila of the Democratic Republic of Congo publicly called for UN peacekeepers to start withdrawing ahead of Congo's fiftieth anniversary of independence in June 2010. The difficult withdrawal of the UN mission in Ethiopia and Eritrea (UNMEE) that occurred after Eritrea abruptly withdrew its consent was also still fresh in the mind of the UN DPKO.

Reasons for the request advanced by the Chadian interlocutors included their dissatisfaction with the slow deployment of the MINURCAT peacekeepers. President Déby had also publicly criticized the peacekeepers for "hiding behind sand bags" and not making populations of eastern Chad safer. They also cited the improvement in the security environment on the ground that would allow the Chadian security forces—including the DIS—to take over from the UN force. Finally, Chadian authorities were frustrated with the slow implementation of infrastructure projects that had been included in the mandate of MINURCAT. In particular, this included the handover of the Abéché camp built under EUFOR but used by MINURCAT, which the Chadian air force insisted it needed to station its newly acquired fighter jets,[62] and where the Chadians wanted to headquarter the new Chad–Sudan monitoring force for the first six months, which the two countries had just agreed to as part of their rapprochement. At that time, many in the international community, including humanitarian organizations, objected that a premature MINURCAT withdrawal would have serious consequences on the security situation of refugees, displaced persons, and humanitarian actors in eastern Chad, and result in the collapse of the DIS police.

However, there were more profound reasons to object to an early withdrawal, many relating to the circumstances in which EUFOR/MINURCAT had been created. The Chadian authorities were always opposed to an international military presence on their territory and had only reluctantly agreed to EUFOR for one year under the conditions that France would provide the bulk of the troops and that the mission would have no political mandate. MINURCAT II—with a UN force set to replace EUFOR—had changed the terms of the deal, and Chad, aspiring to regional power status, did not want to be associated with the type of fragile states that generally host UN peacekeeping operations. Furthermore, Chad had in the meantime considerably rearmed itself—as demonstrated by its victory over the rebels in May 2009[63]—and rebels no longer represented a threat to the regime as they had been deprived of their rear bases across the border, and as Chad and Sudan had at last started an effective rapprochement (discussed in the following).

A Negotiated but Early Exit

From 26 January to 23 April 2010, the UN dispatched to Chad three successive teams to discuss the future of MINURCAT with Chadian authorities. When the first mission initially offered to discuss ways to make the mission more effective, the Chadian authorities reiterated that they wanted the military component to leave, but suggested that they would be open to seeing the civilian presence (including DIS support) remain. However, the UN DPKO found that security conditions on the ground would not allow for such a model. During the next mission, led by DPKO Under-Secretary-General Le Roy, President Déby consented to a limited UN military presence to guard the UN camps from which the MINURCAT civilian component would operate. Chad also agreed to a two-month technical extension to the mandate. This allowed for a third mission, led by acting SRSG Youssef Mahmoud (replacing SRSG Angelo, who completed his assignment on 31 March 2010), to enter into a much longer negotiation, which culminated on 23 April in an agreement or "Aide Memoire" with the Chadians to be transmitted to the Security Council.[64] SRSG Mahmoud described the negotiation as follows:

> There was a visceral distrust of the UN, of peacekeeping...So as a negotiator, that's the first thing I had to address. So basically, I spent the first week listening, and trying to understand why there was this broken relationship with the Government of Chad.[65]

The negotiated agreement was effectively a mission withdrawal plan. This plan included the government of Chad's reappropriation of its primary responsibilities to protect civilians and to ensure the security of humanitarian workers after the departure of MINURCAT, and its appropriation of MINURCAT's benchmarks as outlined in paragraph 25 of Security Council Resolution 1861 (2009). The one-year withdrawal period, proposed to extend to May 2011, would also allow for consolidating and increasing the sustainability of the DIS. This negotiated agreement also served the purpose of the UN mission, avoiding a precipitated withdrawal and a potentially difficult extraction of the mission (UNMEE Eritrea scenario). Finally, it would help the Security Council to avoid a rupture with Chad.

However, these goals were only partially achieved. By unanimously adopting Resolution 1923 on 25 May 2010, the Council decided that the withdrawal period would finish by 31 December 2010. It also reduced the number of infrastructure projects that had been consented to in previous mandates, justifying this decision by noting that the government of Chad had asked for the early departure of the mission. This created an additional challenge for MINURCAT, which could not finish Integrated Security Detachment development projects on time. The trust fund that MINURCAT had set up to support the development of the Integrated Security Detachment would be handed over to United Nations Development Programme (UNDP) and United Nations High Commissioner for Refugees (UNHCR), and would continue to receive some donor funding as the government progressively took ownership of this special police/gendarmerie unit, which it has been calling "the baby of both Chad and the UN."

As the decision to withdraw the mission came from Chad, CAR had had little say in it. The authorities in CAR, unhappy with the fact that EU funding was going to regional MICOPAX forces rather than its own armed forces, expressed interest in the idea of UN troops remaining in CAR—and providing logistical support and training to FACA; however, this option was quickly ruled out. It would take only two weeks for rebel forces to seize the town of Birao from the 100 FACA troops freshly deployed after MINURCAT troops had left.[66]

UN Security Council members who had initially pushed for EUFOR/MINURCAT—primarily France, with support from the United Kingdom and the United States—were seen as largely indifferent to the departure of the mission. France and the EU were happy to end EUFOR after one year and to claim that, in comparison to the shortcomings of the military component of MINURCAT II, it had been a success.[67] The United Kingdom and the United States, faced with financial austerity at home, were pleased to see some of the infrastructure projects cut. However, the Security Council did not trust that the Chadian authorities would fully assume their responsibility to protect civilians as the mission departed, and asked for three progress reports during the last six months of MINURCAT.

The AU remained quiet—in 2010, it did not issue a single communiqué on Chad, focusing instead on the CAR political process and establishing an AU Liaison Office in Bangui.[68] Interestingly, the presence of Libya in the UN Security Council in 2008–2009, and its chairing of the AU from 2 February 2009 to 31 January 2010, did not lead to increased interactions between the UN and the AU on Chad and CAR.

A Sustained Chad–Sudan Rapprochement

The cessation of Chad's consent to the UN peacekeeping mission coincided with a more sincere rapprochement effort between Chad and Sudan initiated at the end of 2009. Many observers, including MINURCAT officials, questioned this new rapprochement at the time, as many past agreements brokered by the region had never been implemented, in spite of the efforts of regional powers and the joint UN–AU mediator for Darfur, Djibril Bassolé. Chad and Sudan may have been encouraged by the prospect of each holding its respective national elections in Spring 2011 and by the referendum on South Sudan self-determination scheduled for January 2011. The ICC indictment of President Bashir also pushed Khartoum toward finding a new common ground with Chad. However, the rapprochement may not have happened without the strong international pressure led by the new US administration and its Special Envoy, Scott Gration. China, which was involved in oil exploitation as well as in other projects in Chad after President Déby gave up his recognition of Taiwan, also supported the rapprochement.[69] The attention of the international community had suddenly shifted from Darfur to the future State of South Sudan, for which some level of collaboration from Khartoum would be needed. The US-led initiative and effective Chad–Sudan rapprochement put both the AU and the UN out of a job.

Both President Déby and President Bashir sent delegations to each other's capitals and made key personnel changes in their entourage that allowed discussions to move forward, which resulted in the signing of a "normalization" agreement in N'Djaména on 15 January 2010—the very day the *Note Verbale* was sent to the UN. This agreement included provisions for the reopening of the border for the first time since 2003 and for the establishment of a 3,000-strong joint border force, which was effectively deployed this time. The ultimate sign of rapprochement was the invitation of President Bashir to N'Djaména for a meeting of the Community of Sahel-Saharan States (CEN-SAD), of which Sudan is a member, despite the ICC arrest warrant and despite Chad being a signatory of the Rome Statute.[70] While a year earlier at the CEN-SAD summit of May 2009 Qaddafi was reportedly pressuring Déby to accept the AU mediation and to not go the UN route,[71] this new summit was the occasion for President Déby to reestablish Chad as a regional power as it took over the CEN-SAD chair.

This Chad–Sudan rapprochement also resulted in additional pressure on the JEM. Chad expelled the JEM in February 2010; it has subsequently lost its main strongholds in North Darfur while being under attack by Sudanese government forces since April 2010. In May 2010, JEM leader Khalil Ibrahim was refused permission to transit through Chad to Darfur and was expelled, without papers, to the Libyan capital, Tripoli. In July 2010, Khartoum returned the favor and sent to Qatar a number of rebel leaders whom Déby wanted expelled from Sudan.[72] In December 2011, JEM leader Khalil Ibrahim was killed in Darfur by the Sudanese army after "escaping" the Libya turmoil a couple of months earlier. Meanwhile in April 2011, Idriss Déby won reelection as the president of Chad. His Patriotic Salvation Movement party captured 113 of the 188 seats in the parliamentary elections. These national elections had been postponed from 2009, and were boycotted by the main opposition parties after their demands for electoral reforms had not been met. Déby's reelection was made possible by a 2005 constitutional reform that had abolished the two-term presidential limit.[73]

The Chad–Sudan rapprochement has since held, as illustrated by the 20 January 2012 marriage of President Déby to the daughter of the notorious Darfuri Janjaweed leader Musa Hilal, in the presence of Sudanese President Bashir.[74] In 2011, the new relations between Chad and Sudan seem not to have been affected by either the birth of the South Sudan state or the fall of Qaddafi's regime, which deprived President Déby of a key ally in the region. Mindful that a hostile relationship with Tripoli could endanger stability in northern Chad and the greater region, the Chadian regime has recognized the new Tripoli regime. However, it is unlikely that the new Tripoli regime could take over Qaddafi's mediator role in the event of a future breakdown in Chadian and Sudanese relations.[75] Chad also reconsidered its August 2010 request for the end of French Opération Épervier, and instead asked France to conduct aerial reconnaissance flights along its northern border with Libya while allowing 950 of its troops to remain stationed in Chad for the time being.[76]

Conclusion

This chapter describes how the relationship between, and respective roles of, the UN and the AU were largely shaped by the powerful states that supported and used the institutions at times when it fit their national and regional interests, but also undermined their work at other times. The formal interactions between the UN and the AU over Chad and CAR were limited, initially by the fact that both the UN Security Council and the AU had their focus on Darfur,[77] and later because, though MINURCAT had been deployed, it was not granted the political mandate that would have allowed it to better coordinate with regional efforts.

The experiences of Chad and CAR provide some insights to the UN–AU relationship, which has since developed on both the political and peacekeeping fronts.[78] Indeed, the deployment of EUFOR/MINURCAT resulted from neither a joint analysis of the situation on the ground nor from an assessment of the comparative advantages of the different organizations. Instead, this chapter explains how the deployment of a peacekeeping mission in Chad and CAR resulted from the circumstantial coincidence of Chadian, Central African, and Western geopolitical interests at the end of 2007. It also highlights how, in the end, both the UN and the AU were sidelined by a Chadian–Sudanese rapprochement dictated by Realpolitik and the shift of international focus away from Darfur to South Sudan. This led to the early withdrawal of a UN peacekeeping mission in Chad and CAR whose primary raison d'être had been the Darfur crisis, and to the AU going quiet—to the point of not issuing a single communiqué—on Chad in 2010.

Beyond the UN–AU relationship, one of the key lessons from the Chad and CAR experience is that, regardless of how ill-conceived a UN peacekeeping mission is, it does not and cannot operate in a vacuum. It is largely dependent on the consent and engagement of the host country, as well as on the sustained support of regional and global powers, particularly the permanent members of the Security Council and the African states holding nonpermanent seats in the Council at the time. The contribution of international peacekeepers is effective only if both these conditions are fulfilled. In the words of SRSG Mahmoud, it must be: "nationally owned, regionally anchored, and internationally supported."

Most lessons to date on the Chad and CAR experience have not focused on the cooperation between international and regional organizations, but have instead been limited to each organization analyzing its own experience within the scope of its mandate. The EU praised its own global and regional approach and the fact that "the political . . . and the humanitarian . . . fields have been both complementary and coordinated, thereby maximizing the EU's impact on the ground."[79] Other lessons have focused on the "bridging force" aspect of EUFOR.[80] Interestingly, in Resolution 1923, the Council also requested that the Secretary-General provide lessons learned from the MINURCAT experience. These lessons included the fact that "consent of a host Government should be nurtured," and that consent is "reversible, especially when the conditions in the country and/or the subregion change significantly during the life of the mission."[81]

The EUFOR/MINURCAT mission was indeed authorized only with the limited consent of the host countries Chad and CAR. However, the success of its mandate to "help create the security conditions conducive to a voluntary, secure and sustainable return of refugees and displaced persons" was largely dependent on addressing the national and regional political root causes of the various conflicts, which was not in the UN mission's mandate. The role played by the joint UN–AU mediator for Darfur, and other AU initiatives aimed at maintaining the link between Khartoum and N'Djaména, should be acknowledged, even if in the end, the pressure exerted by the new US administration may have been the key to the Chad–Sudan rapprochement. However, the absence of an explicit political mandate impeded the UN mission from adequately coordinating with these parallel political processes.

The issue of consent also points to the challenge of keeping the peacekeeping tool relevant in the eyes of host countries, which tend to be protective of their sovereignty and to prefer support for their own capacity-building over large foreign troop deployments. This would require that UN peacekeeping becomes more flexible, and that it further builds on partnerships with regional organizations and powers to deploy appropriate expertise to support the building of host country capacities.[82] Additional challenges come from the fact that unless such efforts are part of a viable political strategy aimed at building accountable and legitimate institutions, they risk unwittingly sustaining or even strengthening autocratic regimes instead of encouraging democratic governance reforms.

There is also much to learn from the fact that the Security Council overlooked the advice of the UN Secretariat, which initially suggested that the conditions necessary for the deployment of a peacekeeping force were not present. The subsequent events may have proven them right, when the inadequacies of the EU and UN forces became evident in the face of the rising banditry and criminality in eastern Chad. Because it was deployed with "no peace to keep," the mission ended up looking like an "exogenously-driven solution for a problem where the issues and root causes lied elsewhere."[83] The perceived hidden agendas that underpinned the genesis of EUFOR/MINURCAT made regional powers all the more suspicious of the UN mission, seen as a Western Trojan horse built when the Council could not get peacekeepers into Darfur.

More broadly, the perceived "instrumentalization" of UN peacekeeping by certain Western powers through the Security Council to push different but converging agendas (preserving allied regimes, putting pressure on the Khartoum regime, or promoting the POC norm) has damaged the credibility of the peacekeeping tool. This issue is not likely to go away, as the permanent membership of the Security Council is increasingly questioned by other member states and as regional organizations such as the AU increasingly assert themselves. In this context, both the UN and the AU have much to gain by building an effective strategic partnership with which to pursue peace and security.

Notes

1. Suyash Paliwal, "The Primacy of Regional Organizations in International Peacekeeping: The African Example," *Virginia Journal of International Law* 51:1 (15 January 2010): 185.
2. S/RES/1778, 25 September 2007.
3. For more background, see Jérome Tubiana, "The Chad–Sudan Proxy War and the 'Darfurisation' of Chad: Myths and Reality," Working Paper, *Small Arms Survey* (Geneva: HSBA, April 2008).
4. International Crisis Group, "Chad: A New Conflict Resolution Framework," *Crisis Group Africa Report* 144:24 (September 2008): 2.
5. For a detailed account, see Thierry Vircoulon, "Oil in Chad: The Fragile State's Easy Victory over International Institutions," *On the African Peacebuilding Agenda*. Available at www.crisisgroup.org/en/regions/africa/central-africa/chad/op-eds/oil-in-chad-the-fragile-states-easy-victory-over-international-institutions.aspx (9 September 2010).
6. Qaddafi created the CEN-SAD in 1998. It became a Regional Economic Community (REC) mandated and recognized by the African Union in 2006. However, with its headquarters in Tripoli, most of its functioning budget paid by Libya, and the direct access to the Mediterranean see it provided through the Misrata free zone, the organization has been largely perceived as under Qaddafi's control.
7. The Summit was also attended by Nigerian President Obasanjo, CAR President Bozizé, and AU Chairperson of the Commission Konaré, as well as Burkina Faso President

Compaoré, who was also at the time chairing the Community of the Sahelo-Saharan States (CEN-SAD).

8. Marc Lacey, "Chad Severs Ties with Sudan as Tensions Escalate," *New York Times*, 14 April 2006.
9. *Sudan Tribune*, "Chad's Deby Accuses African Union of indifference," 18 April 2006.
10. Communiqué of the Peace and Security Council of the AU, at its seventieth meeting held on 12 and 13 February 2007.
11. International Crisis Group, "Chad: A New Conflict Resolution Framework," *Crisis Group Africa Report* 144 (24 September 2008): 15.
12. S/PRST/2008/3, Statement by the President of the Security Council, 4 February 2008.
13. The Contact Group was cochaired by Libya and Congo Brazzaville and included Senegal, Gabon, Chad, Sudan, Eritrea, the Organization of Islamic Cooperation (OIC), MINURCAT and the AU, and also designated France, the United States, and the United Kingdom as part of the group of friends of the Dakar Agreement, allowing them to participate in the monthly meetings.
14. *Sudan Tribune*, "Sudan, Chad Endorse Plan to Monitor Border Joint Border," 29 April 2008.
15. Interview with Senior United Nations official, 22 March 2012.
16. Alexandra Novosseloff and Richard Gowan, "Security Council Working Methods and UN Peace Operations: The Case of Chad and the Central African Republic, 2006–2010," *Center on International Cooperation* (New York: New York University, April 2012).
17. African Union, Communiqué of the 63rd Meeting of the Peace and Security Council on the situation in Darfur, PSC/MIN/Comm(LXIII), 20 September 2006, in New York.
18. S/2006/1019, 22 December 2006.
19. A/55/305–S/2000/809, 21 August 2000.
20. *BBC*, "France Watches Chad-Sudan Border," 5 February 2008.
21. S/RES/1706, 31 August 2006.
22. A compromise solution would later be found with the government of Sudan for a UN–AU Hybrid Mission in Darfur (UNAMID) to take over from existing AU mission AMIS in December 2007.
23. The US Congress had passed the Darfur Peace and Accountability Act (H.R. 3127/S. 1462), which was signed into law by President Bush on 13 October 2006.
24. S/2996/1019, 22 December 2006.
25. Interview with senior Chadian official, 29 February 2012.
26. *Radio France Internationale (RFI),* « Villepin au Tchad et en Afrique du Sud », 30 November 2006.
27. S/2006/1019, 22 December 2006, para. 15.
28. Novosseloff and Gowan, Security Council Working Methods and UN Peace Operations.
29. S/2007/97, 23 February 2007.
30. Kouchner had previously championed the "*droit d'ingerence*," or the right to intervene to stop mass atrocities by using military force, and had previously proposed the establishment of a French-led military-humanitarian corridor from Chad to Darfur before being forced to retreat.
31. *Sudan Tribune*, "Chad Opens Door to Possible Foreign Military Force," 11 June 2007.
32. S/2007/540, Note verbale dated 11 September 2007 from the Permanent Mission of Chad to the United Nations addressed to the Secretary-General, 12 September 2007.
33. S/RES/1778, 25 September 2007.
34. Terry M. Mays, *Africa's First Peacekeeping Operation: The OAU in Chad, 1981–1982* (Westport, CT: Praeger, 2002).
35. Composed of three main rebel groups—the Union of Forces for Democracy and Development (UFDD), the Union of Forces for Democracy and Development-Fundamental (UFDD-F), and the Assembly of the Forces for Change (RFC)—which had announced the creation of a unified military command in December 2007.

36. Other sources also point to the critical role played by Libyan ammunition delivery via French-secured N'Djamena airport, and the support by armed elements from the JEM—including by preventing rebel reinforcements from reaching N'Djamena—as well as by the Zaghawa presidential guards posted in Bangui called upon for support.
37. The arrest and conviction of members of French charity organization Zoé's Ark accused of abducting children by the Chadian authorities at the end of 2007 had raised tensions with the French government. Soon after the February 2008 N'Djamena attacks, Chad and France agreed that the members be transferred to France.
38. *Amnesty International*, "Chad: Government Must Investigate the Enforced Disappearance of Ibni Oumar Mahamat Saleh," 3 February 2012.
39. S/PRST/2008/3, 4 February 2008.
40. Matthew Brunwasser and Elaine Sciolino, "Bulgarian Nurses and Palestinian Doctor Freed from Captivity," *New York Times*, 24 July 2007.
41. *BBC*, "Sudanese rebels 'reach Khartoum,'" 10 May 2008.
42. *Reuters*, "Rebels in Central African Republic Clash with French Forces," 5 March 2007.
43. The only two previous EU missions in Africa were Operation Artemis in eastern Democratic Republic of the Congo (DRC) in 2003 authorized under resolution 1484 (2003), and EUFOR DRC during the 2006 elections authorized under resolution 1671 (2006). As per EUFOR Chad/CAR, the two previous missions had been both short term and in support of a UN Mission.
44. David Lanz, "EUFOR Chad/CAR: A Regional Solution for a Regional Problem?," in "EUFOR Tchad/RCA Revisited," ed. Feichtinger and Hainzl, *An International Review of Peace Initiatives* 22 (October 2009): 39–42.
45. S/RES/1778 (2007), United Nations Security Council Resolution 1778 (2007), 25 September 2007.
46. *Human Rights Watch*, "The Risk of Return: Repatriating the Displaced in the Context of Conflict in Eastern Chad," June 2009.
47. Winrich Kuehne, *How the EU Organizes and Conducts Peace Operations in Africa EUFOR/MINURCAT* (Berlin: Center for International Peace Operations [ZIF], March 2009).
48. The word "Janjaweed" refers to armed men on horseback and designates Sudanese militiamen as primarily members of nomadic Arab tribes.
49. *AFP*, "Chad's Deby Accuses EUFOR of Helping Rebels," 21 June 2008.
50. S/2009/562, 29 October 2009.
51. The initial MINURCAT mandate had envisaged the establishment of a "*Police tchadienne pour la protection humanitaire* (PTPH)" but this title had to be changed to DIS to respond to Chadian objections that it also included gendarmes and to humanitarians objections over the use of the work "humanitarian."
52. S/2009/199, 14 April 2009.
53. S/2010/611, 1 December 2010.
54. Interview with senior Chadian official, 29 February 2012.
55. Annika S. Hansen, *Policing the Peace: The Rise of United Nations Formed Police Units* (Berlin: Center for International Peace Operations [ZIF], May 2011).
56. S/RES/1861, 14 January 2009, para. 6(i).
57. Interview with senior UN official, 23 February 2012.
58. ECCAS is an Economic Community of the African Union for promotion of regional economic cooperation in Central Africa.
59. S/2009/199, 14 April 2009.
60. Following a series of internal conflicts and mutinies in 1996 and 1997, subregional mediation efforts led to the establishment of the Inter-African Mission to Monitor the Implementation of the Bangui Agreements in February 1997. It was replaced in April 1998 by a UN peacekeeping operation, the UN Mission in the Central African Republic (MINURCA).

Following the successful holding of elections in September 1999, MINURCA was withdrawn and replaced by the United Nations Peacebuilding Support Office in the Central African Republic (BONUCA).

61. European Commission, *Annual report The African Peace Facility 2009*, and European Commission, *Annual report The African Peace Facility 2010*.
62. S/2010/217, Report of the Secretary-General on the United Nations Mission in the Central African Republic and in Chad (MINURCAT), 29 April 2010.
63. *BBC*, "Chad Says Rebel Attack Defeated," 7 May 2009.
64. S/2010/217, Report of the Secretary-General on the United Nations Mission in the Central African Republic and in Chad (MINURCAT), 29 April 2010.
65. SRSG Mahmoud speaking at IPI's Special Representatives of the Secretary-General (SRSG) Series, "MINURCAT: The Challenges of an Early Exit" (21 October 2010).
66. *BBC*, "Central African Republic Rebels Seize Birao Town," 26 November 2010.
67. Roland Marchal, "An Assessment of EUFOR Chad/CAR," in "EUFOR Tchad/RCA Revisited," ed. Feichtinger and Hainzl, *An International Review of Peace Initiatives*, 22 (October 2009).
68. Communiqué of the AU Peace and Security Council (CAR) at its 215th Meeting, 8 January 2010.
69. Tubiana, "Renouncing the Rebels: Local and Regional Dimensions of Chad–Sudan Rapprochement," *Small Arms Survey* (Geneva: Graduate Institute of International and Development Studies, March 2011).
70. *BBC*, "Sudan's President Bashir Defies Arrest Warrant in Chad," 21 July 2010.
71. *International Crisis Group*, "Africa without Qaddafi: The Case of Chad," Africa Report N°180, 21 October 2011.
72. *Small Arms Survey*, "Sudan Human Security Baseline Assessment (HSBA)" http://www.smallarmssurveysudan.org.
73. *BBC*, "Chad's President Idriss Deby Re-elected Amid Boycott," 10 May 2011.
74. *Sudan Tribune*, "Chad President to Marry Daughter of Darfur Janjaweed Leader," 30 December 2011.
75. International Crisis Group, "Africa without Qaddafi: The Case of Chad," Africa Report N°180, 21 October 2011.
76. *Jeune Afrique*, "Tchad: la stabilité malgré tout," 4 April 2012.
77. Novosseloff and Gowan, Security Council Working Methods and UN Peace Operations, 29.
78. See for instance PSC/PR/2.(CCCVII), "Report of the Chairperson of the Commission on the Partnership between the AU and the UN on Peace and Security: Towards Greater Strategic and Political Coherence," AU Peace and Security Council 307th Meeting, Addis Ababa, Ethiopia, 9 January 2012.
79. Council of the EU, "Council Conclusions on Operation EUFOR Tchad/RCA," 16 March 2009.
80. Hylke Dijkstra, "The Military Operation of the EU in Chad and the Central African Republic. Good Policy, Bad Politics," *International Peacekeeping* 17:3 (June 2010): 395–407.
81. S/2010/611, 1 December 2010.
82. Senior Advisory Group. *Civilian Capacity in the Aftermath of Conflict*. Independent report, March 2011.
83. SRSG Mahmoud speaking at IPI's Special Representatives of the Secretary-General (SRSG) Series, "MINURCAT: The Challenges of an Early Exit" (21 October 2010).

Chapter 7

Côte d'Ivoire, 2002–2011

*Fabienne Hara and Gilles Yabi**

Introduction

In April 2011, four months after incumbent Ivorian President Laurent Gbagbo rejected the results of elections in which he was voted out from power, United Nations (UN) peacekeepers and French forces attempted to end the political crisis by launching a simultaneous attack on Côte d'Ivoire's security forces and military installations. Within days, Gbagbo's supporters were defeated, the Forces Républicaines de Côte d'Ivoire (FRCI), mostly composed of former rebels from the Forces Nouvelles (FN) insurgency, took full control of Abidjan, and President-elect Alassane Ouattara took office. The decision to intervene was consistent with the enforcement of the unique mandate that the UN had in Côte d'Ivoire during the October and November 2010 presidential elections—its mission (UN Operation in Côte d'Ivoire, UNOCI) was to certify the entire electoral process, including the monitoring of results. In the end, the UN declared Ouattara the legitimate winner. The decision to intervene militarily, in line with the relatively new doctrine of Responsibility to Protect (R2P), was conducted with the UN Security Council's (UNSC) blessing[1] as a response to the dramatic deterioration of the postelectoral humanitarian and security situation and the risk of the country's relapse into civil war.

Since the beginning of the civil war in 2002, the Economic Community of West African States (ECOWAS), the African Union (AU), France, South Africa, and Burkina Faso, had all tried—in turn or in partnerships that consisted of various different combinations—to promote a political resolution of the crisis, including through different power-sharing arrangements and a roadmap to UN-supervised elections. France took an early lead in the mediation process and negotiated the January 2003 Linas-Marcoussis agreement (LMA). While ECOWAS immediately mobilized its support, the presence of millions of West African nationals in Côte d'Ivoire limited its room for maneuver. Nevertheless, both France and ECOWAS made a quick push to "multilateralize" and legitimize their efforts in Côte d'Ivoire, creating a complex security architecture relying

Source: Map No 4312 Rev 3, United Nations, Department of Field Support, Cartographic Section, December 2011

upon a UN peacekeeping mission, a robust French military presence, and a series of "anti-spoiler" measures, including an arms embargo, a sanctions regime, and human rights inquiries. At the end of the long peace process, the UN, supported by ECOWAS, looked to France to take the lead in military action during April 2011, a decision that was a clear indication of the failure of diplomacy by all actors with a stake in the crisis.

During the first phase of the international response to the armed conflict, from September 2002 to mid-2003, France and ECOWAS were the key players. However, as the former colonial power and permanent member of the Security Council had troops on the ground, it took the lead at the diplomatic level in early 2003. Subsequently, the UN became the lead organization following the creation of a peacekeeping mission, operating alongside French forces. After a period of extreme tension between Ivorian forces and French troops in November 2004, the AU increased in significance and South Africa took the lead in mediation efforts. Despite combined actions by both the AU and the UNSC, the peace process stalled and eventually resulted in a return to a regionally brokered solution—and to the direct actors of the conflict—which created the conditions, though not ideal, for presidential elections.

This chapter discusses the experience in Côte d'Ivoire and the main challenges and strategic choices that confronted the joint attempt by various key actors to deal with the Côte d'Ivoire conflict, highlighting the lessons learned in the process. It provides an overview of the background to the conflict, deals with the different stages of the conflict, and discusses the division of labor and the nature of cooperation between UN and regional organizations, ECOWAS and AU.

At the Origins of the Political Crisis and Armed Conflict in Côte d'Ivoire

The Republic of Côte d'Ivoire achieved independence in August 1960 following sixty-seven years of French colonial rule. The nation's first president, Félix Houphouët-Boigny, had previously held several posts in the French government before leading the independence movement. Houphouët-Boigny maintained virtually complete political control over Côte d'Ivoire until his death in 1993, and his party, the Parti démocratique de Côte d'Ivoire–Rassemblement démocratique africain (PDCI-RDA), was, until 1990, the sole constituent of the country's one-party system. During this period, Côte d'Ivoire maintained a close political relationship with France, its former colonial power. This relationship emerged from Houphouët-Boigny's personal willingness to engage with France, especially when compared with some of his regional counterparts, as well as perceived mutual economic advantage, largely through the cocoa trade and public investments. This closeness is most evident in the signing of a defense agreement between the two nations. This pact, which included several secret clauses, obliged France to come to the aid of Côte d'Ivoire's government in the event of external and even internal security threats. Côte d'Ivoire also established itself as a regional business and economic hub during the period, drawing in migrants from surrounding countries (Burkina Faso and Mali being the largest sources of immigration). While this was initially advantageous, these migratory trends would not only later provoke a backlash, but also served to entwine the political destiny of Côte d'Ivoire with that of its neighbors.[2]

The early part of Houphouët-Boigny's rule was largely characterized by stability and economic growth, then dubbed the "Ivorian miracle." During the 1960s and 1970s, the country's per capita GNP rose at an annual rate of 5 percent. Levels of immigration, as well as natural population growth, were consistently high. The population grew from 3 million in 1960 to 4 million in 1970, and by the year 2000 had reached 16 million.[3]

However, by then, prosperity had evaporated. Severe economic difficulties began in the late 1980s and dominated the 1990s. The prolonged downturn was caused primarily by a steep decline in the world price of cocoa, the country's major export, and a failure to adapt economic policies quickly, leading to unsustainable levels of external debt. This translated into a sharp decrease in living standards, rising unemployment, and intercommunal tension, which was often directed at both recent as well as long-established migrants and Ivorians with foreign origins.[4]

It was within this context of a shrinking economy that Houphouët-Boigny's regime faced unprecedented political pressures to move toward democratization. The popular demand for an end to the one-party systems was not limited to Côte d'Ivoire during the late 1980s. Facing strong internal and external pressures, Houphouët-Boigny was forced to accept change and multiparty elections were organized in 1990. The old leader won comfortably. In addition to having kept his incredible personal popularity, the opposition, led by Laurent Gbagbo, also had insufficient time, resources, and freedom to mount a credible alternative. In reality, the nation was still a de facto one-party state. In the wake of the election, opposition leader Gbagbo was put in jail for a short time. The election campaign was also notable for Houphouët-Boigny's pledge to guarantee the citizenship rights of all settled immigrants. This is important because, first, it contrasted starkly with the policies of subsequent governments, and second, the fact it was being made at all was indicative of the issue's salience in the public debate. Houphouët-Boigny appointed for the first time a prime minister. He chose Alassane Ouattara, a respected economist with regional and international experience, to try and fix the grave financial crisis.[5]

Following Houphouët-Boigny's death in December 1993, Henri Konan Bédié, the speaker of parliament and designated constitutional successor, assumed the presidency, though there were a few hours of tension marked by suspicion that Prime Minister Ouattara was also interested in the immediate presidential succession. The rivalry between Bédié and Ouattara in the last two years of Houphouët-Boigny's life was manifestly apparent. President Bédié was less successful than his predecessor at controlling the political system without provoking dangerous divisions within the elites and the society. Within the PDCI, a splinter group emerged, led by Djéni Kobina, who formed the Rassemblement des Républicains (RDR), which became Ouattara's party. The move weakened the PDCI and increased the linking of major political parties with ethno-regional blocks. The PDCI was further associated with the peoples of the Centre (Baoule in particular, Houphouët-Boigny and Bédié's ethnic group), the RDR with "Dioula" northerners,[6] and the Ivorian Popular Front (FPI) with peoples from the West—though this association was looser. In addition, Gbagbo's FPI became increasingly important as their support grew, especially among urban youths frustrated by a severe economic and social crisis.[7]

It is in the context of these developing political pressures that Bédié began to pursue policies based on the doctrine of "ivoirité," described as "a nationalist-qua-ethnic political stratagem disguised as patriotism,"[8] or, put simply, "to be considered genuinely Ivoirian one had to be culturally more southern than northern."[9] This rested on a controversial distinction between "indigenous Ivorians" and "Ivorians of immigrant ancestry" that weaves together antiforeigner and anti-northerner sentiments. The tacit goal of this divisive ethnic politics was to marginalize northerners, lumping them together with the immigrants from Burkina Faso, implying that they too are foreigners or at best Ivorians of immigrant ancestry. Under Bédié, some aspects of this ideology became enshrined in law. In 1994, he introduced a law requiring that a candidate for the presidency "must be Ivorian by birth. He must never have had another nationality. He must never have renounced the Ivorian nationality."[10] This law was clearly targeted at Ouattara who had worked abroad, notably for the International Monetary Fund (IMF), and had done so under a passport from Burkina Faso.[11]

At this time, reports began to emerge of northerners being stopped by police and gendarmerie officers who would hassle them and often take their identity cards on the pretense that they were fake. The idea of *Ivoirité* also filtered into other areas of Ivorian society, such as land tenure, and affected the cohesion of the army as well. Tensions unavoidably grew in the country. With Ouattara barred from contesting the 1995 and 2000 elections, northerners further associated his exclusion from the political battle with attempts to exclude them from citizenship. In December 1999, a successful coup overthrew Bédié and installed General Robert Guéï, a former chief of army staff, as head of state. It was the country's first coup, and a major illustration of the growing political instability and fractures within the armed forces. After promising to "clean the house" and not pretend to presidency after a short transitional period, Gueï decided that he could maneuver to stay in power.[12] He ran in presidential elections in October 2000, after a debate on constitutional reform that was dominated by the issues of conditions of origin attached to the eligibility to presidential function. The Supreme Court announced that many presidential candidates, including Bédié and Ouattara, once more would be barred from running. Ouattara was excluded on the grounds of "his doubtful nationality"; Bédié was barred for his inability to prove "his mental and physical fitness" to run.[13]

Only 37 percent of the electorate voted, and Guéï declared himself the winner, despite preliminary results favoring Gbagbo. After massive protests by Gbagbo's FPI supporters and a shift of allegiances by the security forces toward Gbagbo, Guéï fled the country and Gbagbo was declared president.[14] Gbagbo continued Bédié's policies of *ivoirité*, favoring largely southern FPI supporters at the expense of the largely northern, "mixed heritage" supporters of the RDR. It is in the context of these deep societal divisions and discrimination that, on 19 September 2002, a group of around 700 soldiers—most of whom had fled to Burkina Faso under Gueï and under Gbagbo's rule—attempted a coup d'état, attacking the cities of Abidjan, Bouaké, and Korhogo.[15] The coup failed, and degenerated into a war between government forces and breakaway army troops calling themselves the Mouvement Patriotique de Côte d'Ivoire (MPCI) and claiming to represent the disenfranchised north.

Over this early period, the regional and postcolonial dynamics that were to be observed throughout the peace process were formed and solidified. The important position of Côte d'Ivoire in the international politics of West Africa, as an economic power and source of regional migration, was established by the policies of President Félix Houphouët-Boigny. The presence of millions of Burkinabe, Malians, and other West Africans in Côte d'Ivoire, in addition to its porous borders with neighboring countries such as Liberia and Ghana, meant that Côte d'Ivoire's security was of great regional concern. This is a significant factor in ECOWAS's early efforts to resolve the crisis of 2002 and also in their lack of success.

In addition, the French perception of Côte d'Ivoire as a model ex-colony was reinforced during this period by the comparatively moderate political positions taken by Houphouët-Boigny, and by his personal Francophone leanings. This ensured a closer relationship than was enjoyed by many of the West African postindependence leaders who wanted to show more distance and autonomy from the former colonial power. This relationship accounts for the long-standing French military presence within Côte d'Ivoire, which also served to reduce the incentives of political leaders to strengthen the domestic security force. It was the French military presence, in tandem with the regional importance of Côte d'Ivoire, which contained the outbreak of civil war and dominated the early stages of the peace process. It was France's ability to intervene rapidly that afforded them relevance and momentum in the resulting peace talks.

The key issues that were to define the protracted conflict of the next ten years were also promulgated during this period. Specifically, the issues of nationality, citizenship, and political exclusion acted as the animating principle for much of the violence that was to come. The poisonously xenophobic nature of *ivoirité* that developed rapidly, from Houphouët-Boigny's promise of citizenship rights for all settled foreigners to the enshrining of exclusionary principles in the constitution during the year 2000, paralyzed the ability of the Ivorian political system to resolve disputes and function effectively. It is a fitting reflection on the paralyzed state of Ivorian politics during the period that it is the same candidate who was disbarred in 2000, at the start of the crisis, whose eventual election in 2010 and subsequent installment marks the end of the period and this chapter's coverage of the Ivorian crisis.

Setting the Stage for Multiple Interventions in the Peace Process: Evolution of Roles among France, ECOWAS, AU, and the UN in 2002–2004

Initial Military and Diplomatic Responses to the Outbreak of Conflict in September 2002

Given the importance of Côte d'Ivoire to both the region and its former colonial power, it is unsurprising that the process of conflict resolution became "regionalized" and internationalized so quickly. France was swift to take action, sending in military reinforcements after the failed attack of 19 September 2002 by rebels on Abidjan in the absence of President Gbagbo, who was in Italy. Just three days after the attempted coup, the French began the deployment of *Operation Licorne*, a military operation initially and ostensibly concerned with the protection of the large French community living in the country as well as other Western foreigners. Between 25 and 29 September, French forces evacuated foreigners who were based in Bouaké and Korhogo in the northern half of the territory where MPCI rebels had retreated after failing to take Abidjan.[16] French forces then established themselves in Yamoussoukro and became a de facto buffer between north-based rebels and south-based government forces.[17] By creating a line of demarcation, France attracted accusations of partiality from both sides, with the rebels arguing that the deployment of French troops was preventing them from moving southward to launch a new attack on Abidjan while government forces accused France of preventing them from moving northward to recapture Bouaké from the rebels.

France's military posture clearly froze the positions of the armed protagonists on the ground, who were not able to make any immediate significant military progress. President Gbagbo, who had returned swiftly to Abidjan to lead the resistance against the rebellion, expected a different military response from the former colonial power that had been so close to previous Ivorian governments and had a defense agreement with the Ivorian state in the case of aggression. Gbagbo insisted on the foreign backing of the September 2002 rebellion, pointing to Burkina Faso (under President Blaise Compaoré)[18] and Liberia (under President Charles Taylor).[19] Gbagbo's regime expected direct military support from France to defeat the assailants, not a neutral French deployment to halt hostilities or timid military support limited to logistical assistance to Ivorian forces. The first anti-French demonstrations mounted by radical pro-Gbagbo youths—the "young patriots"—started a few days after these events. The demonstrations were a way to put pressure on French decision makers in favor of the ruling government.[20]

While the decisions on the military front were made exclusively by Paris, the French government immediately encouraged the search for an African political solution to the armed conflict. The regional organization, ECOWAS, which had been active in conflict resolution efforts throughout the 1990s (particularly in Liberia, Sierra Leone, and Guinea-Bissau), was the natural candidate to take the lead on Côte d'Ivoire.[21] President Abdoulaye Wade of Senegal was the chairperson of ECOWAS in September 2002 and his minister for foreign affairs was tasked with early discussions with the Ivorian rebels in their stronghold of Bouake. ECOWAS's first meeting on the crisis was organized in Accra (Ghana) on 29 September (first Accra Agreement), leading to the formation of a high-level contact group composed of the heads of states of Ghana, Guinea Bissau, Mali, Niger, Nigeria, and Togo.[22]

The ECOWAS meeting was attended by eleven heads of states out of fifteen member states, and also by a number of other distinguished observers: President Thabo Mbeki of South Africa, who was the chairperson of the AU, Amara Essy, the interim president of the AU Commission,[23] and Ahmedou Ould Abdallah, the Special Representative of the UN Secretary-General (SRSG) for West Africa. While the decisions were made by ECOWAS heads of state, the statement of Accra stressed the "firm commitment and the support of the Africa Union to Côte d'Ivoire and to ECOWAS in its efforts to defend and protect democracy, constitutional governance, respect of human rights and the rule of law."[24] It was decided during the statements that the special representative of the AU chairperson would be a member of the mediation committee and that the AU would work with ECOWAS in the peace initiatives more generally.[25]

On 17 October 2002, the rebel group MPCI unilaterally signed a ceasefire agreement under which French forces were to enforce the cessation of hostilities until they could be relieved by ECOWAS troops. The Ivorian government later also accepted the principle of the cessation of hostilities through a declaration by President Gbagbo. President Mbeki and a newly appointed special envoy of the AU Commission[26] attended a meeting of the Contact Group in Abidjan on 23 October 2002. The summit decided to appoint President Gnassingbé Eyadema of Togo as coordinator of mediation activities, and determined that ECOWAS had to deploy a "Monitoring Group" quickly—a military mission—tasked with controlling the cessation of hostilities and maintaining the peaceful climate necessary for pursuing dialogue between the rebels and the government.[27] On 29 October, a meeting of the AU in Addis Ababa approved the ECOWAS decision to deploy a Monitoring Group; encouraged by the parties to cooperate with President Gnassingbé Eyadema, the chairperson of the AU and the AU special envoy thanked the French government for accepting to deploy its force on the ceasefire line in the meantime.[28]

Negotiations between the parties started on 24 October in Lomé (Togo) and were conducted by President Eyadema, assisted by the executive secretary of ECOWAS, the special envoy of the AU, and the SRSG for West Africa. The mediation generated a draft of a comprehensive peace agreement, including chapters on preservation of peace, political issues, military and security issues, humanitarian and human rights issues, socioeconomic issues, and implementation of the peace agreement. Negotiations continued in November in Lomé even as the security situation in Côte d'Ivoire was deteriorating, particularly in Abidjan and in the western region bordering Liberia. The Lomé talks led to rapid agreement on military issues but stalled on the political agenda of the rebel groups, who were insisting on the removal of President Gbagbo, a constitutional review and the holding of fresh elections.[29] It was clear from developments on the ground that both sides were more concerned with consolidating their military forces and looking for regional and international allies than negotiating a way to end the violence in good faith.

ECOWAS efforts on the military front continued toward the deployment of a regional force with a meeting of the Defense and Security Commission in Abidjan on 25 October, a meeting of the Mediation and Security Council the following day, a meeting of the army chiefs of staff of the countries contributing to the ECOWAS Force on 6 and 7 November in Abuja (Nigeria), and a meeting on the coordination of international financial and material contributions to the Force held in Paris on 14 November.[30] The ECOWAS force was expected to be composed of 1,264 military personnel, coming from Benin, Ghana, Niger, Senegal, and Togo. The regional organization expressed a financial need of US$18.5 million for the deployment and functioning of the force for an initial period of six months and planned the arrival of at least 1,000 troops by 23 November 2002.[31] The limitation of ECOWAS's planning capabilities and the lack of logistical assets resulted in extreme dependency on Western donors for communication equipment as well as transportation of troops. This severely affected the announced plans of ECOWAS. A deadline of 31 December 2002 for the deployment of the Force was announced during an ECOWAS summit on 18 December in Dakar (Senegal), a few weeks after two new rebel groups had plunged the west of the country into insecurity and chaos.[32] The first troops of the Force would finally deploy in Côte d'Ivoire in April 2003, eight months after the outbreak of the armed conflict. It meant that French Licorne Force was the sole external military force on the ground trying to prevent direct confrontation between various rebel groups and governmental forces assisted by mercenaries and newly formed militias.

The attendance of only three heads of state at the 18 December 2002 ECOWAS summit was a clear indication of the disappearing momentum in the diplomatic efforts of the regional body.[33] While the summit recognized the efforts made by President Eyadema of Togo who had concluded his talks a few days before, and received a promise by President Gbagbo to propose a global peace plan soon, it was actually a turning point in the transfer of primary responsibility for conflict management to the UN. The final declaration of the summit called on the AU, the UN, and the UN Secretary-General to get involved in the resolution of the crisis; it also requested that the Chairman of ECOWAS seize the Security Council so that it could provide support to ECOWAS efforts, and asked France and African countries who were members of the Security Council to ensure that the Council organized, as soon as possible, a meeting on the situation in Côte d'Ivoire.[34] The call by ECOWAS for direct involvement of the Security Council was strongly encouraged by France.[35] By January 2003, France, with the tacit agreement of a divided and weak ECOWAS and a silent AU, had paved the way for a deeper engagement of the UN after the conclusion of a decisive round of peace talks in Linas-Marcoussis (France).

The January 2003 LMA: French Leadership and Monitoring Roles for Regional Organizations and the UN

Five days after the 18 December meeting, which seemed to have reinforced Gbagbo's position, the rebel leader Guillaume Soro had called upon France and the UN to lead negotiations, claiming that the rebels no longer had faith in African efforts to broker peace.[36] France, through the Minister of Foreign Affairs Dominique de Villepin, started discreet talks with various parties with the objective of preparing a grand meeting on the French soil in January 2003. Despite the ambivalent position of President Gbagbo and the declared hostility of most of his supporters in Abidjan to perceived French recognition of the rebel group as a legitimate interlocutor of the international community, French diplomats managed to ensure the participation of all significant political parties and rebel groups in the Linas-Marcoussis peace talks (15–23 January 2003).[37]

The round table was chaired by the Chairman of the French Constitutional Council, Pierre Mazeaud—a close friend of President Jacques Chirac—assisted by Judge Keba Mbaye (Senegal) and a former prime minister of Côte d'Ivoire, Seydou Diarra, as well as the special envoy from the African Union Commission, the executive secretary of ECOWAS, and the SRSG for West Africa,[38] acting as facilitators. It was thus a French-driven initiative with inputs from regional organizations and the UN. However, the shift from ECOWAS to France and gradually to the UN in planning the successful resolution of the Ivorian crisis was clear. The inter-Ivorian talks facilitated by the international community resulted in the signing of the LMA on 23 January 2003 by all Ivorian political forces, including President Gbagbo's party and three rebel groups. The Agreement included the creation of a government of national reconciliation, to be headed by a nonpartisan, consensual prime minister appointed by President Gbagbo, who was expected to delegate substantial powers to the latter, until the end of the presidential term and the holding of elections scheduled for 2005.

The Agreement defined the main tasks of the new government to be formed: prepare a timetable for credible and transparent national elections, restructure the defense and security forces, organize the regrouping and disarmament of all armed groups, and design and implement a number of reforms to resolve the issues that were identified by the participants as being at the core of instability and violence in the country, such as the question of citizenship, the status of foreign nationals, eligibility to run for the presidency of the country, incitement to hatred and xenophobia by certain media, and the land tenure regime. The LMA provided for the establishment of a monitoring committee to be based in Abidjan and composed of representatives of the UN, AU, ECOWAS, the European Commission, the International Organization of the Francophonie (OIF), the Bretton Woods financial institutions, the Group of Eight countries, the European Union (EU), a military representative of the troop-contributing countries, and France.[39] The committee was to be chaired by the UN, not ECOWAS or the AU, another indication of the shift in the distribution of roles within the international community.

The signature of the LMA was immediately followed by a meeting of the heads of state of concerned African countries and France on 25 and 26 January 2003 in Paris, to provide a wide endorsement of the Agreement by the international community. Ten African presidents attended the summit, including Gbagbo, Compaoré (Burkina Faso), Taylor (Liberia), Amadou Toumani Touré (Mali), Abdoulaye Wade (Senegal and ECOWAS chairperson), John Kufuor of Ghana (and next ECOWAS chairperson after Wade), as well as Thabo Mbeki (South Africa and chairperson of AU). UN Secretary-General Kofi Annan was also present and heavily involved in the discussions led by French president Jacques Chirac, host of the summit. President Gbagbo appointed in Paris the former prime minister, Seydou Diarra, to head the new government of national reconciliation and an understanding was reached on the distribution of cabinet posts among the Ivorian parties, under which the key portfolios of defense and the interior were controversially allocated to the rebel movements.[40]

The enthusiasm and hopes of international actors present in Paris contrasted sharply with the tense atmosphere in Abidjan, where supporters of Gbagbo expressed publicly and aggressively their strong opposition to the LMA and the power-sharing formula accompanying it. Youth leaders in Abidjan carried out violent anti-French demonstrations in protest. President Gbagbo back in the country also expressed publicly his reservations about the provisions of LMA, calling them "mere proposals."[41] In the immediate weeks after the peace talks, there were numerous reasons to believe that the implementation of the LMA would be more than difficult and the political fight among President Gbagbo, the rebel groups under the leadership of Guillaume Soro, and the political rivals (former President Bédié and former Prime Minister Ouattara) was intense in anticipation of the planned October 2005 presidential elections.

Making the LMA Work

From Regional Mediation (ECOWAS) to International Peacekeeping (UN)

For months, the Government of National Reconciliation imagined by the LMA remained illusory. The appointed Prime Minister Seydou Diarra was prevented from starting to work by a series of massive, and often violent, demonstrations in Abidjan and other southern towns protesting against the allocation of the ministries of defense and the interior to the rebel movements.[42] French interests and installations were again targeted by pro-Gbagbo militants. While President Gbagbo confirmed the appointment of Diarra as prime minister and asked him to propose a cabinet in early February 2003, he made clear that he intended to retain all his constitutional prerogatives, and that he would not implement those provisions of the LMA that he considered to be incompatible with the country's Constitution. He also rejected the allocation of the defense and interior ministries to the rebel movements.

The ECOWAS Contact Group had to engage in fresh diplomatic efforts to find a way out of the immediate impasse. Presidents Eyadema of Togo, Kufuor from Ghana, Obasanjo from Nigeria, the Interim Chairman of the Commission of the AU, Amara Essy, and the Vice-President of South Africa, Jacob Zuma, met with President Gbagbo in Yamoussoukro on 10 February 2003 and it was only then, as a result of that meeting, that Seydou Diarra was installed as prime minister. It would take another ECOWAS high-level meeting in Accra on 6–8 March, to which all signatories of the LMA were invited, to make progress in the formation of the wider government.[43] ECOWAS Chairman, President Kufuor, led the discussions, which were also facilitated by the head of the freshly created monitoring committee of the LMA representing the UN, the executive secretary of ECOWAS, the special representative of the OIF, and the new special representative of the AU.[44] The attendance of the Accra II summit showed again the high level of regional, continental, and international shared commitment to resolving the crisis, but also the potential drawbacks of having so many external mediators or facilitators.

On the military front, ECOWAS continued to deploy its troops on the ground in the first quarter of 2003 with the crucial logistical support of the French army, both forces having received international legitimacy from the Security Council, which, acting under Chapter VII of the UN Charter, passed Resolution 1464 on Côte d'Ivoire on 4 February 2003. Under the Council resolution, ECOWAS and French forces were mandated to monitor the ceasefire and support the implementation of security aspects of the LMA. After the welcomed signature of a complete ceasefire by the Ivorian armed forces and the rebel groups on the entire territory of Côte d'Ivoire on 3 May 2003, the Council passed the Resolution 1479 that established the UN mission in Côte d'Ivoire (MINUCI), a political mission supported by a small team of military liaison officers. The SRSG, head of MINUCI, and chair of the monitoring committee of LMA, Albert Tévoédjrè, became the primary interlocutor of Ivorian parties while the key military presence remained that of the French Licorne Force, deployed in the most tense and volatile areas in the west and southwest.

At the same time, given the level of hostility demonstrated by the youths mobilized for the defense of Gbagbo's regime, France was keen on adopting a low profile and transferring the mediation work to ECOWAS and the UN. As a permanent member of the Security Council, France was working in New York to ensure that political and material resources were allocated to the UN mission in Côte d'Ivoire so that the burden would be shared by the wider international community. In August 2003, UNSC Resolution 1498 renewed ECOWAS and French forces' authorization for six months. On 13 November 2003, Resolution 1514 extended MINUCI mandate until 4 February 2004. On 24 November, a delegation from ECOWAS led by the Foreign Minister of Ghana went to UN headquarters and conveyed an appeal to the Security Council to consider strengthening the ECOWAS Mission in Côte d'Ivoire (ECOMICI) and transforming them into a UN peacekeeping force.[45] The initiative was a clear recognition by the regional organization of its incapacity to sustain a fully fledged and autonomous peacekeeping force in a large country such as Côte d'Ivoire where the proliferation of armed militias and rearming of both governmental and rebel forces were not pointing to a quick resolution of the conflict.

The Security Council adopted Resolution 1528 on 27 February 2004, establishing the United Nations Operation in Côte d'Ivoire (UNOCI) for an initial period of twelve months, from 4 April 2004. The Council requested the Secretary-General to transfer authority from MINUCI and ECOWAS forces to UNOCI on that date. The mandate of the initial 6,420-strong force, in coordination with the French forces, included observing and monitoring the implementation of the comprehensive ceasefire agreement of 3 May 2003 and movements of armed groups; assistance in disarmament, demobilization, reintegration, repatriation, and resettlement; protection of UN personnel, institutions, and civilians; support for humanitarian assistance, implementation of the peace process; and assistance in the field of human rights, public information, and law and order.[46] French Licorne Forces were to remain as an independent operation authorized by the Council, under the authority of Paris, and expected to act in support of UNOCI upon request from the UN Secretary-General.

From April 2004, the Council continuously renewed UNOCI's mandate, adapting to the ongoing political and security developments in the country. The Security Council held dozens of meetings on the situation in Côte d'Ivoire and voted a long series of resolutions in three broad areas: resolutions on renewal, modification of UNOCI mandates, and strengthening of its military and police components; resolutions on sanctions and restrictive measures (individual sanctions, arms embargo, and ban of exports of rough diamonds); and resolutions on the transitional political arrangements and monitoring of the electoral process.[47] The establishment of UNOCI did not mean the full disengagement of ECOWAS countries on the peacekeeping side. The troops of ECOMICI who were already deployed in Côte d'Ivoire were re-hatted and became the first blue helmets of UNOCI in 2004. Troops and police officers from Benin, Ghana, Niger, Nigeria, Senegal, and Togo had continuously been part of the UN peacekeeping mission along with traditional troop contributors who came in later, such as Bangladesh, Pakistan, India, Jordan, and Morocco.

ECOWAS member countries thus played an important role in giving UNOCI most of its initial military strength. Being part of a UN peacekeeping force, with the associated material conditions, was an attractive option for ECOWAS states that were aware of the financial obstacles to a deployment of a regional force for a long period. The regional organization was simply incapable of maintaining a large enough force in a difficult context such as Côte d'Ivoire, particularly given that a number of member countries (Burkina Faso, Liberia, to a lesser extent Mali and Guinea) could not consider sending troops owing to their perceived sympathy toward Ivorian protagonists or their own internal instability. The status of impartiality associated with a UN operation could provide to the ECOWAS member states present on the ground a better protection against accusations of support to a party of the conflict.

Political and military developments throughout 2004 had significant and lasting consequences on the management of the crisis by the international community. Every aspect of the LMA was a matter of dispute between the three groups of actors: President Gbagbo's camp, FN rebel forces under Guillaume Soro, and the unarmed political opposition led by Alassane Ouattara and Henri Konan Bédié. President Gbagbo strived to keep power in the southern part of the territory while the FN were establishing bases for a durable military, political, economic, and financial organization in the northern half of the country. Both armed protagonists were shielded from each other by a "zone of confidence" monitored by the peacekeeping forces composed of UNOCI and the French Licorne Force. In March 2004, an attempt by the opposition parties to demonstrate in Abidjan and to denounce the non-implementation of the LMA by President Gbagbo was violently put down by the governmental forces and militias. These incidents resulted in 150 deaths, according to the UN.[48]

The government of national reconciliation was systematically paralyzed and the reality of power never shifted from the president to the prime minister as required by the LMA. ECOWAS sought to resolve the dispute once again, taking the initiative by inviting all signatories of the LMA to a meeting of heads of state in Accra on 29 and 30 July 2004. President Kufuor of Ghana and UN Secretary-General Kofi Annan jointly hosted the meeting, attended by eleven heads of state of ECOWAS and also by the presidents of South Africa and Gabon, as well as the president of the AU Commission and the executive secretary of ECOWAS. The summit led to a new agreement, the Accra III agreement, which included measures to address the key obstacles to the peace process, in particular, the criteria for eligibility to the presidency, legislative reforms concerning citizenship, and the Disarmament, Demobilization and Reintegration (DDR) program.

The hopes that were revived by the Accra III agreement would be short lived. By October 2004, tensions were once again high as no party took steps toward the full respect of commitments made before the international community. There was no disarmament on the side of the rebellion and no dismantling of any militia group on the side of Gbagbo. The early signs of a resumption of hostilities were confirmed on 4 November 2004 when President Gbagbo ordered a military operation on FN targets situated in their central and northern strongholds. This blatant violation of the ceasefire was accompanied by the mobilization of pro-Gbagbo youth militias in Abidjan, who attacked the offices of opposition parties and newspapers in an atmosphere of nationalist fervor.[49] The military offensive lasted for only two days, from 4 to 6 November, when a raid by an Ivorian fighter plane unexpectedly targeted an encampment of the French forces in Bouake, killing nine French soldiers and one American citizen and wounding thirty-eight additional French soldiers.

The French reaction, coming from political authorities in Paris, was both swift and decisive. The Licorne Force destroyed almost all of the Ivorian military air fleet in Yamoussoukro and Abidjan, fighter planes as well as helicopters, including those inside the presidential compound in Yamoussoukro. From 6 to 9 November 2004, the Ivorian conflict was transformed into a strange and bloody confrontation between the Ivorian military and youth groups on one side and French forces who were part of a peacekeeping mission on the other.[50]

This quasi-war between France and its former colony claimed dozens of civilian lives and further complicated the international management of the crisis. While the condemnation of the violation of the ceasefire by government forces was shared by ECOWAS, the AU, and the UN, the extent of the unilateral French military retaliation was also met with skepticism and criticism by a number of African personalities. During a quickly organized visit on 11 November by South African President Thabo Mbeki, appointed as an emergency AU mediator, and also endorsed by ECOWAS during a meeting in Abuja (Nigeria), President Gbagbo showed the wreckage of the Ivorian planes destroyed by the French army to underline his point that the conflict was primarily a battle for the independence of Côte d'Ivoire in face of French domination. President Mbeki, a powerful voice of the AU and the champion of the principle of "African solutions to Africa problems," was sensitive to this nationalist line of reasoning proposed by Gbagbo.

Mbeki had been present at several of the earlier ECOWAS meetings, including the initial meeting ten days after the conflict began in September 2002 and the summit in Paris that endorsed the LMA; so his involvement was not without prior interest or knowledge. However, this period, beginning with his initial attempt to save the peace process in November 2004, marked a sea change vis-à-vis the prior France–ECOWAS-led attempts to resolve the crisis. The dominant actors now became the AU, through South African diplomacy, and the UNSC, which passed Resolution 1572 (15 November 2004) imposing an embargo on arms exports to Côte d'Ivoire and creating a regime of individual sanctions (travel bans and asset freezes) on those who were identified as spoilers of the peace process.[51] Essentially, after the repeated failures of ECOWAS leaders, African actors—now the AU supported by the South African heavyweight—retained the lead for mediation efforts to revive the previous peace agreements, while the UNSC, under French direction, maintained support for the peacekeeping mission and activated sanctions to put pressure on the Ivorian actors.

The Rise and Fall of the South African Mediation on Behalf of the AU

The imminent expiration of Gbagbo's presidential term in October 2005 created a new sense of vulnerability among his camp (who had until this point relied on constitutional validity as the cornerstone of their arguments and indeed their whole approach during the peace talks) and a renewed sense of urgency among a fatigued international community. The impetus coming from Mbeki's mediation, as well as Gbagbo's belief that Mbeki would favor his party more than previous peace-brokers, had led to early progress.[52] The first agreement negotiated by Mbeki, signed at Pretoria in April 2005, was (once again) widely hailed as a breakthrough by all those concerned. The five crucial Ivorian actors—the president, Laurent Gbagbo; opposition leaders Alassane Ouattara and Henri Konan Bédié; the leading rebel leader, Guillaume Soro; and the prime minister, Seydou Diarra—all professed their satisfaction with the outcome.[53] Crucially, Mbeki was able to persuade Gbagbo to accept the principle that all political parties signatory to the LMA would be eligible to stand a candidate in the forthcoming presidential election. In effect, this was a guarantee that Ouattara would be permitted to stand for election for the first time. Another essential outcome from the April 2005 meeting was the agreement by the Ivorian parties that the Mediator (Mbeki) will "request the United Nations on behalf of the Ivorian People to participate in the organization of general elections."[54]

This accord was subsequently endorsed by the UNSC, which offered logistical support, specifically broadening its mandate to include a responsibility to assist in the electoral preparations and creating the new position of the "UN high representative for elections in Côte d'Ivoire" as distinct from the SRSG who heads the peacekeeping mission.[55] Unfortunately, the trend of a seemingly perfect political settlement followed by persistent violence that was observed following the LMA was also to be witnessed in the aftermath of the Pretoria agreement. Violence continued, and a massacre in Duekoué (western region) of at least forty-one people[56] was instrumental in drawing international attention to the ongoing challenges of implementation. The signatories of the agreement were recalled to Pretoria on 28–29 July 2005 to review its implementation. They all reiterated their commitment to the peace process, to the holding of elections in October 2005—an aim that was by this point clearly outside the realms of possibility—and overcoming the various problems of implementation. They also agreed in principle on the legitimacy of using UN sanctions to target anyone viewed to be slowing the peace process. Just two months after the signature of the Pretoria II agreement, one of the parties—the FN rebellion of Soro—officially rejected Mbeki's mediation, claiming that the South African diplomacy was biased in favor of President Gbagbo.[57]

UN Secretary-General Kofi Annan, taking note of the continued tensions and the failure of disarmament, was the first to confirm in September 2005 that elections scheduled for October 2005 were to be postponed. As part of this realization and after a tense internal debate on what should happen after the end of the president's constitutional five-year term, Gbagbo's presidency was extended "for twelve months at most."[58] This was a move organized in three steps by the ECOWAS heads of State summit, which made recommendations on 30 September 2005 in Abuja; by the AU's Peace and Security Council, which made decisions on 6 October in Addis Ababa; and by the UNSC, which voted a new resolution (Resolution 1633) on 21 October 2005. The extension was coupled with a vast array of threats concerning the negative consequences that would ensue should the country not be capable of holding a presidential election in late 2006.

Unsurprisingly, Gbagbo's position before and after 30 October was to affirm that it was his constitutional right to remain president until the country was reunified and elections could be organized, irrespective of the international community's decisions. Gbagbo had also openly rejected ECOWAS's legitimacy as a decision maker on the Ivorian dossier before the 30 September extraordinary summit, stating that some ECOWAS member states were involved in the conflict and taking advantage of illegal economic exploitation of the FN-controlled territory.[59] He did not attend the meeting in Abuja and was clearly playing the AU, and more precisely South Africa, against ECOWAS. International actors accepted the extension of Gbagbo's mandate. They had little choice given the prevailing balance of forces in Abidjan. The only option left to them was to accept the status quo while working to divert political and financial resources toward the office of a new prime minister who was expected to act with autonomy from President Gbagbo and his adversaries, and create the conditions for credible elections as quickly as possible.[60]

In December 2005, the regional central bank governor Charles Konan Banny was chosen by African leaders, and with the visible support of French president, to replace Diarra as prime minister.[61] The installation of Banny was coupled with the creation of the International Working Group (IWG) as demanded by the AU Peace and Security Council and endorsed by SC Resolution 1633. Interestingly, while the AU decision on 6 October 2005 stipulated that the Working Group would be chaired by the Minister of Foreign Affairs of the country assuming the AU presidency (Nigeria at that time), the UNSC had decided that the Group would be cochaired by the SRSG.[62] The composition of a subgroup in charge of "daily mediation" gave a striking indication of the ever-heavy diplomatic machinery: the SRSG for Côte d'Ivoire, the UN high representative for elections in Côte d'Ivoire, the special envoy of South Africa still invested as AU mediator, the special representative of the ECOWAS secretary-general, and the special representative of the president of AU Commission. The Security Council also decided that this mediating group would be cochaired by the SRSG, and not just chaired by the special envoy of South Africa.

The change of prime minister, the reinforcement of his prerogatives by Resolution 1633 as well as the creation of an intrusive IWG expected to meet at ministerial level every month in Côte d'Ivoire were clearly aimed at limiting the power of President Gbagbo in the run up to the election that was, theoretically, to be held no later than October 2006. These attempts were met with widespread criticism from Gbagbo's supporters. Tension escalated rapidly after Banny's appointment. In January 2006, the IWG suggested dissolving the Ivorian parliament, whose mandate had expired. This drew an immediate response from Gbagbo's FPI, who called for the immediate departure of French and UN troops accused of carrying out a "constitutional coup."[63] The main UN base in Abidjan was threatened by hundreds of pro-Gbagbo youths[64] and there were several other attacks on UN personnel and vehicles. In response, the UN imposed targeted sanctions, which, though provided for by Resolution 1572 in November 2004, had not been used until that point.[65] While these actions appeared to have a mollifying effect and the following months passed in relative peace, limited progress on disarmament, identification of populations, and voter registration failed to create a climate in which elections could be held.

Throughout 2006, monthly meetings of the IWG marked by antagonistic positions, especially between the French and South African representatives, did not bring solutions to the intractable obstacles that lay on the road toward elections. Despite the support of the IWG for Prime Minister Banny, President Gbagbo retained de facto power. This was particularly so as to control the conditions under which citizen identification, leading to the very sensitive process of voter registration, would take place. UN Secretary-General Kofi Annan organized two meetings, one in Yamoussoukro on 5 July 2006 with Ivorian parties and another in New York on 20 September 2006, attended by AU and ECOWAS leaders, though without President Gbagbo, who declined the invitation.[66] They did not result in any breakthrough in the peace process.

It was clear that no election would take place in October 2006 as prescribed by Resolution 1633, and that new transitional arrangements had to be made to avoid a dangerous uncertainty from November 2006. ECOWAS heads of state met again for an extraordinary summit on 6 October 2006 and recommended a "new transition for a maximum of twelve months starting on 1 November 2006." Although they recommended that President Gbagbo should continue as the head of state, they wanted the prime minister to have "all necessary powers" to lead the peace process, including the "necessary authority on the defence and security forces."[67] On 16 October 2006, the AU Peace and Security Council met at the level of heads of state in Addis Ababa and validated the ECOWAS proposition of a new and "final" transition led by President Gbagbo and Prime Minister Banny whose authority to conduct the electoral and disarmament processes were to be reinforced.

Back to the Direct Local and Regional Actors of the Crisis: The Inter-Ivorian Dialogue and ECOWAS/Burkina Faso's Facilitation

The UNSC—at the end of the chain of regional organizations—adopted Resolution 1721 on 1 November 2006. As expected, the resolution extended the mandate of President Gbagbo for the second time and placed responsibility for managing the crisis in the hands of the prime minister, who "must have all the necessary powers, and all appropriate financial, material and human resources required, as well as full and unfettered authority," and who must be empowered to take "all necessary decisions, in all matters, within the Council of Ministers or the Council of government, by ordinances or decree-laws."[68] It further stated that the prime minister must also have the necessary authority over the defense and security forces.

Immediately after the vote of this resolution, President Gbagbo said he would not implement aspects of the resolution that violated the Ivorian constitution, which had never been put aside by various peace agreements. He promised to propose an alternative solution to the crisis. On 19 December 2006, he unveiled his plan to hold "direct dialogue" with the FN rebellion to negotiate disarmament and reunification of the country, with the facilitation of Blaise Compaoré, President of Burkina Faso, who was to assume chairmanship of ECOWAS from January 2007.[69] During a summit in Ouagadougou on 19 January 2007, the heads of state of ECOWAS expressed their support for the dialogue proposed by Gbagbo and entrusted Compaoré, the incoming chairperson, with facilitating the talks. The change in ECOWAS chairmanship was timely and provided a regional institutional legitimacy to Compaoré as facilitator of Ivorian talks, but Gbagbo chose him because of his well-established influence on the FN political and military leadership, and the role Burkina Faso has been playing in the Ivorian crisis for years.

Representatives of President Gbagbo and the FN began closed-door discussions in Ouagadougou on 5 February. The established tradition of discretion and even secrecy in Burkina Faso's diplomatic politics was maintained throughout the discussions. While the two parties backed by armed forces were undoubtedly the main actors, President Compaoré invited the other key political leaders, Alassane Ouattara and Henri Konan Bédié, in Ouagadougou to seek their views on key issues and also sought contributions from the SRSG and the UN high representative for elections. On 4 March, President Gbagbo and the secretary-general of the FN Soro signed the Ouagadougou Political Agreement (OPA).[70]

The agreement built upon previous peace agreements and Council Resolution 1721 in terms of what needed to be done, but validated a clearer power-sharing arrangement than that under the LMA. The leader of the rebellion, Soro, became the prime minister, serving under his long-time adversary, President Gbagbo. The illusion of a "neutral" and consensual prime minister being given all powers to conduct key processes was abandoned for the first time since 2003. The third key personality in the new framework was President Compaoré, the prime adversary of Gbagbo within ECOWAS whose country, Burkina Faso, had an exceptionally important stake in the evolution of Côte d'Ivoire. On 12 June 2007, Blaise Compaoré set foot on Ivorian soil for the first time in nearly seven years and was warmly welcomed by all Ivorian politicians, in stark contrast with the extremely tense period of 2002–2003.

The OPA was controversial as it bypassed the civilian opposition parties and its fundamental viability rested upon two men, who had previously been mortal enemies, being able to cooperate and implement reforms that had eluded the entire international community. That said, the agreement was received favorably, in part because of a lack of alternatives, and largely because it was the first time major actors in the peace process had independently sought peace. Strategically, it was also well received as Soro was clearly well placed to lead disarmament proceedings, assuming he was so inclined, and in return was to put in place voter registration for the much delayed elections—clearly a position of immense importance for the future of Ivorian politics. The gradual winding down of hostilities that had commenced at the time of the Pretoria agreements was reinforced by the retreat of both sides from their front-line positions near the buffer zone in December 2007.[71] The period that followed, from 2008 to 2010, was a time of both intense bureaucracy (ten UNSC resolutions were passed regarding Côte d'Ivoire in this period), and also of intense practicality. While the elections were again postponed from late 2008 to late 2010, the relative lack of violence ensured that the focus remained on voter registration and electoral preparations more generally.

This was a period of improvement, however small, with crucial advances being made in reunifying the country. The government was able to redeploy soldiers in the north for the first time since September 2002. There was also reasonable progress in voter registration. The downside of the focus that electoral efforts demanded was that it meant UNOCI was forced to spend less time monitoring abuses of human rights and seeking to create a climate of security and justice. There was very limited disarmament beyond those weapons disposed of during the smattering of public ceremonies held over this two-year period. The regional and international actors, as well as the Ivorian leaders, prioritized electoral preparations as in October 2010 the country would have gone ten years without a presidential election. There were also the same significant disincentives for former rebels and pro-Gbagbo militias to disarm, if not more, than there had been in 2005. The long peace process and the power-sharing arrangement between Gbagbo and Soro from 2007 had not reduced the risks of return to violence associated with the holding of the presidential election, the most open and unpredictable of Ivorian history given the participation of all important political leaders, Gbagbo, Ouattara, and Bédié.

Responding to the Violent Postelectoral Crisis: Regional and International Coordination, Collaboration, and Fractures in Crucial Times (November 2010–April 2011)

The Presidential Election

The stakes for 2010 presidential elections were high. For the Ivoirians, it was the culmination of a nearly two-decade-long battle for power and the succession to Houphouët-Boigny. For the international and regional communities, it was a chance to end a frustrating peace process and to start withdrawing from an expensive peacekeeping commitment.[72] Despite the lack of progress in some key elements of the OPA, the announcement of an agreement by the parties on a date for presidential elections was widely welcomed. UNOCI, which had an unusually broad mandate to certify all phases of the electoral process—including identification and registration of voters (completed in July 2009)—certified the final voter's list through the SRSG Choi Young-Jin on 24 September 2010 and the first round of elections was finally scheduled for 31 October.[73]

After a short, two-week campaign, first-round polls were held in what the SRSG characterized as a "generally peaceful and free atmosphere."[74] However, UNOCI did report some increase in militia activity in the lead-up to elections and international forces were forced to increase patrolling during the fragile electoral period.[75] On 6 November, the Constitutional Council announced final results that sent Gbagbo and Ouattara to a second round of elections, with 38 percent and 32 percent of the votes, respectively. Six days later, the SRSG certified these results. The second round of elections showed a marked increase in violent incidents between Ouattara and Gbagbo supporters, particularly during the one-week campaign period in late November. Gbagbo's militants used state media to disseminate xenophobic hate speech and the incumbent president declared a curfew the night before the elections.[76] Meanwhile, the Ouattara camp consolidated its base in the North and received the crucial endorsement of the other key nonarmed opposition leader, former President Bédié from the PDCI, who came third in the first round. Despite news of a united opposition, Gbagbo remained confident of victory. The diplomatic community, operating under the assumption that Gbagbo would only allow the country to go to the polls if he was certain of victory, prepared for few alternative scenarios and made few contingency plans.

Ouattara's victory in the second round took many by surprise. The polling on 28 November was relatively peaceful and monitored by 300 international elections observers, including those from the UN. Gbagbo's allies immediately complained about the transparency of elections in the North. The security situation quickly became tense and, as radical elements of the FPI mobilized, Mr. Ouattara and his supporters took refuge in the Golf Hotel in Abidjan under UN protection. Electoral Commission's President Youssouf Bakayoko announced the results on 2 December from behind UNOCI protection, also at the Golf Hotel. The following day, the Constitutional Council invalidated the commission's announcement by canceling around 600,000 votes from pro-Ouattara strongholds in the North and Centre and declaring Gbagbo the winner.[77] On 4 December, President Gbagbo was sworn in for another term by the president of the Constitutional Council, a close ally, in a strange atmosphere of preparations for violent confrontation with the pro-Ouattara side.

The International Community's Response: Diplomacy and Sanctions First

Initially, SRSG Choi hesitated to make a pronouncement on the elections, fearing that direct involvement at an early stage would forfeit UNOCI neutrality and leverage, as well as jeopardize the safety of international personnel. However, under significant diplomatic pressure, particularly from France, the United States, and Britain, he soon confirmed Ouattara as the winner of the presidential elections with 54.1 percent of the votes.[78] The certification process had included UNOCI staff deployment to various polling centers in order to monitor the process and collect sample results, as well as deployment to the regional tabulation centers and the collection, cross-checking, tabulation, and review of tally sheets for indications of fraud. The SRSG was thus able to determine the validity of the tally sheets and to review the likely impact of the disputed votes. UNOCI found that even of the disputed departments' tally sheets, very few lacked a Gbagbo representative's signature and even if all the contested votes were nullified on this basis, Ouattara would still have won the election.[79]

In early December 2010, all three organizations—UN, AU, and ECOWAS—appeared to be united in calling upon all stakeholders to respect the outcome of the election, as certified by the UN, and they expressed their readiness to isolate those who threatened the peace process, or committed serious violations of human rights and/or international humanitarian law.[80] On 2 December, the Security Council issued a press statement, welcoming the announcement of the provisional results by the Ivorian electoral commission.[81] Shortly afterward, the AU and ECOWAS delivered similar statements. The AU held an extraordinary session on 4 December, and welcomed efforts by ECOWAS and the UNSC, as well as the initiative of the chairperson of the AU Commission, to send former President Thabo Mbeki for emergency consultations in order to find a "legitimate and peaceful solution to the crisis."[82] ECOWAS, chaired by Nigeria, followed with an extraordinary meeting of heads of state on 7 December. They suspended Côte d'Ivoire from the organization under Article 45 of the organization's Supplementary Protocol on Democracy and Good Governance and, endorsing the results certified by the SRSG, they recognized Ouattara as President elect while calling upon President Gbagbo to step down.[83]

However, despite the parties' agreement on the UN role and the mandate provided by UNSC resolutions, the decision of the SRSG to certify the results of the elections and pronounce Alassane Ouattara the winner generated controversy. Within the Security Council, Russia argued vigorously against it as unwarranted interference in a national process, while South Africa and Brazil felt strongly that it was inappropriate for the United States, France, and the United Kingdom to pressure the SRSG to issue an announcement. Such opposition to the certification mandate, which some saw as a pretext for broader opposition to military action to force Gbagbo from power, grew stronger as the crisis wore on.

Meanwhile, Gbagbo continued to reject the results and reiterated his intention to stay in power during his meeting with AU-mandated President Mbeki. Attacks began, with the security forces setting up roadblocks and deploying heavy weapons to positions around the Golf Hotel, where Ouattara, Bédié, and other opposition leaders had sought refuge. Over the ensuing days, security forces sought to lock down pro-Ouattara neighborhoods, including Abobo, Adjamé, Koumassi, and Treichville. The UN increasingly became a target of pro-Gbagbo forces, particularly by militia and armed youths,[84] and Human Rights Watch and the International Commission of Inquiry documented evidence of summary executions and forced disappearances during this period.[85] By the end of the first week of January 2011, the UN reported some 210 deaths from related violence, predominantly committed against those perceived to be aligned with Ouattara, since mid-December.[86]

ECOWAS held a second meeting of heads of state on 24 December, after AU Commission Chair Jean Ping and ECOWAS Commission President Victor Gbeho failed once more to convince Gbagbo to step down and recognize Ouattara as the legitimate president, while imposing tough sanctions and threatening that military force would be employed in the event that other means were exhausted. This show of force and determination by the subregion, however, proved to be the beginning of the end of international consensus on the resolution of the crisis. Within days of the ECOWAS communiqué,[87] a number of ECOWAS members publicly distanced themselves from the threat of force, as they feared that a military intervention could jeopardize the safety of their citizens in Côte d'Ivoire. In addition, the ECOWAS threat to use force lacked credibility. The subsequent meeting of the Chiefs of Defense Staff, on 18–20 January, seemed to confirm the suspicion that an intervention by the region's standby force was not operationally feasible, and that an intervention by a surgical strike force to remove Gbagbo or a larger intervention to protect civilians from ethnic violence would require additional resources.[88]

With West Africa's largest military contributor, Nigeria, heading toward presidential elections of their own, the possibility of an intervention in neighboring Côte d'Ivoire was remote. Within the AU and Security Council, key members used the controversy over the threat to use force to mobilize additional actors to oppose the "West's" position on the departure of President Gbagbo. As the crisis intensified, and after some nine failed high-level or envoy visits to Abidjan between early December 2010 and late January 2011, the AU stepped up its engagement in the crisis and, for a period, occupied the political vacuum left by the diplomatically marginalized ECOWAS and a quiet UNSC faced with its own internal divisions.

The AU adopted a more conciliatory posture in trying to establish a negotiated resolution, including a possible power-sharing agreement led by Ouattara. This approach was driven by South Africa's President Jacob Zuma and backed by former President Mbeki, Gbagbo's old ally President José Eduardo dos Santos of Angola, and others in the region with a strong affinity for Gbagbo's anti-neo-colonialist rhetoric. The AU's subsequent selection of Kenya's Prime Minister Odinga, himself a member of a power-sharing government in Kenya, as the AU's representative on two trips to Abidjan in January sent a mixed message about the possibility of a power-sharing arrangement.

At the AU Summit held during 25–31 January 2011 in Addis Ababa, the establishment of a high-level panel, comprised of heads of state of Burkina Faso, Chad, Mauritania, South Africa, Tanzania, as well as the heads of both the AU Commission and ECOWAS Commission, tasked to review the elections and certification process, as opposed to a clear signal of support for ECOWAS' position, deepened divisions within the AU. The publication of the panel report was delayed several times, reinforcing the impression that the AU was buying time. On the UNSC, Russia and South Africa were particularly insistent on waiting for the AU panel report before taking any further action. Signs of divisions within and among AU, ECOWAS, and UNSC, resulting in an endless series of deferrals to one another, sent the message to President Gbagbo that he still had room to shop for support.

While the Council authorized an additional 2,000 troops on 19 January, and repeatedly extended the temporary redeployment of assets from UNMIL to UNOCI, the response of the Council to direct attacks on the UN mission was remarkably weak.

From 19 January until 3 March 2011, the Council remained silent, even while attacks on UN peacekeepers continued and reports of ethnic and sectarian-based violence worsened. The African voice was split on the Security Council. South Africa's open opposition to the clearly stated position of Nigeria, typically the lead on West African affairs, indicated an intensification of the competition between the two powers for influence on the continent. South Africa's deployment of a military vessel off the coast of Côte d'Ivoire was seen as a direct provocation of Nigeria, bringing the tension between the two governments to a head.[89]

The Choice of the Military Solution Validated by the International Community

More coercive steps appeared to weaken the regime, but not enough to fundamentally shift its strategic calculations or to affect the support of the security forces. In addition to suspension from both the AU and ECOWAS, individual travel bans and asset freezes were implemented by the United States and EU, as well as an embargo on cocoa and coffee exports declared by President-elect Ouattara. These measures were on top of existing UN sanctions that remained in effect.[90] The regime's access to financial resources was severely restricted as the World Bank announced a suspension of both loans and the disbursement of funds to the government, along with the African Development Bank, and a decision by the West African States Central Bank (BCEAO, French acronym) to give authority over transactions to Ouattara considered the legitimate president.[91] The implementation of this measure was undermined by BCEAO head and Gbagbo ally, Philippe-Henry Dacoury-Tabley, and Gbagbo subsequently seized BCEAO assets in the country.[92] In February, Gbagbo nationalized four major international banks, all of whom had already been forced to suspend operations in the country, and he also nationalized the cocoa market in an attempt to circumvent US and EU embargos.[93] The threat of the International Criminal Court (ICC) referral was also real for Gbagbo. While Côte d'Ivoire has not acceded to the Rome Statute, a declaration by the government in 2003 invited ICC jurisdiction and the ICC Prosecutor's office issued a statement on 2 December 2011 declaring that it was under this authority that it was monitoring the situation in the country.[94]

Through February and March, violent confrontations between Ouattara supporters and security forces escalated.[95] The pro-Gbagbo presidential guard, as well as special units of the army, police, and gendarmerie, used heavy weapons, including mortars, and displaced thousands of civilians in Abidjan suburbs. Direct fighting between security forces and former rebel forces was reported on 24 February in Tiapleu, near the Liberian border.[96] Attacks on civilians, particularly in Abidjan and the West, increased dramatically in the first half of March. For Ouattara, it became clear that reconciliation in the divided country would only grow more difficult as this level of conflict and stalemate continued, and that a military option was therefore the only solution. However, in order to implement such a strategy, he was dependent on the international community and his appointed prime minister and head of former rebels, Guillaume Soro. A military confrontation was not without substantial risks. These included the possibility of sparking intercommunal violence, and the likelihood that it would increase Ouattara's dependency on former rebels who had been implicated in abuses (in March 2011, the rebels were renamed as the Republican Forces of Côte d'Ivoire [FRCI]).

The international community soon began to unify around such a military option, particularly after the AU high-level panel visited Côte d'Ivoire and President Zuma realized that the case presented by the Constitutional Council was not credible.[97] While the AU panel did call for the appointment of a new High Representative to facilitate talks again to end the crisis, the report published on 10 March affirmed Ouattara as the legitimate president and did not request a recount of votes, as some had suspected it might.[98] After the AU PSC endorsed the report of the high-level panel on 10 March, the UNSC announced its determination to impose targeted sanctions, on 21 March. The request by ECOWAS to the UNSC to enhance UNOCI's mandate and adopt more stringent sanctions on 24 March made the position of the subregion clear, namely, that the AU had reached its capacity to resolve the crisis, thus putting the responsibility squarely back on the UNSC to act.[99] By 25 March, France and Nigeria had jointly circulated a draft resolution. This joint cooperation proved critical, particularly in light of South African, Chinese, and Russian positions.

As negotiations on the draft resolution proceeded in the Council, the use of heavy weapons by Gbagbo's camp against civilians in densely populated urban areas was becoming an increasing focus of the UN Mission and the UNSC. The limitations of UNOCI in effectively protecting civilians were clear, as peacekeepers were focused on evacuating internationals, protecting the Golf Hotel where Ouattara, Soro, and their allies were isolated, and UN and force protection activities. However, since the UNOCI resolutions already contained strong language concerning the protection of civilians (PoC) under Chapter VII, there were few opportunities to enhance the mission's mandate. Given Russian, Chinese, and South African opposition, there was no significant consideration of language that would have explicitly called for UNOCI to participate in operations to remove President Gbagbo. Instead, the P3 focused on "heavy weapons" and were explicit in authorizing UNOCI to act *preventively* to ensure PoC from heavy weapons.[100]

UNOCI coordinated its operations with the French mission, Licorne, as requested by the UNSG in a letter to President Sarkozy. It was politically important for both the French government and President Ouattara that the French intervention be perceived as legitimately as possible. A stand-alone French intervention, even at the request of Ouattara, would have likely provoked greater negative reactions within the country and the region. Parallel to the negotiations of the UNSC, the UN Secretariat had negotiated the redeployment of Ukrainian attack helicopters to UNOCI to participate in a likely attack on heavy weapons used by the Gbagbo regime in Abidjan. The Secretariat determined that a preemptive strike on heavy weapons, already used against civilians during previous attacks, was within its PoC mandate and that there was therefore no requirement to revise the existing rules of engagement for peacekeepers.

On 4 April, simultaneous attacks were launched by UN and French helicopters on heavy weapon installations at Gbagbo's presidential palace and at least five other installations in Abidjan.[101] The heavy weapon capacity of Gbagbo was neutralized and the UN announced a successful operation. This evidently was a contributing factor to the ultimate success of the FRCI (pro-Ouattara) offensive in Abidjan. The former rebel forces were positioned on the outskirts of Abidjan just days before the UN/French attack on Gbagbo's residence but they had faced significant resistance gaining access to the city. They finally forcibly removed Gbagbo from his fortified bunker at the presidential residence defended by some 200 elite loyal troops. The extent of foreign support in this final phase of the operation remains unclear, but strong public emphasis was placed on the Ivorian face of the capture and transfer of President Gbagbo and his wife Simone to the Golf Hotel.

Once President Ouattara asserted his authority in the country, the international community was quick to lift most sanctions and facilitate access to the resources of the state. The UN and others also called for the accountability of war crimes, crimes against humanity, and other serious human rights violations committed by both sides in the postelection crisis and urged President Ouattara and his government to pursue reconciliation in the country. French and UN forces quickly began to plan their reconfiguration in the country to support the new government, including a significant downsizing of French Licorne.

Lessons Learned from the Management of the Postelectoral Crisis

The last phase of the international intervention not only reveals some interesting partnerships and trends in the area of coordination and cooperation between the UN and regional organizations, but also some overall gaps in the international preparedness to deal with electoral violence. It is clear that conditions for presidential elections were far from ideal, even though they had been delayed several times in order to ensure adequate preparation. UNSC and regional actors insisted upon presidential elections as the only way out of the conflict, but these elections came at the end of a long process characterized by failures of commitment from the Ivorian parties as well as international political neglect of critical reconciliation, reunification, and disarmament issues. Not enough political work had been done to make sure that electoral results would be acceptable by both parties, and little scenario contingency planning was made in this respect. After nine years of civil war, and a political battle that started after Houphouët-Boigny's death in 1993, it could have been better anticipated that neither Gbagbo nor Ouattara, whose militants clashed bloodily on many occasions since the 2000 elections, were prepared to lose these elections.

When the postelectoral crisis erupted, UNOCI was not in a position to stop the violence or even fulfill its robust mandate of PoC. For months, the UN mission consistently failed to deter attacks on civilians, particularly by pro-Gbagbo forces. UNOCI patrols were turned back from lightly armed roadblocks erected by youth groups and irregular forces. ECOWAS was also clearly ill prepared to play a military role, as described earlier, and relied on the French to carry out the final push. The West African organization was in a similar situation in the early stages of the armed conflict back to the September 2002–April 2004 period. As described in the sections earlier, ECOWAS had to rely on the French logistical support to deploy a limited number of troops and could not sustain a peacekeeping force independently from French and the UN. Despite the progress made between 2002 and 2011 in building a regional peacekeeping force as part of the AU Stand-By Force planned by the continental security architecture, ECOWAS—still the most advanced regional organization in this regard—was not capable of projecting a military force when Côte d'Ivoire was on the edge of an unprecedented chaos threatening the entire region.

Before the critical runoff on 28 November 2010, the diplomatic action of ECOWAS was largely delegated to the Facilitator of the Ouagadougou Agreement, President Blaise Compaoré. He did try an ultimate mission to defuse the tensions just the day before the second round, by calling President Gbagbo to renounce his decision to declare a curfew.[102] When it appeared that Gbagbo had decided to refuse defeat, Compaoré and ECOWAS aligned their positions on the verdict of the UN SRSG certification recognizing Ouattara as the winner. The working relationship that had been established between President Compaoré as Facilitator of the OPA and the UN SRSG throughout the last stages of the electoral process played a significant role in ensuring ECOWAS and UN alignments after the vote.[103] Despite the controversy on the interpretation of the certification role reflected in the debates within the Security Council, ECOWAS's full support of the UN certification mandate, and the way it has been exercised by the SRSG, was critical to building a dominant if not universal position on the name of the winner of the election and the need to enforce the result.

Clearly, the divisions within the AU, and the difference of views between Nigeria and South Africa delayed the resolution of the crisis for at least two months. While ECOWAS and the UN had a collaborative interaction in the quest for a solution to the postelectoral crisis, AU hesitations were seen very negatively by ECOWAS leaders. The tensions between the West African influential countries on the Ivorian dossier (led by Nigeria, Burkina Faso, and Senegal) and the Southern Africa group (led by South Africa and Angola) were visible during the January 2011 AU summit in Addis Ababa. ECOWAS leaders clearly expressed their frustrations about seeing African countries from other regional organizations questioning their line on a West African crisis, giving the example of Zimbabwe and Madagascar crises—the resolution of which had always been left to the Southern African Development Community (SADC) and its great power, South Africa. As described earlier, South Africa had been heavily involved in the resolution of the Ivorian conflict, particularly in 2005–2006, and former President Mbeki had progressively been perceived as too sympathetic to Gbagbo's line, possibly also in reaction to an excessive anti-Gbagbo's discourse by France in particular.[104]

During the postelectoral crisis, the French first expressed a deep ambivalence to political and military engagement, and pushed the West African region and the UN to the forefront of responding to the crisis without committing to undertake the necessary actions. However, in the end, the presence of equipped French forces in the country proved to be essential to the UN's ultimate operational success and allowed the UNSC to confidently call upon the UN mission to neutralize heavy weapons. The presence of French forces was also very convenient for ECOWAS, which had threatened military intervention without having the capacity and the necessary unity within the organization to lead a complicated and dangerous military operation against Gbagbo's forces in Abidjan.

Even the UN mission alone was in a fragile position in the last phase of the postelectoral conflict. As in many other UN peacekeeping missions, the UN's capacities came up far short of the ambitious mandate originally given by the UNSC. Whether the decision to target heavy weapons defending Gbagbo with UN attack helicopters alongside French forces represented a major leap in UN peacekeeping is less controversial. Despite the protestations of Russia, China, and South Africa, the UN's steps were not far beyond previous operations, such as those in the Democratic Republic of the Congo (DRC) in 2003 and 2008. Like the operation in Côte d'Ivoire, Artemis in the DRC in 2003 required the engagement of a non-UN, international force and the UN engaged attack helicopters to stop a rebel advance outside of Goma in 2008. With such robust PoC mandates, the concept of impartiality in peacekeeping has evolved substantially, but with very little clear operational guidance, especially from member states.

Conclusion

Ivorian armed conflict ended in April 2011 as a result of recourse to a military solution conducted by those actors who had had boots on the ground for many years (namely the French, UN, and Ivorian rebel forces, who had never disarmed) and finally backed the civilian political leader chosen by the majority of the voters in an internationally certified election. This final intervention gave prime roles to the UN and France, a former colonial power, and no visible part to key regional and subregional players, the AU and ECOWAS. In this context, the case of Côte d'Ivoire was an exception to the current pattern of the Security Council deferring responsibility for and leadership of crisis management in Africa to the AU and regional organizations such as ECOWAS. The mantra of "African solutions to African problems" has bolstered the AU's supremacy in responding to conflicts in the continent. In the case of Côte d'Ivoire, however, the AU was only partially able to apply that supremacy for several reasons: There was a marked interest by France, a permanent member of the Security Council; ECOWAS was limited in its capacity to intervene militarily, while also fearing it would jeopardize the safety of West African nationals living on Côte d'Ivoire's territory; and, the AU failed to get any traction from Gbagbo on a diplomatic solution.

Despite the inability of ECOWAS and the AU to resolve the crisis, a legitimate intervention could not have been conducted without their cooperation; the strong support of ECOWAS, and a degree of acceptance by all members of the AU, who had sent a high level panel to confirm the results of the elections. Security Council Resolution 1975, which authorized the use of force to neutralize heavy weapons, was cosponsored by France and Nigeria, and adopted at the request of ECOWAS. The process of reaching consensus on the Council was anything but smooth. It took four months to get consensus and the response was initially much more chaotic and much less coordinated than it appeared, exposing deep internal divisions both within the Security Council and between the AU and ECOWAS. While both the AU and ECOWAS initially stood firmly by the position that Ouattara had won the elections and Gbagbo had to step down, differences of vision and competition between Nigeria and South Africa prevented consensus within the AU on key diplomatic efforts as well as drove wedges between the two African members within the Security Council.

Through the years, the international strategy failed to address the fundamental cause of the conflict—a fight to the death for the capture of state power. While both sides agreed to a ceasefire and various political agreements from 2003, each remained in control of approximately half of the country and armed to the teeth. Fundamentally, the conflict was a battle between a few individuals for the succession to Houphouët-Boigny, in a context of unprecedented economic and social crisis favoring the explosive political manipulation of regionalism, ethnicity, and national identity in a country forged by old and recent waves of migrations. From late September 2002, the international strategy succeeded only in freezing the frontline and containing violence until the elections.

By the time of elections in October and November 2010, only the identification and registration of all voters had been completed; the other necessary conditions for peaceful elections, including the reunification of the country and disarmament, were not achieved; UN sanctions against spoilers and the arms embargo were only partially enforced, and no serious measures were taken to curb impunity. De facto, the expectation of a final winner-take-all victory through elections became a disincentive to disarmament. Indeed, neither party to the conflict was prepared to lose the elections, or to lose the war.

Notes

*The authors would like to recognize the invaluable research and drafting assistance of Heather Sonner, senior analyst at International Crisis Group, as well as of Maja Bovcon, and Cormac Sullivan in the preparation of this chapter.

1. UNSC resolution 1975 (2011) permitted the use of force in order to neutralize "heavy weapons," and called up Laurent Gbagbo to stand down from the presidency.
2. F. Akindès, *The Roots of the Military Political Crises in Côte d'Ivoire* (Uppsala, Sweden: Nordic Africa Institute, 2004).
3. M. McGovern, *Making War in Cote d'Ivoire* (Chicago, IL: University of Chicago Press, 2010).
4. For further treatment of the interconnectivity of economic decline, land rights, and the mistreatment of recent migrants in late 1980s' Côte d'Ivoire, see D. Chirot, "The Debacle in Côte d'Ivoire," *Journal of Democracy* 17:2 (2006): 63–77.
5. R. Banégas, "Côte d'Ivoire: Patriotism, Ethnonationalism and Other African Modes of Self-Writing," *African Affairs* 105:421 (2006): 535–552.
6. R. C. Crook, "Winning Coalitions and Ethno-Regional Politics: The Failure of the Opposition in the 1990 and 1995 Elections in Côte d'Ivoire," *African Affairs* 96:383 (1997): 215–242.
7. McGovern, *Making War in Cote d'Ivoire.*
8. A. B. Bah, "Democracy and Civil War: Citizenship and Peacemaking in Cote d'Ivoire," *African Affairs* 109:437 (2010): 597–615.
9. Chirot, "The Debacle in Côte d'Ivoire."
10. Ibid.
11. Bah, "Democracy and Civil War: Citizenship and Peacemaking in Cote d'Ivoire."
12. Akindès, *The Roots of the Military-Political Crises.*
13. Ibid.
14. After the immediate postelectoral fighting between the members of the presidential guard of General Guéï and the security forces and civilians who wanted him to accept his defeat and leave, there was a second phase of deadly clashes opposing Gbagbo's militants backed by some security forces and the partisans of Ouattara who demonstrated to demand the organization of a new presidential election.

15. Interior Minister Emile Boga Doudou was killed in the initial hours of the coup in circumstances that remain unclear. Later on, ex-President Guéï, his wife and military aides were also killed by unidentified members of the security forces.
16. Christian Bouquet, *Géopolitique de la Côte d'Ivoire* (Paris: Armand Colin, 2005).
17. Ibid.
18. Blaise Compaoré who was then captain became president of Burkina Faso in October 1987, after his predecessor Thomas Sankara was killed in a military coup. Compaoré had a good relationship with President Houphouët-Boigny, though he also provided support to Ivorian opposition leader Laurent Gbagbo before the latter came to power in October 2000. Relations between Compaoré and Gbagbo deteriorated rapidly probably in response to FPI's intended nationalist policies, which threatened vital interests of Burkina Faso migrants in Côte d'Ivoire and Burkina Faso's interests more generally.
19. Charles Taylor, who started an armed rebellion against Liberian President Samuel Doe in December 1989, was a key actor in the long civil war from 1990 to 1997, when he was elected president. He benefited from the support of Compaoré's regime in the early years of his rebellion.
20. International Crisis Group, *The War Is Not Yet Over* (Brussels: ICG Africa Report N°72, November 2003).
21. In 1999, the Heads of State and Government of ECOWAS adopted the Protocol relating to the Mechanism for Conflict Prevention, Management and Resolution, Peacekeeping and Security.
22. Report of the interim chairperson of the Commission of the African Union on the developments in the situation in Côte d'Ivoire, eighty-seventh ordinary session of the central organ of the mechanism for conflict prevention, management and resolution at ambassadorial level, 4 December 2002, Addis Ababa, Ethiopia. Hugo Sada, "Le conflit ivoirien: enjeux régionaux et maintien de la paix en Afrique," *Politique étrangère* 68:2 (2003): 321–334.
23. The transformation of the Organization of African Unity (OAU) into the AU was in its initial phase when the Ivorian conflict started. The decision to create the AU was made in 1999, the Constitutive Act was adopted in 2000, the decision to create the Peace and Security Council of the AU was made in 2001, and the AU was officially launched only in 2002.
24. Statement of the ECOWAS Extraordinary Summit on Côte d'Ivoire held in Accra, Ghana, 29 September 2002.
25. Report of the interim chairperson of the Commission of the African Union on the developments in the situation in Côte d'Ivoire, op. cit.
26. Former President of Sao Tome and Principe Miguel Trovoada was the special envoy appointed by Essy Amara.
27. Report of the interim chairperson of the Commission of the African Union on the developments in the situation in Côte d'Ivoire, op. cit.
28. Ibid.
29. Bouquet, *Géopolitique de la Côte d'Ivoire.*
30. Report of the interim chairperson of the Commission of the African Union on the developments in the situation in Côte d'Ivoire, op. cit.
31. International Crisis Group, *The War Is Not Yet Over.*
32. International Crisis Group, *Côte d'Ivoire: No Peace in Sight* (Dakar and Brussels: ICG Africa Report N°82, July 2004).
33. Laurent Gbagbo from Côte d'Ivoire, Blaise Compaoré of Burkina Faso, and Pedro Pires of Cape Verde joined the Senegalese president in Dakar.
34. Final statement of the extraordinary summit of the Heads of State and Government of the ECOWAS, 18 December 2002, Dakar. In the first three months after September 2002, the

involvement of the UN was limited to a presidential declaration of the Security Council on 31 October and the participation of the UN Secretary-General through his special representative for West Africa in the first ECOWAS summit in Accra and subsequent mediation efforts. The 31 October Security Council declaration had condemned the attempt against the democratically elected government of Côte d'Ivoire, affirmed its support to the mediation by the ECOWAS Contact Group, and encouraged the international community to provide assistance for the deployment of the ECOWAS Force. See press statement on Côte d'Ivoire by President of Security Council, UNSC/7558, 31 October 2002.

35. Sada, "Le conflit ivoirien: enjeux régionaux et maintien de la paix en Afrique."
36. International Crisis Group, *Côte d'Ivoire: No Peace in Sight.*
37. Ibid.
38. Respectively, Miguel Trovoada, Mohamed Ibn Chambas, and Ahmedou Ould Abdallah.
39. Background of the United Nations Mission in Côte d'Ivoire (MINUCI) is available at:http://www.un.org/en/peacekeeping/missions/past/minuci/background.html
40. The full terms and list of attendance of the LMA can be found here: http://www.issafrica.org/AF/profiles/cotedivoire/linasmar.pdf.
41. See, for example: http://reliefweb.int/node/117915.
42. International Crisis Group, *Côte d'Ivoire: The War Is Not Yet Over*, op. cit.
43. Background of the United Nations Mission in Côte d'Ivoire (MINUCI), op. cit.
44. Respectively Albert Tevoédjrè, Mohamed Ibn Chambas, Lansana Kouyaté, and André Salifou.
45. Background of the United Nations Mission in Côte d'Ivoire (MINUCI), op. cit.
46. Resolution 1528 of the UN Security Council, 27 February 2004.
47. For an analysis of the various UNSC resolutions throughout the peace process and their implementation, see Gilles Yabi, "Côte d'Ivoire," in *Security Council resolutions under Chapter VII: Design, Implementation and Accountabilities: The Cases of Afghanistan, Côte d'Ivoire, Kosovo and Sierra Leone*, ed. Blanca Antonini (Madrid: FRIDE, 2009).
48. "Report of the Commission of Inquiry into the Events Related to the March in Abidjan (Côte d'Ivoire)," op. cit.
49. Third progress report of Secretary General on UN operation in Côte d'Ivoire, S/2004/962, 9 December 2004.
50. International Crisis Group, *Côte d'Ivoire: The Worst May Be Yet to Come* (Dakar and Brussels: ICG Africa Report N°90, March 2005).
51. S/RES/1572, 15 November 2004.
52. See International Crisis Group, *Côte d'Ivoire: Les demi-mesures ne suffiront pas* (Dakar and Brussels: Briefing Afrique N°33, October 2005).
53. James Copnall, "Frail Hope Emerges from Ivorian Deal," *BBC*, 7 April 2005.
54. Pretoria agreement on the peace process in the Côte d'lvoire, 6 April 2005.
55. S/RES/1603, 3 June 2005, created the post of High Representative for elections and defined its mandate to verify "all stages of the electoral process" and assist the Independent Electoral Commission, the Constitutional Council, and other relevant agencies "to help them prevent and resolve any difficulty which may jeopardise the holding of open, free, fair and transparent elections." S/RES/ 1721 (1 November 2006, reinforced the mandate of the High Representative, but after the signature of the March 2007 Ouagadougou political agreement, the Security Council decided to dissolve the High Representative post—as demanded by President Gbagbo, especially—and attribute the certification mandate to the Special Representative of the UN Secretary-General.
56. http://www.iol.co.za/news/africa/dozens-killed-during-clashes-in-ivory-coast-1.242666.
57. International Crisis Group, *Côte d'Ivoire: Les demi-mesures ne suffiront pas.*
58. Ibid.

59. *IRING*, "Côte d'Ivoire: West African Leaders Try to Revive Flagging Peace Efforts," September 30, 2005.
60. International Crisis Group, *Côte d'Ivoire, La paix comme option* (Dakar and Brussels: ICG Africa Report N°109, May 2006).
61. The Central Bank of West African States (Banque centrale des Etats d'Afrique de l'Ouest, BCEAO, French acronym), issues the CFA franc, the common currency shared by former French colonies of West Africa, which maintained a close monetary relation with France.
62. S/RES/1633, 21 October 2005.
63. *BBC*, "Ivorian Party Quits Peace Process," 17 January 2006.
64. Ibid.
65. The sanctions were imposed upon Charles Blé Goudé and Eugene Djué from Gbagbo's "patriotic" movements and zone commander Kouakou Fofié of the Forces Nouvelles.
66. Report of the President of the African Union on the situation in Côte d'Ivoire, sixty-fourth meeting of the Peace and Security Council, 17 October 2006, Addis Ababa, Ethiopia.
67. Ibid.
68. S/RES/1721, 1 November 2006.
69. For a discussion of the Ouagadougou talks and the March 2007 Agreement, see International Crisis Group, *Côte d'Ivoire: Can the Ouagadougou Agreement Bring Peace?* (Dakar and Brussels: ICG Africa Report N°127, June 2007).
70. Ouagadougou Political Agreement, March 2007. Available as S/2007/144, 13 March 2007.
71. See International Crisis Group, *Côte d'Ivoire: Can the Ouagadougou Agreement Bring Peace?*
72. The global financial crisis from 2008 to 2009 had increased pressure from major financial contributors to drawdown peacekeeping commitments across the board.
73. S/2010/537, 18 October 2010.
74. S/2010/600, 23 November 2010.
75. Ibid.
76. Ibid.
77. For a more extensive discussion of the legal arguments, see International Crisis Group, *Côte d'Ivoire: Is War the Only Option?* (Dakar and Brussels: ICG Africa Report N°171, March 2011).
78. The UNOCI certification cell reviewed the voter tally sheets and calculated that Ouattara would have still won with a majority of votes even with the most favorable view on the complaints made by pro-Gbagbo supporters, particularly with respect to unsigned tally sheets.
79. S/2011/211, 30 March 2011.
80. SC/10105, 8 December 2010.
81. SC/10100, 2 December 2010.
82. African Union, Press Statement of the 251st Meeting of the Peace and Security Council (PSC/PR/BR.(CCLI)), 4 December 2010.
83. ECOWAS, ECW/CEG/ABJ/EXT/FR./Rev.2, 7 December 2010.
84. UNOCI press release 951, 18 December 2010; UNOCI press release 954, 28 December 2010; UNOCI press release 955, 30 December 2010.
85. Human Rights Watch report, 5 October 2011; United Nations Human Rights Council, *Report of the independent commission of inquiry on Côte d'Ivoire*, A/HRC/17/48, 6 June 2011.
86. Outside of Abidjan, the situation was also deteriorating, as exemplified by the intercommunal violence that began to take place between the Malinké and Guéré in Duékoué.
87. ECOWAS, ECW/CEG/ABJ/EXT/FR./Rev.0, 24 December 2010.
88. *IRIN*, "Côte d'Ivoire: Briefing on AU and ECOWAS," 15 February 2011.
89. Interview, Civil Society Observer, New York, October 2011.
90. Council of the European Union: 18206/10, 22 December 2010; 18261/10, 31 December 2010; 5361/11, 14 January 2011. UN Security Council resolutions: S/RES/1572, 15 November

2004; S/RES/1643, 15 December 2005; and S/RES/1946 15 October 2010. US and EU travel bans: http://www.google.com/hostednews/afp/article/ALeqM5iSXaXX5kr4UcV_F_gFDkHRxfxjQg?docId=CNG.12330a073a4e5c1c45b564ecbd4f796c.2a1; US cocoa and coffee embargo http://www.google.com/hostednews/afp/article/ALeqM5gPGoXN-nHwBnAi7HJUHjRPaj29jg?docId=CNG.ae92b0aa2b694ca3182261c1f11bfc1a.8b1

91. World Bank statement on Côte d'Ivoire, 2011/278/AFR, 22 December 2010; and UEMOA Communiqué de Presse de la Session Extraordinaire du Conseil des Ministres de l'UEMOA, 23 December 2010.
92. In an embarrassing episode, the director of the BCEAO refused to implement the decision taken by the member states and he was finally forced to resign on 22 January 2011. Ouattara's spokesman estimated that Gbagbo had been able to withdraw US$200 million before Dacoury-Tabley was removed. http://www.aljazeera.com/news/africa/2011/01/20111245575892515.html, 24 January 2011.
93. Four foreign banks were nationalized: British Standard Chartered (UK), BNP-Paribas (FR), Societé Générale (FR), and Citibank (US): http://abcnews.go.com/Business/wireStory?id=12950365#.Ts-NZrJCo4Q (18 February 2011). Statement of Gbagbo spokesman is available at http://blogs.wsj.com/corruption-currents/2011/02/18/gbagbo-nationalizes-ivory-coast-banks-to-reopen-monday/; Gbagbo nationalizes cocoa, 7 March 2011: http://blogs.wsj.com/corruption-currents/2011/03/07/ivory-coasts-gbagbo-attempts-to-nationalize-cocoa-purchases-exports/
94. http://www.icc-cpi.int/NR/rdonlyres/6235122D-87C3–4CDE-9021–032BB93E6B6A/282841/C%C3%B4tedIvoireENG.pdf.
95. Secretary-General's report 2011/211, 30 March 2011; HRW report, 6 October 2011; OCHA humanitarian report #17, 11 March 2011.
96. OCHA humanitarian report # 15, 25 February 2011; Secretary-General's report 2011/211, 30 March 2011.
97. Interviews, West African civil society actor, New York, October 2011; Diplomat interview, New York, September 2011.
98. AU Peace and Security Council Communiqué, PSC/AHG/COMM.1(CCLXV), 10 March 2011.
99. ECOWAS Communiqué A/RES.1/03/11 25 March 2011.
100. UNSC resolution 1975 of 31 March 2011. Emphasis added.
101. "The five installations include Gbagbo's residence where heavy weaponry was destroyed, the republican guard, state TV, the Agban paramilitary base, and the arms depot at Akouedo,"http://www.allwestafrica.com/050420118898.html, 5 April 2011.
102. International Crisis Group, *Côte d'Ivoire: Is War the Only Option?*
103. Both the UN SRSG and the appointed Representative of President Compaoré for the follow-up of OPA based in Abidjan were mentioned in the Ivorian electoral code as recipients of copies of the tallies coming from the polling stations. But only UNOCI had the means to undertake a parallel comprehensive examination of the results as part of the certification process.
104. As mentioned earlier, the monthly meetings of the International Working Group in 2006 were often marked by fierce debates opposing South African and French representatives.

Chapter 8

The Democratic Republic of the Congo, 1996–2012

Tatiana Carayannis

Introduction

August 2011 marked twelve years since the signing of the Lusaka Ceasefire Agreement that ended the second Congo war. It also marked the twelfth anniversary of the establishment of the UN Mission in the Democratic Republic of the Congo (MONUC, Mission de l'Organization des Nations Unies en Rėpublique Democratique du Congo). Yet, the root causes of the wars persist—access to land in eastern Democratic Republic of the Congo (DRC) remains contested, and control over revenues from natural resources remains in the hands of a few. Armed groups, both foreign and domestic, continue to operate with impunity in the eastern DRC and are the source of much of the insecurity in the region. And state institutions remain weak and resource-starved.

Over the last decade and a half, the Congo has witnessed an extraordinary number of attempts by regional and international actors—individuals, states, and institutions—to resolve the largest conflict that Africa has seen since independence. The conflict, however, persists, and at an enormous cost. The most that these attempts have achieved are several partially respected cease-fire agreements. They have failed to end the violence or to reestablish central government authority throughout the DRC.

Today, the DRC transition is at a crossroads. Despite second postconflict elections held in November 2011 that aimed to complete a peace process started in December 2002 during the Inter-Congolese Dialogue at Sun City, a growing number of Congolese feel disenfranchised by a government increasingly reliant on strong-handedness, as its authority rests on weak national and local institutions—a crisis of governance that elections have not solved. In the last two years, little progress has been made on the disarmament and reintegration of Rwandan-backed rebel groups or Mai Mai militias,[1] and until recently, efforts to dismantle and repatriate the Rwandan Hutu FDLR (Democratic Liberation Forces of Rwanda) militia have yielded few decisive results.

Source: Map No 4007 Rev 10, United Nations, Department of Field Support, Cartographic Section, July 2011

Over the last two decades, the notion that regional organizations are better placed and have greater political will to respond to security threats in their own regions has gained wide currency. This reflects both the reluctance of major powers to intervene in African conflicts and the removal of Cold War barriers to regional initiatives. Arguments favoring regional approaches are based on the logic that local threats to peace are more promptly and more effectively dealt with by governments in the affected region. The reasons given are that states in the region are themselves adversely impacted by the war and thus have a vested interest in regional stability; that regional groups' familiarity with local crises and personal relations with warring parties makes them better placed to mediate disputes; and that regional interventions will be perceived as more legitimate by the region than would interventions undertaken by extra-regional actors. Others point to the complex interdependence of states and their interests; the frequently inadequate local resources to solve local problems; and partisan divisions in the region where the conflict is taking place, as evidence suggesting that regional organizations are not necessarily best placed to resolve conflicts in their regions. This chapter seeks to examine responses to the wars in the DRC (or "the Congo") in the context of this debate.

The story of the many efforts to mediate an end to violence in the DRC over nearly two decades is long and complex and has been told in greater detail elsewhere. This chapter analyzes the responses and interactions of the United Nations (UN),[2] the African Union (AU, previously the Organization of African Unity [OAU]), and the Southern African Development Community (SADC) to the three recent Congo wars since September 1996. It draws preliminary conclusions about the roles of the UN and regional organizations in resolving conflicts that involve entire regions, and is organized largely chronologically. The first section of the chapter provides an overview of the origins of the three Congo wars and their international responses. The second section examines the role of the UN and regional organizations in the political transitions and efforts to consolidate peace since 2003. The concluding section offers some thoughts about what this case study may suggest about multilateral approaches to complex hybrid[3] wars and post-conflict peace-building.

Background to the Conflict[4]

The conflict in the Congo is best understood as three interlocking wars. While the Congo wars trace their roots to the Rwanda genocide of 1994, the first war began in September 1996 as an invasion by a coalition of neighboring states of what was then Zaire, and resulted in replacing president Mobutu with Laurent Kabila in May 1997. The second war broke out in August 1998 when a similar configuration of neighboring states some of whom had been Kabila's patrons in the first war, broke with him and attempted a similar ouster, but without their earlier success. It ended with the signing of the Lusaka Ceasefire Agreement in July 1999 by the Kabila government and the Mouvement pour la libération du Congo (MLC) and Rally for Congolese Democracy (RCD, Rassemblement Congolais pour la Démocratie) rebel groups fighting it, the result of a stalemate in the war and considerable external pressure.

In both the first and second wars, neighboring states established local proxy movements in an attempt to put a local stamp on their activities. However, the bulk of Kabila's fighting forces in the first war were foreign (mostly Rwandan), while in the second war, this was less so. In that war, the MLC's forces were largely Congolese trained by Uganda officers, while the RCD forces were integrated with Rwandan troops and commanders.

When the Lusaka Ceasefire Agreement was signed in July 1999, three rival Congolese rebel groups—the MLC and the split factions of the RCD (RCD-Goma and RCD-K/ML)—controlled two-thirds of the DRC's territory. Laurent Kabila's government in Kinshasa, which had itself taken power by force two years earlier, controlled the remaining third. The withdrawal of most foreign troops shortly thereafter created a power vacuum in rebel-held territories, and a third war began behind UN-monitored cease-fire lines in northeastern Congo. This war was fought between ever smaller groups—foreign and domestic—that have since become significant actors in the illicit activities in that region. In June 2003, following a national dialogue and a series of regional agreements, the DRC swore in a Government of National Unity consisting of leaders representing almost every local actor in the wars. This transition culminated in a UN-supported national election in 2006 that narrowly elected Joseph Kabila president after two hotly contested rounds of voting.

Opération Turquoise

The first event to transform an impoverished, yet relatively nonviolent Congolese society into an arena of conflict and war was the genocide of the Rwandan Tutsi in

1994. For several years, the Rwandan Hutu–dominated government led by President Habyarimana, and the Rwandan Patriotic Front (RPF), a Tutsi-led rebel group, had been embroiled in a civil war. The genocide, which began in early April 1994 and lasted for approximately three months, saw Hutu leaders mobilize almost the entire Hutu population in the organized mass murder of up to 1 million Tutsi and "moderate" Hutu. The failure of international interventions in Rwanda has been dealt with elsewhere.[5] For the Congo, what is important is the effect of a variety of policy decisions by the UN in Rwanda, which led to a Security Council cover for the French *Opération Turquoise*.

The loss of ten Belgian peacekeepers in early April 1994 and the deteriorating security situation in Rwanda prompted the UN, at the urging of the Belgian government, to withdraw most of its UN Assistance Mission for Rwanda (UNAMIR I) forces two weeks into the genocide.[6] As word of the massacres got out, France offered to lead a humanitarian mission to the region until the UN could mobilize support for a new operation with a mandate appropriate to the new situation on the ground. On 22 June 1994, UN Security Council Resolution 929 authorized a temporary French mission "for humanitarian purposes in Rwanda until UNAMIR is brought up to the necessary strength."[7] Its mandate was to use "all necessary means" to ensure the humanitarian objectives spelled out in the Security Council's earlier Resolution 925 on UNAMIR[8] though the resolution stressed "the strictly humanitarian character of this operation which shall be conducted in an impartial and neutral fashion."[9]

The first of the 2,500 heavily armed French troops of *Opération Turquoise* began arriving in Goma[10] the following day. Although the Security Council authorized a multinational force under French command and control, it was de facto an exclusively French military intervention.[11] This was problematic, as the Rwandan Hutu–dominated government had received political and financial support as well as military training from the French since 1990. The arrival of French troops in the last weeks of the genocide, while the Habyarimana government was under heavy attack by the RPF, was seen by Rwandan government leaders as an intervention in their favor—so much so that French soldiers were quoted saying they were "fed up of with being cheered along by murderers!"[12] It is not surprising, therefore, that in the absence of adequate communication with the Rwandan rebels during the planning of the mission, and given the close ties between France and the Hutu-dominated regime in Rwanda, the RPF saw the French intervention as an attempt to shore up the weakening *génocidaire* government. These fears would be confirmed. News accounts widely reported that the Mitterrand government had, in fact, continued to ship arms to the Habyarimana government even after the massacres had started. Furthermore, according to one observer close to the mission, there were some in the French government and military who conceived of this mission as an effort to provide assistance to the failing Hutu government.[13]

Opération Turquoise established a so-called Safe Humanitarian Zone in southern Rwanda to which many Hutu leaders, Rwandan military, and civilians retreated. It is estimated that the French intervention did save some Tutsi,[14] although it also jeopardized the lives of retreating UNAMIR I troops. Canadian General Romeo Dallaire, commander of the UNAMIR I forces, recalls that the arrival of French troops led the RPF to retaliate against the UN by attacking the remaining UNAMIR troops left largely helpless with little heavy artillery and no communication with *Opération Turquoise* commanders.[15]

Opération Turquoise had two principal effects that were contrary to its mandate of protection and neutrality: first, it failed to stop the bulk of the massacres of civilians that were still occurring; and second, the operation did not disarm the Hutu militias, known as the Interahamwe, nor the defeated Forces Armées Rwandaises (FAR) units.[16] Instead, it allowed them and their political leaders, along with masses of Rwandan Hutu civilians, to escape across the border into the Congo. These effects resulted in the profound destabilization of eastern Congo.

The First Congo War

The conflict in the Congo has involved at least nine African states and a number of proxy movements with varying degrees of local mobilization and support. The first war began in September 1996 as an invasion by a coalition of neighboring states of what was then Zaire, and succeeded in replacing President Mobutu with Laurent Kabila in May 1997.

The Mobutu regime tried to convince the world that what was happening was a foreign invasion of the Congo, but to little avail. Neither the UN nor the OAU condemned the invading forces, an indication of a general feeling worldwide that Mobutu had to go. The notion that what was happening was largely a revolution against the Mobutu regime gained wide currency in the Western press, which from the start of the war referred to it as a civil war or rebellion. Many Congolese shared this view, even though it was widely known that there were foreign troops fighting in the anti-Mobutu alliance.[17] A young, unemployed Congolese lining up to join the allied rebel forces offered a journalist a sentiment echoed throughout the country: "When it started, we thought Rwanda was the one attacking Zaire. Later, we found out it was a Zairian struggle. I personally believe in the revolution because it's a revolution that is sustained by everyone."[18]

Mobutu failed to obtain any serious military support from abroad, although later US intelligence reports indicated that France had conducted a covert operation to aid Mobutu in the hopes of retaining their influence over the third largest country in Africa,[19] fearing what it no doubt perceived to be a growing American and anglophone hegemony in Africa.[20] The French government reportedly supplied Mobutu with three combat aircraft from Yugoslavia, along with crews and about eighty mercenaries, mostly Serbians, at the cost of US$5 million and in clear violation of an agreement among France, Belgium, and the United States not to sell arms to the Zairian government.[21]

The forces that did the bulk of the fighting for the Mobutu regime were the Interahamwe/ex-FAR, Serbian mercenaries, and National Union for the Total Independence of Angola (UNITA) rebel forces. By the end of 1996, Mobutu's army was being routed and was in full retreat, looting, raping, and killing Congolese civilians along the way. This conduct, on top of years of scarcity and neglect under Mobutu's dictatorship, helps explain why the Congolese people soon welcomed the anti-Mobutu alliance and allowed its young men to be recruited into its ranks. By mid-February 1997, Kabila was showing off more than 10,000 new recruits sporting AK-47s and new uniforms in parades in cities along the eastern border, as more young recruits queued up for hours to enlist.[22]

International action during the first war took the form of weak declaratory UN resolutions on the war, and intense international and regional diplomatic efforts to negotiate Mobutu's exit. Ambassador Mohamed Sahnoun of Algeria was appointed in January 1997 as joint UN–OAU Special Representative for the Great Lakes region, and South African President Nelson Mandela emerged as the principal mediator in the first war. The first meeting between Mobutu's government and the rebels took place in Cape Town on 20 February 1997 and was brokered largely by the United States and South Africa. Despite the presence of high-level envoys from the United States (Assistant Secretary of State for African Affairs George E. Moose and President Clinton's then special assistant on Africa, Susan Rice) and South Africa (Deputy Foreign Minister Aziz Pahad), the talks collapsed and subsequent talks failed to reach agreement. On 17 May 1997, after a failed last-minute effort by Mandela and Sahnoun to produce agreement for another round of talks and facing certain military defeat, Mobutu left the Congo for the last time, and the anti-Mobutu alliance marched into Kinshasa unopposed. This ended the first war.

Mandela's mediation efforts, aimed at ensuring a smooth transition through a negotiated exit for Mobutu, did not include the so-called nonviolent opposition—Congolese nongovernmental organizations (NGOs), churches, and long-time opposition leaders, all of whom had considerable public support in their opposition to the Mobutu dictatorship. By excluding Congolese opposition parties from the negotiations for a transitional government and limiting participation to the forces with guns, mediation efforts in the first war effectively marginalized political leaders who had gained much popularity and legitimacy over the years, especially through their leadership in the National Sovereign Conference of 1993. It also bestowed a considerable degree of international legitimacy on Kabila and the alliance, which only encouraged Kabila, once in power, to ignore later calls by the UN and donors for multiparty politics.

International Preoccupation with Humanitarian Issues

In late 1996 and early 1997, anti-Mobutu alliance forces marched largely unchallenged across the country toward Kinshasa. During this military campaign, the international community was more focused on humanitarian concerns and what it perceived to be a new refugee crisis unfolding in the Congo, than on the presence of foreign troops on Congolese soil whose aim was to overthrow the Zairian government. The anti-Mobutu forces operating in the Congo appeared to have made little distinction between civilians and militias, or among women, children, and men; and the Interahamwe/ex-FAR themselves were accused of having used these civilians as human shields. Hence, while international sentiment saw the retreating Hutu as refugees under fire by advancing rebel forces, and thus in need of international protection, the Rwandan troops saw them as the hard-core perpetrators of the genocide who had not given up on controlling Rwanda, or even on finishing the genocide.

Concerned about the growing insecurity in the region, on October 18, 1996, the UN and the OAU issued a joint call for an international conference on security in the region. On 5 November 1996, the OAU brought together leaders from Uganda, Zambia, Rwanda, Eritrea, Tanzania, Ethiopia, and Cameroon in Nairobi for a regional summit to address the war in the Congo. They called for an immediate cease-fire and reaffirmed their commitment to the OAU principle of respecting the territorial integrity of member states—in this case, the Congo.[23] Although Rwanda joined in these declarations, its new president, Pasteur Bizimungu, had some days earlier made reference to a "Berlin II," suggesting that Congolese borders were not, in fact, sacrosanct.[24]

Meanwhile, Western newspaper and television reports continued to focus on the plight of the "refugees," and on the state of hundreds of lost or orphaned children among them. Calls for an international humanitarian intervention to assist and repatriate these Hutu "refugees" intensified and came not only from the UN and international humanitarian organizations, but also from the OAU. On 9 November 1996, in what appears to have been a compromise between those in favor of a UN intervention and those opposed to it, Security Council Resolution 1078 called on the UN Secretary-General to "draw up a concept of operations and framework for a humanitarian task force, with military assistance if necessary."[25] The resolution stopped short of authorizing a humanitarian intervention, but asked the UN Secretary-General to formulate a plan for one. It also asked the OAU and the states in the region "to examine ways in which to contribute to and to complement efforts undertaken by the United Nations to defuse tension in the region, in particular in eastern Zaire."

On 11 November 1996, the Central Organ of the OAU's Mechanism for Conflict Prevention, Management, and Resolution, held its Fourth Extraordinary Session at the level of ministers in Addis Ababa. Statements from that meeting, as well as an OAU communiqué transmitted to the Security Council on 13 November, emphasized the urgent need for the provision of humanitarian assistance to the "refugees" in the Congo and for their voluntary repatriation to Rwanda.

On 18 February 1997, five months into the anti-Mobutu military campaign and three months before Mobutu relinquished power, the Security Council adopted a five-point peace plan for eastern Zaire. The plan called for the immediate cessation of hostilities; the withdrawal of all external forces, including mercenaries; the respect for the national sovereignty and the territorial integrity of Zaire, and other states of the Great Lakes region; the protection of all refugees and the facilitation of humanitarian assistance; and the peaceful settlement of the conflict through dialogue, elections, and the convening of an international conference.[26] Although this resolution recognized, for the first time, the presence of foreign forces in the Congo and called for their withdrawal, the Security Council stopped short of identifying any one force as the aggressor. An internationally recognized government, albeit an unpopular one, was claiming invasion; yet the UN and the OAU were united in not responding substantively to a clear violation of international law and the UN Charter. The general sentiment seemed to be that a handful of states in the region were doing everyone a favor by assuming the responsibility of ridding Africa of one of its more embarrassing and enduring dictators who had, over several years, hosted insurgency movements aiming to overthrow the governments of its neighbors.

Calls for a Multinational Force

In early November 1996, with pressure mounting for international community action, the Clinton administration began probing the Canadian government for possible interest in leading a mission to the Congo, suggesting that the United States would be willing to support a Canadian-led, but not a "blue-helmet" intervention.[27] Once Canada and the United States reached a minimum agreement over American participation in the mission, on November 15, 1996, Security Council Resolution 1080 authorized a Canadian-led "temporary multinational force to facilitate the immediate return of humanitarian organizations and the effective delivery by civilian relief organizations of humanitarian aid to alleviate the immediate suffering of displaced persons, refugees and civilians at risk in eastern Zaire, and to facilitate the voluntary, orderly repatriation of refugees by the United Nations High Commissioner for Refugees as well as the voluntary return of displaced persons." As part of the resolution, the Security Council noted that these efforts were also requested by regional leaders at the Nairobi Summit on 5 November 1996, and that the Security Council intended "to respond positively on an urgent basis to those requests." The multinational force was not authorized, however, to disarm the Interahamwe/ex-FAR[28] in the Congo. Neither Canada nor the United States wanted to assume responsibility for disarming combatants who were not likely to give up their weapons voluntarily.[29]

At the Security Council discussions on the resolution, the representative of the Zairian government, Lukabu Khabouji N'Zaji, expressed dismay at what he saw to be the Security Council's unresponsiveness to a foreign act of aggression perpetrated against his state by the invading forces of Rwanda and Uganda. He complained about a Security Council double standard in the application of international law, and noted that since it had responded forcefully to Iraq's invasion of Kuwait in August 1990, he could not understand "the Council's reluctance to defend Zaire against a similar aggression."[30] Nevertheless, Canada announced that already twenty countries had committed over 10,000 troops for the mission; and Madeleine Albright reminded the Council of the "shock and horror" of the genocide in Rwanda two years earlier, adding that the international community was now prepared to assist "those most in need."[31]

In spite of the many pronouncements in favor of the mission and mounting pressure from the region, the authorized Canadian-led multinational force was never deployed. By the time the resolution was adopted, the situation on the ground had changed dramatically. As soon as the attacks on the camps started in September 1996, hundreds of thousands of Hutu refugees began marching back across the border into Rwanda.[32] It did not take much for the United States, already reluctant to intervene, to seize upon these events as reason enough for not deploying the multinational force.[33] These two resolutions, 1078 and 1080, adopted within days of each other less than eight weeks into the first war, were the only Security Council actions in 1996 that dealt with the conflict in the Congo. The emphasis of both resolutions was the humanitarian needs of the Hutu "refugee" population; neither one dealt with the presence of foreign troops in the Congo.

The Second Congo War and the Road to Lusaka

The second war broke out in August 1998 when a similar configuration of neighboring states, some of whom had been Kabila's patrons in the first war, broke with him and attempted a similar ousting but without their earlier success.

A draft cease-fire agreement prepared by UN and OAU representatives two weeks into the second war highlighted one of the issues that would plague the region in its efforts to negotiate an end to the violence: how to define the nature of the conflict. Each party to the war interpreted the conflict differently and could not agree on who the belligerents were. This draft agreement identified Angola, DRC, Namibia, Rwanda, Uganda, and Zimbabwe as parties to the conflict—but Rwanda and Uganda had not yet publicly declared their military presence in the Congo, and protested the exclusion of any Congolese rebel groups from the proposed list of signatories. On the other hand, in his continuing efforts to present the war exclusively as a case of foreign aggression by Rwanda and Uganda, Kabila initially denied the existence of an internal rebellion and refused to recognize the Rwandan- and Ugandan-backed RCD as a belligerent. Not surprisingly, the RCD defined this war as a revolution against a dictatorial regime, and argued that the only two fighting were the RCD and the Kabila regime.

At its Eighteenth Summit meeting in Mauritius during 13–14 September 1998, SADC appointed Zambian President Frederick Chiluba to lead the peace effort. Shortly after, the European Union (EU) appointed Aldo Ajello as Special Envoy, and the United States dispatched Ambassador Thomas Pickering, then Undersecretary of State for Political Affairs, and former US senator Howard Wolpe as Special Envoy.

By early 1999, the war had acquired an even greater complexity, as there were now three rebel groups operating in the Congo, collectively controlling over half the country. The RCD had split into two movements as a result of internal disagreements: the RCD-ML (Mouvement de Libération), backed by Uganda, and the RCD-Goma, backed by Rwanda. The MLC, another anti-Kabila armed group, was established with Ugandan support in northern Equateur Province some months after the founding of the RCD.

The second Congo war ended with the signing of the Lusaka Ceasefire Agreement in July 1999,[34] the result of a stalemate in the war and considerable external pressure. Although the Lusaka process was a product of the region, Wolpe and Ajello were deeply involved in the negotiations. Despite the ceasefire agreement, violence among armed groups continued behind the ceasefire lines until the establishment of a government of national unity in 2003, in what some observers refer to as the third war.[35]

The UN was largely prevented from taking a more active role in resolving the conflict due to the reluctance of the major powers, especially the United States, to intervene in such a large-scale and complex regional conflict before a peace agreement was reached. This inaction created a space for a number of local initiatives. Between the outbreak of the war in August 1998 and the signing of the Lusaka Peace Agreement in August 1999, there were twenty-three failed SADC- or OAU-sponsored meetings at the ministerial or presidential level aimed at brokering an end to the war, as well as numerous other unsuccessful efforts by individual leaders in the region. One of the first regional responses was a decision by Zimbabwe, Angola, and Namibia to invoke Kinshasa's recent SADC membership[36] as a reason to launch a SADC military intervention to defend the Kabila government from foreign aggression. Zimbabwe's President Mugabe held the chairmanship of SADC's Politics, Defense, and Security Organ during this time, and used his position to secure a SADC umbrella for Zimbabwe's, Angola's, and Namibia's military intervention to end the war in Kabila's favor. The three countries also justified their actions as an application of the principle of individual and collective self-defense under article 51 of the UN Charter, a justification later affirmed by the Security Council.[37]

This intervention, which did not seek nor receive UN Security Council authorization, is what South African analyst Cedric de Coning earlier called SADC "neo-interventionism"—operations undertaken by subregional groups that intervene not as peacemakers, but as allies of one of the belligerents in the conflict with the aim of influencing the outcome of the war.[38] It deeply divided the subregional organization, as there were members, most notably South Africa, who strongly opposed it. South African leaders felt that Mugabe had hijacked SADC to give a Zimbabwean intervention greater legitimacy. The Organ's decision to intervene militarily was challenged by Mandela, then chair of the SADC Summit. Mandela argued that such decisions should rest with the Summit, as that is the institutional body that represents all community members at the level of head of state. In what appears to have been a power struggle between Mugabe and Mandela for regional dominance, South Africa's preference for nonintervention and SADC neutrality was not heeded. In spite of subsequent attempts to clarify where the final decision-making authority lies on security issues, there still is no consensus among SADC members about which of the organization's decision-making bodies has the ultimate authority in such matters.

A draft cease-fire agreement prepared by UN and OAU representatives for a summit of regional defense ministers held at Victoria Falls on 18 August 1998 demonstrated the problem that would plague the region in mediating a negotiated settlement: how to define the nature of the conflict. Each party to the war interpreted the conflict differently, and consequently, could not agree on who the belligerents were. This draft agreement identified the governments of Angola, DRC, Namibia, Rwanda, Uganda, and Zimbabwe as the belligerents. However, Rwanda and Uganda had not yet publicly declared their military presence in the Congo, and protested the exclusion of any of the Congolese rebel groups from the proposed list of signatories, by walking out of the meeting.[39] In his continuing efforts to present the war exclusively as a case of foreign aggression by Rwanda and Uganda, Kabila initially denied the existence of an internal rebellion and refused to recognize the RCD as a belligerent. Of course, the RCD defined this war as a revolution against a dictatorial regime, and argued that the only two belligerents were the RCD and the Kabila regime, each with its foreign supporters.

A meeting with Kabila and Museveni hosted by Libya's Muammar Gaddafi on 18 April 1999 resulted in the signing of an initial peace agreement. The Sirte Accord called for the deployment of a peacekeeping force, the withdrawal of foreign troops from Congolese soil, and a national dialogue, but resulted only in the withdrawal of Chadian troops from the Congo, as neither the RCD nor its sponsor, Rwanda, was party to the agreement. Although SADC, the OAU, and other regional power brokers continued their efforts to mediate a negotiated settlement during these months, what ultimately brought the warring parties to the negotiating table was a stalemate in the war.

The Lusaka Ceasefire Agreement

The Lusaka Agreement called for the immediate cessation of hostilities within twenty-four hours of its signing. By "hostile action," it meant not only military attacks and reinforcements, but all hostile propaganda as well—an important emphasis in a region where hate speech has incited violence with devastating consequences. Furthermore, the agreement called for disarming foreign militia groups in the Congo, the withdrawal of all foreign forces from the country, and the exchange of hostages and prisoners of war. It also called for the establishment of a Joint Military Commission (JMC) composed of representatives of the belligerents, each armed with veto power. The JMC was to be headed by a neutral chair appointed by the OAU, and charged with ensuring, along with UN and OAU observers, compliance with the cease-fire until the deployment of a UN peacekeeping force mandated to ensure the implementation of the agreement. The signatories of the agreement asked that this mission have both a peacekeeping and a peace enforcement mandate and explicitly asked the Security Council to authorize coercive force, if necessary, to achieve its objectives of disarming the various armed groups.

Most significantly, the agreement also provided for an all-inclusive process, the "Inter-Congolese Dialogue" to produce a new political order for the Congo. The former president of Botswana, Sir Ketumile Masire, was appointed to facilitate that process in December 1999. A key provision was that all domestic parties to the dispute, whether armed or not, were to participate in this dialogue as equals. The inclusion of the non-violent political opposition and of civil society groups was a positive element, and in sharp contrast to the previous exclusion of these groups from earlier mediation efforts in the DRC.

The strengths of the Lusaka Agreement were several:

- It recognized the overlapping layers of interstate and intrastate actors involved in the second war.
- It was signed by almost all major parties to the dispute, including foreign governments and rebel groups.
- It recognized the need for an internal healing process among Congolese—an inter-Congolese dialogue in anticipation of forming an interim government.
- It affirmed a rarely applied principle that all parties (except the Mai Mai), including government and civil society, would participate on the basis of equal status.
- It recognized the security concerns of Congo's neighbors regarding insurgency movements seeking to overthrow their governments out of bases in the Congo.

The weakness of the agreement was that it froze the status quo and distinct zones of influence controlled by different rebel factions and their patrons—the MLC and Uganda in the northwest; in the east, Rwanda and the RCD (and more recent proxies such as the National Congress for the Defence of the People [CNDP]); and to a lesser extent, Uganda and increasingly fragmented proxies in the northeast. However, the greatest failure of the agreement was leaving out the Mai Mai. The Mai Mai were neither represented at the peace negotiations in Lusaka nor were they mentioned as participants in the internal dialogue. This, despite being supported by Kinshasa and at one point declared to be a part of the new Congolese army. This missed opportunity continues to plague efforts to mediate and consolidate peace today, as the Mai Mai continue to fight in the Kivus.

The Inter-Congolese Dialogue

The Lusaka Agreement envisioned a six-week-long national dialogue with armed and unarmed Congolese groups about the future institutions and interim government of the Congo as a parallel process to the disarming of armed groups and the departure of foreign armies. Until his assassination, Laurent Kabila repeatedly refused to cooperate not only with the UN, but also with the dialogue's facilitator, President Masire. Kabila never accepted the actual implementation of the agreement's provision that all parties, including the government, would enjoy the same status in the inter-Congolese dialogue. He quarreled with Masire over the start date of the negotiations and eventually shut down the facilitator's office in Kinshasa. Kabila also tried to exploit Anglophone–Francophone rivalries in Africa by accusing Masire—an Anglophone—of being biased in favor of Uganda and Rwanda, and demanded that another facilitator—a Francophone—be appointed.

Joseph Kabila, once in power in January 2001 following Laurent Kabila's assassination, initially took steps to revive the Lusaka process, and on 4 May 2001, two weeks before the Security Council's visit to the region, the Lusaka Agreement signatories met again in Lusaka and signed a Declaration on the Fundamental Principles. The Inter-Congolese Dialogue finally got started with a preparatory meeting in Gaborone between 20 and 24 August 2001, attended by representatives of all signatories to the Lusaka Agreement and the Congolese nonviolent political opposition and civil society, as well as observers from the UN, OAU, SADC, EU, and the JMC. After some disagreements over who would participate in the talks and on their venue, they agreed that the national dialogue would be held in Addis Ababa for a period of six weeks beginning on 15 October 2001.

The talks opened as planned at the UN Economic Commission for Africa (ECA) conference hall in Addis Ababa. Citing financial constraints, Masire limited participation to only eighty representatives rather than the original 330 agreed to in Gaborone. This played into Kinshasa's stall tactics and after just three days into peace talks, Kinshasa walked out of the meetings in protest that not all parties were represented. Kinshasa insisted that Mai Mai be included in the talks, a proposal strongly opposed by the Congolese rebel groups who argued that only parties included in the Lusaka Agreement should be invited to participate in the dialogue. Kinshasa's objective was to stack the deck in its favor by pushing the participation of groups it could easily manipulate.

Two months later, on 6 December 2001, Nigeria hosted a preparatory meeting for the internal Congolese dialogue, under UN auspices. This Abuja meeting resulted in a compromise on the Mai Mai question, with agreement to give the Congolese militia six of the approximately 300 seats at the national dialogue. Another round of UN-sponsored informal talks aimed at confidence-building among the parties in preparation for Sun City was held in Geneva during 4–7 February 2002. This time, it was the RCD who walked out of the talks, calling the meeting a total failure. At issue, again, was the Mai Mai question. The RCD accused Kinshasa of violating the Lusaka Ceasefire Agreement by continuing to support the Mai Mai militias who were neither bound by nor respected the cease-fire.

The national dialogue finally reopened in South Africa's Sun City on 25 February 2002 initially without the participation of one of the principal actors, the MLC, which complained that the government had stacked the deck in its favor by sending bogus civilian opposition parties. Eventually, all of the actors participated in the talks which lasted for a total of fifty-two days.[40] Despite numerous efforts by South Africa, the dialogue failed to achieve even a general agreement between the key actors. An agreement for a transitional power-sharing arrangement in which Joseph Kabila would remain president and MLC leader Jean-Pierre Bemba would be named prime minister was signed by the government and the MLC, but this was rejected by the Rwanda-backed RCD-Goma and the political opposition. On leaving Sun City, Masire acknowledged that "we are leaving Sun City without fully realizing all our goals."[41]

Observers have put partial blame on the facilitation, which never quite understood the dynamics and underlying relationships between the negotiating parties, a shortcoming that Masire's inability to speak French did not help. Masire also permitted Kabila's stall tactics to continually derail the process. Masire faced another problem—funding. By May 2000, several weeks after he had been appointed, he still had not received the US$6 million pledged from international donors for his office. Of course, the parties themselves were to blame for the failures of Sun City for neglecting the continued violence—or the emerging third war—in eastern DRC, focusing instead on negotiating government positions for themselves. Despite these failings, the talks produced dozens of meaningful resolutions establishing such institutions as a Truth and Reconciliation Commission—negotiated institutions that could potentially provide the basis for a durable peace rather than having to reinvent the wheel. We will not know this, however, until there is a thorough assessment of their failed implementation.

The escalating violence between rival Rwandan and Ugandan proxy forces in the east prompted the appointment of two UN Special Envoys, who played a much more proactive mediation role than Masire—former Senegalese prime minster and seasoned politician Mustafa Nyasse, and a former Eritrean diplomat, Haile Menkerios, who had dealt with the Kabila alliance during the first war and was thus familiar with the region's geopolitics. The resulting Pretoria Agreement, which was brokered by Nyasse and Thabo Mbeki in December 2002, established an all-inclusive framework for the "1+4" transitional government of national unity that was eventually seated in 2003 and which led to the country's first free, national election in 2006.

From MONUC to MONUSCO

In 2010, four years after Congo's landmark post-conflict national election in 2006, the UN Mission in the Congo entered its fourth, and some expect, final phase as the renamed MONUSCO (UN Stabilization Mission in the Congo). Phase one was the initial UN deployment of a small observer mission in 1999 following the second Congo war that erupted in August 1998. Its initial mandate, authorized by Security Council Resolution 1279, was to support the implementation of the Lusaka Ceasefire Agreement.

Phase two coincided with the political transition in the Congo begun in 2003. By 2004, MONUC had grown into a substantial integrated mission with the mandate to support the Government of National Unity and the transition, and the complex and expensive national electoral process held in 2006.

The mission's third phase began in 2009 when, in keeping with its reinforced mandate, MONUC entered a more robust peacekeeping phase, focusing largely on the unfinished business of the stabilization of eastern Congo. A series of joint military operations with the Congolese national armed forces against armed groups in the east yielded mixed results and came under heavy criticism for their failure to protect civilians. Most significantly, these joint military operations, conducted with a national army known for human rights abuses, exposed the operational tensions in the mission's multiple mandates called for in Resolution 1856.

The UN mission entered its fourth and final phase on 28 May 2010, when the UN Security Council adopted Resolution 1925, substantially reconfiguring the UN mission in the Congo and reframing the force as a stabilization mission. Resolution 1925 authorized the withdrawal of up to 2,000 troops from the country, further concentrated the mission's attention on civilian protection and military operations in the east, and established a reserve force that could react, in principle, to incidents throughout the country. Coming on the heels of efforts by the Congolese government to see a substantial reduction in the UN's presence, Resolution 1925 marked the beginning of a process, which, barring the resumption of regional hostilities, many believe will culminate in the mission's departure.

The Origins of the UN Mission in the DRC

There were encouraging signs for substantive UN involvement in Central Africa coming out of the Security Council in late 1998 and early 1999. UN Security Council statements soon after the second Congo war broke out commended the region's diplomatic efforts for a peaceful settlement, and called for the withdrawal of all foreign forces in the Congo.[42] The Security Council President's Statement of 11 December 1998 said that the Security Council was "prepared to consider, in the light of efforts towards peaceful resolution of the conflict, the active involvement of the United Nations, in coordination with the OAU, including through concrete, sustainable and effective measures, to assist in the implementation of an effective ceasefire agreement and in an agreed process for a political settlement of the conflict."[43] There were other signs that could have been interpreted by the region as a greater willingness of the UN to help enforce peace agreements negotiated by the region. Security Council Resolution 1208, on the plight of refugees in African conflicts, adopted a month earlier on 19 November 1998, called on African states to develop procedures to separate refugees from "other persons who do not qualify for international protection afforded refugees or otherwise do not require international protection" and urged African states to "seek international assistance, as appropriate," to do this. UN Resolution 1234, adopted on 9 April 1999, supported SADC's regional mediation efforts by name, and for the first time since the second war began, made a clear distinction between invited and noninvited forces in the Congo. This was in contrast to the Lusaka Agreement that made no such distinction.

Once the agreement was signed in Lusaka, UN Security Council Resolution 1258, on 6 August 1999, welcomed the agreement and authorized an observer mission to the

Congo. However, the Security Council did not grant this mission the enforcement mandate requested by the signatories to the Lusaka Agreement, nor did they authorize the force size they expected. The UN deployed ninety military liaison officers to the headquarters of the belligerents for three months to assist the JMC in the peace process, and to determine when there might be sufficient security guarantees to deploy a larger UN force. In defending this preliminary action against critics who argued it was insufficient, a UN spokesperson noted that although small in number, "these [military liaison officers] MLOs will contribute to confidence-building among the parties and represent the vanguard of further UN involvement."[44] The Congolese mission at the UN pushed hard for this resolution, and even embarked on a successful campaign to lobby African members of the Security Council and other nonpermanent members through the Non-Aligned Movement (NAM) caucus. The Congo viewed a UN intervention as being very much in its interest, both because Kinshasa recognized that it would not easily defeat the Rwandan military and because as long as Rwanda claimed that it had security concerns, it would generate international sympathy. It was, therefore, hoped that a UN intervention would help eliminate the principal justification for Rwanda's presence in the Congo.[45]

Once this small technical assessment team was deployed, the Security Council adopted Resolution 1279 on 30 November 1999 authorizing the United Nations Observer Mission in the DRC (MONUC). MONUC would be constituted by the earlier deployment of military liaison personnel and increased by an additional 500 military observers.[46] Its mandate included that of the earlier technical assessment team, the "observation of the ceasefire and the disengagement of forces" (paragraph 5d) and "to facilitate the delivery of humanitarian assistance" (paragraph 5e). The deployment of the force was to occur in three phases, conditional on the security situation on the ground. Phase I, the deployment of military liaison officers to the headquarters of all the signatories to the agreement to help coordination, had already been launched under Resolution 1258. The deployment of military observers inside the Congo, authorized by Resolution 1279, to monitor compliance with the peace agreement constituted phase II.

In January 2000, the warring parties met in New York under the auspices of the UN Security Council during "Africa month"—an initiative of US Ambassador Richard Holbrooke who held the Security Council presidency during that month.[47] This was a public relations victory for Kabila. The Security Council accorded him all of the trimmings reserved for a head of state, while the rebel leaders or their representatives sat in the gallery. On 24 February 2000, the Security Council adopted Resolution 1291 extending MONUC's mandate for another six months and expanded the force to 5,537 military personnel, including 500 observers and appropriate civilian staff. The resolution gave the mission the authority, under Chapter VII, "to take the necessary action . . . to protect United Nations personnel . . . ensure the security of and freedom of movement of its personnel, and protect civilians under imminent threat of physical violence." Kabila, demonstrating his long-standing suspicion of Westerners, supported the resolution only on the condition that the UN force would be composed solely of troops from the South, preferably from Africa, and reserved the right to reject or approve any of the contributions. The size of the force authorized was criticized again as far too small to effectively monitor a peace agreement with multiple belligerents in a country with little infrastructure.

Eventually, agreement was reached on the condition that the authorized force would constitute only a second phase, with a larger force deployed in a subsequent phase.[48] Frequent cease-fire violations and Kinshasa's continued refusal to allow the UN unfettered access made deployment of phase II difficult and the monitoring of the disengagement of forces nearly impossible. Because of these difficulties, the OAU deployed 30 "neutral verification teams" inside the Congo in November 1999 for a year to help monitor the cease-fire pending the deployment of MONUC observers.[49] President Kabila assured a Security Council mission to the Congo led by Ambassador Holbrooke between 4 and 8 May 2000—the first of a series—that Kinshasa would fully cooperate with MONUC, while criticizing the UN for "failing to condemn the presence of uninvited troops" in the Congo.[50] Disagreements over where to colocate the JMC and MONUC, and the MLC's refusal to withdraw its forces as mandated by phase II further delayed deployment.[51]

A devastating clash between Ugandan and Rwandan troops in Kisangani that began on 5 June 2000 resulted in thousands of civilian casualties and neither inspired confidence at the UN that there would soon be any peace to keep, nor favored calls for a more robust UN force in the Congo. A strongly worded resolution adopted by the Security Council on 16 June expressed "outrage" at the fighting, called for the immediate demilitarization of Kisangani and the withdrawal of foreign troops from the country, and, for the first time, directly accused Uganda and Rwanda of violating "the sovereignty and territorial integrity of the Democratic Republic of the Congo" and asked Uganda and Rwanda to "pay reparations for the loss of life and the property damage they have inflicted on the civilian population in Kisangani."[52] Discussions with American and other officials led to the conclusion that this resolution was driven primarily by French animus toward Rwanda. The American position was that this resolution would severely undermine the Lusaka process in two ways. First, because it gave primacy to the withdrawal of foreign forces over the promotion of internal dialogue and the disarmament of armed groups, and, therefore, would only serve to harden the resistance of the Kinshasa hard-liners to disarming Army for the Liberation of Rwanda (ALiR) (Interahamwe/ex-FAR). Second, because it privileged the foreign forces supporting Kinshasa, therefore undoing the balance reflected in the Lusaka Agreement's failure to distinguish between Kinshasa's foreign allies and the foreign allies of the rebel groups. Since the adoption of this resolution, the Kinshasa government has repeatedly emphasized the specific reference to Rwanda and Uganda, which has made progress on foreign troop withdrawal more difficult. Indeed, to date, there has been virtually no movement on the ground in this direction. Today, Ugandan and Rwandan troops have left Kisangani, but the RCD-Goma continues to maintain a presence there despite repeated UN calls to demilitarize the city.

Laurent Kabila's assassination on 16 January 2001 removed some of the obstacles to further MONUC deployment, as his twenty-nine-year-old son and successor, Joseph Kabila, soon consented to the full deployment of UN forces. On 22 February 2001, Security Council Resolution 1341 demanded that "Ugandan and Rwandan forces and all other foreign forces withdraw" from the Congo, and asked that a timetable for that withdrawal be prepared within the next three months.

On 26 April 2001, six workers with the International Committee of the Red Cross were killed by armed groups near Bunia, leading then Security Council President, UK

Ambassador Sir Jeremy Greenstock, to note that the incident "made us not just worry about the safety of humanitarian and other UN international workers, but also for the peace process in the Congo."[53] Moreover, Uganda's anger at the accusations made against Ugandan officials in the April 2001 UN Report on Resource Exploitation in the DRC led Museveni to declare Uganda's unilateral withdrawal from the Congo and from the Lusaka Agreement. However, as Kamel Morjane, the UN's special representative for the Congo noted, Uganda's withdrawal would not threaten the peace process: "If the government decides to withdraw its forces from the Congo, it's always favorable. This is in line with the Lusaka Agreement."[54] Museveni did not follow through on his threat.

It was in this climate that the Security Council, this time led by French Ambassador Jean-David Levitte, visited the Central African region in mid-May 2001 to assess efforts to implement the peace plan. On the day the delegation was due to arrive in Kinshasa, Kabila repealed Decree 194, imposed by his father to restrict political party activity. This high-level delegation determined that "the cease-fire is holding and the parties to the conflict, with one exception, have disengaged their forces in accordance with the agreement they have signed."[55] The Security Council delegation took the opportunity of MONUC's imminent receipt of two fast patrol boats to announce that MONUC was reopening the vast Congolese river network. What the delegation failed to mention was that there was a third war emerging in eastern Congo. This violent, popular rebellion against the Rwandan occupation pitted the Mai Mai in alliance with ALiR (Interahamwe/ex-FAR), the Burundian Hutu insurgents, and the FDD (Forces pour la Défense de la Démocratie),[56] all supported by Kinshasa, against the RCD-Goma, the Rwandans, and to a lesser extent, against the now defunt Front de libération congolais.[57]

On the basis of the Security Council mission's report, the Security Council decided that disengagement was nearly complete, and on 15 June 2001, adopted Resolution 1355 authorizing preparations for the deployment of phase III including plans for the voluntary disarmament, demobilization, repatriation, reintegration, and resettlement (DDRRR) of all armed groups in the Congo. The role of the UN in this process, as spelled out in a joint communiqué signed by all the parties at the conclusion of the Security Council's visit to the region in May 2001, is that of an "impartial arbiter."[58] The UN is responsible for coordinating all aspects of the DDRRR process, while international humanitarian agencies are responsible for the screening of génocidaires and war criminals and turning them over to the international tribunal investigating the Rwanda genocide.[59] The role of the UN and the OAU, therefore, is one of coordination and monitoring. The rest is conditional on the voluntary compliance of the armed groups. In other words, the foreign armed militia fighters in the Congo are asked to voluntarily give up their arms and demobilize, and to voluntarily return to their countries of origin. Enforced compliance is not in the mandate established by the UN or the OAU.

MONUC's Chapter VII mandate was initially a Chapter "6 1/2" mandate—its enforcement capability is limited to the protection of its own personnel, that of humanitarian relief workers, and some Congolese civilians. It was not authorized to disarm armed militias by force. The problem with voluntary compliance, however, is that many of these armed groups can be expected to go underground to avoid giving up their weapons, a fact noted by the UN as early as June 2001.[60]

MONUC troops were gradually deployed in previously blocked areas, and as of 30 September 2002, 4,309 out of the authorized 5,537 uniformed personnel had been deployed.[61] Despite its relatively small numbers, MONUC had established a noticeable presence in some key cities in the country. Its riverboat units patrolled some of the country's waterways, thus encouraging the movement of people and goods, and it provided over US$700,000 worth of relief support, mostly in the form of air transport for relief workers, after the devastation caused by the eruption of Mount Nyiragongo in Goma on 17 January 2002.

Calls for a multinational force were more successful in 2003 than in 1996, after a series of talks with regional actors brokered by Pretoria in December 2002 led to the withdrawal of foreign forces from the DRC. The withdrawal of Ugandan troops from Ituri created a power vaccum in Northeastern DRC that precipitated a deadly spate of factional fighting between ethnic-based militias controlled by the Hendu and Lendu ethnic groups, themselves proxies for some of the departing foreign forces. In the spring of 2003, several thousand civilians fleeing the violence in the town of Bunia sought refuge around the MONUC compound housing 700 Uruguayan peacekeepers, who proved unable to stop the violence. As tensions and public outcry at MONUC's inability to respond effectively mounted, in May 2003, the UN Security Council authorized the deployment of an EU-led International Emergency Multinational Force named Operation Artemis, to Ituri. Authorized under a UN Chapter VII mandate, Artemis was to be an interim force for three months to stabilize the region and give MONUC time to be reinforced. Since then, most of the UN's 17,000 military personnel in the DRC have been deployed in eastern Congo.

Responses to the Third Congo War and Continued Violence in Eastern DRC

Since the signing of the Lusaka Agreement, there was relatively little violence or combat along the cease-fire lines between Kinshasa-controlled and rebel-controlled regions. Violence and the accompanying humanitarian disaster were largely limited to the struggle between Mai Mai–ALiR (now FDLR)–FDD forces against Rwanda and the RCD and the violence in the northeast. A bilateral agreement signed between Kinshasa and Kigali in Pretoria on 30 July 2002 resulted in the complete withdrawal of Rwandan forces in return for Kinshasa's promise to dismantle the Hutu militias and hand them over to Rwanda. A similar cease-fire agreement with Kampala in Luanda on 6 September 2002 resulted in the withdrawal of Ugandan forces. While the withdrawal of foreign troops paved the way to the formation of a government of national unity and to the first national elections in 2006, it also created a power vacuum in the east, and a significant increase in violent, anarchic conflict between ever smaller groups that no major actor effectively controls. This violence persists to this day.

Despite two national elections since the transition, there is little evidence in DRC that a liberal political order is emerging through independent courts, free media, and civil society. Without these accompanying institutional transformations from the institutional legacies of war, the legacy of fear prevails. Election processes provided an opportunity to build the institutional building blocks and structures that support democratization, but this failed to happen. It is difficult to mitigate violence around elections when preexisting grievances have not been addressed in the period between the first and second post-conflict elections.

The bulk of the ongoing violence is concentrated in eastern Congo, where the implementation of the March 23 Agreements between the government and armed groups in the Kivus remains at a standstill. New alliances of convenience between residual Congolese and foreign armed groups and between them and Congolese army officers are locked in fierce competition for control over lucrative mining interests. These intense rivalries have devastating consequences on civilian populations in the region. Attacks on civilians routinely include sexual violence, lootings, and abductions, and continue to result in one of the highest rates of displacement in Africa today.

In North and South Kivu provinces, targeted Armed Forces of the Democratic Republic of Congo (FARDC, Forces Armées de la République Démocratique du Congo) military operations against the FDLR with the support of MONUSCO have had limited results in neutralizing the FDLR, which continued its reprisal attacks against civilian populations.

The Lord's Resistance Army

Moreover, the Lord's Resistance Army (LRA) continues to operate among northeast DRC, Central African Republic, and southern Sudan. The group routinely attacks civilians and is accused of carrying out a repeat of its "Christmas massacres" of December 2008 again in December 2009, when it killed over 100 civilians in remote villages in Haut- and Bas-Uélé. Of concern also is the impact that the 2011 referendum process in Sudan might have on the LRA dynamic. Joint FARDC and Uganda People's Defence Forces operations targeting the LRA continue, with MONUSCO logistical support. The regional threat presented by the LRA, however, and the remoteness of northern Orientale province have severely challenged MONUSCO's increasingly limited resources and its ability to effectively protect civilians targeted in reprisal attacks.

In recent years, much of UN–AU cooperation in the region has focused on the fight against the LRA and efforts to apprehend or kill its leader, Vincent Kony. Several AU summits highlighted the regional threat posed by the LRA and the Kampala summit in July 2010 announced that the AU would coordinate regional action. A meeting of international stakeholders held in Bangui in October 2010 under AU auspices and chaired by President Bozizé established a series of proposals for the AU initiative against the LRA. This initiative consists of two actions: the appointment in November 2011 of former Mozambican diplomat Francisco Madeira as the AU special envoy for LRA and the creation of a regional force (renamed the Regional Intervention Force or RIF) to track down the LRA.

In practice, this initiative has had limited success thus far. First, the subsequent creation of a Joint Coordinating Mechanism (JCM) composed of ministers from the region reduced the special envoy's role to largely a coordinating one. Second, the RIF was not a new force but rather re-hatted Ugandan troops with US support already involved in the hunt for Kony. Third, tensions among states in the region, in particular between DRC and Uganda, remain, and have strained the regional effort.

The UN response to the LRA shifted in 2011 from MONUSCO to supporting the AU regional initiative through its recently established political mission for Central Africa,

United Nations Regional Office for Central Africa (UNOCA), and SRSG Abou Moussa, who has been playing a coordinating role. UNOCA was requested, in coordination with the United Nations Office to the African Union (UNOAU), to engage with the AU and facilitate cooperation between the UN and the AU on the LRA. As the focal point for the UN's response to the LRA threat, on 10 and 11 October 2011, UNOCA hosted a meeting of the UN presence in Central Africa to discuss ways of strengthening a coordinated approach to UN support for peace endeavors in the region, and more actively addressing cross-border threats to regional security, including the LRA. However, as recently as June 2012, Moussa appealed to the Security Council to actively support the implementation of the UN regional strategy and the AU Regional Cooperation Initiative, as the international funding that the AU had hoped for has not been forthcoming.

The CNDP and March 23 Movement

In November 2008, in response to Laurence Nkunda's growing CNDP rebellion, the UN Secretary-General announced a high-level UN–AU mediation effort, headed by former Nigerian President Obasanjo. This dual-hatted mediation effort was greeted with cautious optimism that this would bring about the focused and comprehensive international political approach that had been lacking in the postelectoral period, but it was soon overtaken by events on the ground. The arrest of Nkunda by the Rwandan government in January 2009 (the result of Nkunda's growing national ambitions and increased international pressure on Kigali), and the three-way deal among Rwanda, DRC, and Nkunda's chief of staff General Bosco Ntaganda to cooperate in pursuing the FDLR, caught the international community—and Obasanjo—by surprise. The sudden and rapid rapprochement between the two governments and their joint operations (led largely by Rwandan forces) against the FDLR, while welcomed by the international community, were met with caution in the DRC and, in some cases, seen as an alarming indication that Rwandan forces were back in the country.

The 2011 election proved challenging for the UN and stabilization efforts as MONUSCO had barely half of the international resources devoted to elections than MONUC had in 2006. Moreover, the compressed election calendar and large-scale voter fraud and intimidation, particularly by CNDP forces in this election, eroded President Kabila's earlier powerbase in the Kivus. The Kagame–Kabila "deal" quickly unraveled after the elections and the subsequent emergence of the Rwandan-backed March 23 Movement (M23) rebellion[62] led by Bosco Ntaganda has created renewed insecurity and instability in the region.

Regional frustration with MONUSCO's failures to eradicate the FDLR—seen by many Congolese as pretext for Rwanda's continued interference in eastern DRC—has led to a call for the establishment of a "neutral" regional force under the auspices of the until recently largely dormant and under-resourced International Conference on the Great Lakes Region. While there have been some initial offers to contribute troops to this regional force from some regional actors (Tanzania and South Africa), it is yet to be seen whether others will contribute troops, for what mandate precisely, and how this neutral force will relate to the existing UN presence of 19,000 UN troops already on the ground. A mini-summit held in New York in the margins of the UN General Assembly in September 2012 yielded few clues about how this crisis will be resolved. Furthermore, while there is mounting international pressure for Rwanda to end its support for M23, it is not clear whether this crisis has a military solution.

As of this writing, there are also calls for the appointment of a UN–AU special envoy again as there is an emerging consensus among Congo analysts that efforts to end the violence in DRC have deeply neglected politics and in particular Rwanda's real interests in the region. Recent years have focused on military solutions (LRA, FDLR) with mixed results. There is thus an urgent need for a comprehensive political framework that would address a key issue in the ongoing cycle of violence and that is Congo's relationship with Rwanda.

Conclusion

The UN peacekeeping and now stabilization mission in the DRC, despite being the largest and most expensive mission fielded to date, was initially strongly resisted by the Security Council.

It took the region to convince the Security Council that external intervention was necessary. The regional powerbrokers who mediated the Lusaka Ceasefire Agreement recognized the limitations of a divided region in undertaking the implementation of the agreement. During pre-Lusaka discussions about an OAU-led, inter-African peacekeeping force for the Congo, OAU Secretary-General Salim Ahmed Salim acknowledged publicly that his organization lacked the capacity to successfully undertake such an operation.[63] In addition to constraints in capacity, members of the OAU supported widely divergent policies in the Congo wars—some supported Kinshasa, some the rebels, and some opted for neutrality. It was virtually impossible to obtain agreement on a common policy, leaving aside the absence of capacity and means.

For SADC, there were similar concerns about resources and capacity. South Africa, the region's dominant economy, made it clear that it had no intention of carrying the financial burden of a regional peacekeeping force. "I think there is a growing consensus that any DRC mission should not be just a SADC affair. We want other western countries to join in. We know if it is just SADC then South Africa will be left to underwrite the whole deployment. We do not want the DRC buck to stop here."[64]

Although largely absent as an institutional force from the first war, SADC responded in a significant way to the later wars in the Congo. That response has taken three forms: mediation, military intervention, and advocacy with the international community. Many of the efforts to mediate a peaceful settlement during the second Congo war were SADC-driven and much of the mediation in both wars was undertaken by leaders in the SADC region. President Mandela was especially instrumental in the Mobutu–Kabila negotiations in 1996–1997, and President Chiluba led regional efforts to pressure the parties into signing a cease-fire agreement. While some SADC powerbrokers were, from the beginning, deeply committed to achieving a cease-fire, clearly others were motivated by the belief that military victory was unlikely or would be too expensive.

One lesson from these wars and attempts to end them, therefore, is that when an entire region is deeply divided by war, it cannot effectively enforce the peace, even if it has been successful in reaching a negotiated settlement. In other words, combatants cannot enforce the peace against themselves. They can participate in peacemaking, and ultimately must do so, but if there is to be peace enforcement, others will have to do it. Moreover, in an interstate war of the magnitude and complexity of the Congo wars, building the peacekeeping capacity of regional organizations alone is unlikely to lead to successful peace enforcement. Hence, while the closeness of regional and subregional groupings to local conflict areas gives them the vested interests to seek stability in their region, this close proximity is a double-edged sword. If DRC today is any example, regional leaders will back opposing interests in the war. Thus, we must not automatically assume that "backyard operations" will lead to peace; in the case of the Congo, they have prolonged and exacerbated the war.

A second lesson one can draw from the Congo wars about regional solutions is that despite deep regional divisions, regional actors can (and did) initiate and successfully negotiate agreements to end conflicts in which large and important portions of that region are themselves participants in the conflict. However, the lessons from the Congo also suggest that the more regionally based the conflict is in terms of state actors involved in it, the more difficult the task of mediation becomes without external partners—partly due to capacity constraints but mostly due to the need for external guarantors and credible, punitive threats for noncooperation. In each case in the DRC, the winning formula for brokering agreements was stepped-up regional engagement, often led by South Africa, backstopped by high-level UN support (either in the form of peacekeeping or special envoys, eventually both), and sharply increased US diplomatic pressure on Rwanda, Uganda, and the DRC. In DRC, the problem has not been negotiating agreements but in ensuring their implementation once they have been signed.

Moreover, the DRC experience and frustration with international (in-)action to end the violence reminds us that consent still matters, which makes the implementation of political mandates all that more difficult. Closer UN–regional cooperation here is critical. However, in the DRC, neither the UN nor the AU has had an effective political strategy toward DRC, while powerful states in the region have. There is an urgent need to identify a clear and productive division of labor between international and regional actors that would best produce and sustain the comprehensive political framework for building a sustainable peace currently lacking in the DRC.

Notes

1. The Mai Mai (or Mayi Mayi) are Congolese civilian "self-defense" militias in the Kivus who mobilize to fight foreign occupation. They have no common leadership or coordination.
2. When referring to the United Nations, one must always be aware that there are, in effect, three UNs: the secretariats (UN as independent actor), the member states (UN as forum for debate), and the networks of NGOs and think tanks that advocate and inform policy. (Thomas G. Weiss, Tatiana Carayannis, and Richard Jolly, "The 'Third' United Nations," *Global Governance* 15 (2009): 123–142.) In many cases, UN secretariats are aware of issues and needs in conflict situations but cannot mobilize member states to act appropriately or in a timely manner. In this chapter, unless specified otherwise, UN action refers to member states' decisions at the Security Council.

3. Complex hybrid wars combine elements of civil (or intrastate) war, interstate war, and cross-border insurgencies. The term "regional war" is often a misnomer as some of the production of violence in these wars can be located outside the region. See Tatiana Carayannis, "The Complex Wars of the Congo: Towards a New Analytic Approach," *Journal of Asian and African Studies* 38:2–3 (2003): 232–255. Reprinted in Rose Kadende-Kaiser and Paul J. Kaiser, *Phases of Conflict in Africa* (Willowdale, ON: de Sitter Publications, 2005).
4. Much of this background is drawn from Tatiana Carayannis and Herbert F. Weiss, "The Democratic Republic of Congo, 1996–2002," in *Dealing with Conflict in Africa: The United Nations and Regional Organizations*, ed. Jane Boulden (New York: Palgrave Macmillan, 2003), pp. 253–303, and from Tatiana Carayannis, "Challenges of Peacebuilding in the Congo," Background paper. *Centre for Humanitarian Dialogue*, July 2009.
5. See Gérard Prunier, *The Rwanda Crisis: History of a Genocide* (New York: Columbia University Press, 1995); Linda Melvern, *A People Betrayed: The Role of the West in Rwanda's Genocide* (New York: Zed Books, 2000); J. Matthew Vaccaro, "The Politics of Genocide: Peacekeeping and Disaster Relief in Rwanda," in *UN Peacekeeping, American Policy, and the Uncivil Wars of the 1990s*, ed. William J. Durch (New York: St. Martin's Press, 1996), pp. 367–407; Philip Gourevitch, *We Wish to Inform You that Tomorrow We Will Be Killed with our Families: Stories from Rwanda* (New York: Farar, Straus, and Giroux, 1998); Scott Peterson, *Me against My Brother: At War in Somalia, Sudan, and Rwanda* (New York: Routledge, 2000); Bruce D. Jones, *Peacemaking in Rwanda: The Dynamics of Failure* (Boulder, CO: Lynne Rienner, 2001); United Nations, "UN Report of the Independent Inquiry into the Actions of the United Nation during the 1994 Genocide in Rwanda," 15 December 1999.
6. UNAMIR forces were mandated to help implement a cease-fire agreement and transitional arrangements. On 21 April 1994, the UN Security Council voted to reduce its UNAMIR forces by 90 percent, to 270 troops. France voted in favor of the withdrawal.
7. Six weeks earlier, on 6 May, Security Council resolution 918 authorized UNAMIR II, a redeployment of 5,500 UN troops with a Chapter VII humanitarian mandate, and imposed an arms embargo on Rwanda. However, delays in contributions meant that UNAMIR II was not deployed until August, three months later, just as *Opération Turquoise* was withdrawing its forces.
8. Resolution 925 was adopted on 8 June 1994 to extend UNAMIR's mandate for another six months, until 9 December 1994. Its mandate required UNAMIR to protect internally displaced persons (IDPs), refugees, and civilians by establishing "secure humanitarian areas," and "provide security and support for the distribution of relief supplies and humanitarian relief operations."
9. UN Security Council resolution 929 was adopted on 22 June 1994.
10. Goma is in eastern Congo, across the Congo–Rwanda border.
11. Within days, in what was a quid pro quo for each power, the Security Council authorized similar operations for the United States in Haiti and for Russia in Georgia.
12. Patrick de Saint-Exupery, "Rwanda. Les assassins racontent leurs massacres," *Le Figaro*, 29 June 1994. Quoted in Prunier, p. 292.
13. See Prunier's account of *Opération Turquoise* in Prunier, *The Rwanda Crisis*, pp. 281–311. Prunier was a member of the French Crisis Unit that supported the operation.
14. Jones, *Peacemaking in Rwanda*, p. 123.
15. Romeo A. Dallaire, "The End of Innocence: Rwanda 1994," in *Hard Choices: Moral Dilemmas in Humanitarian Intervention*, ed. Jonathan Moore (Lanham, MD: Rowman and Littlefield, 1998), pp. 71–86.
16. Once out of power, known as "the ex-FAR."
17. In fact, the principal pro-democracy NGOs in the Congo, the Comité national des organisations non-gouvernementales au développement, issued a statement shortly after

the war started, confirming the presence of Rwandan and Ugandan troops fighting alongside the Banyamulenge in the Congo. *Info-Zaire* newsletter, "Feuillet d'information produit par la Table de Concertation sur les Droits Humains au Zaire," No. 121 (26 November 1996).

18. James C. McKinley, Jr., "Zaire's Rebels Win New Converts," *New York Times*, 21 February 2001.
19. For a discussion of French fear of US dominance in Africa, see Howard W. French, "France Fear U.S. Advance in Africa," *New York Times*, 4 April 1997, and Gérard Prunier, "Operation Turquoise: A Humanitarian Escape From a Political Dead End," *Centre de la Recherche Scientifique*, unpublished paper (December 1995).
20. "France Linked to Defense of Mobutu" *New York Times*, 2 May 1997.
21. Yugoslav government officials and Geolink, a Paris-based telecommunications company, allegedly ran the French covert operation. "France Linked to Defense of Mobutu," *New York Times*, 2 May 1997.
22. "Zaire's Rebels Win New Converts," *New York Times*, 21 February 2001.
23. Press Statement by the Regional Summit on the Crisis in Eastern Zaire, 5 November 1996. Reprinted by United Nations Department of Humanitarian Affairs, Integrated Regional Information Network (IRIN).
24. *Info-Zaire* newsletter, 26 November 1996.
25. Under the resolution, the objectives of the task force include "short-term humanitarian assistance and shelter to refugees and displaced persons in eastern Zaire, assisting the United Nations High Commissioner for Refugees with the protection and voluntary repatriation of refugees and displaced persons, and establishing humanitarian corridors for the delivery of humanitarian assistance."
26. United Nations, Security Council resolution 1097, 18 February 1997.
27. For an account of the process that led to the decision to authorize the Canadian operation, including the debates within the Canadian government and between Canada and the United States, see John B. Hay, "Conditions of Influence: An Exploratory Study of the Canadian Government's Effect on U.S. Policy in the Case of Intervention in Eastern Zaire." Unpublished MA thesis submitted to the Faculty of Graduate Studies and Research, The Norman Paterson School of International Affairs, Carleton University, Ottawa, Ontario, May 1998. Also see, James Appathurai and Ralph Lyshysyn, "Lessons Learned from the Zaire Mission," *Canadian Foreign Policy* 5:2 (Winter 1998): 93–105.
28. Now the FDLR, although nearly two decades after the Rwanda genocide, looks very different from the earlier ex-FAR/Interahamwe, as only a few of the FDLR's commanders are hardcore *genocidaires*. Many in the FDLR rank and file were too young to have been involved in the 1994 genocide.
29. Although Rwanda eventually went along with the proposed intervention, it objected to any efforts to repatriate Hutu refugees that were not authorized to disarm them first. Humanitarian NGOs were also insisting upon disarmament as a necessary condition for humanitarian relief efforts.
30. United Nations, Security Council Press Release of 3713th meeting, SC/6291, 15 November 1996.
31. Ibid.
32. Those Rwandan Hutu who remained in the Congo were probably largely made up of Interahamwe/ex-FAR, their families, and some ordinary civilians who had either been forced or volunteered to withdraw westward to escape the advancing forces of the anti-Mobutu alliance.
33. The mission was abandoned in spite of arguments by United Nations High Commissioner for Refugees (UNHCR) and humanitarian relief organizations questioning the numbers of refugees actually returning to Rwanda, *Info-Zaire* newsletter, 26 November 1996.

34. The MLC and the RCD signed in August, as a leadership quarrel within the RCD had held up its signing since neither faction's leaders could agree on who should sign for the movement. Eventually, that disagreement was overcome by having all 50 founding members of the RCD become signatories.
35. Tatiana Carayannis, "The Complex Wars of the Congo: Towards a New Analytic Approach," *Journal of Asian and African Studies* 38:2–3 (2003): 232–255.
36. The DRC became a member of SADC on 28 February 1998.
37. Security Council Resolution 1234, 9 April 1999.
38. Cedric de Coning, "Neo-Interventionism: An African Response to Failed Internationalism," *South African Yearbook of International Affairs*, 1999–2000, quoted in *Whither Regional Peace and Security? The DRC After the War*, ed. Denis Kadima and Claude Kabemba (Pretoria: Africa Institute of South Africa, 2000), pp. 15–16.
39. See International Crisis Group, *Africa's Seven Nation War* (International Crisis Group DRC Report no. 4, 21 May 1999).
40. For an account of the Sun City negotiations, see Paule Bouvier and Francesca Bomboko, *Le Dialogue Intercongolais* (Paris: L'Harmattan, 2004).
41. Integrated Regional Information Network report, 22 April 2002.
42. See United Nations, Statement by the President of the Security Council, S/PRST/1998/26 (31 August 1998) and United Nations, Statement by the President of the Security Council, S/PRST/1998/36 (11 December 1998).
43. S/PRST/1998/36, 11 December 1998.
44. United Nations, Integrated Regional Information Network, "UN Military Officers Prepare for Deployment," 9 September 1999.
45. Interview with André Kapanga, Congolese ambassador to the UN under Laurent Kabila, and the authors, 4 April 2002.
46. South Africa's Institute for Security Studies has correctly noted that MONUC is "[a]rguably the most complicated and ambitious post-Cold War experiment in the creation of peace from chaos with fairly modest resources." Jakkie Cilliers and Mark Malan, *Peacekeeping in the DRC: MONUC and the Road to Peace*, Monograph no. 66 (Halfway House: Institute for Security Studies, October 2001), Executive Summary, p. 3. Given the size of the country and the number of different combatants, domestic and foreign, one could well amend "fairly modest" to "inadequate"—both in terms of its mandate and size.
47. During this "Africa Month," the Security Council also discussed the problem of the AIDS pandemic in Africa, an unprecedented step which moved the Council closer to a broader conceptualization of security. In an equally unusual development, Holbrooke invited Vice-president Al Gore to address the Council on the issue of AIDS.
48. Interview with André Kapanga and the authors, 14 March 2002.
49. *Entrepreneur*, 18–24 October 2001, p. 4.
50. United Nations, "Report of the Security Council Mission to the Democratic Republic of the Congo, 4–8 May 2000," S/2000/416.
51. MLC leader Jean-Pierre Bemba, fearing a power vacuum in Equateur Province, insisted that he would not withdraw unless the UN deployed a force large enough to guarantee the security of over 100,000 people in villages MLC forces had "liberated." "I think this UN and the international community only cares about my army withdrawing, but do not care if the black Congolese are massacred by the Interahamwe and government forces." Jean-Pierre Bemba, quoted in United Nations, Integrated Regional Information Network report 2 May 2001. The reason he mentions the Interahamwe—usually associated with the conflict in the Kivus—is that Kabila had deployed Hutu battalions in the FAC to the Equateur front where they were considered by the MLC as being Kinshasa's best soldiers. These Rwandan Hutu soldiers were mobilized by the Kabila regime, largely from UNHCR camps, both in the Congo and Congo-Brazzaville shortly after the second Congo war started.

52. Security Council Resolution 1304, 16 June 2000. The Security Council also asked the Secretary-General "to submit an assessment of the damage as a basis for such reparations."
53. United Nations, Integrated Regional Information Network report, 30 April 2001.
54. "Uganda Pulls Out of Peace Pact Intended to End Congo Civil War," *New York Times*, 30 April 2001.
55. The exception was Bemba's Front de libération congolais, the now defunct and short-lived Museveni-initiated alliance between the MLC and the RCD-ML in north Kivu. United Nations, "Report of the Security Council Mission to the Great Lakes Region, 15–26 May 2001," Addendum, Annex I, paragraph 4.
56. The FDD is the military wing of the Burundian Hutu party Conseil National pour la Défense de la Démocratie (CNDD).
57. The Front de libération Congolais was the short-lived alliance between the MLC and the RCD-ML in north Kivu initiated by Uganda which at that time backed both rebel groups.
58. United Nations, "Report of the Security Council Mission to the Great Lakes Region, 15–26 May 2001," Addendum, Annex III, paragraph 11.
59. This process would be facilitated by a radio and print media information campaign undertaken by "the UN, the OAU and the signatories" (paragraph 16) on the incentive packages for those with arms to give them up.
60. United Nations, "Eighth Report of the Secretary-General on MONUC, 8 June 2001," S/2001/572, para. 106.
61. On 4 December 2002, Security Council resolution 1445 expanded the number of troops authorized to 8,700.
62. Two reports of the UN Expert Group on DRC have established Rwandan government support for the M23 rebellion, despite protests to the contrary by Kigali. For all of the Expert Group's reports, see http://www.un.org/sc/committees/1533/egroup.shtml.
63. International Crisis Group, *Africa's Seven Nation War*, p. 8.
64. A South African defense official, quoted in United Nations, Integrated Regional Information Network, "Military Apprehensive ahead of DRC Peacekeeping," 27 August 1999.

Chapter 9

Liberia

Katharina Coleman

Introduction

The Liberian civil war has historical roots dating back to the nineteenth century, when the modern state of Liberia was formally created by freed US slaves who were "repatriated" to Africa by the American Colonization Society. The subsequent domination of Liberian politics and society by "Americo-Liberians" only ended in 1980, when former Master Sergeant Samuel Doe came to power following a coup. Popular enthusiasm for seeing an "indigenous" Liberian in power waned as the Doe regime revealed itself to be authoritarian, violent, and biased toward Doe's own ethnic group, the Krahn.[1] The Doe era thus added escalating ethnic tensions among indigenous Liberians to the long-standing animosity between indigenous and Americo-Liberians.

The proximate cause of Liberia's extended civil war, however, was Charles Taylor's protracted struggle to gain and subsequently maintain power in Liberia. Taylor initiated an armed rebellion against Doe in 1989, and despite Doe's death in 1990, Taylor continued to lead the National Patriotic Front of Liberia (NPFL) in an armed struggle for control of Liberia until he was elected to the country's presidency in 1997. From 1999 onward, Taylor was himself challenged by armed rebellions. This second phase of Liberia's civil war ended with Taylor's resignation and exile to Nigeria in August 2003, the 2005 democratic election of Ellen Sirleaf to Liberia's presidency, and Taylor's 2006 extradition to face trial for war crimes and crimes against humanity before the Special Court for Sierra Leone in The Hague.

The division of labor between global and regional actors responding to the conflict differed dramatically between the two phases of the war. Both phases witnessed a military intervention by the Economic Community of West African States (ECOWAS) and a subsequent United Nations (UN) deployment, but the modalities of these deployments and how they related to each other were fundamentally different. In the first phase, the ECOWAS operation was a long-term deployment and the UN committed only a small monitoring mission. In the second phase, ECOWAS deployed an interim

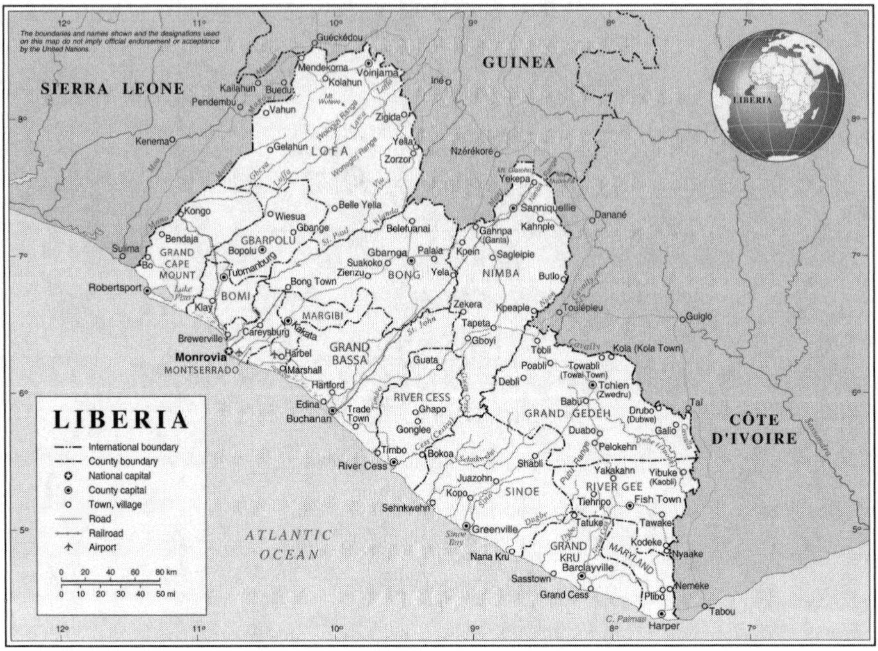

Source: Map No 3775 Rev 7, United Nations, Department of Peacekeeping Operations, Cartographic Section, October 2010

force that was replaced by a UN follow-on mission. It is thus tempting to see the two phases of Liberia's civil war as illustrating the evolution from one model of UN–regional cooperation in conflict management to another.

However, this chapter cautions against moving too quickly from observing the differences in the division of labor between the UN and ECOWAS to concluding that a new and potentially generalizable model of cooperation had been adopted by either these organizations or their individual member states. In both phases of the Liberian war, international cooperation was arrived at in an ad hoc manner resulting more from circumstances and negotiation than from an application of a general model. Admittedly, the first pair of ECOWAS and UN interventions was presented as instantiating a new model of cooperation. Nevertheless—and only partially because of the failures of this "model"—the 2003 division of labor was again a political compromise reached through interstate negotiation. While shaped by lessons from the 1990s, it ultimately reflected not a consensus conception for improved UN–ECOWAS cooperation but a political bargain reflecting the interests and relative power of two key states, the United States and Nigeria. Thus, the Liberian case suggests that it may be misleading to think in terms of general models of cooperation between the UN and regional organizations in conflict management: The precise "model" of cooperation is renegotiated on a case-by-case basis in each new conflict.

This chapter proceeds as follows. The first section focuses on the first experience of ECOWAS–UN cooperation for conflict management in Liberia. It provides an overview of ECOWAS and UN efforts before offering an account of how this division of labor emerged. The second section examines the division of labor that emerged between ECOWAS and UN in the second phase of Liberia's civil war. It highlights the importance of three interrelated factors in shaping this new division of labor (early UN engagement in the emerging crisis, ECOWAS insistence on a limited military role, and interstate bargaining about the distribution of conflict-management responsibilities) before summarizing key developments in Liberia after 2003. The conclusion reflects on the lessons of this case study.

ECOWAS and UN Cooperation in the 1990s

Taylor crossed into Liberia from Côte d'Ivoire in December 1989, and by June 1990, the NPFL controlled some 90 percent of the countryside and was besieging Monrovia.[2] In July 1990, Liberia's UN ambassador asked the Security Council to address the conflict,[3] and Doe also appealed to the ECOWAS Standing Mediation Committee (SMC) for assistance. The SMC responded on 7 August 1990 by calling for an immediate cease-fire in Liberia and for an ECOWAS Ceasefire Monitoring Group (ECOMOG) to help implement this cease-fire.[4] On 24 August, some 2,600–3,500 ECOMOG troops were deployed to Liberia, landing under hostile fire because Taylor had rejected the cease-fire.[5] ECOMOG established a beachhead, and secured Monrovia by November. Its strength increased, reaching about 6,000 troops in October 1990 and expanding further in subsequent years to peaks of over 12,000 troops.[6] By contrast, the UN Observer Mission in Liberia (UNOMIL) only began in September 1993 and its strength never exceeded 370 troops. Neither deployment proved able to end the Liberian civil war, which despite thirteen cease-fires and peace accords effectively continued until 1997, when Taylor won the Liberian presidency in elections monitored by both ECOWAS and the UN.[7]

ECOWAS and UN Conflict-Management Efforts

ECOMOG states distinguished themselves by their responsiveness to the Liberian crisis and by their commitment to addressing it. Just twenty-four days elapsed between Doe's appeal to the SMC and the latter's creation of ECOMOG, and seventeen days later thousands of ECOMOG troops were deployed to Liberia. Their hostile reception prompted an increase in force levels rather than a withdrawal, and ECOMOG remained in Liberia throughout the seven years of conflict and into its aftermath. Nigeria, ECOMOG's largest troop contributor, estimated in 1999 that it had lost 500 soldiers and spent US$8 billion in Liberia.[8]

Yet, ECOMOG had three core weaknesses. First, it was biased against the NPFL and thus unable to act as an impartial mediator in Liberia. As the contemporary Nigerian ambassador to Liberia acknowledged, Nigeria in particular largely envisioned the intervention as an enforcement action against Taylor: "We went into Liberia to help Doe to crush the rebellion."[9] Taylor thus had little reason to trust ECOMOG's neutrality either in facilitating peace negotiations or in implementing the terms of a peace accord.

Second, the ECOMOG deployment was arguably illegal. It was launched without a UN Security Council mandate even though under the UN Charter "no enforcement action shall be taken . . . by regional agencies without the authorization of the Security Council."[10] It was also created by the SMC rather than the ECOWAS Authority of Heads of State and Government, the only ECOWAS body legally entitled to make such a decision. The Authority makes decisions by consensus, and since Tayor enjoyed the support of ECOWAS members Côte d'Ivoire and Burkina Faso, consensus on an operation opposing Taylor was impossible. The SMC's creation of ECOMOG effectively circumvented the Authority.[11] Finally, ECOMOG was under-resourced, raising problems of inadequate force levels, insufficient equipment, and corruption among ECOMOG troops both at the level of individual soldiers augmenting their pay and in terms of a more systematic exploitation of Liberia's resources. One result was an inability to militarily defeat the NPFL in the Liberian countryside, which not only prolonged the conflict but also complicated it as ECOMOG began to encourage local factions to join in the fight against Taylor, thus multiplying the number of conflict parties.[12] Another consequence was a loss of local legitimacy for ECOMOG, which critics in Monrovia charged was an acronym for "Every Car Or Moving Object Gone."[13]

ECOMOG cooperation with the UN was slow to emerge. Although Nigeria suggested in August 1990 that the Security Council should lend its "considerable moral support" to ECOMOG and "generously contribute materially" to its success,[14] the Security Council neither authorized nor funded ECOMOG. It undertook no independent action, either. Eventually, in January 1991, it "commended" ECOWAS efforts in a Presidential Statement.[15] In November 1992, it repeated this commendation in Resolution 788, which also imposed an arms embargo on Liberia but exempted ECOWAS forces from this restriction.[16] On 22 September 1993, following the signing of the Cotonou Peace Agreement by Liberia's major conflict parties on 25 July, the Council authorized UNOMIL, "emphasising . . . that the Peace Agreement assigns ECOMOG the primary responsibility of supervising . . . [its] implementation and envisages that the United Nations role shall be to monitor and verify this process."[17] A UN observer mission was one of two tools envisaged in the Cotonou Agreement to remedy the problem of perceived ECOMOG partiality, the second being a call for "an expanded ECOMOG which includes the forces of ECOWAS Member States and African troops from outside the West African region."[18]

Even when it did emerge, cooperation with the UN did not substantially remedy ECOMOG's weaknesses. It had some positive effects on the ECOMOG's international legitimacy, though arguably not its legality. UNOMIL's deployment could not remedy ECOMOG's weak legal basis or resolve the political divisions within West Africa that led to ECOMOG's creation through the SMC rather than the Authority. However, the fact that the UN was willing to co-deploy with ECOMOG signaled global endorsement of the regional force, even though UNOMIL's monitoring role also suggested a certain mistrust of it.[19]

Cooperation with the UN did not, however, remedy ECOMOG's resource scarcity. UNOMIL's mission was to monitor progress under the Cotonou Agreement, not to assist ECOMOG. With an initial authorized strength of 303 military observers, 20 medical officers, and 45 military engineers, all of whom were barred from "participation in enforcement operations," UNOMIL could offer ECOMOG little military support.[20] Indeed, UNOMIL relied on ECOMOG for its own security, adding to the regional force's military responsibilities. UNOMIL's budget was separate from ECOMOG's and included no subsidies for the regional force. For one ECOMOG officer, UNOMIL's presence thus merely highlighted ECOMOG's lack of resources: "the difference was too striking to see between UNOMIL observers in their four-wheel drive air-conditioned cars as opposed to the few ECOMOG... transport badly needing repairs."[21] Resolution 866 did authorize the establishment of a Trust Fund for ECOMOG, but by 31 August 1997, contributions only totaled US$25.6 million, a paltry sum compared with Nigeria's US$8 billion expenditure or even with UNOMIL's total received contributions of US$96.6 million.[22] Moreover, Trust Fund resources were targeted at diversifying ECOMOG and thus overwhelmingly allocated to new ECOMOG contributors rather than existing ones.[23] The resulting "disparities in the incomes of the UN-sponsored 'expanded ECOMOG' personnel with several hundred US dollars each month, as against about $150 in ECOMOG pockets, was [sic] a dampener on the morale of troops exposed to the same environment, pressures, and danger."[24]

Moreover, UNOMIL failed to provide a credible corrective to ECOMOG's perceived partiality. Legally, the authority relationship between UNOMIL and ECOMOG was underspecified: the Cotonou Agreement and Security Council Resolution 866 created parallel missions without robust coordination mechanisms. Consequently, UNOMIL had no formal leverage over ECOMOG's actions: "At the crucial point of interface with the ECOMOG Field Commander, [UNOMIL Head] Gordon-Somer's precedence was unclear; however, it was certain that the ECOMOG Commander held final authority over his own forces."[25] Moreover, the relationship between ECOMOG and UNOMIL was poor: UNOMIL's resources aroused envy, the UN's late arrival to "monitor" a peace that ECOMOG had fought to produce created resentment, and early attempts at independent action by UNOMIL's Chief Military Observer "simply irritated... [ECOMOG's Field Commander], who then found it difficult, if not impossible, to co-operate with him."[26] Most importantly, UNOMIL's reliance on ECOMOG for security and other support made effective independent monitoring impossible. Observing UNOMIL's dependence, and consequent acquiescence to ECOMOG impositions such as curfew times and roadblocks, "many Liberians saw UNOMIL as subordinated to ECOMOG."[27] On the international stage, UNOMIL salvaged some of its own and ECOMOG's reputation simply by failing to criticize ECOMOG. As one UNOMIL member put it, "we would just keep patting them on the back and say what a great job they were doing."[28] Liberian observers were not misled, however: "UNOMIL quickly lost the trust of local factions which had remained wary of ECOMOG."[29] Partly as a consequence, when the Cotonou Agreement began to collapse, UNOMIL observers came under attack. By August 1994, a kidnapping of UNOMIL personnel had led to the mission's withdrawal from western Liberia, and by January 1995, UNOMIL was largely restricted to Monrovia, where it would essentially remain until the mission was terminated in September 1997.[30]

The Ad Hoc Emergence of the First "Model" of ECOWAS–UN Cooperation

With UNOMIL's deployment, the UN self-consciously and explicitly broke new ground in terms of its cooperation with regional organizations for conflict management.

Security Council Resolution 866 noted that UNOMIL was "the first peace-keeping mission undertaken by the United Nations in cooperation with a peace-keeping operation already set up by another organisation."[31] In January 1995, Secretary-General Boutros Boutros-Ghali argued that if cooperation "experiments" in Liberia and Georgia succeeded, they might "herald a new division of labor between the UN and regional organizations, under which the regional organization carries the main burden but a small UN operation supports it and verifies that it is functioning in a manner consistent with positions adopted by the Security Council." Wisely, Boutros-Ghali added a caution: "The political, operational and financial aspects of the arrangement give rise to questions of some delicacy. Member States may wish at some stage to make an assessment, in the light of experience in Liberia and Georgia, of how this model might be followed in the future."[32]

While UNOMIL was hailed as experiment, however, it was not primarily created as such. The division of labor between ECOWAS and the UN was less a product of principled creative innovation than a result of negotiations reflecting the interests and bargaining power of three key actors.

The first actor was the NPFL. In mid-1990, it had rejected both ECOWAS and UN intervention, calculating that it could seize power in Liberia as long as no foreign forces interceded. ECOMOG's deployment prevented the NPFL's victory and forced it to accept ECOWAS-sponsored peace initiatives in Bamako (November 1990), Banjul (December 1990), and Lomé (February 1991), all of which ultimately failed to end the conflict. Convinced of ECOMOG's intention and ability to thwart the NPFL, Taylor changed tactics. From September 1990 onward, the NPFL's position was generally that it would welcome a UN peacekeeping force but that it rejected ECOMOG as unacceptably biased—though in March 1991, Taylor also raised the possibility of "supplementing" ECOMOG with a UN peacekeeping force.[33] However, Liberia's ECOMOG-supported Interim Government of National Unity (IGNU) roundly rejected the notion of replacing ECOMOG with a UN force, though it conceded that the regional force might be diversified so that Taylor would "not have to disarm to Nigerian and Ghanaian soldiers only."[34] The next four Peace Accords (Yamoussoukro I–IV, June–October 1991) all retained a central implementation role for ECOMOG. In October 1992, the NPFL launched a full-scale attack code named Operation Octopus on Monrovia, determined to secure a military victory and thus obviate the need for further negotiations. Although almost successful, the attack was ultimately repulsed by ECOMOG forces and allied Liberian factions.[35] By March 1993, the NPFL was in retreat and in disarray.[36] It continued to insist on a UN replacement of ECOMOG as a condition of peace, but did so from a position of relative weakness.[37] Yet, the NPFL was not fully defeated and had amply proven its ability to disrupt Liberian peace processes. It thus had to be brought into any credible peace agreement.

The second key actor was ECOMOG, led by Nigeria and only partially responsive to broader ECOWAS input.[38] Nigeria, West Africa's most populous and (in terms of GDP) richest state, had spearheaded ECOMOG's initial deployment. Its motivations included a desire to demonstrate regional leadership and Nigerian dictator Ibrahim Babangida's friendship with Doe, but, like other ECOMOG states, Nigeria was also concerned about the safety of its nationals in Liberia, the potentially debilitating impact of the Liberian conflict on West Africa, and the fact that the NPFL included "Libyan-trained dissidents" from several other West African states, raising "the spectre of Liberia as a permanent regional revolutionary base."[39] ECOMOG states—notably Nigeria—were hostile to the NPFL, and remained so in 1993. By then, however, the prolonged fighting in Liberia (including the costly effort to repulse Operation Octopus) had generated "ECOMOG fatigue" among key regional states—including Nigeria, where the Liberian effort was increasingly unpopular, and democratization pressures forced Babangida to resign in August 1993.[40] Nigeria and other ECOMOG states were therefore less committed to an exclusive ECOMOG role in implementing a peace agreement than they had been in previous Liberian negotiations. As they firmly noted in November 1992, however, a possible UN role had to enhance ECOMOG's position rather than undermine it.[41]

The third actor was the UN, where enthusiasm for a Liberian operation was distinctly limited. A full UN peacekeeping force for Liberia was only briefly considered in July/August 1990. At the time, there were public calls—including from Liberia's foreign minister—for the United States to take emergency military action to bring peace to Liberia.[42] The United States had no desire to do so, since the end of the Cold War had curtailed its strategic interests in Liberia, tensions between Iraq and Kuwait were mounting, and the Liberian conflict received only limited coverage in the US media.[43] Instead, the United States announced on 31 July that it was "examining what role the United Nations can play in resolution of this conflict."[44] The initiative faltered when the three African nonpermanent Security Council members failed to support a UN operation: Côte d'Ivoire, because it hoped for an outright NPFL victory, and Zaire and Ethiopia, because they feared setting a precedent for intervention.[45] ECOMOG's deployment then allowed the United States to abandon proposals for a UN force. By mid-1993, when the Cotonou Agreement was negotiated, the conflicts in Bosnia and Somalia had shown the limitations of UN peacekeeping and the UN's financial crisis had begun.[46] There was no desire among Security Council members to authorize a large-scale UN peacekeeping force for Liberia. Secretary-General Boutros-Ghali also preferred to see Liberia as "a good example of systematic cooperation" between the UN and ECOWAS, in which the global organization should play only a "supporting" role.[47]

Yet, the Security Council could not altogether avoid greater involvement in the Liberian conflict. Operation Octopus and its associated atrocities—notably the killing of five American nuns on 31 October 1992—licited global attention.[48] Heavy-handed ECOMOG tactics, including aerial bombing of NPFL positions, also raised international concerns. Most prominently, US Assistant Secretary of State Herman Cohen commented: "Unfortunately, [ECOWAS] is no longer a neutral party…I think the next step…will be U.N. intervention to provide a neutral party to try to bring about a political solution."[49] The US State Department quickly repudiated the comments, insisting that it saw no "reason to replace the ECOMOG force with a U.N. peacekeeping force,"[50] but pressure for greater UN involvement was mounting. On 19 November, the Security Council's unanimous decision to impose an arms embargo on Liberia (but exempt ECOMOG) recognized the conflict as a threat to international peace and security. It also resulted in the dispatch of a Special Representative of the Secretary-General (SRSG) to Liberia. Trevor Gordon-Somers began intensive consultations with the conflict parties, and in May 1993, suggested that he might "recommend a U.N. observer presence to monitor and balance ECOMOG's planned supervision of disarmament and encampment."[51] His diplomatic efforts culminated in the UN-sponsored peace talks in Geneva during 10–17 July 1993 and helped pave the way for the Cotonou Agreement on 25 July—which called for precisely the kind of observer mission Gordon-Somers had advocated. The request was politically hard for the UN to deny. Boutros-Ghali's 2 August report to the Security Council diplomatically affirmed that the UN had already played a "major role" (in humanitarian assistance), suggested that it could assume a "larger role," and argued that an observer mission was "crucial" while remaining only "supportive in nature."[52] His 9 September Concept of Operations proposed a distinctly modest mission anchored by 303 military observers.[53] The Security Council accepted this Concept on 22 September.[54]

The Decline of the Cooperation "Model"

Like previous Liberian peace accords, the Cotonou Agreement quickly collapsed. The installation of a transitional government, stipulated to take place within thirty days of the signing of the Agreement, was delayed until May 1994 as factions argued about the allocation of key cabinet positions.[55] These disputes raged within as well as between factions, and caused one major conflict party (United Liberation Movement of Liberia for Democracy [ULIMO]) to split into two hostile factions in 1994.[56] New factions also emerged, including the Liberian Peace Council, which by April 1994 was fighting the NPFL in eastern Liberia. Meanwhile, disarmament and demobilization efforts of former combatants suffered from the absence of mechanisms for reintegrating soldiers into society, and ECOMOG struggled to attract substantial new troop contributions while deployment "fatigue" led existing contributors (including Nigeria) to dramatically reduce their commitments.[57] By June 1994, the UN Secretary-General noted that "the continuing hostilities of recent months have led to new population displacements."[58] Two months later, he reported that "the situation in Liberia ha[d] further seriously deteriorated...ECOMOG [was] still not fully deployed and UNOMIL ha[d] recently withdrawn from the western region."[59] ECOMOG subsequently enlarged its presence, notably because Nigeria (under the dictatorship of Sani Abacha, who overrode popular discontent) increased its troop contribution to some 9,000 troops by 1996.[60] It took three more years and four further peace accords before this phase of the Liberian civil war ended, and it did so in part because a rapprochement between Taylor and Abacha helped make the prospect of an election that Taylor was likely to win acceptable to Nigeria.

UNOMIL remained deployed throughout this period, but its role was marginal. As noted, from January 2005, the mission was largely confined to Monrovia.[61] Its authorized strength was reduced from the initial 348 military personnel to just over 160 in November 1995 and 92 in November 1996.[62] Its actual strength did not always reach the authorized levels, partly because of lack of interest by potential troop contributors. UNOMIL's nadir came in May 1996, when fighting in Monrovia led to the evacuation of 88 of its then 93 military observers and the systematic looting of its vehicles and other equipment.[63] The mission subsequently recovered, albeit modestly, and played a positive role in facilitating the 1997 elections.[64] Nevertheless, UNOMIL's contribution to conflict resolution was modest—and the "model" of cooperation pioneered by ECOWAS and the UN attracted little praise. Indeed one commentator argued in 1997 that the experience "exemplifies how burden-sharing [between the UN and regional organizations] can undermine peace and security and exacerbate a civil war." His title captured a widespread reaction to what appeared to be finally the end of the Liberian civil war: "Successful" Elections in Liberia: Hold the Applause."[65]

ECOWAS and UN Cooperation in the 2000s

In the 1997 election, Taylor's National Patriotic Party won 75.3 percent of the votes, twenty-one of Liberia's twenty-six Senate seats, and forty-eight of the sixty-four seats in the House of Representatives.[66] This result owed much to Liberians' desire for peace, and their recognition that Taylor would reignite the conflict if denied political power. Unsurprisingly for a government elected with the slogan "he killed my Pa, he killed my Ma, I will vote for him,"[67] Taylor's regime soon faced armed challenges. In April and August 1999, the Justice Coalition of Liberia, composed of Liberian dissidents living in Sierra Leone and allied with local militias opposing Sierra Leone's Taylor-supported Revolutionary United Front (RUF) government, launched incursions through Guinea into Liberia's Lofa County.[68] In early 2000, Justice Coalition of Liberia members and other dissidents merged to form the armed group Liberians United for Reconciliation and Democracy (LURD). Denied full support from Sierra Leone, LURD gained a foothold in Guinea and in July 2000, launched a new incursion into Lofa County, ultimately establishing its military presence in western Liberia.[69] The Movement for Democracy in Liberia (MODEL), initially a LURD splinter group, emerged in 2002 with Côte d'Ivoire's support and in early 2003, crossed from Côte d'Ivoire into eastern Liberia.[70] By May 2003, LURD and MODEL controlled "nearly two thirds of the country" and threatened Monrovia.[71]

International efforts to mediate the conflict were unsuccessful. The Mano River Union (comprising Liberia, Sierra Leone, and Guinea) held a series of ministerial and lower-level meetings from mid-2001 onward and a summit in Rabat during 27–28 February 2002, but the effort failed to contain the escalating violence.[72] ECOWAS sponsored an unsuccessful inter-Liberian peace dialogue in March 2002.[73] In September 2002, the African Union, ECOWAS, the European Union, France, Ghana, Morocco, Nigeria, the United Kingdom, the UN, and the United States formed the International Contact Group on Liberia to "involv[e] the international community further in efforts to resolve the Liberian crisis,"[74] but despite four official meetings in 2002–2003, the conflict persisted. On 4 June 2003, the Liberian conflict parties and other Liberian and international actors (including the Contact Group) convened in Accra for cease-fire negotiations under ECOWAS auspices, facilitated by former Nigerian head of state Abdulsalami Abubakar. On 17 June, these negotiations produced a cease-fire agreement, which was premised on Taylor's promise to relinquish power to a transitional government and intended to allow the parties to negotiate a comprehensive peace agreement. By 28 June, however, UN Secretary-General Kofi Annan reported "flagrant violations of the ceasefire" and warned of "a major humanitarian catastrophe" in Liberia, citing the civilian casualties of fighting in Monrovia, the disruption of international relief efforts due to the violence, cholera outbreaks, and food shortages.[75]

Thus, although Taylor was now the target of rebellion rather than the challenger, the political and military situation in Liberia bore considerable similarities to circumstances in 1990. An autocratic ruler faced a military challenge supported by some of Liberia's neighboring states, rebel groups controlled much of the countryside and threatened Monrovia, diplomatic efforts to end the violence failed, and the conflict had dire humanitarian consequences. Two key factors that had shaped international responses in 1990 were also replicated. First, the United States was again unwilling to lead a military intervention, despite its historical ties to Liberia and despite the fact that many Liberians would have welcomed its deployment. The George W. Bush administration was preoccupied with Iraq, and there was substantial opposition within Congress to any expenditure of US military resources in Liberia.[76] US officials thus "responded to mounting calls for U.S. military intervention by stating that they were studying the issue."[77] Second, Nigeria was again the key player in formulating the regional response to the crisis. Ghana, Senegal, and Mali were important potential troop contributors and Guinea's position was critical because as LURD's key supporter it held leverage over the rebel group. However, Nigeria accounted for 57 percent of the total armed forces in ECOWAS states other than Liberia, 58 percent of their combined GDP, 54 percent of their population, and 45 percent of their military expenditure.[78] Its regional preeminence was further enhanced by the debilitating turmoil in Côte d'Ivoire, by most measures the region's second largest state and the traditional leader of francophone West Africa. The precedents for ECOWAS military activity without Nigerian leadership were not encouraging: a 1998–1999 deployment in Guinea-Bissau fielded only 712 troops,[79] and the Côte d'Ivoire deployment announced in October 2002 numbered only 1,200 troops in April 2003.[80] A robust ECOWAS intervention in Liberia was thus feasible only if Nigeria agreed to provide the force's military backbone. As in 1990, moreover, there was speculation that a personal friendship between the Nigerian and Liberian heads of state might influence Nigeria's position: in 2003, this centered around allegations that Nigerian President Olusegun Obasanjo had "a personal relationship with Charles Taylor's sister."[81]

Yet, the conflict-management roles ECOWAS and the UN played in Liberia in the 2000s differed dramatically from the division of labor in the 1990s. When the first elements of the ECOWAS Mission in Liberia (ECOMIL) deployed on 4 August 2003, they did so with a UN mandate that established the operation's legality and international legitimacy, with an international commitment to provide logistical support, and with a guaranteed exit strategy. Security Council Resolution 1497 of 1 August 2003 authorized the establishment of a "Multinational Force in Liberia to support the implementation of the 17 June 2003 ceasefire agreement..., to help establish and maintain security in the period after the departure of the current President and the installation of a successor authority...and to secure the environment for the delivery of humanitarian assistance." It permitted this Force to take "all necessary measures to fulfil its mandate," and provided for the "necessary logistical support" to the ECOWAS elements of the Multinational Force. Crucially, moreover, it committed the UN to deploy a "longer-term United Nations stabilization force to relieve the Multinational Force...no later than 1 October 2003."[82] There were no prerequisites for this UN operation. The ECOWAS deployment was thus explicitly and unconditionally an interim measure. In the event, ECOMIL was deployed for less than two months and reached a maximum strength of 3,600 troops. It was replaced by UN Mission in Liberia (UNMIL), which peaked at almost 16,000 troops in 2005 and remains deployed as of June 2012.

This new division of labor was not simply a reaction to the failings of the 1990s "model" of cooperation. It was a political bargain shaped less by the lessons of the past than by the current interests, constraints, and incentives of key actors. Three principal factors produced this bargain: early UN engagement during the escalating crisis; Nigerian (and therefore ECOWAS) insistence on a strictly limited conflict management role; and intense negotiations between the United States and Nigeria, reflecting both states' interests and relative power and deftly shaped by UN Secretary-General Kofi Annan. The following sections discuss each of these factors in turn before offering a fuller empirical description of ECOWAS and UN conflict-management efforts since 2003.

Early UN Engagement

The UN did not take the international lead in responding to the resurgent conflict in Liberia, ceding the diplomatic initiative first to the Mano River Union and then to ECOWAS. However, the Security Council was seized with the situation in Liberia and the UN was actively engaged in the diplomatic conflict-management efforts.

Even after UNOMIL was withdrawn in September 1997, the situation in Liberia remained on the Security Council's agenda. This was partly because a small UN Peacebuilding Support Office in Liberia (UNOL) was established in November 1997, which provided a conduit of information back to UN headquarters. More important, however, was the Taylor government's involvement in Sierra Leone's ongoing civil war and the illegal trade in Sierra Leonean diamonds. Sierra Leone's RUF benefited from Taylor's support from the very beginning of its armed rebellion in 1991. In 1997, a coup brought it to power, and the Security Council responded by imposing sanctions on Sierra Leone.[83] By 2000, the Council recognized that an illicit trade in diamonds continued to fuel violence in Sierra Leone,[84] and in 2001, a Council-commissioned Panel of Experts confirmed that much of this trade occurred with "the permission and involvement of Liberian government officials at the highest levels."[85] In response, the Security Council imposed sanctions on Liberia, demanded that it cease its assistance to the RUF and its participation in the diamond trade, and mandated the Secretary-General to submit regular reports on Liberia's compliance with these demands.[86] The Council reaffirmed both mechanisms in 2002, mandating a second Panel of Experts to conduct "a follow-up assessment mission" of Liberia's compliance.[87]

While the objective of these interactions was to monitor Liberia's role in Sierra Leone, they also ensured that the Security Council remained seized of developments in Liberia. For example, Mexico (a nonpermanent Council member in 2002–2003) served as Chair of the Sierra Leone Sanctions Committee, and became alarmed at the growing instability in Liberia after a sanctions-related visit to West Africa in June–July 2002.[88] Similarly, an October 2002 Secretary-General's report on Liberia's still-incomplete compliance with Council demands regarding Sierra Leone also noted that Liberia's "ongoing conflict continues to take a huge toll on the Liberian population."[89] This avenue of engagement proved important in eliciting a Security Council reaction to the conflict in

Liberia despite the antipathy several Council members reserved for the Taylor regime. Liberia's 1999 *note verbale* to the Council protesting the incursions into Lofa County as Guinean acts of aggression failed to secure a sympathetic response.[90] By December 2002, however, a Security Council Presidential Statement identified the escalating violence in Liberia as a threat to international peace and security.[91] In May 2003, the Council announced that it would dispatch a diplomatic mission to four West African countries including Liberia, where the mission would be to urge parties to engage in cease-fire negotiations.[92]

Simultaneously, the UN supported other bodies' diplomatic efforts to address the situation in Liberia. Both the Security Council and Secretary-General Annan—who as a Ghanaian had a particular interest in the West African region—commended the Mano River Union for its efforts to address the conflict.[93] The UN was a founding member of the International Contact Group on Liberia, participating in its meetings from September 2002 onward through a representative of the Secretary-General.[94] It was also represented at the ECOWAS-sponsored Accra negotiations in June 2003, and the resulting agreement provided for UN officials to join ECOWAS diplomats in monitoring the ceasefire. The UN accepted this role and responded positively though cautiously to an ECOWAS request for the use of a UN helicopter to transport the Joint Verification Team.[95]

Thus, by the time the Accra cease-fire collapsed, the UN was deeply implicated in international efforts to respond to the Liberian crisis—and therefore expected to react to the renewed violence. Annan added to these expectations when he formally (and therefore publicly) not only warned the Security Council of the ceasefire violations and impending humanitarian catastrophe but also requested "that the Security Council take urgent action to authorize the deployment to Liberia of a highly trained and well-equipped multinational force, under the lead of a Member State... [and] authorized under Chapter VII of the Charter of the United Nations."[96]

Two days later, Annan went a step further and suggested that the United States should be at the forefront of the UN-authorized response: "There are lots of expectations that the US may be prepared to lead this force, of course that is a sovereign decision for them to take, but all eyes are on them."[97] Annan's position was widely shared. Among Liberians, Taylor announced that he would welcome US troops, a LURD negotiator suggested that "the Americans can lead the [intervention] force, and the West Africans can play a supporting role," and civilians sought to shame the United States into intervening by placing the bodies of conflict victims before the US embassy in Monrovia.[98] Internationally, the British UN ambassador and head of the Security Council mission scheduled to visit West Africa suggested that the United States would be a "natural candidate" to lead an intervention in Liberia.[99] The French Foreign Minister also argued for an international force in Liberia, adding "let's see which nations have a tradition in the region. I am thinking particularly of what the US is ready to do."[100] ECOWAS Executive Secretary Mohamed Ibn Chambas concurred: "We need to see the United States at this point rise up to this occasion."[101]

Facing these unwelcome pressures, US Secretary of Defence Donald Rumsfeld commented only that the administration was considering "a range of options" in Liberia, a response US officials maintained consistently for the next month.[102] Yet, the existing UN engagement in Liberia made it impossible for the United States to ignore the crisis and increased pressure for it to respond. Lessons from the past—including from previous deployments in Liberia—also mattered. For example, Rumsfeld echoed the rhetoric of the 1990s in suggesting a reliance on regional conflict management, commenting that African militaries were "well-trained. We've helped equip them, and to the extent they've been deployed I've been told they've handled themselves well."[103] By 2003, such claims rang hollow—but it was the political mobilization of actors, rather than simply past experience, that foreclosed the option of once again delegating responsibility to the subregion. Annan insisted publicly that "notwithstanding the commendable efforts of ECOWAS, broader international action is urgently needed to reverse Liberia's drift toward total disintegration."[104] The United Kingdom and France, both permanent Security Council members, publicly supported an international military effort. On 7 July, the Security Council's own mission to West Africa recommended that "the Security Council should urgently consider authorizing an international stabilization force."[105] In making this recommendation, the mission explicitly cited "the ECOWAS appeal for troops and other support from outside the region," thus highlighting arguably the most crucial mobilization of all—and the second key factor in the emergence of the 2003 division of labor.

ECOWAS Insistence on a Limited Role

Unlike in the 1990s, in 2003, ECOWAS refused to accept primary responsibility for military conflict management in Liberia. A critical reason for this refusal was the position taken by Nigeria, and more specifically Nigerian President Olusegun Obasanjo. Though a civilian head of state, Obasanjo's autonomy in crafting Nigerian foreign policy had already been noted in 2001 by Howard Jeter, the US ambassador to Nigeria, and it was further cemented by Obasanjo's reelection in April 2003.[106] Three core considerations affected Obasanjo's position on Liberia.

First, Nigeria had a national interest in seeing the Liberian crisis resolved. Ideologically, Obasanjo and other Nigerian policy makers held the "personal belief that West Africa is Nigeria's backyard; that Nigeria has the right and responsibility to deal with any troubled turf within the confines of this sub-regional fence."[107] Pragmatically, the 1989–1997 Liberian war had been a major source of regional instability whose implications were still palpable in 2003. It had led to internal wars (notably in Sierra Leone) and interstate tensions: in 2003, Liberia, Guinea, Côte d'Ivoire, and Sierra Leone were fomenting one another's rebellions. There were some 257,000 Liberian refugees in West Africa in late 2002, and Liberia hosted 65,000 refugees from other regional states, especially Sierra Leone and Côte d'Ivoire.[108] Protracted conflict resulted in dismal economic performances in several West African states, a proliferation of small arms in the region, and a mobilization of fighters moving from one conflict to the next: "When a country finally achieves a peace treaty, the guys who make a living through the barrel of their guns seep across the border to the next country."[109] Nigeria was outside of the immediate arc of instability' since refugees, combatants, and conflict spill-overs were concentrated in Liberia, Guinea, Sierra Leone, Côte d'Ivoire and (for refugees) Ghana. However, it was affected by the instability, and had spent US$12 billion on regional conflict management between 1990 and 2003.[110]

Second, Nigerian domestic politics precluded another long-term military deployment in Liberia. The prospect was deeply unpopular among Nigerians, many of whom felt that their country had already sacrificed for regional security and received scant international recognition in return.[111] Within the Nigerian military in particular, "the overwhelming majority of Nigerian officers who served in Liberia under ECOMOG bitterly oppose[d] the new deployment."[112] Obasanjo summarized the prevailing sentiment: "We spent well over $12bn, when we were in Liberia and Sierra Leone for well over 12 years. The world did not acknowledge that, not even in terms of giving us debt relief for the contribution we made…When we went into Liberia before nobody gave us support. And we lost well over 1,000 Nigerians."[113] International criticism of these interventions was widely perceived as adding insult to injury. There were also financial considerations. By the end of its first deployment, "60–65 percent of the ECOMOG equipment from Liberia was unserviceable."[114] Equipping and funding a new deployment was an unwelcome burden at a time when Nigeria faced large budget deficits; by 2003, it had a total external debt stock of US$34.6 billion, representing 126 percent of its export earnings.[115] Finally, there was a perceived need to keep Nigerian troops available for domestic deployments. In 2002, the military had been used to contain conflict in Nigeria's Plateau state, and in early 2003, violence had flared in Delta State. By July 2003, the situation there was serious enough to affect Obasanjo's calculations of which army units could be deployed to Liberia.[116]

Third, there were potent global and bilateral foreign policy incentives for a Nigerian military intervention in Liberia. Globally, one of Obasanjo's key foreign policy objectives was to restore Nigeria's international prestige, which the dictatorships of the 1990s had severely tarnished.[117] He also had two more concrete aims: "Obasanjo's ultimate goal, aside from positively influencing donors and creditors, is to secure a permanent seat on the UN Security Council."[118] By 2003, Obasanjo had made little progress toward these aims: Nigeria's external debt increased to US$34.6 billion from US$29 billion in 1999,[119] there was no international consensus on creating an African, permanent Security Council seat, and even if there had been, Egypt and South Africa were contesting Nigeria's claim to this seat. Responding to international calls for military intervention in Liberia would earn Nigeria goodwill and highlight a commitment to international peace and security befitting of a Security Council member.[120] Conversely, failure to respond to the Liberian crisis would damage Nigeria's international reputation. Like many Nigerians, international observers saw Liberia as being in Nigeria's "backyard" and expected Nigeria to respond to the crisis.[121] Leading an intervention in Liberia might also cement the "special relationship" with the United States that Nigeria had sought since its transition to democracy in 1999.[122] Since the United States was under international pressure to lead a military response to the crisis but reluctant to do so, a Nigerian deployment might earn US gratitude—and potentially support on debt relief and Security Council reform. As discussed in the following, it could also be used to extract US resources, not only in terms of logistic and financial assistance for the deployment itself but also in the form of additional longer-term US military aid.

These complex incentives produced two results. First, Nigeria was very active in diplomatic efforts to defuse the escalating Liberian crisis. The unsuccessful ECOWAS-backed dialogue among the Liberian parties in March 2002 was a Nigerian initiative, a Nigerian was Chief Mediator at the June 2003 Accra negotiations, and behind the scenes, Obasanjo joined other West African leaders in pressuring Taylor to resign from power.[123] When the Special Court for Sierra Leone announced on 4 June 2003 that it had indicted Taylor for war crimes, Obasanjo braved international and domestic criticism to offer Taylor asylum. He explained his motivations in confidence to Western diplomats: "Nigeria would make the sacrifice of accepting Taylor because his removal from Liberia could be the most important single step toward peace in West Africa... [I]f Taylor feels compelled to remain in Liberia because of the war crimes charges, he will fight to the end... [and] not hesitate to spend others' lives in the process."[124] Second, when diplomatic efforts failed, Obasanjo advocated a *joint* intervention force: Nigeria would deploy to Liberia, but only with international logistical and financial assistance *and* with military support from allies beyond West Africa, notably the United States. Obasanjo justified this position succinctly: "it is in our backyard, it is our problem. But it is not our problem alone. It is in fact Africa's problem, and it is the world's problem."[125] This stance fundamentally shaped the official ECOWAS position conveyed to the Security Council Mission to West Africa in late June:

> ECOWAS hoped to be ready to secure the ceasefire by creating a buffer zone through the deployment of a stabilization force, but they needed financial and logistical assistance from the international community... [Moreover,] an international stabilization force, led by a State outside the region, was needed urgently to deploy alongside an ECOWAS force. The [ECOWAS] Executive Secretary hoped the United States might consider involvement in such a force.[126]

Negotiating a Division of Labor

The division of labor that actually materialized in Liberia from the confluence of pressure for a robust UN-authorized and US-led response to the crisis, US unwillingness to assume a military leadership role, and the Nigerian-inspired ECOWAS proposal for a joint West African and global intervention, was a hard-fought compromise that took time to emerge. The Accra cease-fire collapsed in late June 2003 but Security Council Resolution 1497, which authorized ECOMIL and promised UNMIL, was only adopted on 1 August. Nonpermanent Security Council members Mexico and Germany both noted the delay,[127] and Annan commented that he hoped the resolution presaged "a new political will that, I think, has been absent among the international community."[128] A key reason for this delay was that the division of labor between regional and international actors was a matter of intense dispute, notably between Nigeria and the United States.

ECOWAS signaled its willingness to deploy 3,000–3,600 West African troops to Liberia in late June.[129] Nigeria was central to this effort, and on 9 July, Obasanjo confirmed his willingness to commit two Nigerian battalions (some 1,500 troops) to Howard Jeter, the US Ambassador to Nigeria.[130] One battalion would come from within Nigeria and the other redeployed from the UN mission in Sierra Leone.[131] On 12 July, the United States was informed that Nigerian Brigadier-General Festus Okwonko had been selected as Force Commander, that Nigeria's two battalions could deploy "on short notice," and that 3,000 ECOWAS troops were available "with Nigeria, Ghana and Mali shouldering most of the load in the beginning."[132]

However, there were two preconditions for deploying these troops. First, they "needed financial and logistical assistance from the international community" to deploy.[133] ECOWAS Executive Secretary Chambas specified that "per diem, airlift, logistical and equipment assistance would be needed for most troop contributing countries."[134] West African governments looked to the United States for this support. Tellingly, in a 2002, discussion with US Ambassador Jeter about a possible Nigerian troop contribution to the ECOWAS force in Cote d'Ivoire, the Nigerian Defence Minister had insisted on US support, "saying the Europeans always "promise heaven and earth' but never come through."[135] For a Liberian deployment, Nigeria sought logistical and financial support from the United States, including a commitment that Nigerian troops redeployed from Sierra Leone would continue to be compensated at UN levels: "he did not want his soldiers receiving less pay for Liberia's greater danger."[136] Obasanjo also requested a more indirect form of compensation: in 2001, US Special Forces had helped train two Nigerian battalions for deployment in Sierra Leone, and Obasanjo sought similar training for five additional battalions in exchange for a Liberia deployment.[137] The second precondition was that ECOWAS troops would not deploy alone. The ECOWAS proposal was for a global multinational force in which the 3,000–3,600 West African troops would be joined by some 2,000 troops from outside the region, including the United States.[138] This was crucial for Nigeria, and in a 9 July conversation with US Ambassador Jeter, Obasanjo made "a strong pitch for American boots on the ground, stating that this would be of tremendous military and psychological value in making all armed groups behave."[139]

The United States balked at both preconditions. In terms of financing, some US funds were forthcoming, but they did not meet Nigeria's expectations. Annan publicly acknowledged the impasse on 31 July: "Ten million dollars was offered by the U.S., which, obviously, the Nigerians have indicated is not enough."[140] The ECOWAS cost estimate for the deployment reportedly exceeded US$100 million.[141] Nigeria's foreign minister was unapologetic about the fact that this bargaining delayed the deployment of Nigerian troops to Liberia: "We made it clear from the beginning that we needed assistance in their deployment, in terms of logistics, in terms of funding. All the cards are not in Nigeria's hands."[142]

The possible US military role in Liberia was a subject of intense negotiations between Nigeria and the United States, including during President Bush's five-nation visit in Africa in early July. On 14 July, two days after his return, Bush publicly raised the *possibility* of a US deployment to Liberia: "we want to help ECOWAS, it may require troops, but we don't know how many yet."[143] He insisted, however, that "any commitment . . . would be limited in size and limited in tenure" and that no US troops would deploy until Taylor kept the promise he had made during the Accra cease-fire negotiations to relinquish power and leave Liberia. Taylor, however, had already indicated that he would not leave Liberia until US troops deployed, allegedly "to avoid further unrest."[144] Moreover, in a private conversation with US Assistant Secretary of State for African Affairs Kansteiner on 12 July, ECOWAS Executive Secretary Chambas had rejected the idea of a two-step deployment led by ECOWAS and with US troops following after Taylor departed.[145] As a possible compromise, Kansteiner suggested that a Marine Expeditionary Unit might be anchored off the Liberian coast during the ECOWAS deployment, ready to land immediately following Taylor's departure. Indeed, on 29 July, the 2,200-strong 26th

Marine Expeditionary Unit arrived off the Liberian coast, with orders not to land until Taylor had left the country.[146] Even this limited military role was opposed by Deputy Secretary of Defence Paul Wolfowitz and the Joint Chiefs of Staff, "on the grounds that no direct U.S. interests [were] at stake in Liberia and that U.S. forces [were] spread thin by the wars in Afghanistan and Iraq and other commitments around the globe."[147] Obasanjo's public reaction, meanwhile, was scathing: "I like that. If your house is on fire and somebody says, 'Here I am, I have my water, a fire engine. Now when you put out your fire I will come in.' I wonder what sort of help that is. With all due respect."[148]

With Nigeria insisting on more financial and military support than the United States was willing to give, the United States' solution (echoing its approach in July 1990) was to turn to the UN. It countered the ECOWAS proposal for a global multinational force by advocating a brief, US-supported ECOWAS deployment that would be replaced by a UN peacekeeping operation. Indeed, the press conference at which Bush announced a possible US deployment to Liberia was a joint photo opportunity with UN Secretary-General Annan. At the meeting preceding that press conference, Bush had presented the US proposal: "I told the Secretary General that we want to help, that there must be a U.N. presence, quickly, into Liberia. He and I discussed how fast it would take [sic] to blue helmet whatever forces arrived, other than our own, of course. We would not be blue helmeted. We would be there to facilitate and then to—and then to leave."[149]

Annan, who in late June had advocated a single US-led multinational force, recognized the need to bargain. As a consummate diplomat, he sought to nudge all parties beyond the offers they had already made:

> The understanding which is emerging now is for the ECOWAS forces to send in a vanguard of about 1,000 to 1,500 troops... After that... President Taylor will leave Liberia, and then the force will be strengthened, hopefully with U.S. participation, and additional troops from the West African region. Eventually, U.N. blue helmets will be set up to stabilize the situation... and once the situation is calmer and stabilized, U.S. would leave and the U.N. peacekeepers would carry on the situation.

In fact, Nigeria had not agreed to a vanguard deployment without the United States, Taylor's commitment to leave Liberia was at best tenuous, and the United States had not agreed to participate in the multinational force or to remain in Liberia until the situation there was stable. The United States resisted Annan's prodding, but Nigeria was forced to make concessions.

Once the US Marines arrived off Liberia's coast, continued Nigerian inaction became harder to defend. Thus, a BBC interviewer chided Obasanjo: "there are 4,500 US troops sitting at sea, off the coast... They are waiting for you, they are saying when the West African peace force goes in, they will then be prepared to come in."[150] Annan added to the pressure. On 28 July, he pronounced himself "very pleased" with the positioning of the US Marines, "which should accelerate the deployment of the ECOWAS forces."[151] On 29 July, he outlined to the Security Council "a three-phased deployment of international troops to Liberia, which would include an ECOWAS vanguard force."[152] To the media, he argued that it was "absolutely essential to accelerate the deployment of the 'vanguard force' to pave the way for the early deployment of the MNF [multinational force]."[153] On 30 July, he asked the Security Council to "approve, speed up and dispatch the vanguard of the West African ... force to Liberia."[154] Annan balanced his remarks by consistently calling for a multilateral force to follow the "vanguard" troops. However, he also pressed ECOWAS to deploy immediately, without full clarity on the composition of the multinational force or the US role within it.

In this context, on 30 July, the United States tabled the draft resolution on that, despite a controversial clause on the non-extradition of peacekeepers to the International Criminal Court, became Security Council Resolution 1497 on 1 August. The resolution called for a Multinational Force rather than an ECOWAS deployment, and for logistical support of "the forward ECOWAS elements" of this Force.[155] It offered no guarantees of the composition of the Multinational Force, but it did provide a firm commitment for a UN follow-on force by 1 October, despite objections from "several Council diplomats" that this was an "unrealistic deadline."[156] Nigeria accepted the compromise and on 31 July, ECOWAS Heads of State "approved the deployment into Liberia of the Vanguard Interposition Force."[157]

ECOWAS and UN Roles

ECOMIL's advance guard of some 200 Nigerian troops arrived in Liberia on 4 August, growing to over 700 troops by 11 August, when Taylor, facing the growing deployment, LURD and MODEL forces outside Monrovia, and US Marines off the city's coast, reluctantly relinquished power to Vice President Moses Blah and departed into exile in Nigeria.[158] On 14 August, members of the US Marine Expeditionary Unit landed to help ECOMIL secure Monrovia and permit the delivery of humanitarian aid to the city.[159] ECOMIL and the US presence also provided crucial political and military stability, facilitating the signing of a Comprehensive Peace Agreement (CPA) by Liberia's conflict parties on 18 August. The CPA called for a continued ECOMIL "Interposition Force" pending the arrival of a UN "Stabilization Force,"[160] and ECOMIL continued to expand, reaching 3,550 troops by 10 September and extending its presence beyond Monrovia to facilitate the withdrawal of armed factions. As ECOMIL grew, the US Marines redeployed to their ships but continued to provide operational support.[161] On 19 September, responding to the CPA and fulfilling its commitment under Resolution 1497, the Security Council established UNMIL, "request[ing] the Secretary-General to transfer authority from the ECOWAS-led ECOMIL forces to UNMIL on 1 October 2003."[162] The transfer of authority took place as envisioned, with UNMIL incorporating ("rehatting") all 3,600 ECOMIL troops.[163] The US Marine Expeditionary Unit was withdrawn, its last members departing on 30 September. From October 2003 onward, therefore, the responsibility for military peacekeeping in Liberia fell exclusively to the UN.

UNMIL was (and at the time of writing remains) a large and multifaceted mission. Its initial mandate was to help implement the 17 June Ceasefire Agreement and the CPA, support "humanitarian and human rights assistance" and security-sector reform in Liberia, and protect UN staff and facilities as well as "civilians under imminent threat of physical violence, within its capabilities."[164] To fulfill these tasks, UNMIL was mandated under Chapter VII of the UN Charter (thus allowing a robust use of force) and authorized to include up to 15,000 military personnel and 1,115 civilian police officers. It therefore expanded beyond the re-hatted ECOMIL troops, fielding 8,806 uniformed personnel from 48 states in December 2003, approaching 16,000 uniformed personnel by August 2004, and maintaining these force levels into 2006 thanks to some 60 personnel-contributing countries.[165]

Over this period, the political and military situation in Liberia gradually improved. Blah relinquished power to a National Transitional Government in October 2003; in November 2004, all armed Liberian factions were formally disbanded, and 2005 saw democratic elections in which Ellen Johnson Sirleaf won Liberia's presidency. Thus, in September 2005, the Security Council requested the Secretary-General to prepare "recommendations on a drawdown plan for UNMIL."[166] In his March 2006 reply, however, the Secretary-General noted that while "UNMIL ha[d] completed many aspects of its initial mandate... the security situation in Liberia and in neighbouring countries remain[ed] fragile and key unfinished tasks need[ed] to be urgently completed in order to ensure sustainable peace and stability in the country."[167] Over 182,000 Liberian refugees remained in West Africa; 37,000 demobilized ex-combatants required placement in reintegration programs; only 1,442 police officers had been trained; governmental authority was "still limited in most parts of the country"; the police and judiciary "remain[ed] very fragile and underdeveloped"; the state lacked effective control over Liberia's natural resources; basic services such as water and electricity were absent "in many parts of the country"; high rates of poverty, unemployment, and criminality posed security challenges; the government was US$3.2 billion in debt; and instability in Côte d'Ivoire posed "a significant external threat to the stability of Liberia."[168] The Secretary-General concluded that UNMIL "remain[ed] indispensable during the consolidation phase" and recommended only a modest and gradual reduction of UNMIL's military personnel.[169] The Security Council responded by extending UNMIL's mandate without requiring force reductions, but requested the Secretary-General to "review his recommendations for a drawdown plan for UNMIL and to present further recommendations in his next regular report... on UNMIL's progress."[170]

The exchange presaged major themes in UNMIL's development over the subsequent years. With UNMIL's assistance, Liberia has continued to make progress. In March 2006, Taylor was definitively removed from Liberian politics through his extradition from Nigeria to face trial for war crimes and crimes against humanity before the Special Court for Sierra Leone, where he was convicted and sentenced to a fifty-year jail term in May 2012. Liberia's Truth and Reconciliation Commission was created in 2006, held extensive public hearings in 2008–2009, and published its findings in 2009–2010. In 2010, Liberia qualified for some US$4.6 billion in debt relief through the IMF and World Bank's Heavily Indebted Poor Countries Initiative, and, gradually, Liberian refugees returned to the country and socioeconomic indicators such as life expectancy and literacy rates improved.[171] 2011 saw a second set of democratic elections in which Sirleaf won a second presidential term. Nevertheless, the situation in Liberia remained fragile. As one report noted in June 2012,

> Despite marked improvements, numerous grievances that plunged Liberia into [its] bloody wars... remain evident: a polarised society and political system; corruption, nepotism and impunity; a disheveled security sector; youth unemployment; and gaps and inconsistencies in the electoral law. The November 2011 election was the country's second successful postwar voting exercise but [also] exposed its deep fault lines.[172]

Reflecting these challenges, UNMIL has contracted only gradually despite regular Security Council insistence on planning the mission's drawdown. It still numbered 7,922 troops and 1,266 police offices in April 2012, when the Secretary-General suggested it might contract to 3,750 troops by 2015.[173]

Conclusion

The two phases of Liberia's civil war saw two very different divisions of labor between ECOWAS and the UN in terms of conflict management. In the first phase, a large, long-term ECOWAS deployment was belatedly paired with a small UN observer mission. In the second phase, a robust but explicitly short-term ECOWAS deployment was promptly replaced with a large and multifaceted UN follow-up operation that remains deployed at the time of writing.

It is tempting to see these two divisions of labor as showcasing an evolution from one model of cooperation between the UN and regional organizations to another. The temptation is made stronger by the fact that the first division of labor was explicitly presented as breaking new ground in regional and global cooperation—and by the fact that the dismal performance of this first "model" more than merited the invention of a new one.

Yet, in both the first and the second phases of the Liberian civil war, the division of labor between ECOWAS and the UN was a product of ad hoc negotiations, state interests, and state power. Actors did draw lessons from earlier experiences: in 2003, few West African or global actors had any interest in replicating the inefficiencies of the division of labor of the 1990s. However, the arrangement that emerged between ECOWAS and the UN in 2003 did not reflect a new consensus on a better way of cooperating to address the Liberian conflict. ECOWAS actors would have preferred a multinational force with a large regional role and strong US participation to the two-step deployment of ECOMIL and UNOMIL. UN-based actors called for a US-led multinational force, possibly with a UN follow-on mission. Neither of these options was realized because the United States refused to play the roles they would have required of it. Thus, it is only in retrospect that the 2003 division of labor appears like a new model of cooperation. At the time, it was simply a political compromise.

This does not mean that the Liberian case study offers no generalizable lessons about the nature of UN–regional cooperation in conflict management. Its first lesson is that whatever cooperation emerges will almost certainly be the result of intense interstate bargaining—indeed, it is arguably not in the interest of powerful states to commit themselves in advance to any particular model of cooperation. The second lesson is that past experiences do matter, because they affect what states perceive to be in their interests in the new conflict situation. Third, international mobilization matters, both by creating a general impetus to address a crisis and by suggesting which state(s) have primary responsibility for responding. The relevant state may not comply but it may be pressured into taking another, less costly action: The United States did not lead a multinational force into Liberia, but it threw its diplomatic weight behind a UN operation—briefly in 1990 and decisively in 2003. Fourth, international civil servants can play an important role in nudging interstate negotiations in particular directions. Kofi Annan fueled claims that the United States should lead a Liberian intervention but ultimately also helped pressure Nigeria to accept the United States' compromise solution. Thus, highlighting the fact that divisions of labor in conflict management are likely to be negotiated on a case-by-case basis does not prevent a search for regular patterns—but it focuses attention on patterns in the negotiations rather than in their outcomes.

Notes

1. 'Funmi Olonisakin, "Liberia," in *Dealing with Conflict in Africa: The United Nations and Regional Organizations*, ed. Jane Boulden (New York: Palgrave Macmillan, 2003), p. 113.
2. Katharina Coleman, *International Organisations and Peace Enforcement: The Politics of International legitimacy* (Cambridge: Cambridge University Press, 2007), p. 75.
3. Nina Wilén, *Justifying Interventions in Africa: (De)Stabilizing Sovereignty in Liberia, Burundi and the Congo* (Basingstoke: Palgrave Macmillan, 2012), p. 56.
4. ECOWAS, *Official Journal of the Economic Community of West African States* 21 (1992): 6–7.
5. Festus B. Aboagye, *ECOMOG: A Sub-Regional Experience in Conflict Resolution, Management and Peacekeeping in Liberia* (Accra: Sedco, 1999), p. 143. David Wippman, "Enforcing the Peace: ECOWAS and the Liberian Civil War," in *Enforcing Restrain: Collective Intervention in Internal Conflicts*, ed. Lori Fisler Damrsch (New York: Council on Foreign Relations, 1993), p. 168. Estimates of initial deployment numbers vary among these and other sources.
6. Coleman, *International Organisations and Peace Enforcement*, p. 73. Aboagye, *ECOMOG*, pp. 90, 144. International Institute for Strategic Studies (IISS), *The Military Balance, 1997/98* (London: IISS, 1997), p. 250.
7. For details on Liberia's ceasefires and peace accords, see *Accord: An International Review of Peace Initiatives—The Liberian Peace Process, 1990–1996*, ed. Jeremy Armon and Andy Carl (London: Conciliation Resources, 1996), pp. 37–82.
8. Herbert Howe, *Ambiguous Order: Military Forces in African States* (Boulder, CO: Lynne Rienner, 2001), 145.
9. Coleman "Innovations in 'African Solutions to African Problems': The Evolving Practice of Regional Peacekeeping in Sub-Saharan Africa," *Journal of Modern African Studies* 49:4 (2001): 529.
10. United Nations (UN), *Charter* (§53.1)
11. Wippman, "Enforcing the Peace," pp. 167–168. Coleman, *International Organisations and Peace Enforcement*, pp. 78–80.
12. William Reno, *Warlord Politics and African States* (Boulder, CO: Lynne Rienner, 1998), pp. 104–105. Howe, *Ambiguous Order*, pp. 154 and 158–159. Alpha Sesay, "Liberia: ECOMOG Mobilized ULIMO Fighters to Fight against Charles Taylor in Liberia and to Attack AFRC/RUF in Sierra Leone, Former ULIMO Fighter Testifies," 7 June 2010, http://www.charlestaylortrial.org/2010/06/page/2/.
13. Stephen Ellis, "Profiteering from War," *Weekly Mail and Guardian (South Africa)*, 25 July 1997.
14. *Letter from the Permanent Representative of Nigeria to the United Nations Addressed to the Secretary-General*, 9 August 1990, S/21485.
15. United Nations Security Council (UNSC), *Note by the President of the United Nations Security*, 22 January 1991, S/22133.

16. UNSC, *Resolution 788*, 19 November 1992.
17. UNSC, *Resolution 866*, 22 September 1993.
18. Liberian Conflict Parties, *Cotonou Agreement*, 25 July 1993, §3.2, accessed 30 May 2012, http://www.unhcr.org/refworld/docid/3ae6b5796.html.
19. Coleman, *International Organisations and Peace Enforcement*, pp. 102–103.
20. UNSC, *Resolution 866*, §3.h.
21. Aboagye, *ECOMOG*,174.
22. UNSC, *Final Report of the Secretary-General on the United Nations Observer Mission in Liberia,* 12 September 1997, S/1997/712, 4.
23. UNSC, *Resolution 866*, §6.
24. Aboagye, *ECOMOG*, p. 174.
25. John Mackinlay and Abiodun Alao, "Liberia 1994: ECOMOG and UNOMIL—Response to a Complex Emergency," *United Nations University Occasional Paper Series*, No. 2 (1995): 16.
26. David Francis, Mohammed Faal, John Kabia, and Alex Ramsbotham, *Dangers of Co-deployment: UN Co-operative Peacekeeping in Africa* (Aldershot: Ashgate, 2005), pp. 128–129. Aboagye, *ECOMOG*, p. 174.
27. Mackinlay and Alao, "Liberia 1994," 16.
28. Coleman, *International Organisations and Peace Enforcement*, p. 102.
29. Clement Adibe, "The Liberian Conflict and the ECOWAS-UN Partnership," *Third World Quarterly* 18:3 (1997): 478.
30. UNSC, *Sixth Progress Report of the Secretary-General on the United Nations Observer Mission in Liberia,* 26 August 1994, S/1994/1006, 3. UNSC, *Eighth Progress Report of the Secretary-General on the United Nations Observer Mission in Liberia,* 6 January 1995, 4.
31. UNSC, *Resolution 866.*
32. Boutros Boutros-Ghali, *Supplement to An Agenda for Peace: Position Paper of the Secretary-General on the Occasion of the Fiftieth Anniversary of the United Nations,* 3 January 1995, A/50/60-S/1995/1, §86.
33. "Liberian Anti-Government Force Calls for Peace Talks," *Xinhua General News Service*, 21 September 1990. "Liberian Peace Plan Offered; President Carter Asked to Act as Mediator," *PR Newswire*, 14 March 1991.
34. "Liberia Cannot Send West African Peacekeeping Force Away: Sawyer," *Agence France Presse*, 28 August 1991.
35. Sesay, "Liberia."
36. Peter da Costa, "Liberia: Main Warring Faction in Disarray," *Inter Press Service*, 5 March 1993.
37. Moyiga Nduru, "Liberia: United Nations Urged to Deploy Blue Berets," *Inter Press Service*, 7 May 1993.
38. Francis et al., *Dangers of Co-deployment*, p. 131.
39. International Crisis Group (ICG), "Liberia: The Key to Ending Regional Instability," *Africa Report No. 43*, 24 April 2002. Herbert Howe, "Lessons of Liberia: ECOMOG and Regional Peacekeeping," *International Security* 31:3 (1996/7): 150.
40. Adibe, "The Liberian Conflict and the ECOWAS-UN Partnership," 479.
41. Peter da Costa, "Liberia: Fighting Peters Out as Leaders Head for Weekend Conclave," *Inter Press Service*, 4 November 1992.
42. "U.S. Peacekeeping Force Proposed," *Associated Press*, 20 July 1990.
43. Howe, "Lessons of Liberia," 150–151.
44. George Gedda, "U.S. Weighs Asking for UN Peacekeeping Force in Liberia," *Associated Press*, 31 July 1990.
45. Wippman, "Enforcing the Peace," 165.

46. The momentous loss of 18 US Rangers in Somalia only occurred on 3 October, but US and global disenchantment with UN peacekeeping was already palpable in the previous months.
47. UNSC, *Report of the Secretary-General on the Question of Liberia,* 12 March 1993, S/25402, §40.
48. Robert McFadden, "Five U.S. Nuns Are Shot to Death While Trapped by Liberian War," *New York Times*, 1 November 1992.
49. "U.S. Official Takes Firm Stance on U.N. Intervention in Liberia," *Houston Chronicle*, 11 November 1992.
50. "Liberia: U.S. Insists It Backs Peacekeeping Force," *Inter Press Service*, 12 November 1992.
51. Peter da Costa, "Liberia: United Nations, United States Urged into the Breach," *Inter Press Service*, 14 May 1993.
52. UNSC, *United Nations Secretary-General, Further Report on Liberia*, 2 August 1993, S/26200, §§16 and 18.
53. UNSC, *United Nations Secretary-General, Report on Liberia*, 9 September 1993, S/26422, §18.
54. UNSC, *Resolution 866.*
55. UNSC, *Fourth Progress Report of the Secretary-General on the United Nations Observer Mission in Liberia*, 18 May 1994, S/1994/588, §§3–9.
56. Max Ahmadu Sesay, "Bringing Peace to Liberia," in *Accord: An International Review of Peace Initiatives—The Liberian Peace Process, 1990–1996*, ed. Jeremy Armon and Andy Carl (London: Conciliation Resources, 1996), p. 14.
57. Adibe, "The Liberian Conflict and the ECOWAS-UN Partnership," 478–480.
58. UNSC, *Fifth Progress Report of the Secretary-General on the United Nations Observer Mission in Liberia*, 24 June 1994, S/1994/760, §41.
59. UNSC, *Sixth Progress Report of the Secretary-General on the United Nations Observer Mission in Liberia*, §29.
60. IISS, *The Military Balance 1997/98* (London: IISS, 1997), p. 250.
61. UNSC, *Eighth Progress Report of the Secretary-General on the United Nations Observer Mission in Liberia*, p. 4.
62. UN, *Liberia–UNOMIL: Facts and Figures,* accessed 15 December 2011 at http://www.un.org/en/peacekeeping/missions/past/unomilF.html.
63. UNSC, *Seventeenth Progress Report of the Secretary-General on the United Nations Observer Mission in Liberia*, 21 May 1996, §§19 and 28.
64. UNSC, *Final Report of the Secretary-General on the United Nations Observer Mission in Liberia*, §30.
65. Eric Berman, "'Successful' Elections in Liberia: Hold the Applause," *UN Watch,* August 1997.
66. UNSC, *Twenty-Fourth Progress Report of the Secretary-General on the United Nations Observer Mission in Liberia*, 13 August 1997.
67. ICG, "Liberia: The Key to Ending Regional Instability," 13.
68. Ibid., 3 and 40.
69. Ibid., 4–5.
70. ICG, "Tackling Liberia: The Eye of the Regional Storm," *Africa Report N°62* (30 April 2003): 10–11 and 19–25.
71. UNSC, *Report of the Secretary-General to the Security Council on Liberia*, 11 September 2003, 2–3.
72. ICG, "Liberia: The Key to Ending Regional Instability," 25. UN, *Report of the Secretary-General to the Security Council on Liberia*, 11 September 2003, 2.
73. ICG, "Liberia: The Key to Ending Regional Instability," 25.

74. UNSC, *Report of the Secretary-General to the Security Council on Liberia*, 11 September 2003, 2.
75. Kofi A. Annan, *Letter Dated 28 June 2003 from the Secretary-General Addressed to the President of the Security Council*, 28 June 2003.
76. Nicolas Cook, *Liberia: Transition to Peace*, CRS Report for Congress No. RL32243, last updated 28 October 2004, 35 and 43–44.
77. Ibid., p. 35.
78. Calculated from data in the World Bank World Development Indicators & Global Development Finance database.
79. Eric G. Berman and Katie E. Sams, *Peacekeeping in Africa: Capabilities and Culpabilities* (Geneva: UN Institute for Disarmament, 2000), pp. 131–138.
80. "ECOWAS Approves Beefed-up ECOMICI Contingent," *UN Integrated Regional Information Networks (IRIN)*, 8 April 2003.
81. ICG, "Liberia: The Key to Ending Regional Instability," 25.
82. UNSC, *Resolution 1497*, 1 August 2003, §§1–5.
83. UNSC, *Resolution 1132*, 8 October 1997.
84. UNSC, *Resolution 1306*, 5 July 2000.
85. UNSC, *Resolution 1343*, 7 March 2001.
86. UNSC, *Resolution 1343*.
87. UNSC, *Resolution 1408*, 6 May 2002.
88. "Aguilar-Zinser Advocates 'Limited, Constructive Engagement' with Liberian President Taylor to Address Regional Instability in West Africa," formerly classified cable, now officially released in full, July 2002.
89. UNSC, *First Report of the Secretary-General Pursuant to Security Council Resolution 1408 (2002) Regarding Liberia*, 22 October 2002, 5.
90. Neh Dukuly-Tolbert, *Letter Dated 11 August 1999 from the Permanent Representative of Liberia to the United Nations, Addressed to the Secretary-General*, 12 August 1999.
91. UNSC, *Statement by the President of the Security Council*, 13 December 2002.
92. UNSC, *Letter Dated 5 May 2003 from the President of the Security Council Addressed to the Secretary-General*, 6 May 2003.
93. "Security Council Salutes Agreement by West African Heads of State," *Associated Press Worldstream*, 28 February 2002.
94. "Liberia; New Contact Group, New UN Representative," *UN IRIN*, 18 September 2002.
95. UNSC, *Letter Dated 18 June 2003 from the SG Addressed to the President of the SC*, 19 June 2003.
96. Kofi A. Annan, *Letter Dated 28 June 2003 from the Secretary-General Addressed to the President of the Security Council*, 28 June 2003.
97. Christophe de Roquefeuil, "Washington Considering Sending Troops to Liberia," *Agence France Presse*, 1 July 2003.
98. Emmanuel Goujon, "Calls for Peacekeepers in Liberia," *Courrier Mail* (Queensland, Australia), 30 June 2003. Jonathan Paye Layleh, "African Leaders Seek U.S. Peace Force in Liberia Ahead of Visit by U.S. President," *Associated Press Worldstream*, 30 June 2003. Jonathan Paye-Layleh, "Liberians Urge US to Halt War after Shelling Kills Nine Civilians," *The Independent (London)*, 27 June 2003.
99. Edith Lederer, "Britain Suggests the United States Intervene in Liberia," *Associated Press Worldstream*, 25 June 2003.
100. "France Wants International Force to Halt Liberia Killing," *The Sunday Times (Perth, Australia)*, 29 June 2003.
101. Dave Clark, "West African Leaders Urge UN to Approve Liberia Peace Force," *Agence France Presse*, 29 June 2003.

102. Jonathan Paye Layleh, "African Leaders Seek U.S. Peace Force in Liberia Ahead of Visit by U.S. President," *Associated Press*, 30 June 2003.
103. Layleh, "African Leaders Seek U.S. Peace Force in Liberia."
104. Kofi A. Annan, *Letter Dated 28 June 2003 from the Secretary-General Addressed to the President of the Security Council*, 28 June 2003.
105. UNSC, *Report of the Security Council Mission to West Africa, 26 June-5 July 2003*, 7 July 2003, §47.
106. Howard Jeter, "Nigeria: Obasanjo Foreign Policy," confidential cable, 7 May 2001.
107. Howard Jeter, "Nigeria: Obasanjo's Liberia Policy Gets Mixed Reviews," confidential cable, 1 August 2003.
108. U.S. Committee for Refugees and Immigrants, *U.S. Committee for Refugees World Refugee Survey–Liberia*, 1 June 2003, accessed 24 January 2012 at http://www.unhcr.org/refworld/docid/3eddc48a6.html.
109. Jeff Drumtra, "West Africa's Refugee Crisis Spills across Many Borders," *Migration Information Source*, 1 August 2003.
110. Gavin Esler, "Interview with President Obasanjo of Nigeria," 29 July 2003, accessed 25 January 2012 at http://news.bbc.co.uk/go/pr/fr/-/2/hi/programmes/newsnight/3106961.stm.
111. Ojieh Chukwuemeka Ojione, "Public Opinion and Foreign policy: Analysing Nigerian Reactions to the Asylum Offered Former President Charles Taylor of Liberia," *African Journal of International Affairs* 11:1 (2008): 71–97, 84.
112. Jeter, "Obasanjo's Liberia Policy Gets Mixed Reviews."
113. Ikechukwu Eze and Brimah Kamara, "Nigeria Loses 1,000 Soldiers, $12b to Liberian War," *Vanguard (Lagos)*, 30 July 2003.
114. Howard Jeter, "In Depth Discussion on ECOWAS Capacity Building," confidential cable, 1 June 2001.
115. World Bank data.
116. Human Rights Watch, "Nigeria: The Warri Crisis: Fueling Violence," 17 December 2003, 4, accessed 22 January 2012 at http://www.unhcr.org/refworld/docid/402f6e7d4.html. Howard Jeter, "Nigeria: Two Battalions Can Deploy Quickly to Liberia–But Need Help," confidential cable, 25 July 2003.
117. Kunle Ajayi, "Nigeria's Foreign Policy and Image Crisis," *African Journal of Public Administration and Management* 16:2 (2005): 50–63, 55.
118. Howard Jeter, "Nigeria: The Obasanjo Administration at Two Years—A Work in Progress," confidential cable, 13 June 2001.
119. World Bank data.
120. "Nigeria to Seek Permanent Seat on the UN Security Council," *This Day*, 13 October 2003.
121. Gavin Esler, "Interview with President Obasanjo of Nigeria," 29 July 2003, accessed 25 January 2012 at http://news.bbc.co.uk/go/pr/fr/-/2/hi/programmes/newsnight/3106961.stm.
122. Jeter, "Obasanjo's Foreign Policy," 7 May 2001.
123. ICG, "Liberia: The Key to Ending Regional Instability," 25. Howard Jeter, "Nigeria: Obasanjo Seeking U.S. Approval for GON Offer of Asylum to Taylor," confidential cable, 19 June 2003.
124. Jeter, "Obasanjo Seeking U.S. Approval for GON Offer of Asylum to Taylor."
125. Gavin Esler, "Interview with President Obasanjo of Nigeria," 29 July 2003, accessed 25 January 2012 at http://news.bbc.co.uk/go/pr/fr/-/2/hi/programmes/newsnight/3106961.stm.
126. UNSC, *Report of the Security Council Mission to West Africa, 26 June-5 July 2003*, 7 July 2003, §42.
127. UNSC, *Security Council—4803rd Meeting, 1 August 2003*, verbatim record, 3–4.
128. Edith M. Lederer, "Security Council Authorizes Multinational Force for Liberia," *Associated Press*, 1 August 2003.

129. Precise figures vary between sources. See UN, *Report of the Security Council Mission to West Africa, 26 June-5 July 2003*, 7 July 2003, §42, and Jonathan Paye Layleh, "African Leaders Seek U.S. Peace Force in Liberia Ahead of Visit by U.S. President," *Associated Press Worldstream*, 30 June 2003.
130. Howard Jeter, "Nigeria—President Obasanjo Confirms Taylor's Asylum Offer and Nigeria's Commitment to Deploy," confidential cable, 9 July 2003.
131. Jeter, "Two Battalions Can Deploy Quickly to Liberia."
132. Howard Jeter, "Nigeria: Abubakar On ECOWAS Liberia Force," confidential cable, 22 July 2003.
133. UN, *Report of the Security Council Mission to West Africa, 26 June-5 July 2003*, 7 July 2003, §42.
134. Howard Jeter, "ECOWAS EXSEC Chambas Discusses Next Steps on Liberia with A/S Kansteiner," confidential cable, 22 July 2003
135. Howard Jeter, "Domestic Security Concerns and Budget Woes Preclude GON Contribution to Cote D'Ivoire Force," confidential cable, 15 November 2002.
136. Jeter, "Two Battalions Can Deploy Quickly to Liberia."
137. Ibid.
138. UN, *Report of the Security Council Mission to West Africa, 26 June-5 July 2003*, 7 July 2003, §42.
139. Jeter, "President Obasanjo Confirms Taylor's Asylum Offer."
140. Edith M. Lederer, "Annan Calls on West Africans to Announce Date for Peacekeeping Deployment to Liberia," *Associated Press*, 31 July 2003.
141. Reed Kramer, "Bush Makes Symbolic Shift on Liberia, but Dying Continues," *AllAfrica*, 28 July 2003.
142. Colum Lynch, "Annan Presses Nigeria on Peacekeepers; U.N. Chief Concerned about Reports of Worsening Situation in Liberia," *Washington Post*, 30 July 2003.
143. U.S. Newswire, "Remarks by the President and United Nations Secretary General Kofi Annan in Photo Opportunity," transcript of remarks, 14 July 2003.
144. "In the News: Bush Visits Africa" *Voice of America*, 13 July 2003.
145. Jeter, "ECOWAS EXSEC Chambas Discusses Next Steps on Liberia."
146. Col. Blair Ross, "The U.S. Joint Task Force Experience in Liberia," *Military Review* (May–June 2005), 62–64. Reed Kramer, "Bush Makes Symbolic Shift on Liberia, but Dying Continues," *AllAfrica*, 28 July 2003.
147. Reed Kramer, "Bush Makes Symbolic Shift on Liberia, but Dying Continues," *AllAfrica*, 28 July 2003.
148. Gavin Esler, "Interview with President Obasanjo of Nigeria," 29 July 2003, accessed 25 January 2012 at http://news.bbc.co.uk/go/pr/fr/-/2/hi/programmes/newsnight/3106961.stm.
149. U.S. Newswire, "Remarks by the President and United Nations Secretary General Kofi Annan in Photo Opportunity," transcript of remarks, 14 July 2003.
150. Gavin Esler, "Interview with President Obasanjo of Nigeria," 29 July 2003, accessed 25 January 2012 at http://news.bbc.co.uk/go/pr/fr/-/2/hi/programmes/newsnight/3106961.stm.
151. "UN Secretary-General 'very pleased' with United States Decision to Position 'Appropriate Military Capabilities' Off Liberian Coast," *M2 Presswire*, 28 July 2003.
152. SGR_875_2003Liberia.
153. Colum Lynch, "Annan Presses Nigeria on Peacekeepers; U.N. Chief Concerned about Reports of Worsening Situation in Liberia," *Washington Post*, 30 July 2003.
154. "Still No Sign of Peacekeepers for Liberia, Annan Presses Security Council to Act," *AllAfrica*, 30 July 2003.
155. UNSC, *Resolution 1497*, §§1, 3.
156. Felicity Barringer, "U.S. Draft Asks UN to Back Liberia Force," *New York Times*, 1 August 2003.

157. ECOWAS, *Final Communiqué*, Accra, 31 July 2003, §13, accessed 11 June 2012 at www.ghanaweb.com/GhanaHomePage/NewsArchive/artikel.php?ID=40289.
158. "Liberia; Nigerian Troops Arrive but Delay Entry to Monrovia, Some Fighting Still Reported," *UN IRIN*, 4 August 2003. Dave Clark and Emmanuel Goujon, "Liberia's Taylor Hands Over Power, Prepares for Exile," *Agence France Presse*, 11 August 2003.
159. Ross, "The U.S. Joint Task Force Experience in Liberia," 64–65.
160. *Comprehensive Peace Agreement between the Government of Liberia and the Liberians United for Reconciliation and Democracy (LURD) and the Movement for Democracy in Liberia (MODEL) and Political Parties* signed in Accra, Ghana, on August 18, 2003, Definitions and §§III–IV.
161. Ross, "The U.S. Joint Task Force Experience in Liberia," 65.
162. UNSC, *Resolution 1509*, 19 September 2003, §1.
163. UN, "'Re-hatting ECOWAS Forces as UN Peacekeepers: Lessons Learned," *Report for the Workshop on Lessons from ECOWAS Peacekeeping Ops 1990–2004*, held at the Kofi Annan International Peacekeeping Training Centre, Accra, Ghana, 10–11 February 2005.
164. UNSC, *Resolution 1509*, §3.
165. UN data, available at www.un.org/en/peacekeeping/resources/statistics/contributors.shtml.
166. UNSC, *Resolution 1626*, 19 September 2005, §13.
167. UNSC, *Tenth Progress Report of the Secretary-General on the United Nations Mission in Liberia*, 14 March 2006, S/2005/159, §20.
168. UNSC, *Tenth Progress Report of the Secretary-General on the United Nations Mission in Liberia*, §§ 11–40.
169. UNSC, *Tenth Progress Report of the Secretary-General on the United Nations Mission in Liberia*, §72.
170. UNSC, *Resolution 1667*, 31 March 2006, §5.
171. UNSC, *Special Progress Report of the Secretary-General on the United Nations Mission in Liberia*, 16 April 2012, S/2012/230, §17.
172. ICG, "Liberia: Time for Much-Delayed Reconciliation and Reform," *Africa Briefing* 88 (12 June 2012): 1.
173. UNSC, *Special Progress Report of the Secretary-General on the United Nations Mission in Liberia*, §66 and page 19.

Chapter 10

Sierra Leone

Shawna Meister

Introduction

Sierra Leone recently marked the tenth anniversary of the end of its eleven-year civil war, an important milestone in its post-conflict history. The war, which erupted in early 1991 and was officially declared over in 2002, was characterized by episodes of intense fighting alongside periods of relative calm, rebel uprisings, military coups, as well as shifting outside interventions. The conflict developed regional dimensions as fighting spilled over into neighboring countries, while some countries exploited Sierra Leone's instability and natural resources. The war was infamous for its brutalization and mutilation of the people, the role of "blood diamonds," and the 500 United Nations (UN) peacekeepers who were taken hostage. Now, however, with a decade of relative calm in a neighborhood of regional problems, Sierra Leone has demonstrated remarkable progress toward sustainable peace.

The end of Sierra Leone's war has largely been credited to the substantial engagements made by both the Economic Community of West African States (ECOWAS) and the UN. ECOWAS, the regional organization, officially intervened in the conflict in mid-1997, while the UN's primary entry point came in late 1999. During the conflict, each organization's independent efforts to achieve peace encountered difficulties; a brief attempt at co-deployment faced its own challenges and turned into a hand-over mission. On the ground, UN and ECOWAS actions and inactions at times endangered the people and prolonged the conflict, while organizational dynamics and the international climate affected decision making at the institutional level. During the post-conflict period, the differences between each organization's capacities to consolidate peace have been more strikingly evident, with the UN undertaking the primary peace-building role, while ECOWAS has contributed assistance and support. Yet sustained, long-term organizational involvement has been important to Sierra Leone, since countries emerging from conflict have a tendency to relapse back into war within five to ten years.[1]

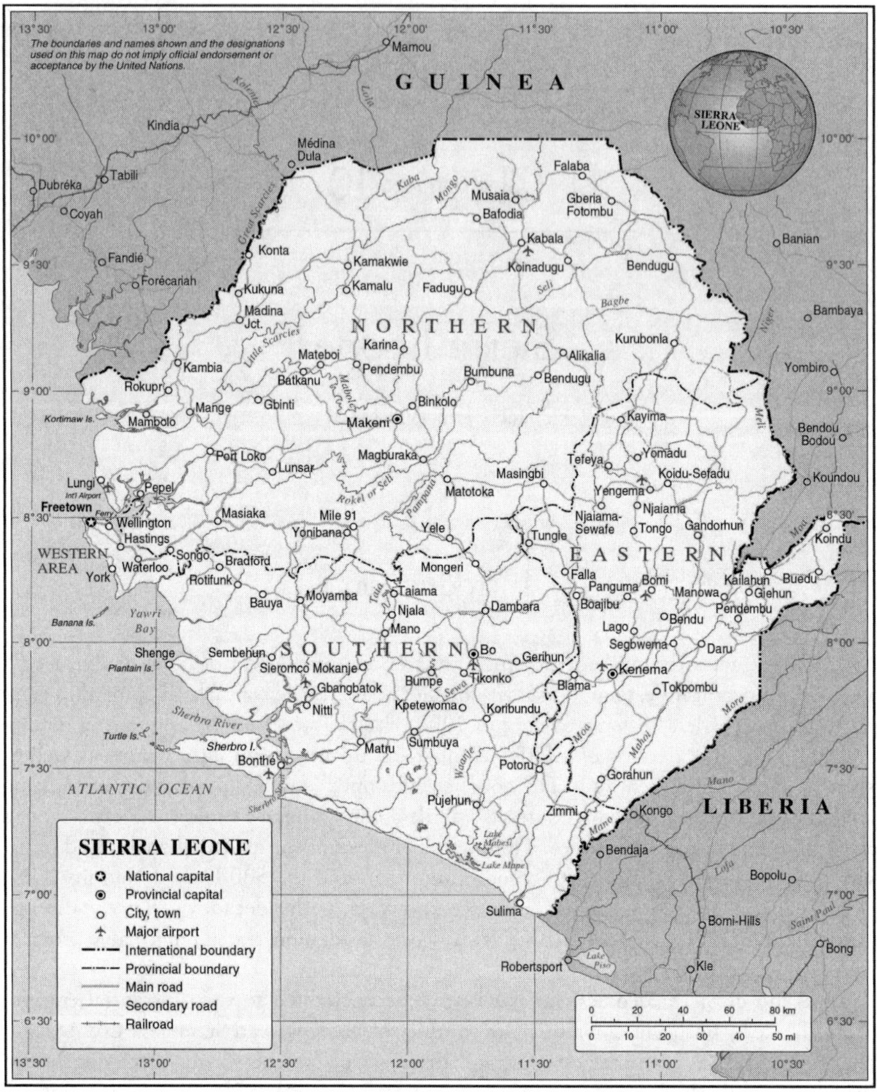

Source: Map No 3902 Rev 5, United Nations, Department of Peacekeeping Operations, Cartographic Section, January 2004

Given the extensive independent and joint efforts of the UN and ECOWAS in Sierra Leone, and the considerable time elapsed thus far (2012) without a return to major fighting, this case presents an opportunity to analyze a broad spectrum of challenges and successes associated with UN and regional organization engagement. The chapter begins by giving a brief background of the conflict, and then outlines the outbreak of war leading up to the May 1997 military coup. The next section analyzes ECOWAS and UN activity throughout the remainder of the conflict, and is followed by a section on the post-conflict period. The conclusion then discusses key findings, offers reflections on ECOWAS and UN engagement and cooperation, and poses questions for future consideration.

Background of the Conflict

Many of the causes contributing to both Sierra Leone's conflict and its continuing challenges in the post-conflict period were decades if not two centuries in the making.[2] In 1787, Freetown, the current capital of Sierra Leone, was established as a British colony for freed slaves (*Krios/Creoles*) joined by British citizens, and it developed largely independently of the surrounding rural areas. In the fashion of British indirect rule, the residents of Freetown created a governing structure focused almost entirely on the urban business elites.[3] Generally, interaction between Freetown and the rural areas was limited to conducting trade. At the end of the nineteenth century, as colonial powers solidified their territorial claims in Africa, the British declared the rural areas a Protectorate in 1896. The loss of independence for rural populations, followed by the requirement to pay taxes to the British, led to a rural uprising two years later. The consequence of this uprising was widespread replacement of rural chiefs with those loyal to the Freetown Government and the partitioning of rural communities. Many of the newly appointed "paramount chiefs" engaged in poor governance practices and alienated many young "non-native" men (outsiders), since chiefs often determined the status and rights of men in the community.[4] By the time Sierra Leone achieved independence in 1961, disgruntled youth, the patron–client relationship between chieftaincies and Freetown, government bias favoring elites, and the rural–urban divide had become entrenched. These problems continued to be an undercurrent of the unrest during the postindependence period and the civil war.[5]

From Independence to Civil War

Sierra Leone achieved independence on 27 April 1961. Although various issues marred its first few years of self-governance, it was political rule under Siaka Stevens from 1968 to 1986 that paved the way for the country's decline into instability.[6] Stevens amended the constitution to a one-party system, making it illegal to challenge the president. His consolidation of power involved the diversion of revenues, foreign aid, and decision-making power to himself. This effectively removed the ability of state institutions to provide services to the people. In some cases, such as that of the central bank, Stevens's tactics removed an institution's ability to function all together.[7] Businesses were unwilling to invest in the country, resulting in significant capital flight. Stevens, government elites, and rural chiefs accumulated personal revenue through corruption and mismanagement of diamond mining and other resource sectors.[8] The only structure to remain remotely intact was the army, though it did so not as a functioning military force but rather as a co-opted pay-off scheme intended to prevent further dissention and keep the military on Stevens's side.[9]

When Stevens retired in 1986, his hand-picked replacement, President Joseph Momoh, attempted to address some of Sierra Leone's problems. However, he was unable to reverse the effects of Stevens's actions and in fact continued many of Stevens's corrupt practices.[10] Within five years of Momoh taking office, the country had next to no infrastructure; the army was seriously debilitated and politicized; a centralized government was ruled by an entrenched, corrupt elite in Freetown while a large number of paramount chiefs abused their powers in the rural regions; the country was divided between both ethnic tribes and urban–rural populations; its diamond and mineral resources were being exploited; and the majority of its impoverished population was substantially alienated, particularly its youth and those in the rural areas.[11]

In addition to these internal problems, the immediate trigger of Sierra Leone's conflict involved a regional element. Charles Taylor, a rebel leader waging war in neighboring Liberia, looked to exploit Sierra Leone's instability for several reasons. He wanted access to its diamonds to fund his war, he sought retribution against Momoh for aiding in Taylor's 1988 capture and arrest, and he wanted to disrupt the Economic Community of West African States Monitoring Group (ECOMOG) military forces that were using Sierra Leone as a base to fight against Taylor in Liberia.[12] He intended to use conflict to achieve these goals. Thus, a long history of internal problems combined with external exploitive interests laid the foundations for the beginning of Sierra Leone's civil war in 1991.

Conflict Erupts

In March 1991, the Revolutionary United Front (RUF) rebels, led by Foday Sankoh, launched their first attacks from Liberia into the Kailahun district of Sierra Leone. Sankoh, an ex-Sierra Leone Army (SLA) corporal, had met Taylor in 1988 while they were both undergoing guerilla training in Libya. Taylor pushed Sankoh to set up the RUF, providing substantial military and financial support.[13] During the RUF's first year, it carried out extreme abuses of civilians, recruited child soldiers, and took over large sections of the rural areas, including control of many of the diamond mines.[14]

While the rural areas were under RUF attack, a group of army officers—increasingly disgruntled with their poor pay, training, and equipment—launched a coup in Freetown on 29 April 1992. President Momoh fled the country and Captain Valentine Strasser became the new military head of state, promising to end the conflict and to hold elections.[15] Strasser brought in Executive Outcomes, a private South African mercenary group, to combat the RUF, and he requested assistance from the UN, which sent Felix Mosha, Special Envoy of the Secretary-General, to attempt mediation with the RUF. Despite Strasser's efforts, the RUF rejected the UN's offer of mediation, the conflict continued, and elections never occurred, leading to the January 1996 coup that installed Captain Julius Maada Bio in power.[16] Bio upheld the promise for elections, which seated Ahmad Tejan Kabbah as president on 29 March 1996. On the combat front, Executive Outcomes made headway against the RUF and began training the *kamajors* (civil defence forces created by rural communities), greatly improving *kamajor* defence and combat skills.[17]

The Abidjan Peace Agreement

The combined efforts of the *kamajors* and Executive Outcomes pushed most of the RUF back to the borders and regained some of the rebel strongholds. Facing potential defeat, Sankoh entered into peace negotiations with Kabbah.[18] The negotiations briefly brought together the UN, ECOWAS, the Organization for African Unity (OAU), and the Commonwealth of Nations (hereinafter the Commonwealth) to work on an agreement. The UN appointed Berhanu Dinka as the UN Special Envoy to Sierra Leone to help the mediation. Amara Essy of Côte d'Ivoire represented ECOWAS and led the negotiations, while Akyaaba Addai-Sebo, a member of the organization International Alert and a friend of Taylor and Essy, represented the RUF. Essy proved instrumental in bringing both sides together, leading to the eventual signing of the Abidjan Peace Agreement on 30 November 1996.[19] Under the terms of the accord, the two sides agreed, inter alia, to a ceasefire and the disarmament, demobilization, and reintegration (DDR) of combatants. The agreement also called for the withdrawal of Executive Outcomes after the deployment of a Neutral Monitoring Group, allowed the RUF to become a political party, and gave RUF members immunity from prosecution for crimes committed as rebels.[20]

Despite the Agreement, poor cooperation, ongoing distrust, and the questionable neutrality of various representatives tainted the negotiations. Observers and participants of the peace talks reported that Addai-Sebo continually worked to derail Dinka's efforts, that Essy appeared to favor the RUF due to his friendship with Addai-Sebo, and that Sankoh and Essy did not trust Dinka. Additionally, Côte d'Ivoire was allegedly supporting the RUF.[21]

Ultimately, the accord did not hold; this was largely due to Sankoh and the RUF's failure to implement it and the signatories' failure to uphold their role as guarantors, but was also due to Kabbah releasing Executive Outcomes before the monitoring group was created. The private army presence was both controversial (being mercenaries) and expensive (their overall cost was estimated at US$35 million).[22] Their exit in January 1997 weakened the security situation, leading to the 25 May 1997 coup by a former soldier, Major Johnny Paul Koroma. He quickly formed the Armed Forces Revolutionary Council (AFRC), banned political parties and the *kamajors*, suspended the constitution, and invited the RUF into Freetown to join his government.[23] Sierra Leone again descended into conflict.

ECOWAS/ECOMOG Intervention

Nigerian-Driven ECOMOG Intervention

Although the May 1997 coup received international condemnation––including statements issued by the UN, the OAU, the Commonwealth, and the European Union (EU)—the first attempt to reverse the coup came from a country rather than an organization.[24] Since 1991, Nigeria had stationed a small contingent of troops in Freetown under the terms of a bilateral status of forces agreement, in part at the request for protection by Momoh—a military school friend of then Nigerian President General Ibrahim Babanginda—and in part as a military staging ground for Nigerian-ECOMOG forces operating in neighboring Liberia.[25] General Sani Abacha, president of Nigeria, following a 1993 coup, continued to maintain the military presence and later had some of the forces act as personal protection for Kabbah.[26] It was in this context that, after the coup, Kabbah called upon Abacha to intervene and reinstate him to power. On 2 June, deploying additional troops and using a Nigerian gunboat already positioned in the waters off Freetown, Abacha attacked the AFRC in Freetown. Intense fighting ensued, killing and injuring over a hundred civilians, but Nigerian forces were unsuccessful in ousting the AFRC–RUF junta.[27]

Not willing to lose Sierra Leone to the junta, Abacha, as the presiding ECOWAS Chairman, turned to ECOWAS to pursue military intervention. Abacha's quest to return peace and a democratic government to Sierra Leone contrasted starkly with his brutal military dictatorship at home. He hoped that by ending the conflict, he would improve his poor international reputation, particularly since Nigeria was under US, Commonwealth, and EU sanctions. He also wanted to extend Nigeria's regional dominance, and thus saw intervention in Sierra Leone as an opportunity to demonstrate Nigeria's security and leadership capabilities.[28]

At the same time, other actors also were pressuring ECOWAS to intervene. The OAU, at odds with its own noninterventionist principles, authorized ECOWAS to "restore the constitutional order," while the UN Security Council endorsed the OAU appeal.[29] Officially, these statements signaled that both organizations were not planning to take action even while they directed ECOWAS to do so. Unofficially, it appeared that both organizations were willing to let any actor—including a military dictator—step in. Despite the negative international sentiment felt for Abacha, the UN remained silent regarding Nigeria's unilateral operation. Similarly, the OAU circumvented the Nigerian issue by legitimizing the operation by tying it to ECOWAS, labeling it an "ECOWAS-led" intervention.[30]

It was not until 26 June 1997 that ECOWAS issued an official statement condemning the coup. This was issued at a special emergency meeting on Sierra Leone held in Conakry, Guinea. Tensions between regional rivals were high as Abacha pushed for the use of force while others, particularly Côte d'Ivoire and Ghana, wanted to pursue a diplomatic solution.[31] ECOWAS eventually decided on a combined approach of three initiatives: dialogue between a Committee of Four (Côte d'Ivoire, Ghana, Guinea, and Nigeria) and the AFRC–RUF to work on resolving the crisis, use of sanctions, and use of force.[32] Thus, it was the combination of internal pressure from Nigeria and external pressure from the OAU and the UN that prompted ECOWAS to engage in the Sierra Leone conflict.

The first initiative, dialogue, broke down by July 1997 when Koroma declared his intention to remain in power.[33] At the ECOWAS annual summit in Abuja on 28–29 August 1997, members then decided to enact the second initiative, the imposition of regional sanctions. The measures restricted travel, authorized the freezing of funds for "members of the illegal regime," and banned the supply of petroleum, arms, and military equipment to Sierra Leone.[34] ECOWAS also instructed the Committee of Five (expanded to include newly elected president of Liberia, Charles Taylor) to request that the Security Council apply universal sanctions. In order to implement the ECOWAS measures, the regional organization launched the third initiative, authorizing the extension of ECOMOG I (the Liberian operation) to ECOMOG II (the Sierra Leone operation), which had a mandate to use "all necessary means" to enforce the embargo.[35] The Nigerian forces, along with a small number of Ghanaian and Guinean troops in Sierra Leone, now officially operated under the ECOMOG mandate and ECOWAS directives. The force has been aptly termed "Nigerian-ECOMOG," given that Nigeria provided over 90 percent of the troops.[36]

ECOWAS' level of engagement in Sierra Leone during this time was in large part subject to the dynamics of its members.[37] Nigeria's domineering and militaristic approach aggravated two ongoing and largely overlapping internal splits, one between Francophone and Anglophone countries, and one between Nigeria and those opposed to Nigeria's use of power. While countries like Guinea—which was experiencing the spillover effects of the Sierra Leone conflict—supported military intervention, Côte d'Ivoire, Burkina Faso, and Ghana were critical of Nigeria's actions, with some going as far as openly stating that they supported the RUF.[38] This was not far from fact since it was known that Burkina Faso and Liberia (along with Libya) were supplying soldiers to the conflict, as well as financing and equipping the rebels.[39]

UN Sanctions and the Conakry Peace Accord

Despite ECOWAS' internal issues, the Committee of Four/Five met with the Security Council and the Secretary-General to push for UN sanctions.[40] Until this point, the lack of the political will to intervene on the part of the Council reflected the reservations of some Council members after the experiences of Somalia and Rwanda, in spite of several years of pressure from Secretary-General Kofi Annan and the United Kingdom for Council action.[41] With the additional push from the region, more than six years into the war, the combination of external and internal pressure prompted the Council to produce its first effort to address the conflict–sanctions Resolution 1132 (8 October 1997). Primarily drafted by the United Kingdom, the sanctions measures included an arms and petroleum embargo and travel restrictions on the junta, and also established a Sanctions Committee (the 1132 Committee).[42] In contrast to ECOWAS, the Council did not enact financial or comprehensive trade restrictions, out of concern about the potential humanitarian impact.[43]

The Council's move was a small sign of cooperation, given that it expected ECOWAS—authorized under Chapter VIII—to implement the sanctions. ECOWAS was not looking for the UN to step in. Although some ECOWAS members wanted a stronger UN presence to help counter Nigerian dominance, the overall regional sentiment was, as expressed at a December 1997 ECOWAS meeting on conflict resolution, that "Africans should take responsibility for their own destiny."[44] ECOWAS, particularly Nigeria, wanted to achieve success on its own.

The expansion to a universal UN embargo proved to have a brief coercive effect on the AFRC–RUF. Feeling the constraints, representatives of the junta agreed to meet with representatives from the UN, ECOWAS, ECOMOG, and the Committee of Five, resulting in the negotiation of the 23 October 1997 Conakry Accord.[45] Also known as the ECOWAS six-month peace plan, it called for immediate cessation of hostilities, DDR of ex-combatants, immunity from prosecution for those involved in the May coup, reinstatement of President Kabbah the following year, and a power-sharing agreement with the junta. Additionally, the plan called for UN support in the form of military observers (MILOBs).[46]

However, the Conakry Accord fell apart on several fronts. From the start, negotiations had been acrimonious due to the heavy-handed tactics of Nigeria's foreign minister, Tom Ikimi (representing the Committee of Five).[47] The agreement also called for ECOMOG to supervise disarmament and demobilization, but ECOMOG's role as a combatant in the fighting created distrust among the AFRC–RUF and unwillingness to disarm.[48] Finally, the combatants did not intend to uphold their commitments. Koroma announced his intention to stay in power, while rebels began stockpiling arms and spreading propaganda against Kabbah.[49] By the end of 1997, fighting had resumed between the AFRC–RUF and the Nigerian-ECOMOG forces.

Nigeria's Military Solution

On 6 February 1998, Nigerian-ECOMOG forces launched a full-scale attack on AFRC–RUF forces in Freetown, with intense fighting lasting for several days. ECOMOG forces managed to push the junta into the rural areas where the *kamajors* continued to fight the rebels while AFRC's Koroma fled to Liberia.[50] Civilians were again caught in the cross fire as the fleeing AFRC–RUF took their vengeance out on the rural people. "Many thousands of Sierra Leonean civilians were raped, deliberately mutilated, or killed outright in a campaign by the AFRC/RUF between February and June 1998 alone."[51]

When the news of the attack reached the Security Council, several members immediately accused the Committee of Five—which had been meeting with the UN at the time of the attack—of "deceiving the UN for not informing them of ECOMOG's intentions."[52] Although the attack undermined the credibility of ECOWAS and brought its oversight capabilities into question in the eyes of the Council,[53] the UN did not initially respond. Three weeks later, the Security Council President made it clear that the decision to use force fell under the authority of the UN. ECOMOG was to "foster peace and stability in Sierra Leone, in accordance with relevant provisions of the Charter of the United Nations."[54]

The attack was equally surprising to ECOWAS members. Having repeatedly insisted that ECOMOG refrain from use of force against the junta (an injunction strongly reiterated during an ECOWAS meeting only six weeks earlier), they were outraged at Nigeria's unauthorized move.[55] Nigeria claimed that its attack fell under ECOMOG's self-defence provisions, but various sources indicate that Nigeria had planned the attack in advance in retribution for losses they suffered during the 1997 coup.[56] The limited support Nigeria had inside ECOWAS was damaged. At a May 1998 ECOWAS meeting, members either refused to send or delayed sending additional troops in response to Nigeria's request to help diversify ECOMOG. On the ground, the few other troop-contributing countries sometimes disobeyed orders from Nigerian commanders, disagreeing with Nigeria's combative interpretation of ECOMOG's mandate.[57]

Nigeria's actions and its command of ECOMOG also distanced other actors from assisting ECOWAS during this time. For many, helping the regional organization or ECOMOG meant indirectly supporting a military dictatorship, particularly one under various bilateral and multilateral sanctions (see earlier). The United States, for example, limited its support to ECOMOG forces, providing relatively small donations in the form of equipment and logistics. Likewise, the United Kingdom, although the biggest advocate for intervention in the conflict, refused to provide ECOMOG with any type of assistance while Abacha chaired ECOWAS.[58]

In the context of ongoing poor funding, and equipment and supply shortages, Nigerian commanders siphoned off substantial amounts of funds intended for the operation.[59] Inadequate pay often delayed by several months led many soldiers to engage in various forms of looting from civilians. This included taking part in illicit diamond mining, either in cooperative arrangements with the RUF or after ECOMOG had taken over the mining areas from the rebels.[60] Thus, among the population, the response to Nigerian-ECOMOG forces fluctuated between gratitude and dislike. They appreciated that ECOMOG was willing to intervene and fight the rebels when no one else would, but the ongoing heavy and sometimes indiscriminate attacks wounded or killed many, and when not fighting, many soldiers often carried out their own abuses on civilians.[61]

Return to Civilian Rule

Despite criticisms of the attack, its impact on the conflict was significant. The 13,000-strong ECOMOG force regained control of Freetown and much of the country, allowing for the return of Kabbah and a civilian government on 10 March 1998.[62] This signaled a tentative potential for peace, triggering a response in New York. On 5 February 1998, the Security Council requested that Secretary-General Annan establish a Trust Fund for Sierra Leone and outline a plan for future UN involvement. With Resolution 1156 (16 March 1998), the Council welcomed Kabbah's return by ending the oil embargo.[63] On 13 July 1998, the Council authorized Annan's recommendation for a UN Observer Mission in Sierra Leone (UNOMSIL) through Resolution 1181. Initially intended to deploy 70 MILOBs (it only reached 50), UNOMSIL was mandated to monitor DDR as well as the military and security situation.[64] The resolution again placed the burden of peacekeeping on ECOMOG, as it was to provide security and assist UNOMSIL in its DDR efforts.

This first cooperative effort between the two organizations in Sierra Leone faced difficulties on the ground. Neither organization adequately prepared its missions for interaction or coordination. Personnel began carrying out "unhealthy comparisons" of each mission's duty assignments, command hierarchy, and operational procedures, straining the UNOMSIL–ECOMOG relationship.[65] Furthermore, UNOMSIL's small size and observer status were inadequate to monitor the entire country and the DDR of 32,000 combatants. In reality, UNOMSIL was the UN response to the increasing criticism of the world body for not doing enough in Africa. The operation symbolized UN involvement without making any substantial commitments—financially, militarily, or in human costs.[66] However, UNOMSIL's presence in Sierra Leone would be short-lived.

The AFRC–RUF forces still operated in parts of Sierra Leone and continued to receive substantial support from Liberia and Burkina Faso. Throughout 1998, they began rebuilding their forces and retaking parts of the country, gradually moving toward Freetown. Information gathered during November and December indicated that an attack on the capital was imminent.[67] As the situation deteriorated, UNOMSIL began evacuating their personnel and by the end of December, all of UNOMSIL as well as the Special Representative of the UN Secretary-General (SRSG) had left.[68] The UN had abandoned ECOMOG and Sierra Leone. Beginning on 6 January 1999, Freetown once again experienced a devastating attack by the AFRC-RUF. ECOMOG suffered significant troop losses and lost nearly all the ground they previously had gained. Through fierce fighting and the deaths of thousands of civilians, ECOMOG retook Freetown by mid-February, but was unable to regain control of the country.[69]

Co-deployment—UN Intervention

Role Reversal Part I: The Lomé Accord

The inability of ECOMOG to re-extend its authority throughout Sierra Leone reinforced the status of the ongoing civil war as a perpetual stalemate between the junta and ECOMOG, with ECOWAS countries footing the costs, while civilians and ECOMOG soldiers paid a bigger price with their lives. After the attack, several ECOWAS members—either disgruntled with Nigeria or unable to maintain contributions to ECOMOG—began advising Kabbah that they intended to reduce support for the operation and pressured him to start negotiations with the rebels.[70] Likewise, Nigeria, which had lost over 800 of its soldiers in the January 1999 battle, told Kabbah that it would not attempt to regain control of the remainder of the country, stressing that dialogue was the next step. The United Kingdom and the United States—also incurring mounting costs due to their ongoing efforts to end the conflict—advised Kabbah to enter into talks with the RUF.[71] Sierra Leonean citizens, too, were weary of the ongoing war and many were ready for Kabbah to engage in some form of dialogue to end the fighting.[72]

Sierra Leone's civil society led the way toward dialogue, holding broad-based peace consultations with both Sankoh and Kabbah in the spring. This opened the doors to a May 1999 cease-fire and then peace negotiations carried out by the SRSG, ECOWAS, OAU, and ambassadors from the United States and the United Kingdom.[73] With ECOMOG's continued presence in question and pressure from regional and international actors mounting, Kabbah signed the Lomé Peace Accord with the RUF on 7 July 1999. The Accord, largely drafted by the United States, was the most comprehensive agreement to date; it included improvements on specifics around DDR and repatriation and resettlement, provisions for human rights, establishment of a truth and reconciliation commission, a proposition for co-deploying two peacekeeping forces comprised of UNOMSIL and ECOMOG, and a call for an exit timetable for ECOMOG dependent upon a restructured SLA.[74]

However, when the details of the Accord were made public, the immediate reaction of various organizations was to criticize its controversial concessions.[75] Lomé included a power-sharing arrangement with RUF leader Sankoh—named vice president of the proposed government—the transformation of the RUF into a political party, and impunity for the rebels. Secretary-General Annan could not agree with the amnesty granted to the rebels, thus had the SRSG to Sierra Leone, Francis Okelo, add a stipulation to the agreement that there could be no immunity for acts of genocide, crimes against humanity, or other violations of international humanitarian law.[76] In describing the situation, Olonisakin explains that, for the UN, pressure to sign came with the realization that as only one of ten signatories the UN was "forced into a position where it could not obstruct what seemed the only real chance for peace for those involved."[77] For Sierra Leone, Lomé was the potential for peace; for the stakeholders, it was the potential exit strategy.[78]

The Lomé negotiators made little attempt to incorporate provisions to deal with some of the root causes of the conflict that had intensified during the war (such as the marginalized urban and youth populations), and rebel exploitation of diamond mining was effectively legitimized through Sankoh's other appointment in the agreement, that as chairman of natural resources.[79] The agreement called for a greater UN role in Sierra Leone, specifically requesting the Security Council to revise UNOMSIL's mandate to meet the needs of the agreement. Lomé's dependence on the UN and ECOWAS/ ECOMOG, however, quickly ran into significant difficulties due to the inability of both organizations to agree on how co-deployment would occur.[80]

Role Reversal Part II: ECOMOG to UNAMSIL

After the failure of the Conakry Agreement, the UN was more willing—if initially only in small increments—to step up support for Lomé and UN engagement with the conflict. In the months before and after the Lomé negotiations, the Security Council supported revising the mandate and concept of operations of UNOMSIL, while in August 1999, Annan outlined a proposed "division of labour" to Nigeria for co-deployment of their respective forces.[81] However, Nigeria's new president, Olesugen Obasanjo, informed Annan that in light of the "gradual return to peace," he was planning a phased withdrawal of Nigeria from ECOMOG beginning in August 1999.

Obasanjo's decision to withdraw from ECOMOG so soon after Lomé reflected the transformation occurring within Nigeria. With the death of General Abacha in 1998, Nigeria's May 1999 elections transitioned Nigeria to a democratically elected government under Obasanjo—whose election campaign was premised on the withdrawal of Nigerian troops from Sierra Leone.[82] Nigeria's reasons for leaving included the high operational costs (estimated at US$1 million a day), the profound unpopularity of the war with Nigerians due to the mounting casualties, and a general combat weariness—at this point, Nigeria had been involved in several African peacekeeping missions.[83] Nevertheless, Obasanjo recognized Nigeria's importance to ECOMOG, and he and other ECOWAS members approached the UN to either finance or take over the ECOMOG mission. The UN declined both proposals.[84]

Deeply concerned that Nigeria's withdrawal would create a security vacuum, President Kabbah convinced Obasanjo to delay his plans.[85] To offset Nigeria's impending departure, Annan submitted a proposed concept for a UN peacekeeping mission to the

Security Council in his 29 September 1999 report, while the United Kingdom pushed for its establishment from the inside. The Council responded on 22 October 1999 with Resolution 1270, which authorized the establishment of the United Nations Mission in Sierra Leone (UNAMSIL), and stressed the need for cooperation between ECOMOG and UNAMSIL.[86] Authorized at a troop size of 6,000, UNAMSIL's mandate called for absorbing UNOMSIL and, among other things, assisting in DDR, providing security for UN personnel, and monitoring the ceasefire. ECOMOG's primary responsibility would be to carry out peacekeeping and provide security. Although appreciative of the Council's decision, Sierra Leone's representative at the UN, Ibrahim Kamara, reminded the Council during the adoption of Resolution 1270 that 6,000 troops would not be an equal substitute for ECOMOG and appealed to the Council to "to do everything in its power to ensure that ECOMOG remains in Sierra Leone for the time being."[87]

The opportunity for heightened organizational cooperation was lost when Nigeria restarted its phased withdrawal from ECOMOG in December 2000. Lack of financial and logistical support was a major factor in its departure, but equally so were concerns over how the UN would handle failure or success in Sierra Leone. On 29 December 2000, Assistant-Secretary General Hédi Annabi reported to the Council that Nigeria's decision to withdraw was based on the concern that the simultaneous existence of two missions with different mandates, forces, and operational capacity meant that the UN could shift problems and blame ECOMOG if something went wrong.[88] Furthermore, several ECOWAS members felt that the UN undervalued their efforts and was attempting to take credit for the years of work that ECOWAS and ECOMOG had put into Sierra Leone.

To a certain extent, the perception that the UN wanted credit was correct. Sierra Leoneans and Africans had been criticizing the UN for years for not doing more in the country and other African conflicts in general.[89] By 1999, RUF atrocities and the use of "blood diamonds" to finance the conflict were receiving increased media attention, resulting in international pressure on the UN to do something.[90] Action in Sierra Leone could help promote the organization, improve its credibility, and tap into a potential UN "success." Thus, the failure to better define the partnership roles and operational outcomes of each mission, along with ECOMOG's financial and logistical constraints, impeded cooperation between the two organizations and contributed to Nigeria's and hence ECOMOG's eventual exit. This inability to work out a long-term co-deployment strategy with ECOWAS prompted deployment of the first UN peacekeeping mission to Sierra Leone—shifting the peacekeeping burden to an unprepared UNAMSIL.

In the early months of 2000, while Nigeria focused on withdrawing its forces and the UN scrambled to launch UNAMSIL, the security situation in Sierra Leone remained precarious. UNAMSIL's original mandate was premised upon ECOMOG's long-term participation, but ECOMOG's early exit reduced the time needed for UNAMSIL to reach full strength.[91] Annan's reports to the Council frequently described rebels disarming UNAMSIL peacekeepers or preventing them access to sections of the country, as well as rebel leaders refusing to allow their troops to participate in the DDR process.[92] Additionally, some rebels feared participating in DDR because they were not confident in UNAMSIL's ability to protect them against combatants that had not yet demobilized.[93] Attempting to improve the situation, on 7 February 2000, with strong pressure from the United Kingdom, the Council authorized Annan's January recommendations to increase UNAMSIL to 11,100 troops, through Resolution 1289.[94] Two months later, the UN again augmented the mission's size by re-hatting nearly 4,000 ECOMOG troops into UNAMSIL.[95]

Despite these efforts, UNAMSIL was "spread too thin on the ground."[96] Furthermore, the re-hatted ECOMOG troops, which had come from a very different mandate and command structure, were not properly informed as to their new role, mandate, and procedures under UN command. Poor communication and coordination already occurring within the rushed UNAMSIL operation further aggravated these issues.[97] Well aware of UNAMSIL's weaknesses, the rebels took advantage of ECOMOG's final departure on 1 May 2000 by staging several attacks in Sierra Leone and eventually taking 500 UN peacekeepers hostage.[98]

UN Engagement

UN Peacekeepers and UN Credibility Taken Hostage

The May 2000 hostage taking provoked strong national and international condemnation, along with two immediate concerns—to secure the release of the hostages and to reestablish the security situation within Sierra Leone. Secretary-General Annan recognized the importance of cooperating with ECOWAS and regional leaders, given their regional expertise and influence, and called upon them to take the lead in negotiations.[99] Talks, however, began with a less than desirable mediator, Liberia's President Charles Taylor, a key external backer of the conflict. Yet, his connections to the RUF and his long-standing relationship with Sankoh made him indispensable. As early as 4 May, Taylor proved his influence, when his discussions with Sankoh resulted in the release of a small helicopter crew the following day.[100] ECOWAS members at a 9 May mini-summit on Sierra Leone in Abuja subsequently mandated Taylor to lead the negotiations for the release of the hostages. Through his efforts, the majority of hostages were released by the end of the month.[101]

On the second concern, reestablishment of the security situation came with a swift intervention by British forces. This initially began on 8 May 2000 as an evacuation mission of foreign nationals from Freetown. Realizing, however, that the UN mission itself was at risk of failing and that the humanitarian situation could again become volatile, the British Government expanded its force's mandate to the protection and reinforcement of UNAMSIL and Sierra Leone government forces.[102] Their quick reaction and "over-the-horizon" display of force off the coast of Freetown sent the message to the rebels that the British were willing and capable of full engagement, contributing to the rebels' intimidation and later willingness to disarm. British deployment also allowed UNAMSIL to redeploy troops to other critical areas in Sierra Leone, and gave them enough time to bring in more UN reinforcements.[103]

The United Kingdom's actions nonetheless added to the already growing negative image of UNAMSIL and the UN created by the hostage taking. The capture of 500 peacekeepers in a country that at the time had just over 9,000 UN deployed troops yet failed to employ its mandate to "take the necessary action to ensure the security and freedom of movement of its personnel" called into question the UN and UNAMSIL's capabilities.[104] The United Kingdom's unilateral intervention and its refusal to place its troops under UNAMSIL in the weeks after the incident gave the impression that a major world power and a Security Council member also lacked confidence in the organization.[105] A few months after the May 2000 incident, when the British eventually contributed personnel to UNAMSIL, many received key placements within the operation. This aggravated tensions with other troop-contributing countries, particularly India, Nigeria, and Jordan, as it appeared that Western countries were making the high-level decisions while others did the dangerous ground work. This became a key reason for Jordan withdrawing its troops from UNAMSIL in October 2000.[106]

Restoring UN Credibility, Diminishing ECOWAS Presence

After the May humiliation, what could have led to a UN exit from Sierra Leone instead led to a long-term, scaled-up engagement by the organization. Within weeks of the hostage taking, the Council authorized a troop increase for UNAMSIL to 13,000, and did so again on 30 March 2001 to 17,500 troops—the organization's largest peacekeeping force at that time.[107] This allowed UNAMSIL to extend itself throughout the country, improving both security and the DDR process, which resumed in August 2000. Additionally, the greater numbers and the better trained and equipped forces became a confidence-builder among Sierra Leoneans and UN forces.[108] The Council also gave the force a stronger mandate, authorizing UNAMSIL "to deter and, where necessary, decisively counter the threat of RUF attacks by responding robustly to any hostile actions or threat of imminent and direct use of force."[109]

To investigate the problems faced by UNAMSIL, Secretary-General Annan sent a "high-level multi-disciplinary assessment team" to Sierra Leone in June 2000.[110] This and other outside assessments indicated a wide range of issues, including insufficient logistical equipment support, low troop contributions, poor coordination and communication both internally and externally, improper transitioning of incoming troops, rapid changes in structure and size, command and control problems.[111] Improvements in these areas formed the basis to many of Annan's subsequent recommendations to the Council.

The first of several Council responses included finally tackling the financial basis and one of the long-standing root causes of the conflict—the illicit diamond trade. UN estimates put RUF earnings from the illegal market between US$25 million to US$125 million per year.[112] On 5 July 2000, the Security Council issued Resolution 1306, which added an import ban on Sierra Leonean diamonds to the Chapter VII mandate.[113] It included an important directive, calling for the 1132 Committee (see earlier) to assess the link between the diamond market and the illegal arms trade. It also established a Panel of Experts to gather information and report to the Committee on violations.

Initially, the sanctions had little impact. The Panel of Experts' first report in December 2000 indicated that diamonds were smuggled into and sold from Liberia.[114] Three months later, the Council placed an embargo on diamonds sold from Liberia, "regardless of origin."[115] Although many ECOWAS members were upset with the sanctions—either defending Taylor or ignoring the resolution—the measures had a strong coercive effect on Liberia.[116] Taylor attempted to halt diamond exports and distanced Liberia from Sierra Leone's diamond trade, significantly weakening the RUF. Equally important, the Council had demonstrated its resolve regarding Sierra Leone by sanctioning one country due to sanctions-breaking in another country.[117]

The change in Council activity toward Sierra Leone was driven, in part, by the efforts of the United States and the United Kingdom. After the May crisis, each pressed for sanctions on Sierra Leone and Liberia, pushed for troop increases to UNAMSIL, and helped rally support behind international funding for the country.[118] In October 2000, the United Kingdom led a Security Council Mission to Sierra Leone to investigate ways in which the Council could improve the UN's role on the ground.[119] The visit brought out innovative recommendations that would guide future UN work (such as establishing a mission-coordinating mechanism).[120] Equally important, the visit directly connected Council members to the issues on the ground and helped strengthen its relations with national and regional efforts.

Increased UN activity in Sierra Leone also was an effort to address perceptions of diminished credibility. The May 2000 crisis overshadowed the future of other UN peacekeeping missions, in particular one planned for the Democratic Republic of the Congo (DRC).[121] UN missions could not risk falling apart in a "comparatively" manageable conflict, such as Sierra Leone, if the organization wanted to deploy missions for bigger and more complex conflicts, such as the DRC. The UN needed a success in Sierra Leone. Thus, it was timely when the *Report of the Panel on United Nations Peace Operations* (Brahimi Report), which assessed the state of UN peacekeeping, was released in August 2000.[122] It frequently referenced UNAMSIL problems throughout its analysis of broader peacekeeping efforts, and as Olonisakin points out, "tied the future of UNAMSIL to UN peacekeeping reform."[123] Sierra Leone became the test case for new strategies.

Despite ECOMOG's departure, ECOWAS continued working with the UN in Sierra Leone. The regional organization contributed significantly to the mediation of the Abuja I (November 2000) and Abuja II (May 2001) cease-fire agreements alongside the UN SRSG, while Nigeria assisted in security-sector reform.[124] Despite these efforts, ECOWAS was financially unable to keep pace with its previous military activity. This was highlighted by its inability to create and deploy a rapid-reaction force of only 1,796 troops, which it had promised to the UN in March 2001, due to a lack of funds.[125] Overall, ECOWAS activity in Sierra Leone significantly dropped after 1 May 2000.

Nevertheless, Sierra Leone benefited from the increased UN attention and from those actors that did not want to see the UN mission fail. Rebels were feeling pressure from the growing numbers of UNAMSIL troops, the UK presence, and attacks by Guinean forces in retaliation for cross-border RUF incursions on Guinean territory, while much of the RUF leadership had been imprisoned.[126] International donations to DDR significantly increased after May 2000 (although they never reached half of the required amount), and by the end of the program in January 2002, an estimated 72,000 combatants had gone through the process.[127] It was among this backdrop that Kabbah officially declared the civil war over on 18 January 2002, while plans for May elections were underway.

Post-Conflict Period

An atmosphere of trepidation and optimism throughout Sierra Leone preceded the 2002 elections. More than ten years of broken cease-fires, failed peace accords, resurgences of violence, and coup d'états had diminished faith in the possibility of real peace. However, there were several reasons to believe that this time was different. Many of the rebel leaders either were in prison or in exile, disarmament and demobilization of ex-combatants had been completed, over 17,000 UN personnel were deployed throughout the country, and the primary external contributor to the conflict, Charles Taylor, had largely disengaged from the RUF and was facing his own problems in Liberia.

Leading up to and during the elections, Security Council Resolution 1389 (16 January 2002) instructed UNAMSIL to provide, among other things, security, monitoring, public information dissemination, and voter registration assistance for the elections.[128] ECOWAS provided support in the form of a thirty-member delegation of electoral observers.[129] As provided for by the Lomé Agreement, the rebels participated in the elections through the formation of a political RUF Party. Despite a few clashes between different political supporters, mostly in Freetown, the elections were relatively peaceful and were considered free, fair, and transparent, resulting in the reelection of Kabbah to power on 14 May 2002.[130]

After May, the UN began planning for its disengagement, but unlike similar missions, UNAMSIL's departure was predicated on "effective consolidation of State authority" and "peace and stability" throughout Sierra Leone, not successful elections.[131] Sierra Leone was far from this reality. Over the next three years, UNAMSIL remained to assist the government as well as trained police and government forces in these objectives, handing over the missions' responsibilities in phases to improve the transition to state authority. Nonetheless, the Council was anxious to scale down the operation, and although there were security concerns, UNAMSIL had met the Secretary-General's benchmarks for withdrawal; thus, its mission was concluded on 31 December 2005.[132]

Peacekeeping to Peace-Building

UNAMSIL's exit, like the elections three years earlier, did not end UN engagement in Sierra Leone. The absence of major conflict did not mean stability, and peace consolidation would need active strategies, particularly in addressing root causes to the conflict. Kabbah's government was making progress. Diamond mining areas were under better control, recognized by the nonrenewal of the Council's diamond sanctions on 4 June 2003, and government authority extended throughout most of the country.[133] However, significant issues remained, including problems in monitoring and enforcing the diamond certification scheme, poor logistical support for the security sector, high youth unemployment, and continuing corruption. Regionally, the fragility surrounding Liberia's upcoming elections and the potential for spillover effects also posed a threat to Sierra Leone's peace.[134]

Given these issues, Sierra Leone benefited from the international climate surrounding the UN in 2004–2005. Long-term post-conflict peace-building was gaining increasing importance alongside continuing debates about UN utility in addressing conflicts.[135] Sierra Leone thus was a country in which the UN could demonstrate its value in peace-building.[136] Recognizing the "importance of continued UN support" in Sierra Leone, the Security Council established the UN Integrated Office in Sierra Leone (UNIOSIL) with Resolution 1620 (31 August 2005) to replace UNAMSIL on 1 January 2006. UNIOSIL was to help consolidate peace, particularly in capacity-building and preparation for the August 2007 elections.[137] Also in 2006, Sierra Leone became one of two country cases placed on the agenda of the newly created UN Peacebuilding Commission (PBC).[138] Although it faced start-up issues, the PBC brought increased attention to practical issues in Sierra Leone, such as youth unemployment, and helped to facilitate progress during Freetown's energy crisis in 2007.[139]

Political tensions and several outbreaks of violence tested Sierra Leone's peace during the August and September 2007 elections. The eventual peaceful transfer of power to the winning opposition was in part due to the efforts of UNIOSIL, the PBC, and ECOWAS. UNIOSIL maintained a "visible" UN presence and assisted the National Electoral Commission, while the PBC liaised with those on the ground, reporting concerns to the Security Council.[140] To promote a peaceful outcome prior to the tense September run-off vote, ECOWAS sent a high-level delegation on 1 September to talk to the candidates.[141]

The most recent mission change by the UN in Sierra Leone occurred with the replacement of UNIOSIL by the UN Integrated Peacebuilding Office in Sierra Leone (UNIPSIL) on 30 September 2008. In 2012, UNIPSIL, with approximately seventy staff, promoted national reconciliation, human rights, good governance, and constitutional reform.[142] On the part of ECOWAS, although the organization has provided assistance in different areas throughout the post-conflict period, it has remained largely in the background relative to the UN.[143]

Political tensions remain a primary source of volatility in Sierra Leone, as neither past President Kabbah or current President Koroma has been able to solidify a national unity government.[144] Furthermore, intense fighting between different party supporters continues to be a problem. Recently, on 7 February 2012, friction increased as Sierra Leone People's Party (SLPP) supporters accused the All People's Congress (APC) of rearming and deploying ex-combatants to some of the outlying regions.[145] Outside of politically related violence, the Secretary-General's latest reports consider Sierra Leone relatively calm; however, he cautions that illicit drug trafficking, organized crime, youth, and corruption remain as primary threats to peace-building.[146] In New York, despite the UN's strong post-conflict commitment, the ongoing funding shortfalls for its efforts expose the diminishing interests of members and their willingness to back up their commitments.[147]

Conclusion

Both ECOWAS and the UN were instrumental in ending Sierra Leone's eleven-year civil war, reinforcing the idea that the complexities of many African conflicts demonstrate a need for responses from both regional and international organizations.[148] At the same time, each organization's intervention was largely independent of the other's, each experienced serious setbacks, both lacked capacity and support in many areas, and political will fluctuated—all of which impeded their efforts to address the conflict, and at times to cooperate.[149] In contrast, significant differences in capacity and experience made partnership in the post-conflict period nearly absent, even though prolonged UN engagement has proved important in maintaining peace. The Sierra Leone case thus brings out several understandings pertinent to ongoing or future UN–regional organization interactions.

Having a powerful member within each organization working to "champion" intervention in Sierra Leone proved important to institutional engagement. Nigeria initiated the ECOMOG force and the United Kingdom activated the UN, and both had the resources to engage. Powerful actors also had their drawbacks. Nigeria's ability to commandeer ECOMOG often forced decisions, resulting in disjointed and at times contradictory forms of engagement from ECOWAS. Furthermore, though ECOMOG had a strong and immediate impact, the changing interests of ECOWAS members (particularly Nigeria) and their limited state capacities meant that reliable and sustained engagement was inhibited. On the other hand, the UN's broader membership and power base greatly subdued UK efforts, partly delaying action in Sierra Leone until another powerful actor (the United States) came on board. Overall, a champion with means and influence appears to be important to engagement; yet, powerful members may choose to operate outside of their respective organizations and mandates, thus undermining organizational legitimacy.

At the UN, beyond British and American interests in Sierra Leone, the changing international climate also affected political will. Despite an opportune entry point after Nigerian-ECOMOG's takeover of most of the country in February 1998, the Council's response was a small symbolic observer force that left when the situation worsened. Yet, the declining security situation as Nigerian-ECOMOG troops withdrew, which culminated in the May 2000 hostage taking, instead resulted in the deployment of the UN's then-largest peacekeeping force, which was followed by more than ten years of post-conflict engagement. By 2000, several UN failures, growing criticism from members' constituents, and questions surrounding UN efficacy all were important to altering political will. A key factor was that success or failure in Sierra Leone became connected to success or failure for other UN missions.

The argument that regional actors inherently have the political will to address conflicts happening in their backyard is somewhat overstated in the Sierra Leone case. True, Nigeria was willing to intervene—but for personal and political gain, not because it was a regional imperative. Furthermore, ECOWAS did very little to address the regional connections to the conflict, while some of the known contributors to the war formed part of the committees and negotiating teams working on peace. Impartiality was in question during each negotiated peace agreement and with ECOMOG actions. This suggests that it may be difficult for regional organizations to be impartial either in a regional conflict situation or when addressing regional factors affecting the conflict. The UN itself was late in addressing the regional connections (e.g., diamonds and Taylor) in Sierra Leone, suggesting that its reliance on regional action may contribute to an inability to see or an unwillingness to deal with the regional dynamics of a conflict once a regional actor is involved.

The UN's disapproval of Nigeria and Nigerian-ECOMOG's use of force did not deter it from letting ECOWAS carry the burden of peacekeeping for nearly three years. This raises an interesting question and an area for further analysis—whether Nigerian-ECOMOG forces had the right to employ force in (collective) defence of Sierra Leone under Article 51 of the UN Charter when the UN was unwilling to do so.[150] States under threat or in a conflict situation may be less concerned with obtaining permission from an organization that is doing little to help them. At the same time, the UN offers a form of "international oversight" that can deter vigilante-style actions from actors that seek permission after the fact.

The Sierra Leone case also gives insights into military solutions to conflicts. ECOMOG had combat-willing and regionally experienced troops, along with Nigerian leadership that, although controversially, was willing to employ force.[151] Supporting ECOMOG at the beginning of the conflict might have ended the conflict sooner, but the trade-off would have been an imposed military solution. For UNAMSIL, a stronger UN mandate and willingness to use force might have deterred the May 2000 attacks (or at least enabled a defensive response), but this would have required a different type of UN operation. Ultimately, the post–May 2000 UNAMSIL force with a stronger mandate, comprising re-hatted experienced and willing ECOMOG troops under more effective oversight, had better results. This suggests that improved responses to conflict may come when the UN and regional organizations make use of each other's strengths. Interestingly, however, the UK presence proved an effective deterrent *without* having to employ significant force, as the junta viewed it as credible, having the means and willingness to use force. An area for further analysis in peace operations is thus examining the ability of a "credible" force to deter fighting and convince belligerents to pursue political solutions.

Another issue related to cooperation was the need by both organizations to "own the success of peace." This had implications on the ground, as neither organization was capable of addressing the conflict on its own, while co-deployment turned into a poorly transitioned hand-over and re-hatted mission. Thus, how successes and failures of co-deployment will be attributed among participating organizations may outweigh the need or willingness to cooperate and partner with each other.

During Sierra Leone's post-conflict period, sustained, long-term attention remains important to maintaining peace in the presence of internal and external destabilizers. Here, the UN currently is better suited to peace-building activities. It has the experience and expertise, and possesses greater resources. ECOWAS, although making efforts, lags significantly behind in its peace-building capacity. On the other hand, the substantial UN presence limits ECOWAS opportunities to gain peace-building knowledge, which will be important when the UN decides to leave.

The Sierra Leone case demonstrates that there are useful and effective cooperative opportunities for UN and regional organizations to address African conflicts. Important challenges remain, however, both to independent and joint efforts. As both organizations seek to address their weaknesses, where will this leave the UN–ECOWAS relationship? How should each organization make use of its limited resources, given that some resources are being diverted to improving areas in which the other organization already has developed? For instance, will this resolve or add to the imbalance between ECOWAS military strengths and UN political and peace-building capabilities? For

Sierra Leone, the dual responses were not always helpful, but ten years of relative peace suggest that the efforts of all involved eventually not only ended the civil war, but laid the ground work for the consolidation of peace.

Notes

1. Michael W. Doyle and Nicholas Sambanis, *Making War and Building Peace: United Nations Peace Operations* (Princeton, NJ: Princeton University Press, 2006), p. 1.
2. For a detailed review of Sierra Leone's history and conflict, see David Keen, *Conflict & Collusion in Sierra Leone* (New York: James Currey Publishers, 2005); J. Peter Pham, *The Sierra Leonean Tragedy: History and Global Dimensions* (New York: Nova Science Publishers Inc., 2006).
3. Pham, pp. 13–22.
4. Paul Jackson, "Chiefs, Money and Politicians: Rebuilding Local Government in Post-war Sierra Leone," *Public Administration and Development* 25:1 (2005): 53–54; Barry Riddell, "Sierra Leone: Urban-elite Bias, Atrocity & Debt," *Review of African Political Economy* 32:103 (2005): 116; Pham, pp. 20–21.
5. For instance, see International Crisis Group, "Liberia and Sierra Leone: Rebuilding Failed States" (Africa Report, 2004), No. 87; William Reno, "Political Networks in a Failing State: The Roots and Future of Violent Conflict in Sierra Leone," *International Politics and Society/ Internationale Politik und Gesellschaft* 10:2 (2003): 44–66.
6. Keen, p. 17.
7. Pham, pp. 41–47.
8. J. Andrew Grant, "Diamonds, Foreign Aid and the Uncertain Prospects for Post-conflict Reconstruction in Sierra Leone," *The Round Table* 94:381 (2005): 451–452; Keen, pp. 58–59.
9. Pham, pp. 41–47.
10. Reno, 56–59; Riddell, 120–123.
11. Riddell, 115–117.
12. Adekeye Adebajo, *Building Peace in West Africa: Liberia, Sierra Leone, and Guinea-Bissau* (Boulder, CO: Lynne Rienner Publishers, 2002), p. 82; Robert Mortimer, "From ECOMOG to ECOMOG II," in *Africa in World Politics: The African State System in Flux*, ed. John W. Harbeson and Donald S. Rothchild (Boulder, CO: Westview Press, 2000), pp. 189–191.
13. Mortimer, pp. 189–190; Pham, pp. 43, 83–86.
14. For instance, see Human Rights Watch (HRW), *Sierra Leone, Sowing Terror: Atrocities against Civilians in Sierra Leone* (1998).
15. 'Funmi Olonisakin, *Peacekeeping in Sierra Leone: The Story of UNAMSIL* (Boulder, CO: Lynne Rienner Publishers, 2008), 14–15.
16. Anatole Ayissi, Robin Poulton, and United Nations Institute for Disarmament Research, *Bound to Cooperate: Conflict, Peace and People in Sierra Leone* (New York: United Nations Institute for Disarmament Research, 2006), p. 39.
17. Keen, pp. 198–199.
18. Olonisakin, *Peacekeeping in Sierra Leone*, pp. 15–16; Pham, p. 118.
19. Adebajo, p. 86.
20. The Abidjan Accord can be found at http://www.sierra-leone.org/abidjanaccord.html. Solomon E. Berewa, *A New Perspective on Governance, Leadership, Conflict and Nation Building in Sierra Leone* (Bloomington, IN: Author House, 2011), p. 120.

21. Adebajo, p. 86; Berewa, pp. 117–119; James O. C. Jonah, "The United Nations," in *West Africa's Security Challenges: Building Peace in a Troubled Region*, ed. Adekeye Adebajo and Ismail O. D. Rashid (Boulder, CO: Lynne Rienner Publishers, 2004), p. 333.
22. Mortimer, p. 196; Pham, p. 113.
23. Adebajo, pp. 86–87; Pham, pp. 118–124.
24. Amnesty International, "Sierra Leone: A Disastrous Set-Back for Human Rights (AI Index: AFR 51/05/97)" (1997): 5–8, AI Index: AFR 51/05/97; United Nations Security Council (UNSC), S/PRST/1997/29 (27 May 1997).
25. 'Funmi Olonisakin, "Lessons Learned from an Assessment of Peacekeeping and Peace Support Operations in West Africa" (Kofi Annan International Peacekeeping Training Centre [KAIPTC], Accra, Ghana, 2008), pp. 14–16.
26. Abass Bundu, *Democracy by Force? A Study of International Military Intervention in the Civil War in Sierra Leone from 1991–2000* (Parkland, FL: Universal Publishers, 2001), pp. 72–74.
27. Amnesty International, "Sierra Leone: A Disastrous Set-back for Human Rights," p. 5; Pham, pp. 128–129.
28. Adebajo, pp. 92–93; David J. Francis, "Peacekeeping in a Bad Neighbourhood: The Economic Community of West African States (ECOWAS) in Peace and Security in West Africa," *African Journal on Conflict Resolution* 9:3 (2009): 97–98; Conciliation Resources et al., "Nigerian Intervention in Sierra Leone" (1997), http://www.c-r.org/sites/www.c-r.org/files/NigerianIntervention_199710_ENG.pdf (accessed 3 February 2012).
29. Organization of African Unity (OAU), "Decisions Adopted by the Sixty-Sixth Ordinary Session of the Council of Ministers [CM/Dec.330–363 (LXVI)]" (1997); UNSC, S/PRST/1997/42 (6 August 1997); UNSC, S/PRST/1997/29; UNSC, S/PRST/1997/36 (11 July 1997).
30. Bundu, p. 75; "OAU Gives Go-ahead for Use of Force in Sierra Leone," *Mail and Guardian*, 4 June 1997, http://reliefweb.int/node/30881 (accessed from Relief Web, 3 May 2012).
31. Adebajo, p. 87; Pham, p. 129.
32. ECOWAS, "Final Communiqué" (26 June 1997), ECOWAS Meeting of Foreign Ministers; Adebajo, pp. 87–88.
33. Adebajo, p. 87.
34. ECOWAS, "Decision of Sanctions against the Junta in Sierra Leone" (Abuja, Nigeria, 28–29 August 1997), Twentieth Session of the Authority of Heads of State and Government.
35. The Committee eventually grew to seven, adding Togo and Burkina Faso. ECOWAS, "Decision of Sanctions," art. 7.
36. Ghana and Guinea contributed approximately 600 troops each, Mali contributed 500, and the remainder of the 13, 000 from Nigeria. Adebajo, p. 91.
37. Inexperience also played a role, as Liberia was ECOWAS' only other "peacekeeping" effort at the time.
38. John M. Kabia, "Regional Approaches to Peacebuilding: The ECOWAS Peace and Security Architecture" (paper presented at BISA-Africa and International Studies ESRC seminar series: African Agency in International Politics, University of Birmingham, 2011); Olonisakin, "Lessons Learned," p. 18.
39. Bundu, pp. 74–75; Olonisakin, "Lessons Learned," p. 18.
40. United Nations Secretary-General (UNSG), Letter dated 7 October 1997 from the Secretary-General addressed to the President of the Security Council (S/1997/776) (7 October 1997).

41. Keen, p. 204; Olonisakin, "Lessons Learned," p. 15; Peacekeeping Best Practices Unit, "Lessons Learned from United Nations Peacekeeping Experiences in Sierra Leone" (United Nations Department of Peacekeeping Operations, 2003), p. 6.
42. A targeted sanctions list was released on 8 January 1998. See the Committee Press Release SC/6464. UNSC, S/RES/1132 (8 October 1997); Adebajo, p. 88.
43. David Cortright and George A. Lopez, *The Sanctions Decade: Assessing UN Strategies in the 1990s* (Boulder, CO: Lynne Rienner Publishers, 2000), p. 171.
44. "Continental Alignments: ECOWAS Conflict Resolution Summit," *Africa Research Bulletin: Political, Social and Cultural Series* 34:12 (1998): 12922; Jonah, p. 326.
45. Cortright and Lopez, p. 172; Pham, pp. 130–131.
46. The Conakry Accord can be found at http://www.sierra-leone.org/conakryaccord.html.
47. According to Adebajo, "Ikimi reportedly told the AFRC that they should either surrender power or they would be flushed out of Freetown. He told them he was not there to negotiate but to reach a timetable for their departure." Adebajo, p. 88.
48. Kabia, np.
49. Keen, p. 216.
50. Pham, pp. 131–132.
51. Keen, p. 219. Human Rights Watch, Summary; UNSG, *Fifth Report of the Secretary-General on the Situation in Sierra Leone* (S/1998/486) (9 June 1998), para. 15.
52. Jonah, p. 331.
53. The Nigerian ground commander, Colonel Maxwell Khobe, had permission from his Nigerian superior to intervene at any time as part of a "defense-offense" strategy, thus bypassing the organizational command structure. Jonah, pp. 331–332.
54. UNSC, S/PRST/1998/5 (26 February 1998).
55. "Continental Alignments," 12921–12922; Keen, p. 219.
56. Additionally, Nigeria placed its Liberian ECOMOG contingents on standby at the Sierra Leone border, which surged across to join in the attack. Mortimer, p. 198; Adebajo, p. 88; Pham, pp. 131–132.
57. Adebajo, pp. 89, 91; "Continental Alignments," 13105.
58. Adebajo, p. 94; Keen, pp. 245, 248.
59. Kabia, np; Olonisakin, "Lessons Learned," pp. 30–31.
60. J. Andrew Grant, "Natural Resources, International Regimes and State-building: Diamonds in West Africa," *Comparative Social Research* 27:1 (2010): 232–233.
61. Amnesty International, "1998—A Year of Atrocities (AFR/51/22/98)" (1 December 1998): 12–13, AFR/51/22/98; Jonah, p. 331.
62. Keen, p. 219.
63. UNSC, S/RES/1156 (16 March 1998); UNSC, S/PRST/1998/5.
64. UNSG, S/1998/486, paras. 66–69; UNSC, S/RES/1181 (13 July 1998).
65. Peacekeeping Best Practices Unit, p. 33.
66. Olonisakin, "Lessons Learned," p. 15.
67. Authors Keen and Olonisakin state that some UN officials, UNOMSIL, and ECOMOG continued to report that the situation in Sierra Leone was stable while humanitarian organizations and others on the ground indicated that the situation was in fact worsening. Keen, pp. 224–227, 249; Olonisakin, *Peacekeeping in Sierra Leone*, p. 32; "Sierra Leone: No Surrender, No Deal," *Africa Confidential* 40:2 (1999): 1–3.
68. Pham, pp. 137–138; UNSG, *Special Report of the Secretary-General on the United Nations Observer Mission in Sierra Leone* (S/1999/20) (7 January 1999), para. 6.
69. As ECOMOG began to regain control of Freetown, it went on a rampage of vengeance, carrying out executions and human rights abuses on civilians believed to be connected to the rebels. Corinne Dufka, "Getting Away with Murder, Mutilation and Rape: New

Testimony from Sierra Leone" (Human Rights Watch 11:3(A) [1999]), I. Summary; Pham, p. 140; Peacekeeping Best Practices Unit, pp. 4–5.

70. Pham, p. 140.
71. Keen, pp. 250–251.
72. Olonisakin, *Peacekeeping in Sierra Leone*, pp. 34–35.
73. In particular, the Inter-Religious Council of Sierra Leone was instrumental in helping both sides engage in discussions. David J. Francis, "Torturous Path to Peace: The Lomé Peace Agreement and Post-war Peacebuilding and Reconstruction in Sierra Leone," *Security Dialogue* 31:3 (2000): 362; Pham, p. 141.
74. The Lomé Accord can be found at http://www.sierra-leone.org/lomeaccord.html. David J. Francis et al., *Dangers of Co-deployment: UN Co-operative Peacekeeping In Africa* (Burlington, VT: Ashgate, 2005), p. 141.
75. Francis, "Tortuous Path," 364–367; Olonisakin, *Peacekeeping in Sierra Leone*, pp. 39–40.
76. UNSG, *Seventh Report of the Secretary-General on the United Nations Observer Mission in Sierra Leone* (S/1999/836) (30 July 1999), para. 7.
77. Olonisakin, *Peacekeeping in Sierra Leone*, p. 40.
78. Francis et al., p. 141.
79. Francis, "Tortuous Path," 361–364; Reno, 55–56.
80. Adebajo, p. 100; Jonah, p. 330.
81. UNSC, S/RES/1245 (11 June 1999); UNSC, S/RES/1260 (20 August 1999); UNSG, *Eighth Report of the Secretary-General on the United Nations Observer Mission in Sierra Leone* (S/1999/1003) (28 September 1999), Sec. VII.
82. Pham, p. 141; UNSG, S/1999/1003, para. 36.
83. Jonah, pp. 329–331; Keen, p. 250.
84. Jonah, p. 330.
85. UNSG, S/1999/1003, para. 38.
86. 'Funmi Olonisakin and Comfort Ero, "Africa and the Regionalization of Peace Operations," in *The United Nations and Regional Security: Europe and Beyond*, ed. Michael C. Pugh and Waheguru P. S. Sidhu (Boulder, CO: Lynne Rienner Publishers, 2003), p. 28; UNSG, S/1999/1003, para. 62, sec. VII; UNSC, S/RES/1270 (22 October 1999).
87. UNSC, 4054th Meeting (S/PV.4054) (22 October 1999), 6.
88. Jonah, pp. 330–331.
89. Olonisakin and Ero, pp. 245–246; Olonisakin, "Lessons Learned," p. 15.
90. Virginia P. Fortna, *Does Peacekeeping Work?: Shaping Belligerents' Choices after Civil War* (Princeton, NJ: Princeton University Press, 2008), p. 68; Grant, "Natural Resources," 236; Olonisakin, "Lessons Learned," p. 16.
91. Peacekeeping Best Practices Unit, p. 34; UNSG, *Fifth Report of the Secretary-General on the United Nations Mission in Sierra Leone* (S/2000/751) (31 July 2000), para. 55.
92. UNSG, *First Report of the Secretary-General on the United Nations in Sierra Leone (UNAMSIL)*, (S/1999/1223) (6 December 1999), sec. III, IV; UNSG, *Second Report on the United Nations Mission in Sierra Leone* (S/2000/13) (11 January 2000), sec. II; UNSG, *Third Report on the United Nations Mission in Sierra Leone* (S/2000/186) (7 March 2000), sec. III, IV.
93. Keen, p. 261.
94. Adebajo, pp. 140–141; UNSG, S/2000/13, Sec. III; UNSC, S/RES/1289 (7 February 2000).
95. Keen, p. 262.
96. Peacekeeping Best Practices Unit, p. 11.
97. Peacekeeping Best Practices Unit, p. 31; UNSC, *Report of the Security Council Mission to Sierra Leone* (S/2000/992) (16 October 2000).

98. A second trigger to the RUF attack was UNAMSIL's announcement in April 2000 that it would begin disarming rebels in the Kono district, both a rebel stronghold and a diamond producing area. Keen, p. 262; UNSG, *Fourth Report of the Secretary-General on the United Nations Mission in Sierra Leone* (S/2000/455) (19 May 2000), para. 56.
99. UNSG, "Comments to the Press" (4 May 2000). http://www.un.org/news/ossg/sgcu0500.htm (accessed from The Secretary-General, off the cuff [May–August 2000] on 9 May 2012).
100. Olonisakin, *Peacekeeping in Sierra Leone*, p. 74; UNSG, S/2000/455, para. 72.
101. "Highlights of the African summit text on S. Leone," *Agence France-Presse* (9 May 2000). http://reliefweb.int/node/63723 (accessed from Relief Web, 8 May 2012); Olonisakin, *Peacekeeping in Sierra Leone*, p. 77.
102. Paul Williams, "Fighting for Freetown: British Military Intervention in Sierra Leone," *Contemporary Security Policy* 22:3 (2001): 156–160.
103. Keen, pp. 272–273; Olonisakin, *Peacekeeping in Sierra Leone*, pp. 63–64; UNSG, S/2000/455, para. 69.
104. UNSG, S/2000/455, para. 23; UNSC, S/RES/1270. para. 14.
105. Additionally, the United Kingdom's small force but significant display of power made UNAMSIL appear unnecessary. Comfort Ero, "A Critical Assessment of Britain's Africa Policy," *Conflict, Security & Development* 1:2 (2001): 57; Olonisakin, *Peacekeeping in Sierra Leone*, pp. 64–69.
106. India also withdrew due to tensions between its force commander, Major-General Vijay Jetley, and Nigerian troops, culminating in his leaked letter to the Secretary-General in which Jetley accused Nigerian troops of sabotaging the mission. Adebajo, pp. 100–101; Keen, pp. 265–266; Olonisakin and Ero, p. 248.
107. UNSC, S/RES/1299 (19 May 2000); UNSC, S/RES/1346 (30 March 2001).
108. Keen, p. 272.
109. UNSC, S/RES/1313 (4 August 2000). para. 3(b).
110. UNSG, S/2000/751, para. 53.
111. UNSG, S/2000/751; UNSC, S/2000/992; Peacekeeping Best Practices Unit; Olonisakin, *Peacekeeping in Sierra Leone*.
112. Sierra Leone Panel of Experts, *Report of the Panel of Experts Appointed Pursuant to Security Council Resolution 1306 (2000), Paragraph 19, in Relation to Sierra Leone* (S/2000/1195) (December 2000), para. 1.
113. UNSC, S/RES/1306 (5 July 2000).
114. Sierra Leone Panel of Experts, S/2000/1195, paras. 81, 86, and 157.
115. UNSC, S/RES/1343 (7 March 2001).
116. Adebajo, pp. 72–73.
117. Olonisakin, *Peacekeeping in Sierra Leone*, p. 78.
118. The change in US policy in Sierra Leone was the result of its new Ambassador to the UN, Richard Holbrooke. His focus on the continent was symbolized during his January 2000 presidency of the Security Council, when he dedicated the month's work to Africa. Keen, p. 271; Olonisakin, *Peacekeeping in Sierra Leone*, pp. 94–96; Thomas G. Weiss et al., *The United Nations and Changing World Politics* (Boulder, CO: Westview Press, 2009), p. 6.
119. Olonisakin, *Peacekeeping in Sierra Leone*, p. 96; UNSC, Letter dated 20 September 2000 from the President of the Security Council addressed to the Secretary-General (S/2000/886) (21 September 2000).
120. UNSC, S/2000/992, sec. IV.
121. UNSC, *Security Council Mission Visit to the Democratic Republic of the Congo, 4–8 May 2000*, (S/2000/416) (11 May 2000), para. 71; Williams, 160–161.

122. Panel on United Nations Peace Operations (Lakhdar Brahimi), *Report of the Panel on United Nations Peace Operations (A/55/305–S/2000/809) (Brahimi Report)* (United Nations, 2000).
123. Olonisakin, *Peacekeeping in Sierra Leone*, pp. 92–93.
124. Adebajo, p. 102; Peacekeeping Best Practices Unit, p. 15.
125. Peacekeeping Best Practices Unit, p. 8; UNSG, *Ninth Report of the Secretary-General on the United Nations Mission in Sierra Leone* (S/2001/228) (14 March 2001), para. 2.
126. Adebajo, p. 103.
127. Keen, pp. 275, 287.
128. UNSC, S/RES/1389 (16 January 2002).
129. ECOWAS, "ECOWAS Observers for Sierra Leone (No. 29/2002)" (2 May 2002). http://news.ecowas.int/ (accessed from ECOWAS Press Release, 29 May 2012).
130. The RUF Party did not win any seats. UNSG, *Fourteenth Report of the Secretary-General on the United Nations Mission in Sierra Leone* (S/2002/679) (19 June 2002), para. 6.
131. UNSC, S/RES/1436 (24 September 2002). Preambular paras. 5, 8.
132. Olonisakin, *Peacekeeping in Sierra Leone*, p. 123; UNSG, *Fifteenth Report of the Secretary-General on the United Nations Mission in Sierra Leone* (S/2002/987) (5 September 2002), paras. 12–13; UNSG, *Twenty-third Report of the Secretary-General on the United Nations Mission in Sierra Leone* (S/2004/724) (9 September 2004), paras. 12–14; UNSC, S/RES/1610 (30 June 2005), para. 1.
133. UNSC, Press statement on Sierra Leone diamond embargo by Security Council president (SC/7778; AFR/634) (5 June 2003).
134. Refer to UNSG, *Twenty-fifth Report of the Secretary-General on the United Nations Mission in Sierra Leone* (S/2005/273) (26 April 2005).
135. The report of the Secretary-General's High-level Panel on Threats, Challenges and Change was released in 2004 followed by the UN World Summit in 2005. Both focused on UN effectiveness, international security, and ways to improve UN responses. Secretary-General's High-level Panel on Threats, Challenges and Change, *A More Secure World: Our Shared Responsibility* (UN Department of Public Information, 2004); United Nations General Assembly, *2005 World Summit Outcome*, (A/RES/60/1), 16 September 2005.
136. Some at the UN felt that Sierra Leone was too far along in its post-conflict process to warrant additional peace-building efforts, while others felt that it was a good candidate for success. Personal interview conducted with a member of the PBC, March 2009.
137. UNSC, S/RES/1620 (31 August 2005).
138. The PBC was one of the major outcomes from the 2005 UN World Summit.
139. Personal interviews conducted with members of the PBC, March 2009.
140. UNSG, *Fifth Report of the Secretary-General on the United Nations Integrated Office in Sierra Leone*, (S/2007/704) (4 December 2007). Personal interview conducted with a member of the PBC, March 2009. UNSG, S/2007/704, para. 7.
141. ECOWAS, "ECOWAS Dispatches Ministerial Delegation to Sierra Leone (No. 80/2007)" (31 August 2007). http://news.ecowas.int/ (accessed from ECOWAS Press Release, 3 June 2012); UNSG, S/2007/704, paras. 2–6.
142. UNSC, S/RES/1829 (4 August 2008).
143. Olonisakin, "Lessons Learned," p. 42.
144. Personal interview conducted with a member of the PBC, March 2009.
145. UNSG, *Report of the Secretary-General on the United Nations Integrated Peacebuilding Office in Sierra Leone* (S/2012/160) (14 March 2012), sec. II (A).
146. UNSG, S/2012/160, sec. II (A).
147. Elizabeth Drew and Alex Ramsbotham, *Consolidating Peace: Liberia and Sierra Leone (Accord: An International Review of Peace Initiatives)* (Conciliation Resources, March 2012), pp. 60–63.

148. The United Kingdom also was significant in helping end the conflict.
149. Additionally, this was only ECOWAS' second peacekeeping intervention and the second UN–ECOWAS joint operation, Liberia being the first. Therefore, inexperience played a factor in responding to the conflict.
150. Jonah, pp. 332–333.
151. Olonisakin and Ero, p. 246.

Chapter 11

Somalia

Paul D. Williams

Introduction

Between January 1991, when military dictator and president of the Somali Democratic Republic Mohamed Siad Barre's regime was ousted, and early 2012, when a new set of principles were adopted to determine the shape of Somalia's future government, a broad range of conflict-management initiatives failed to bring either stability or peace to Somalia. Indeed, Somalia in early 2012 was in much the same situation as it had been in early 1991: There was no legitimate central government, the country was politically fragmented, its people endured extreme poverty and various forms of armed conflict, it was awash with arms (despite an international arms embargo), there were intense food security and environmental challenges, and the country lacked even the most basic infrastructure. Not surprisingly, a large proportion of Somalis fled the country. In sum, since 1991, Somalia has become the infamous poster child of state failure; the world's collapsed state *par excellence*.[1]

Despite being at the top of the state failure charts, addressing Somalia's plight was never a priority for most international actors from outside the Horn. In contrast, Somalia was always an important issue for its neighbors, most notably Ethiopia and Kenya. However, these neighbors seemed to prefer dealing with a fractured and weak state rather than run the risk of a powerful Islamist regime taking power throughout Somalia and renewing its territorial claims related to a Greater Somalia. In this context, Somalia has been the site for an unprecedented array of conflict-management initiatives conducted by external actors––most prominently Somalia's neighbors, the United Nations (UN) and regional organizations, principally the Intergovernmental Authority on Development (IGAD) and the African Union (AU)—as well as a variety of local actors. Somalia has witnessed UN peacekeeping operations, a US-led peace enforcement mission, unilateral military operations (by Ethiopia and Kenya), sanctions (a UN arms

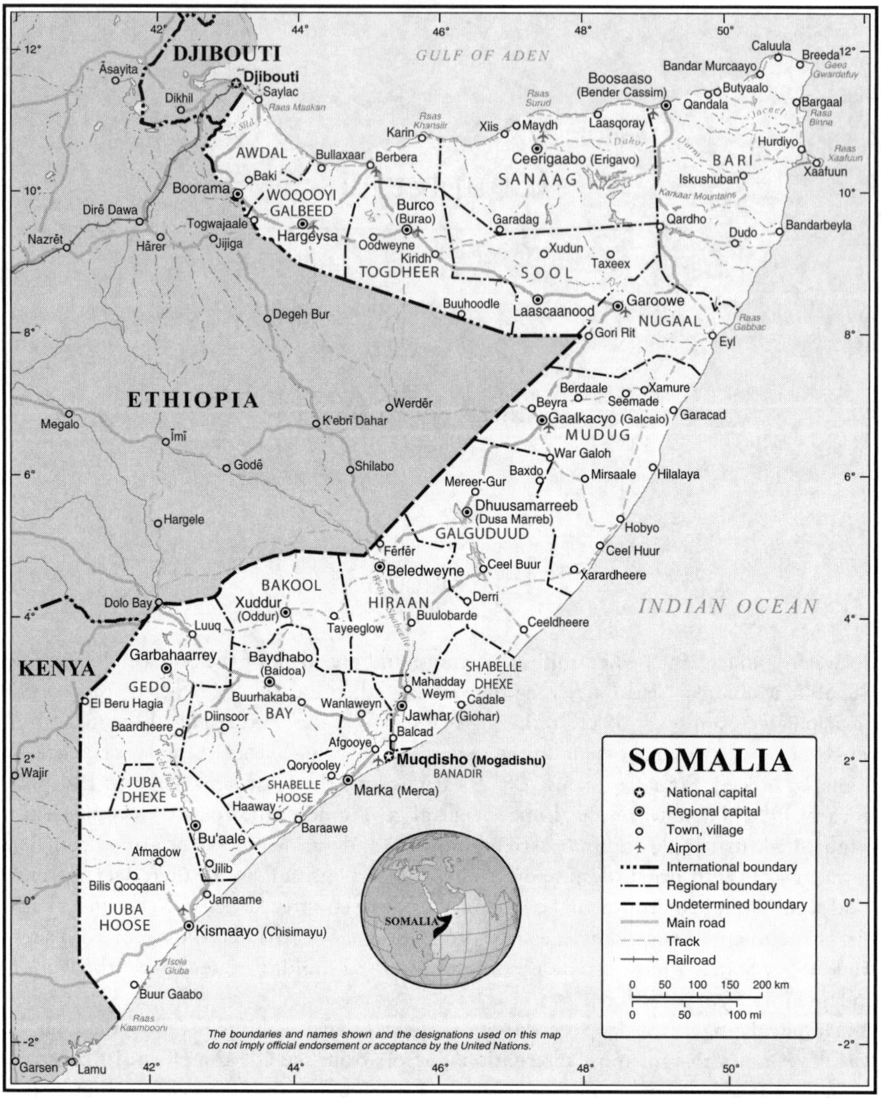

Source: Map No. 3690 Rev. 10, United Nations, Department of Field Support, Cartographic Section, December 2011

embargo and sanctions against Eritrea for supporting certain Somali armed groups), the AU's biggest ever military mission—a counterinsurgency/VIP protection mission dressed up as "peacekeeping"—multinational counter-piracy operations, targeted assassinations and drone strikes/raids by special forces from various states, as well as pretty much every variety of multilateral diplomatic initiatives, many of which have been based outside the country.

This chapter provides a broadly chronological analysis of the complex series of conflict-related events in Somalia's recent history as well as the various interactions between the UN and regional organizations in their attempts to manage Somalia's various conflict dynamics. It focuses on the period following late 2004, when the Transitional Federal Government (TFG) emerged from the IGAD-sponsored Somalia National Peace and Reconciliation Conference held in Kenya, until mid-2012.[2] During this period, the UN, AU, and IGAD all tried to maintain Somalia's territorial integrity and build a strong central government—although they did so for different reasons and with different priorities.[3] An important instrument in this process since early 2007 was the African Union Mission in Somalia (AMISOM), a primarily military operation that was the hybrid result of inputs from a wide range of external actors. While the vast majority of African states voted with their feet and refused to contribute to the mission, by mid-2012, AMISOM had made considerable military progress, in large part because of the support it received from external donors as well as distinct military campaigns by Ethiopian and Kenyan forces. However, for all the progress on the military track, AMISOM will stand or fall based on whether legitimate and effective political authorities can be established in Mogadishu, and if Somalis can agree among themselves about what "Somalia" is and how it should be governed. Because genuine consensus was lacking on these fundamental issues, international conflict-management initiatives floundered. A major factor in the initiatives' dismal results is that they usually proceeded in a top-down manner; they failed to invest the resources necessary to deal with the scale of Somalia's problems; they were often impatient; and they were regularly hijacked by locals keen to use external state-building and peace-building initiatives for their own parochial political and/or economic advantage.

Six Myths

International conflict-management initiatives in Somalia took place in a context heavily influenced by some widespread myths about what had happened in the country and what might help to "fix" it. International mythology had depicted Somalia as an anarchic and chaotic land plagued by war, famine, disease, and banditry that had not only attracted all manners of international terrorists and spawned huge columns of refugees, but had more recently become the epicenter of a piracy epidemic. There is a grain of truth in some of these descriptions, but they miss a few crucial points.

The first myth was that the absence of a central government meant that the country was left in a state of complete anarchy. In fact, while Somalia may have lacked a central government between 1991 and 2004, it was never devoid of governance structures. Indeed, Somalis had become quite adept at manufacturing "governance without government," and were thus at the "forefront of a poorly understood trend—the rise in informal systems of adaptation, security, and governance in response to the prolonged absence of a central government."[4]

A second myth was that Somalia was continually at war with itself, and that the violence there was either chaotic/random/indiscriminate or all down to clan politics. In reality, the patterns of political violence with which international conflict-management initiatives had to grapple were much more complex. One typology identified twelve distinct forms of armed conflict dynamics based on the scale of fighting and the actors involved, namely, civil war, foreign forces at war, proxy wars, subnational polities at war, communal clashes, standing clan militias at war, paramilitaries at war, war economies (where actors use violence for economic gain), piracy, Islamists at war, private militias and security forces, and armed criminality/banditry.[5]

The idea that Somalis could enjoy peace and development only if a strong central government was resurrected was a third influential myth. Not only had peace and development occurred in some parts of the country in the absence of a centralized national government (namely, Somaliland, but also to a lesser extent Puntland), but international attempts at state-building had actively generated new forms of domestic conflict—this time between groups who sought to profit from these external projects and those who thought a strong central government was a major part of Somalia's problems. Some opposed the resurrection of a central government because they believed that corrupt politicians fighting over centralized power was the root cause of Somalia's modern-day problems. Others objected because they thought that a new government might threaten the coping strategies that they had developed in its absence; that is, since some people were doing reasonably well without a central government, they were generally happy for things to stay that way.

A related myth, prevalent among the relevant international organizations, held that a top-down peace-building/"pick a winner" approach could actually deliver an effective central government. This idea persisted, despite being tried repeatedly and consistently failing to produce the desired results. In contrast, Ken Menkhaus has neatly summarized what appears to be the real lesson of the last two decades of peacemaking initiatives in Somalia:

> The single most important conflict-sensitivity lesson from Somali-inhabited regions of the Horn of Africa actually emanate from Somaliland and northeastern Kenya. In both of those areas, a high and durable level of peace has been forged, despite daunting obstacles. It has been crafted via partnerships between coalitions of civic and social authorities (clan elders, women's market groups, religious leaders, business leaders) and a local government authority that is "willing but not able" to govern, and which views civic engagement in conflict mitigation and governance as an opportunity, not a threat. That in turn makes local communities active stakeholders in their own governance and security, and produces an organic and effective set of systems of community policing that are unquestionably the most powerful source of peace and security in the Eastern Horn of Africa.[6]

A fifth myth suggested that Somalia's "ungoverned spaces"—to use the Pentagon's terminology—should be the principal concern of those actors engaged in the US-led "war on terrorism." In fact, local Somalis were a lot less worried about transnational terrorism than most Western governments assumed.[7] In practice, the majority of Somalis were much more concerned with acts of terrorism committed against civilians within Somalia, which were perpetrated by both insurgents and government forces alike. Moreover, the generally militarized approach of several external powers actually drummed up greater levels of support for extremist groups, making Somalia a more attractive destination for international Jihadists in the late 2000s than it was in the aftermath of 11 September 2001 ("9/11"). As Menkhaus has persuasively argued, at least before the Ethiopian intervention that installed the TFG in Mogadishu in late 2006, there were six main factors that made Somalia a less attractive base for terrorist organizations than some Western states feared.[8] First, terrorist cells and bases are much more exposed to international counterterrorist action in zones of state collapse where US Special Forces could violate state sovereignty regularly and with impunity. The US air strikes in January 2007 and March 2008 against al-Qa'ida suspects in Somalia were a case in point. Second, areas of state collapse tend to be inhospitable and dangerous, particularly for foreigners. Consequently, since few foreigners choose to reside in such environments, foreign terror cells will find it very difficult to blend into the local population and retain the degree of secrecy necessary to conduct their activities. A third factor is the double-edged nature of the lawlessness that accompanies situations of state collapse: While lawlessness reduces the risk of apprehension by law enforcement agencies, it increases the likelihood that terror cells will suffer from more common crimes such as kidnapping, extortion, or assassination. As Menkhaus suggests, "it appears that lawlessness can inhibit rather than facilitate certain types of lawless behavior."[9] A fourth problem is that any terrorists would be susceptible to betrayal by Somalis looking to ingratiate themselves with the US authorities. Fifth, Somalia represents an environment in which it is very difficult to stay neutral and outside the interclan rivalries. Relatively mundane activities such as hiring personnel or renting buildings will inevitably be seen as evidence of taking sides, and once this perception has been established, the external actor in question becomes a legitimate target of reprisals by rival clans. Finally, the collapse of the Somali state has left it without the usual array of "soft" Western targets such as embassies and businesses. As a result, Somalia was more likely to be used as a transit point for materiel than to act as a more permanent base for cells. Even terrorists, it would seem, require a degree of political order to conduct their activities. The "security paradox" identified by Menkhaus is that, at least in the short term, attempts to resurrect effective state institutions in Somalia might create an environment that is more, not less, conducive to terrorist cells basing themselves in the country.

The sixth and perhaps biggest myth of all was that Somalia was a genuine, Westphalian state, which was temporarily broken and just needed "fixing." In reality, governance structures in Somalia had only conformed to the idea of Westphalian statehood for a few decades between 1960 and 1991. In truth, "Somalia" itself was a contested concept, a political argument about where the genuine boundaries of the Somali nation lay. Somalia, the UN member state after 1960, has been the historical exception rather than the rule. As a result, perhaps conflict-management initiatives should not automatically have been geared to resurrecting the exception.

The TFG Is Established

The TFG was established in late 2004 as the successor of the Transitional National Government that had emerged in 2000 out of the Somali National Peace Conference (alternatively known as the "Arta Process," named after the town in Djibouti where it was held).

The TFG was the product of the IGAD-led Somali National Peace and Reconciliation Conference, or "Mbagathi Process" (after the Kenyan town where discussions were eventually held). The process began in December 2001 at a time when IGAD was trying to take a more proactive role in conflict management in the region's two key cases of Somalia and Sudan. In Somalia, the process started with two parallel sets of talks between the Transitional National Government and the Somali Restoration and Reconciliation Council (SRRC) in Nakuru, Kenya, and in Gode, Ethiopia. Mediated by Kenyan diplomats, the talks unfolded in three phases, ultimately producing the TFG. In October 2002, the parties were able to agree to the Eldoret Declaration on federal government structure and Cessation of Hostilities. In February 2003, phase two began when the talks were relocated to Mbagathi, outside Nairobi. After several months of wrangling, a draft charter was eventually produced on 15 September 2003, but in October, the talks closed down. Phase three began in May 2004 when a new round of talks were launched, and between August and October, the constituent parts of what would become the TFG took shape: a Transitional Federal Charter was adopted and a Transitional Federal Parliament was selected, which duly chose Abdullahi Yusuf Ahmed as the president in October 2004 for a five-year transitional period. The TFG was inaugurated in December 2004 and immediately gained international recognition. In contrast to the earlier Transitional National Government, which had been dominated by the Mogadishu-centered Hawiye clan, the TFG's top leaders and security forces were dominated by members of a coalition between Yusuf's Majerteen/Darood clan (based in Puntland) and the Abgal/Hawiye clan. This group was generally pro-Ethiopian, pro-federalist, and anti-Islamist.[10] The TFG moved into the Somali town of Jowhar and then Baidoa in June 2005.

IGASOM: The Peace Operation that Never Was

Newly inaugurated President Abdullahi Yusuf wasted no time in calling for external assistance. Shortly after assuming office, he visited Addis Ababa to ask the AU to deploy 20,000 peacekeepers to help him consolidate his government and disarm some 55,000 militiamen.[11] Although the AU did not carry out Yusuf's request for a 20,000-strong force, in January 2005, IGAD proposed the deployment of a 10,500 strong Peace Support Mission to Somalia (known as IGASOM), which would facilitate the return of Somalia's TFG to Mogadishu.[12] Interestingly, IGAD's charter did not explicitly include a provision for deploying such a peace operation, although advocates suggested that Article 7(g) could perhaps be used as the legal basis.[13] On 12 May 2005, the AU's Peace and Security Council endorsed IGAD's proposal and duly authorized the deployment of IGASOM, requested the UN Security Council grant an exemption to the arms embargo imposed against Somalia in order to facilitate the deployment of the mission, and stressed the need for AU member states and the UN to provide IGASOM with political, financial, and logistical support.[14] Later that year, the Peace and Security Council also made clear that it envisaged the deployment of an AU peace operation to take over from IGASOM.[15] In spite of support from both IGAD and the AU, it quickly became obvious that not only did IGAD lack the bureaucratic capabilities to assemble such a force, but few states actually wanted to provide the necessary troops, in part because of the hostility the idea generated inside Somalia. As a result, the IGASOM proposal died.

What prompted this regional involvement in Somalia? The short answer is the combination of instability within the country, the UN's general neglect of the situation after 1995, and the specific concerns of Somalia's neighbors, particularly Ethiopia. The central difficulty was that the regional organizations concerned, IGAD and the AU, lacked the capabilities necessary to deal with the problems they faced.[16] (Most of their attention focused on developments in south-central Somalia in general and Mogadishu in particular, although in late 2005, the AU did briefly respond—negatively—to Somaliland's request for membership.)[17] It was notable that the AU generally followed IGAD's lead on Somali issues. This was in step with the emerging practice at the AU Peace and Security Council, which generally deferred to subregional preferences when making its decisions. Both organizations were also heavily influenced by Ethiopia's preferences: first about the configuration of the TFG, and later about how to respond to the takeover of Mogadishu by the Islamic Courts.

The Islamic Courts Take Mogadishu

With the TFG now on Somali soil but unable to establish a presence in the capital city, a major alteration of the political terrain occurred on 5 June 2006 when the Union of Islamic Courts took control of Mogadishu.[18] It did so by defeating the newly formed Alliance for Peace Restoration and Combat Against Terror (APRCT), described by one respected analyst as "a group of U.S.-backed militia leaders posing as a counterterrorist coalition."[19] The Islamic Courts had begun operating in Somalia in early 1994. Their primary function was to provide law and order as well as a degree of security for commerce within certain zones. Initially established in northern Mogadishu, they subsequently spread south and ceased to operate in the north of the city from early 1998. After a lull in their fortunes coinciding with the establishment of Somalia's Transitional National Government of Abdiqasim Hassan Salad (see earlier), the Courts enjoyed a revival in 2003 under the leadership of Sheikh Sharif Sheikh Ahmed. Politically, the Courts represented a "broad mosque," bringing together individuals from the moderate and fundamentalist ends of the Islamic spectrum.

Shortly after taking control of Mogadishu, the court leaders announced the formation of a Supreme Council of Islamic Courts (SCIC) with an individual who met Osama bin Laden in early 2001, Hassan Dahir Aweys, as its head. The SCIC also opposed the proposed IGAD operation as tantamount to a foreign invasion by Ethiopia. On the positive side, the sea and airports were reopened, rubbish and roadblocks were cleared from the streets, squatters were evicted from government buildings, and the city enjoyed a degree of stability unparalleled for well over a decade.

While Mogadishu's residents may have enjoyed the newfound stability, other actors were distinctly worried about the SCIC takeover. In response to the rise of the courts and subsequent collapse of the APRCT, the United States led an initiative to establish an informal International Contact Group to coordinate international responses to Somalia.[20] This was part of the US effort to reconstruct a strong central government in Somalia as part of its plan to capture or kill those individuals involved in bombing its embassies in Nairobi and Dar es Salaam in 1998, and to deny al-Qa'ida a safe haven in Somalia. Washington's key concern on the latter score was probably that Aweys' protégé Adan Hashi Farah Ayro was the key leader of *al-Shabaab* (the Youth), which since 2003 had been broadcasting its links with al-Qa'ida, assassinating rivals, and kidnapping and murdering foreigners in Somalia.[21] However, the problem for the United States was that, despite the SCIC's connections with al-Qa'ida, Washington's public denunciation of the courts as being dominated by terrorists, and its dismissal of the Union of Islamic Courts' achievements (notably, bringing a semblance of order to Mogadishu), outraged many Somalis.[22]

Enter Ethiopia (Again)[23]

The other state that was seriously concerned with developments in Mogadishu was Ethiopia. During August 2006, Ethiopian troops entered Baidoa to support the TFG authorities and protect a buffer zone in case more radical voices within the SCIC gained the upper hand and incited irredentist violence in eastern Ethiopia. Ethiopian Prime Minister Meles Zenawi articulated the logic behind Ethiopia's move shortly after the SCIC's takeover of Mogadishu. "We are aware of course," Meles said,

> that the Union of Islamic Courts is a union of desperate forces. There are those Somalis who have supported the establishment of such courts because of the desperation that came as a result of the absolute chaos and lawlessness in Mogadishu. So, in a sense, for many supporters of these courts, the issue is one of order and stability. We understand their desire and we have nothing against that desire...As regards the implications of the resurgence of terrorist groups within Somalia, on the security and stability of Ethiopia, naturally, like any country, we reserve the right to defend ourselves against all attempts to destabilize our security and stability.[24]

It was in this turbulent political context that the idea of an African peacekeeping force was resurrected when UN Security Council Resolution 1725 (6 December 2006) authorized IGAD and AU member states to "establish a protection and training mission in Somalia." This was probably designed to give the Ethiopian National Defence Force a plausible exit strategy from Mogadishu. The force was mandated to monitor the progress of, and ensure the safe passage of those involved in the political dialogue between the SCIC and the TFG authorities; to maintain security in Baidoa; to protect members of the TFG as well as their key infrastructure; and to train the TFG's security forces and help reestablish the national security forces of Somalia.

On 10 December, however, Sheikh Sharif made clear the SCIC's intention to recapture Baidoa from the TFG.[25] Two days later, the SCIC's military chief, Sheikh Indha'adde, and his (*al-Shabaab*) deputy, Sheikh Muktar Robbow, issued an ultimatum to the Ethiopian troops to leave the country or face forcible expulsion, and began moving their forces toward Baidoa.[26] A brief war of (often confusing and contradictory) words followed and fighting broke out between the SCIC forces and Ethiopian troops near Baidoa on 20 December. Here, in a single battle, Ethiopian forces quickly killed hundreds of ill-prepared Somali youths who had been sent to stop them by the SCIC leadership. By 29 December, Ethiopian and TFG soldiers had installed the TFG in Mogadishu. The SCIC's forces were routed and their leaders and militia scattered across the country. As they retreated, the US air force attacked SCIC forces in an unsuccessful attempt to kill al-Qa'ida operatives thought to be working with them.[27] At this stage, the Ethiopians were estimated to have approximately 15,000 troops in Somalia, concentrated in Baidoa and Mogadishu.

The Ethiopians claimed that their military operation was an example of collective defense under Article 51 of the UN Charter since it took place at the behest of the TFG, which was at the time the internationally recognized authority for Somalia.[28] Regardless of the legal arguments, Islamists around the world depicted Ethiopia as a crusading state, which had, with Western collaboration, engaged in what one respected scholar called, "the ultimate provocation."[29] Meles Zenawi was depicted as the modern-day Abraha, "the would-be Ethiopian destroyer of Islamic holiness."[30] On 5 January 2007, for example, Osama Bin Laden's deputy, Ayman al-Zawahiri, issued a video-taped message entitled, "Help Your Brothers in Somalia!" which called for Jihadists to supply fighters, money, and expertise against Ethiopia.[31]

Enter the AU

It was at this point that the AU's Peace and Security Council revived the idea of a peacekeeping force but called upon the UN to provide financial and other support for what was now called AMISOM.[32] AMISOM was supposed to comprise about 8,000 troops "supported by maritime coastal and air components, as well as an appropriate civilian component, including a police training team."[33] Most of these additional components never materialized or turned up very late. The first AU troops, a battle group from Uganda, arrived in early March and were immediately greeted with mortar and rocket attacks.

AMISOM was mandated, among other things, to support dialogue and reconciliation in Somalia by assisting with the security of all those involved in the process; to protect TFG institutions and provide security for key infrastructure; to assist in the reestablishment of national Somali security forces; and to provide security for the delivery of humanitarian assistance and the repatriation of refugees and displaced persons. Conspicuously absent from the mandate was the need to protect local civilians (other than members of the TFG). In the same way that the AU had looked to succeed the initial IGASOM deployment, it was envisaged that AMISOM would work to create conditions in which a UN peace operation could be deployed.[34] By February 2007, Ethiopia had already withdrawn one-third of its troops and was planning to withdraw another third.

It was also widely noted that Ethiopia broke the AU Peace and Security Council's internal procedures when it shepherded AMISOM's authorization through the institution. Despite being a key party to the conflict under discussion, the Ethiopian representative played a crucial role in the debate to establish AMISOM. Under Article 8.9 of the *Protocol Relating to the Establishment of the Peace and Security Council of the African Union* (9 July 2002), Ethiopia's representative should have withdrawn from the deliberations after the briefing session.[35] Article 8.9 states:

> Any Member of the Peace and Security Council which is party to a conflict under consideration by the Peace and Security Council shall not participate either in the discussion

> or the decision making process relating to that conflict or situation. Such Member shall be invited to present its case to the Peace and Security Council as appropriate, and shall, thereafter, withdraw from proceedings.

Instead, the Ethiopian representative even sought to chair the meeting, arguing that her country was not a party to the conflict. This statement was apparently greeted with open laughter within the meeting chamber and prompted one representative to ask what protocol the Ethiopian representative had been reading. After an hour of argument, it was decided that the representative from Gabon would chair the final part of the meeting but the Ethiopian representative continued to participate.[36]

Just over one month after the AU authorized AMISOM, its decision was endorsed by UN Security Council Resolution 1744 (20 February 2007). Although there was clear consensus within the UN's Department of Peacekeeping Operations that Mogadishu was not a conducive environment for a blue helmet peace operation, the Security Council relented to the idea of an African force, despite being well aware that the AU lacked the capabilities needed to carry out such a mission. Part of the explanation for the UN Security Council's decision was the sense that it had effectively abandoned Somalia for the previous decade and so needed to be seen to act.[37]

By April 2007, the situation for Mogadishu's civilians was dire. TFG security forces were engaged in looting, assaults, and political assassinations of suspected insurgent sympathizers, while Ethiopian troops did much the same as well as conducting indiscriminate attacks (often artillery shelling) on residential neighborhoods that they suspected of harboring insurgents.[38] Not surprisingly, many civilians ran away. Aid agencies estimated that more than 400,000 residents were displaced in April 2007 alone with a further 300,000 already internally displaced. By 2008, the number had grown to 1.3 million.[39]

AMISOM was left floundering in the middle of this mess. By mid-June 2007, it was staffed by just over 1,600 Ugandan soldiers (the sole troop-contributing country) who maintained a 24/7 presence at just four locations in Mogadishu: the airport, KM-4 traffic circle, Villa Somalia (the presidential residence), and the new seaport. Most of the force was based at its headquarters in the airport. Perhaps uniquely in the world of peace operations, AMISOM's mission headquarters was actually located outside Somalia, in Nairobi. Not surprisingly, therefore, its force commander regularly complained about the lack of political leadership on the ground.[40]

Between mid-July and the end of August 2007, the TFG organized a national reconciliation congress in Mogadishu in a rather transparent attempt to gain some local legitimacy outside Yusuf's own clan base. It achieved little, not least because many of the insurgents were from the Hawiye clan and they interpreted the latest struggle as a Darood-led TFG trying to reassert its dominance over the primarily Hawiye city of Mogadishu. As a result, the SCIC's leaders refused to participate in the TFG congress and instead held their own version in Asmara between 6 and 12 September. This ended with the formation of the Alliance for the Re-Liberation of Somalia (ARS). The consensus did not last long and the ARS soon split into two factions: a more moderate wing led by Sheikh Sharif Sheikh Ahmed and Sharif Hassan moved to Djibouti (ARS-Djibouti), while a more hard-line group led by Hassan Dahir Aweys remained in Eritrea (ARS-Asmara). The two factions were deeply divided over whether or not to engage with the TFG. When in May 2008 Sheikh Sharif agreed to begin talks with the TFG, the intra-ARS struggle turned violent.

The Djibouti Peace Process

By the end of March 2008, Ethiopian officials claimed that they had reduced the number of their troops in Somalia to approximately 2,500, mostly based around Mogadishu and Baidoa. At this stage, the operation was costing Ethiopia about US$1 million per day.[41] This was financially and politically unsustainable and Ethiopia had to find an exit strategy quickly. It came in the form of the Djibouti peace process. This process was facilitated by the UN Secretary-General's Special Representative, Ambassador Ould Abdallah, and unfolded in four rounds of talks, which officially began in May 2008. It culminated in a series of agreements signed between the TFG and the ARS-Djibouti faction led by the two Sharifs on 9 June, 26 October, and 25 November, respectively.[42]

The political impetus for the process came from Ethiopia, which was seeking a way to withdraw its soldiers from Mogadishu, save face, and leave behind at least potentially stable (and non-irredentist) authorities. To that end, Ethiopia "placed heavy pressure on the Yusuf wing of the TFG to embrace the accord, and when this failed it pressured Yusuf to resign [see below], clearing the way for the formation of a new government."[43] Among other things, the 9 June Agreement endorsed the territorial integrity of Somalia, requested a cease-fire, and established a Joint Security Committee and High-Level Committee to oversee political cooperation.[44] It also called for Ethiopian withdrawal, and the replacement of Ethiopian troops with a UN international stabilization force (ISF) (which must not include soldiers from any of Somalia's neighbors) to deploy within 120 days. The stabilization force was to be made up of troops "from countries that are friends of Somalia excluding neighbouring states" (para.7a) and "UN forces" (para.7b). Naturally, the signatories also called for external actors to fund the plan and for an international conference to be held within six months, aimed at addressing Somalia's reconstruction and development.

On 26 October 2008, during a third round of talks, both parties reaffirmed their commitment to political cooperation and reconciliation in a Joint Declaration in Djibouti. This set out the modalities for the implementation of a cessation of hostilities between the two sides. On 25 November, they also signed an agreement involving plans to reconfigure the TFG, including by doubling the size of its parliament to incorporate members of the ARS-Djibouti and civil society groups (see in the following).

The ISF that Never Was

The Ethiopian withdrawal from Mogadishu left the very real prospect of a security vacuum, and it was far from clear that AMISOM and the TFG's own security forces would be able to defeat the insurgents. After various appeals for support from the AU, in mid-November 2008, the UN Secretary-General Ban Ki-moon recommended that an ISF of "approximately two brigades" be deployed to Mogadishu.[45] Intended to unfold in four phases, the ISF was supposed to support the implementation of the Djibouti Agreement and create conditions for the deployment of a multidimensional UN peacekeeping operation.[46] Phase 1 would involve deployment to Mogadishu, while in Phase 2, the ISF would monitor and verify the withdrawal of Ethiopian forces from the city. These two phases were scheduled to take place "within six months" (paragraph 44). In Phase 3, the force would conduct stabilization operations in Mogadishu in order to facilitate the consolidation of the TFG's authority. Phase 4 involved the transition to a UN multidimensional peacekeeping operation of "22,500 troops operating in five brigade-sized sectors throughout southern and central Somalia."[47] At this stage, there were approximately 1,000 Ethiopian soldiers and 3,400 AMISOM troops in Mogadishu.

By mid-December, however, the Secretary-General had to inform the UN Security Council that while he still believed only "a multinational force" was "the right tool for stabilizing Mogadishu," only fourteen of the fifty countries approached had responded to his request for contributions. Of these, only two offered funding (the United States and the Netherlands). None of them pledged any troops or offered to assume the lead nation role. He went on to note that this was particularly "disappointing" since it stood "in such sharp contrast to the exceptional political will and commitment of military assets which Member States have shown in respect of the fight against piracy."[48] (In December 2008, the European Union [EU], North Atlantic Treaty Organization [NATO], and a variety of other countries engaged in various maritime security operations off the coast of Somalia to stem the rise in piracy.)

With the death of the ISF concept, the Secretary-General explored other options to prepare for the security vacuum expected to arise after the Ethiopians withdrew. In addition to advising that the UN continue its contingency planning for a potential UN peacekeeping operation, he proposed three steps.[49] First, AMISOM should be reinforced. This should be done through bilateral support to the troop-contributing countries (Uganda and Burundi); through support at the mission level in the area of logistical, medical, and engineering capabilities; and through the transfer of some US$7 million worth of assets from the UN peacekeeping mission in Eritrea and Ethiopia (UNMEE), including prefabricated accommodation, electricity generators, air-conditioning units, ablution units, and soft-skin vehicles. Moreover, the UN should bolster its support for AMISOM by providing an additional logistics support package and continuing to assist AU planning and deployment preparations through its Planners team in Addis Ababa. Second, the UN should build the capacity of the Djibouti Agreement signatories to restore the security sector and the rule of law. In the short term, this should involve training and equipping 5,000 joint TFG/ARS-Djibouti forces, a 10,000-strong Somali Police Force, and other justice and corrections personnel. The third step was for the Security Council to consider establishing a maritime task force, perhaps as part of the ongoing antipiracy operations. Not only could this support AMISOM's operations but it could host a quick-reaction force to support AMISOM peacekeepers and could serve as an operational platform for any envisaged UN peacekeeping operation.

In light of these developments, the AU decided not to withdraw AMISOM and on 22 December, the AU Peace and Security Council extended AMISOM's mandate for a further two months (16 January to 16 March), called on the UN Security Council to deploy an ISF as well as a support package for AMISOM, and subsequently a UN peacekeeping operation to take over from AMISOM.[50] In November 2007, however, UN Secretary-General Ban Ki-moon had made clear his view that deploying UN peacekeepers to Somalia was "neither realistic nor viable"—indeed, the security situation was so bad that it was not even possible to send a UN technical assessment team.[51] Since there was virtually no hope of UN blue helmets being deployed, the AU made very clear that it wanted the UN to pay for AMISOM in the interim, not least they argued because AMISOM had been endorsed by a UN Security Council resolution.

TFG Version 2.0

By the end of 2008, the situation in Mogadishu looked grim and the current international strategy of supporting President Yusuf's TFG was foundering. A ray of hope appeared on 29 December, however, when, after much international pressure, TFG President Yusuf resigned, thereby ending a months-long stand-off with the prime minister.[52] This paved the way for the reconstruction of a new TFG. Unfortunately, this turned out to be just as corrupt and factionalized, and almost as ineffective as its predecessor. However, at the time, it was thought to offer a real window of opportunity to make political progress. This reconfiguration of the TFG was precipitated by the earlier deals as part of the Djibouti process and, crucially, the departure of Ethiopian forces, which completed their withdrawal from Mogadishu on 13–14 January 2009. Residents of northern Mogadishu poured into the streets to celebrate an Ethiopian departure that few believed would occur. On 26 January 2009, Ethiopian soldiers departed Baidoa and on the same day ARS-Djibouti merged with the largely moribund TFG.

On 31 January 2009, Sheikh Sharif's political career came full circle when the former leader of the SCIC was elected president of Somalia's new TFG (by 293 votes to Masla Siyaad's 126). After nearly a month of negotiations, the reconfiguration of TFG version 2.0 was complete. Thanks to a rather hasty and arbitrary process of selection, it now included 39 cabinet ministers and 550 parliamentarians, most of whom lived abroad and who lacked genuine domestic constituencies. On 13 February, President Sharif had selected a new prime minister, Omar Abdirashid Sharmarke, to replace Hassan Hussein Nur Adde, the man with whom he had negotiated the Djibouti accord. This decision was driven by clan calculus, in part as a means of keeping Puntland in the new TFG.[53] Not long afterward, the TFG extended its original five-year mandate (which was set to expire in August 2009) for an additional two years. In his first few months in office, Sheik Sharif made significant efforts to bring the Islamist opposition into dialogue but was rebuffed.

Within Mogadishu, TFG version 2.0 was largely dependent upon AMISOM troops for its survival and on external, primarily the UN and Western, actors for its finances and the training and arming its own security forces.[54] This fed local impressions that the TFG was "more accountable to . . . the international community for its survival, than on the Somali people, a perception that continu[ed] to undermine trust in the TFG."[55]

For its part, with the departure of Ethiopian soldiers, AMISOM was left with only highly unreliable and poorly trained TFG security forces to battle *al-Shabaab* militia for control of Mogadishu's various districts. The situation was made even more difficult because some of the TFG forces trained by EU states would promptly defect or desert shortly after being deployed into Mogadishu. This led to serious levels of mistrust between AMISOM and TFG security forces when they were meant to be partners fighting the same enemy.[56] By this stage, AMISOM was comprised of approximately 4,000 troops from Uganda and Burundi and a small number of police officers. Even though it was still less than half its authorized strength, the AU was totally incapable of managing a deployment of this size. As a consequence, the creation of the UN Support Office for AMISOM (UNSOA) was an absolutely crucial development. In Resolution 1890 (16 January 2009), the UN Security Council had authorized its Department of Field Support to establish UNSOA in order to deliver a logistics capacity support package to keep AMISOM afloat.[57] (Between mid-2008 and mid-2012, AMISOM received nearly US$800 million from the UN—in addition to the nearly US$40 million pledged to the UN's AMISOM Trust Fund between 2009 and 2011.[58]) This was seen as critical to achieving even a semblance of operational effectiveness for AMISOM and as preparation in case a UN operation was required.

Arguably, the most controversial aspect of AMISOM's operations was its indiscriminate use of force, including mortars and artillery, in response to *al-Shabaab* attacks. This may have been directly responsible for several hundred civilian deaths and led to calls from a variety of NGOs for AMISOM to give much greater attention to civilian protection.[59] Interestingly, it had also drawn criticism from Sheikh Sharif, who accused AMISOM of committing war crimes when he was still head of the ARS-Djibouti wing.[60]

Faced with little local support, a struggling AMISOM, a concerted assault from the forces of ARS-Eritrea, *al-Shabaab* and al-Qa'ida, and lacking the security forces necessary to control even most of its own capital city, the new TFG sought to extend its power base by cultivating allies elsewhere.[61] The Declaration of Cooperation between the TFG and Ahlu Sunnah Wal Jama'a (ASWJ) was the major example of this outreach. Signed in Nairobi on 21 June 2009, this agreement covered political, security, humanitarian, and development affairs and was an attempt by the TFG to open up another front against *al-Shabaab* forces in the south of the country. ASWJ was an old religious group that focused on providing free education in the mosques, but in late 2008, it became involved with armed attempts to resist *al-Shabaab*'s efforts to capture the central Somali towns of Dusamareb, Gelinsor, and Guricel. Worried about the extreme Islamist agenda being peddled by *al-Shabaab*, ASWJ allowed militia fighters raised by a group of *Habir-Gedr* businessmen to operate under its official banner in order to resist. These fighters also received support from Ethiopian troops stationed in Galgadud and Mudug. Since then, ASWJ had continued to rely on Ethiopian military and financial support.

A formal agreement was signed between the TFG and ASWJ on 15 March 2010 in Addis Ababa. Accordingly, the TFG agreed to integrate ASWJ's administration (ASWJ was given 39 government positions) and security forces into its structures in conformity with the Transitional Federal Charter and the spirit of the Djibouti Agreement. Among other things, the two groups also agreed to "fight against terrorism and extremism and for the reconstitution of the Somali nation" and "extremist ideologies that are alien to Somali values, culture and traditional Islamic practice" through the establishment of a National Advisory Council of Ulemas.

Ban's Plans at the UN

While all this was going on, the AU and UN were debating what to do about AMISOM. In April 2009, as stipulated in UN Security Council Resolution 1863, UN Secretary-

General Ban Ki-moon submitted a report to the Security Council setting out four options to help achieve the UN's strategic objective of ending violent conflict and laying the foundations for sustainable peace and a return to "normality."[62] On the political track, the key was to support the peace process and foster national reconciliation by building capacity for local governance, drafting a constitution and integrating human rights into all aspects of the process. On the security track, the priorities were to create conditions in which the process of rebuilding state institutions could take root, especially "a legitimate locally owned and developed national security apparatus." On the recovery track, the key was to move beyond the current humanitarian emergency and provide basic services (including water, health, and education).[63] *Option A*: "Transition from AMISOM to a UN peacekeeping operation" envisaged a 22,500-strong UN peacekeeping operation acting under Chapter VII of the UN Charter taking over from AMISOM, described as a "high risk" option. Moreover, the Secretary-General noted that when in February 2009 the Department of Peacekeeping Operations had asked sixty member states whether they would be willing to contribute troops to such an operation, only ten responded, all negatively.[64] *Option B*: "Staying the current course" envisaged a UN support package for AMISOM until the Somali National Security Force could secure Mogadishu on its own, described as a "pragmatic" option. *Option C*: "Staying the current course with a 'light footprint' in Somalia" entailed the support package outlined in Option B as well as establishing a UN Political Office for Somalia and a UNSOA in Mogadishu, described as the "prudent" option. *Option D*: "Engagement with no international security presence" was intended to serve as a contingency plan in case of an AMISOM withdrawal (intentional or forced).

The Secretary-General's preferred approach was "incremental... whereby the United Nations would pursue its strategic objectives... while continuing to work towards the deployment of a peacekeeping operation at the appropriate time."[65] During what the Secretary-General called Phase 1, Option B would be carried out; during Phase 2, Option C would be practiced. Only during Phase 3 would it be appropriate to enact Option A. Option D would remain the contingency plan in case of AMISOM withdrawal. This approach resonated with some of the relevant advocacy groups. Refugees International, for instance, argued that "Further, talk of deploying a UN peacekeeping operation should be put on hold [because it] would be a polarizing and destabilizing symbol of foreign meddling on Somali soil."[66] At the other end of the spectrum, however, Gérard Prunier argued that insisting on a continued or increased AMISOM presence "would be a mistake" since AMISOM's impact was counterproductive: It was not strong enough "to make a strategic difference" but was large enough to bolster *al-Shabaab's* "nationalist arguments" accusing "the new president of betrayal."[67]

Ending the Transition

While the focus of some seven years of diplomacy had been to support the TFG, it was not forgotten that the "T" in TFG stood for "Transitional." At some point, the TFG had to be brought to a close and a permanent government established. As noted earlier, the TFG's original mandate had been five years (until August 2009). However, TFG version 2.0 had essentially given itself a stay of execution for another two years. It was in this context that AMISOM, IGAD, and UN Political Office for Somalia (UNPOS) signed a memorandum of understanding in Nairobi on 28 April 2010 in which they agreed that their efforts to support the TFG would be more effective if they could share information, coordinate while respecting each other's comparative advantages, develop joint programs where possible, and avoid duplication of effort. They also agreed that the TFG had to give way to a permanent government structure. It was the beginning of the end for the TFG.

Nevertheless, first things first: In 2010, the TFG and AMISOM were facing sustained assaults from *al-Shabaab* insurgents. To improve its chances of taking control of all of Mogadishu, in July 2010, IGAD called for AMISOM's troop levels to be raised to 20,000.[68] This figure was later assessed by the UN's Military Staff Committee to be too high and the UN Security Council endorsed a troop increase from 8,000 to 12,000 in Resolution 1964 (22 December 2010). Predictably, potential African troop-contributing states did not rush to send more troops to Mogadishu and it was left to Uganda and Burundi to increase their own troop levels. (They had finally reached the authorized strength of 8,000 in late 2010 following terrorist bombings carried out by *al-Shabaab* in Kampala in July 2010. AMISOM was now called on to increase its numbers still further but other contingents promised by Djibouti, Sierra Leone, and Nigeria among others failed to materialize.)

It was not until mid-2011 that the TFG openly recognized the need to do something about its transition status. However, at first, it simply extended its own tenure even further. In the Kampala Accord signed between the president of the TFG and the speaker of the Transitional Federal Parliament on 9 June 2011, they agreed to defer elections of the president and speaker for twelve months after August 2011; the prime minister would then resign within 30 days and the president would subsequently appoint a new prime minister, who would then appoint a new cabinet which reflected the 4.5 formula for power sharing.[69]

Not surprisingly, many of the various donor states supporting the TFG were furious, having little to show for their investment and now facing the prospect of being stuck for an additional twelve months with a corrupt, incompetent, and still largely illegitimate government. The mood was captured succinctly in the July 2011 report of the UN Monitoring Group on Eritrea and Somalia, which delivered a damning verdict on the TFG. It concluded:

> The principal impediments to security and stabilization in southern Somalia are the Transitional Federal Government leadership's lack of vision or cohesion, its endemic corruption and its failure to advance the political process. Arguably even more damaging is the Government's active resistance to engagement with or the empowerment of local, de facto political and military forces elsewhere in the country. Instead, attempts by the Government's leadership to monopolize power and resources have aggravated frictions within the transitional federal institutions, obstructed the transitional process and crippled the war against Al-Shabaab, while diverting attention and assistance away from positive developments elsewhere in the country.[70]

This assessment seemed about right, but once again developments on the ground influenced international conflict-management policies. On this occasion, the news was positive, inasmuch as in August 2011 AMISOM and TFG forces succeeded in forcing *al-Shabaab* fighters to officially retreat from their positions in central Mogadishu. Initially, they retreated only as far as the outskirts of the city and some settlements just outside Mogadishu, such as Marka, Balaad, and Afgoye, from where they continued to launch various guerrilla-style attacks and assassinations as well as suicide bombings. By mid-2012, however, *al-Shabaab* forces had also been pushed out of these satellite settlements.

After much pressure from its external donors, the TFG finally agreed to the Roadmap on Ending the Transition, which was signed on 6 September 2011. The delegates included members of the Transitional Federal Institutions (TFIs), Puntland State of Somalia, Galmudug State of Somalia, and ASWJ. The authorities in Somaliland were notably absent. The Roadmap sought a definitive end to the transitional period in Somali politics before 20 August 2012. It did so by focusing on four priority tasks: security, the constitution, reconciliation, and good governance. It also granted the TFG an additional year because it would have been politically impossible to completely tear up the earlier Kampala Accord. The principles for the Roadmap's implementation were defined as: (1) Somali ownership—they would be led by the TFG and the preference would be to hold all meetings inside Somalia; (2) inclusivity and participation—they would involve all sectors of society (elders, women, youth), regional entities, civil society organizations, as well as religious and business leaders; (3) the meetings would be well resourced, by following a Resource Mobilization Plan that made international financial support contingent on seeing results related to the four priority tasks; and (4) that the roadmap would be monitored on a regular basis to ensure compliance. Some critics were not impressed with what they saw as yet another deferral of the issues, with one dubbing it a "roadmap to nowhere."[71]

Events on the ground in Somalia got even more complicated in October 2011, when Ethiopian and Kenyan forces entered Somalia in a pincer-type movement designed to pressurize *al-Shabaab* in conjunction with AMISOM's attempts to push the insurgents out of Mogadishu. The Ethiopians did roughly what they had done many times previously and pushed into central Somalia and the strategic towns of Belet Weyne, which it took from *al-Shabaab* forces in December, and Baidoa, which fell in February 2012. The new development was Kenya's Operation *Linda Nchi* (Swahili for "Protect the Nation"). Following the famine-induced mass exodus of refugees streaming across the Somali–Kenya border and the kidnapping of several foreign nationals along the same frontier, Kenyan authorities increased fortifications along the border and deployed troops into Somalia with the stated aim of preventing *al-Shabaab* operations in Kenya by creating a buffer zone up to the settlement of Afmadow. Operation *Linda Nchi* took place with the concurrence of the TFG (and support in the Kenyan parliament),[72] although reports appeared that suggested Sheik Sharif was publicly critical of the Kenyan "invasion."[73] The Kenyan operation unfolded along three primary axes: with a push toward Kismayo; from the border crossing at Liboi through the Somali border town of Dhobley, toward the *al-Shabaab* stronghold of Afmadow; and from the northern Kenyan border town of Elwaq into Somalia's Gedo region. Estimates suggested that some 2,400 Kenyan troops crossed into Somalia, that they had met stiff local resistance, that they suffered an unclear number of fatalities, and that their deployment was costing approximately US$180 million per month.[74]

By the end of the year, it seemed like progress was finally being made in terms of ironing out the details of how to end the TFG. Between 21 and 23 December 2011, the Somali National Consultative Constitutional Conference took place in Garowe, Puntland. Facilitated by the UN's Special Representative and involving the same signatories as the Roadmap, it produced the Garowe Principles on 24 December 2011. These dealt with the two core issues of (1) the structure, size and basis of representation, and selection criteria for the new federal parliament under the new federal constitution; and (2) the adoption of the new federal constitution by a (temporary) constituent assembly and its size, structure, and criteria for selection. The overall point was to adopt a provisional new Constitution and establish a new, smaller, and more representative Parliament and elections for the positions of speaker and deputies (on 20 July 2012) and president (20 August 2012). It was agreed that the National Constituent Assembly would be based on the 4.5 formula, consist of a maximum of 1,000 delegates of which 30 percent must be women, and that all its tasks should be completed by 30 May 2012, at which time it would dissolve. A bicameral legislature was to be established on 21 August 2012. The new Somali Federal Parliament was to have 225 members, 20 percent women, and would come into being in June 2012 for a term of four years. Members of the new federal parliament would "be nominated by recognized traditional elders assisted by qualified civil society members" (Principle 2e) and would be sworn in on 15 June 2012. For its initial term, the new parliament would be selected on the basis of the 4.5 formula. But Principle 2(c)ii stated that "The 4.5 formula shall never become the basis for power sharing in any future political dispensation after the above mentioned term concludes."

The signatories also agreed to continue their discussions on how to implement the transition at a later date, and during 15–17 February 2012, a second conference was convened, which produced the Garowe II Principles on 18 February. These concluded that Somalia would have a two-chamber parliament: The lower house would have 225 seats (with at least 30 percent going to women), while the upper house would have 54 seats (three members for each of Somalia's eighteen administrative regions, which were to be the same ones as in 1991 when Siad Barre was overthrown). This would come into effect by August 2012. The National Constituent Assembly was to have 1,000 members, at least 30 percent of whom must be women, and who would be selected by Roadmap signatories assisted by traditional leaders and civil society and based on the 4.5 formula.

Later that month, the UN Security Council approved an increase in AMISOM's troop strength to 17,731 in Resolution 2036 (22 February 2012). This reflected AMISOM's new strategic and military concepts of operations. These documents were developed in a collaborative process during December 2011 and January 2012 and involved representatives from the AU, UN, IGAD, the TFG, Uganda, Burundi, Ethiopia, Kenya, the United States, and the United Kingdom. In sum, AMISOM adopted a new force posture based around four land sectors. Sector 1, Mogadishu, involved some 9,500 troops from Ugandan and Burundi; sector 2, in southwest Somalia, involved some 4,200 troops from the re-hatted Kenyan force[75] as well as a new battalion from Sierra Leone; sector 3, centered on the town of Baidoa, comprised some 2,500 Ugandan and Burundian troops supported by Ethiopian forces; and sector 4, focused on the town of Belet Weyne, northeast of Mogadishu, would be monitored by the arrival of roughly 1,000 Djiboutian soldiers supported by Ethiopian forces. During the first half of 2012, AMISOM forces, with the help of Ethiopia, TFG, and friendly clan militias, gained considerable ground from *al-Shabaab*. By mid-2012, the focus of attention was on whether the port city of Kismayo, *al-Shabaab*'s new center of gravity, could be captured before the end of the transition period in late August.

Conclusion

In light of the preceding analysis, several conclusions can be drawn about the role of the UN and regional organizations in Somalia's protracted crisis as well as the relationships between them. The first issue concerns the reasons for the UN's involvement. After a long period of neglect, UN engagement with Somalia increased from late 2004 because of its formal recognition of the TFG as Somalia's legitimate government. In addition, the dire security and humanitarian situation on the ground, as well as Ethiopia's military operations and the AU's call for help made it impossible for the UN to continue to ignore what was happening. However, because neither the UN Security Council nor the Secretariat thought the circumstances in Mogadishu were right for a blue helmet peacekeeping operation, UN support for conflict-management activities came through the tiny UNPOS and more practically through UNSOA, which provided essential support to AMISOM.

The motives prompting regional arrangements to engage with Somalia varied according to the institution. As discussed earlier, in the early 2000s, IGAD engaged in more proactive forms of peacemaking in both Sudan and Somalia, albeit with a strong Kenyan lead and considerable assistance from its external friends, perhaps most notably the United States, the United Kingdom, and Norway. The new AU was also far more proactively engaged with conflict-management initiatives than its predecessor, and Somalia was a regular feature of its discussions prompted by IGAD and President Yusuf himself. While the League of Arab States played little more than a bit part in Somalia's drama, both the EU and NATO played significant roles in support of AMISOM and the TFG's attempts to build effective security forces. The EU's Africa Peace Facility provided crucial financial assistance to pay AMISOM troops their allowances and it also conducted a training program based in Uganda. From December 2008, it also conducted antipiracy operations off the coast of Somalia. Unfortunately, these were not coordinated with AMISOM's operations on land, and revealed that the EU was more concerned with securing its trade routes and tourists than it was with fixing the root causes of the problem onshore. After the release of its new strategy for the Horn of Africa in late 2011, support to AMISOM and ending the transition process in Somalia was an important part of meeting its new strategic objectives for the region.[76] In comparison, NATO played a lesser but significant role by providing strategic airlift to support AMISOM troop-contributing countries and some subject-matter experts to assist the AU Peace Support Operations Division's work on AMISOM. Since late 2008, NATO also engaged in various counter-piracy operations; in June 2009, the Alliance became a member of the International Contact Group on Somalia.

Not surprisingly, these international organizations interacted in complex ways, in part because they did not always share the same analysis of the problems posed by Somalia's crisis and hence disagreed about the potential solutions. From early 2007 onward, the interactions between the African regional organizations (AU and IGAD) and the UN converged around the need to support the TFG, principally through AMISOM, and attempts to make the TFG more inclusive, accountable, and legitimate. This strategic objective remained broadly constant, although in late 2008, it was thought that a reconfiguration of the TFG and Yusuf's expulsion were required. Such coordination as existed between these entities tended to occur in an informal and ad hoc manner until the signing of the memorandum of understanding among the UN Political Office for Somalia, IGAD, and AMISOM in April 2010. Arguably, the chief driver of their interactions seemed to be how best to respond to changing events on the ground, most notably in Mogadishu, and the poor performance of the TFG, upon which all their strategies depended. The other important driver was the fact that while the African regional organizations brought an important degree of political legitimacy to external conflict-management activities, they were unable to engage in effective political action because they lacked the necessary military, bureaucratic, and financial capabilities to carry it out without major support from a range of other actors, most notably the UN, the United States, and the EU.

But for all this activity, what was the overall impact of their policies? The record between 2004 and mid-2012 suggests that the answer is, not much. The proposed solution to Somalia's problems, the TFG, proved corrupt, factionalized, incompetent, and illegitimate in the eyes of many locals. As a result, it took nearly eight years for it to restore a reasonable degree of order to Mogadishu, let alone the rest of Somalia. Arguably the most significant role played by these international organizations was in providing the international recognition necessary to turn a coalition of Somali armed factions, which included key members of the SCIC, into the country's transitional government. This had a major impact on the country's conflict dynamics in Mogadishu and beyond. In terms of affecting outcomes on the ground, however, it was the Ethiopian military that had the greatest impact through its forcible installation of the TFG into Mogadishu, its shattering of the SCIC, and through its very presence as a useful recruiting tool for *al-Shabaab* during 2007 and 2008 in particular.

Somalia's crisis also unfolded at a time when there were intense international debates over the appropriate relationship between the UN and regional arrangements in general and the AU in particular. This usually boiled down to a debate over how to interpret Chapter VIII of the UN Charter and whether the AU should receive special treatment from the UN because African crises consumed such a large proportion of the Security Council's agenda.[77] In this case, it was notable that AMISOM was deployed prior to receiving explicit authorization from the UN Security Council. Although UN Security Council Resolution 1725 (6 December 2006) had endorsed IGAD's deployment plan for the IGASOM mission (transmitted to the Council in mid-October 2006), it did not envisage the circumstances present in Mogadishu in early 2007. In particular, while UN Security Council Resolution 1725 authorized a force with a mandate to "ensure free movement and safe passage of all those involved with the dialogue process," that is, personnel from both the TFG and the Union of Islamic Courts (operative paragraph 3), the AU Peace and Security Council authorized AMISOM in January 2007 in a completely different political context—one in which the process of dialogue had been stopped by Ethiopia's campaign to forcibly insert the TFG into Mogadishu, and where several thousand Ethiopian soldiers were seen as an occupying power by many local Somalis. In this sense, AMISOM was primarily an AU initiative that received post facto endorsement from the UN Security Council one month later (in Resolution 1744). A second conclusion about the UN–regional relationship in this case was that both IGAD and the AU proved incapable of establishing and deploying a sizeable peacekeeping operation without major external assistance. Thus, the UN and other external donors proved indispensable for the running of AMISOM—something that advocates that the "African solutions" mantra would do well to remember. Indeed, in this case, AMISOM looked less like a genuinely pan-African solution to Somalia's crisis than a pact between Ethiopia and Uganda (and later Burundi) to keep a lid on Somalia's most volatile Islamic extremists. Ultimately, most African states simply voted with their feet and did not send troops to Mogadishu.

This conclusion also holds lessons about the relative division of labor between the UN and regional organizations in the Horn of Africa. Because both the AU and IGAD were shown to lack the capacity to conduct robust peacekeeping without major amounts of external assistance, several advocates for a strong international force being deployed to Mogadishu (notably, the Bush administration) looked to the UN instead. They were foiled because the Security Council, the UN Secretariat, and ultimately almost all the potential troop-contributing countries decided that attempting to conduct a UN peacekeeping operation in Mogadishu was a bad idea. As a consequence, supporters of regional peacekeeping must be careful to keep their ambitions in line with what these organizations can actually deliver on the ground.

Notes

1. For example, Somalia was ranked at the top of the Fund for Peace/*Foreign Policy* magazine Failed States Index from 2008 to 2012. It was ranked third in 2007, seventh in 2006, and fifth in 2005 when the Index was started. See http://www.fundforpeace.org/global/?q=fsi. In early 2008, the Brookings Institution ranked Somalia at the bottom of its Index of State Weakness in the Developing World. See http://www.brookings.edu/reports/2008/02_weak_states_index.aspx.
2. For background on events during the 1990s and earlier, I recommend the following publications: For general historical background, I. M. Lewis, *A Modern History of the Somali* (Oxford: James Currey, 4th edition, 2002). On the history of mediation efforts, Interpeace, *A History of Mediation in Somalia since 1988* (Nairobi: Interpeace, May 2009). On the international peace operations deployed between 1992 and 1995, John L. Hirsch and Robert B. Oakley, *Somalia and Operation Restore Hope* (Washington, DC: US Institute of Peace Press, 1996). On developments in the northwest specifically, Mark Bradbury, *Becoming Somaliland* (Oxford: James Currey, 2008). For a foreign aid worker's perspective on life in Somalia after the departure of UN peacekeepers, John S. Burnett, *Where Soldiers Fear to Tread* (London: Bantam, 2006).
3. An alternative view, proposed by Ken Menkhaus, suggested the "most promising formula for success in state building in Somalia [in part because it is already practiced across much of the Horn] is some form of 'mediated states' in which the government relies on partnership (or at least coexistence) with a diverse range of local intermediaries and rival sources of authority to provide core functions of public security, justice, and conflict management in much of

the country." Ken Menkhaus, "Governance without Government in Somalia," *International Security* 31:3 (2006/07): 78.

4. Ibid., 74.
5. Ken Menkhaus, *Conflict Analysis: Somalia* (Nairobi: UN Political Office for Somalia, February 2011, updated December 2011), pp. 10–14.
6. Ibid., p. 42. See also Accord, *Whose Peace Is It Anyway? Connecting Somali and International Peacemaking* (London: Conciliation Resources, 2010).
7. See Kenneth J. Menkhaus, "Somalia and Somaliland," in *Battling Terrorism in the Horn of Africa*, ed. Robert I. Rotberg (Washington, DC: Brookings Institution Press, 2005), pp. 23–47; Ken Menkhaus, *Somalia: State Collapse and the Threat of Terrorism* (London: IISS Adelphi Paper No. 364, 2004).
8. Menkhaus, "Somalia and Somaliland." Interestingly, the US intelligence community had made roughly the same assessment. See US Military Academy, Combating Terrorism Center, *Al-Qaida's (mis)Adventures in the Horn of Africa* (New York: West Point, 2007), at http://www.ctc.usma.edu/posts/al-qaidas-misadventures-in-the-horn-of-africa.
9. Menkhaus, "Somalia and Somaliland," p. 40.
10. Ken Menkhaus, *Somalia: A National and Regional Disaster?* (UNHCR, April 2009), pp. 1–2, at http://www.unhcr.org/refworld/pdfid/49f180d82.pdf.
11. Sally Healy, *Lost Opportunities in the Horn of Africa* (London: Chatham House, Horn of Africa Group Report, 2008), p. 22.
12. IGAD, "Communique on Somalia," issued in Abuja, Nigeria, 31 January 2005.
13. Article 7 on IGAD's Aims and Objectives states that the institution will: 7(g) Promote peace and stability in the subregion and create mechanisms within the subregion for the prevention, management, and resolution of inter and intrastate conflicts through dialogue. Signed March 1996, at http://www.igad.int/etc/agreement_establishing_igad.pdf.
14. AU, PSC/PR/Comm. (XXIX), 12 May 2005.
15. AU, PSC/Min/Comm. (XXXIV)–(i), 3 July 2005.
16. For a discussion of IGAD's weaknesses in the field of conflict management, see Sally Healy, *Peacemaking in the Midst of War: An Assessment of IGAD's Contribution to Regional Security in the Horn of Africa* (London: LSE Crisis States Working Paper No. 59, April 2009). On the AU, see Paul D. Williams, *The African Union's Conflict Management Capabilities* (Council on Foreign Relations Working Paper, 2011), at http://www.cfr.org/african-union/african-unions-conflict-management-capabilities/p26044.
17. The story is well covered in International Crisis Group, *Somaliland: Time for African Union Leadership* (Nairobi: ICG Africa Report N°110, 23 May 2006).
18. For details, see Roland Marchal, "Islamic Political Dynamics in the Somali Civil War," in *Islamism and Its Enemies in the Horn of Africa*, ed. Alex de Waal (Bloomington, IN: Indiana University Press, 2004), pp. 132–139; Cedric Barnes and Harun Hassan, "The Rise and Fall of Mogadishu's Islamic Courts," *Journal of Eastern African Studies* 1:2 (2007): 151–160; Healy, *Lost Opportunities in the Horn of Africa*, pp. 23–24.
19. Menkhaus, "Governance without Government in Somalia," p. 76. The ARPCT was formed in February 2006, apparently with considerable assistance (of some US$2 million) from the US Central Intelligence Agency in return for help tracking down those individuals responsible for the US embassy bombings in Nairobi and Dar es Salaam in 1998. See, for example, Bronwyn E. Bruton, *Somalia: A New Approach* (New York: Council on Foreign Relations, Special Report No. 52, March 2010), p. 7; Shaul Shay, *Somalia: Between Jihad and Restoration* (New York: Transaction Publishers, 2011), p. 189.
20. By early 2012, the group had held twenty-one meetings. Its participants included Austria, Belgium, Canada, China, Denmark, Djibouti, Egypt, Ethiopia, Finland, France, Germany,

Italy, Japan, Kenya, Republic of Korea, Malaysia, the Netherlands, Norway, Qatar, Saudi Arabia, Somalia, South Africa, Spain, Sudan, Sweden, Switzerland, Turkey, Uganda, United Arab Emirates, United Kingdom, United States, African Development Bank, AU, EU, Islamic Development Bank, IGAD, League of Arab States, Organization of Islamic Cooperation, NATO, UN, and the World Bank.

21. Ayro was killed in a US air strike in Somalia on 1 May 2008.
22. See, for example, Abdi Ismail Samatar, "Ethiopian Invasion of Somalia, US Warlordism and AU Shame," *Review of African Political Economy* 34:111 (2007): 158; Healy, *Lost Opportunities in the Horn of Africa*, p. 25.
23. Since August 1996, Ethiopian troops had engaged in a series of military incursions aimed at degrading Islamist bases in Somalia, particularly those of *al-Ittihad al-Islami*, which Ethiopia's Prime Minister Meles Zenawi believed were fermenting trouble in eastern Ethiopia.
24. *Ethiopian Herald*, 30 June 2006, cited in Haggai Erlich, *Islam and Christianity in the Horn of Africa* (Boulder, CO: Lynne Rienner, 2010), p. 168.
25. Ibid., p. 166.
26. Barnes and Hassan, "The Rise and Fall of Mogadishu's Islamic Courts," 156.
27. Mark Bradbury and Sally Healy, "Endless War," in Accord, *Whose Peace Is It Anyway?*, p. 14.
28. For a discussion of the legal dimensions, see Zeray W. Yihdego, "Ethiopia's Military Action against the Union of Islamic Courts and Others in Somalia," *International and Comparative Law Quarterly* 56:3 (2007): 666–676. On the politics of the process of international recognition, see Anonymous, "Government Recognition in Somalia and Regional Political Stability in the Horn of Africa," *Journal of Modern African Studies* 40:2 (2002): 247–272.
29. Erlich, *Islam and Christianity in the Horn of Africa*, p. 176.
30. Ibid., p. 7.
31. The subsequent number of foreign Jihadist fighters who came to Somalia was the subject of much debate. Estimates of several hundred seem to be the most reliable.
32. AU, PSC/PR/Comm. (LXIX), 19 January 2007.
33. Ibid., para. 9.
34. See AU Press Release, "AU Mission in Somalia Agreement Signed," 6 March 2007, at www.ethioembassy.org.uk/news/press%20releases/AU%20Mission%20in%20Somalia%20Agreement%20signed.htm.
35. The *PSC Protocol* came into force on 26 December 2003 (after ratification by twenty-seven of the fifty-three AU members) and the Peace and Security Council officially began work on 16 March 2004 at the ministerial level in the margins of the 4th Ordinary Session of the AU Executive Council.
36. Author's confidential interviews: AU official, Addis Ababa, May 2007, and former Ethiopian official, Washington, DC, March 2008.
37. The UN had been deeply engaged in Somali affairs between 1992 and March 1995 when its peacekeeping operation, the UN Operation in Somalia (UNOSOM) II, departed. After that, the UN's presence in Somalia was almost entirely humanitarian (through various UN agencies). The minimal political engagement that occurred was via the UN Political Office for Somalia (UNPOS). Established in April 1995, UNPOS comprised of a small team of civilians based in Nairobi because Somalia was thought to be too dangerous. UNPOS was overseen by the UN's Department of Political Affairs and only relocated some of its personnel to Mogadishu in January 2012.
38. See, for example, *Somalia: Shell-Shocked—Civilians under Siege in Mogadishu*, 19:12(a) (New York: Human Rights Watch, August 2007).

39. Menkhaus, *Somalia: A National and Regional Disaster?*, p. 3.
40. Solomon Dersso, *Somalia Dilemmas: Changing Security Dynamics, but Limited Policy Choices* (Pretoria: ISS Paper No. 218, October 2010), p. 14.
41. Wikileak Cable 08ADDISABABA855, 31 March 2008, para. 4.
42. For an overview, see Apuuli Phillip Kasaija, "The UN-led Djibouti Peace Process for Somalia, 2008–2009," *Journal of Contemporary African Studies* 28:3 (2010): 269–274.
43. Menkhaus, *Somalia: A National and Regional Disaster?*, p. 7.
44. Although the Agreement is dated 9 June 2008, it was not actually signed until 19 August 2008.
45. Subsequent UN–AU planning cohered around an ISF of approximately 6,000 troops.
46. S/2008/709, 17 November 2008, paras. 31–43.
47. Ibid., para. 47.
48. S/2008/804, 19 December 2008.
49. Ibid., Annex.
50. AU, PSC/MIN/Comm.4 (CLXIII), 22 December 2008, para. 19.
51. *BBC News Online*, "Somalia Peacekeepers 'Not Viable,' " 9 November 2007, available online at http://news.bbc.co.uk/go/pr/fr/-/2/hi/africa/7086367.stm.
52. In frustration with President Yusuf, in November and December 2008, IGAD and the AU endorsed sanctions against Yusuf and his associates. Given Yusuf's ill health, a travel ban preventing his medical care visits to Nairobi was probably instrumental in his decision to resign. Kasaija, "The UN-led Djibouti Peace Process," 273.
53. Since both Nur Adde and Sheikh Sharif are members of the same Hawiye clan-family. Sharmarke, on the other hand, hails from the Majerteen clan of the Darood clan-family, the same clan as former President Abdullahi Yusuf. Menkhaus, *Somalia: A National and Regional Disaster?*, pp. 7–8.
54. For an overview, see International Crisis Group, *Somalia: The Transitional Government on Life Support* (Washington, DC: Africa Report No. 170, 21 February 2011).
55. Dersso, *Somalia Dilemmas*, p. 10.
56. Author's confidential communication with AMISOM official, May 2011.
57. UNSOA provided the delivery of rations, fuel, general stores, and medical supplies; engineering and construction of important facilities; health and sanitation; medical evacuation and treatment services and medical equipment for AMISOM medical facilities; communications and information technology; information support services; aviation services for evacuations and troop rotations; vehicles and other equipment; and capacity-building. Report of the UN Secretary-General, *Support to African Union Peacekeeping Operations Authorized by the United Nations* (A/65/510-S/2010/514, 14 October 2010), para. 30.
58. Figures are from the UN's Advisory Committee on Administrative and Budgetary Questions.
59. Author's confidential communication with Inter-Agency Standing Committee Somalia Protection Cluster partner member in Nairobi, September 2010.
60. Specifically, Sheikh Sharif complained that: "AMISOM has been using tanks and heavy artillery indiscriminately against the population of Mogadishu. As a result, according to the latest estimates, over 100 people, including children, women, and elderly have been killed; more than 300 others have been wounded, and about 3000 have fled their homes, where Ethiopian troops and the TFG militias have been looting their homes . . . It is obvious that AMISOM had used unnecessary force and targeted heavily populated quarters and markets far away from the fighting area(s) which can only be taken as deliberate mass killing. Since AMISOM had not come with the consent of the Somali people, lately we have been spending a significant amount of time and efforts to convince our people to accept AMISOM as a peace keeping force, but the latest terror has seriously damaged the image of

the mission of AMISOM in Somalia . . . We consider this AMISOM action as a war crime; therefore, we urgently request the UN as well as AU to send an impartial fact find [sic.] mission at the earliest possible time to investigate these atrocities and swiftly bring the culprits to justice." Sheikh Sharif Sheikh Ahmed, Chairman ARS, "AMISOM Brutality in Somalia," unpublished letter addressed to the UN Secretary-General, the presidents of the AU, Uganda, and Burundi, officials from the League of Arab States, the Organization of Islamic Conference, and various human rights organizations, 29 September 2008, copy in author's possession.

61. In mid-March 2009, Osama bin Laden had described Sheikh Sharif as a "surrogate of our enemies," and consequently his "authority was null and void" and "he must be dethroned and fought." Cited in Erlich, *Islam and Christianity in the Horn of Africa*, p. 182. *Al-Shabaab* made a formal declaration of allegiance to al-Qa'ida on 2 February 2010.
62. S/2009/210, 16 April 2009, paras. 48–80.
63. Ibid., para. 42.
64. Ibid., para. 55.
65. Ibid., para. 82.
66. Refugees International, *Somalia: Political Progress, Humanitarian Stalemate* (Washington, DC: Refugees International Field Report, 3 April 2009), p. 3.
67. Gérard Prunier, "Somalia: Beyond the Quagmire," *Open Democracy* (25 February 2009): 6.
68. At the Fifteenth Extra-Ordinary Session of the IGAD Assembly of Heads of State and Government, Addis Ababa, 5 July 2010.
69. The 4.5 formula suggests that power should be shared between the four main clan-families of Somalia (Darod, Digil-Rahanweyn, Dir, and Hawiye) as well as with the minority clans, which make up the 0.5.
70. *Report of the Monitoring Group on Somalia and Eritrea Pursuant to Security Council Resolution 1916* (2010) (UN doc. S/2011/433, 18 July 2011), p. 12.
71. Michael A. Weinstein, "Somalia: A Roadmap to Nowhere," 22 September 2011, http://www.garoweonline.com/artman2/publish/Somalia_27/Somalia_A_Roadmap_to_Nowhere.shtml.
72. A joint communiqué dated 18 October 2011 and signed by the Kenyan foreign minister and Somali deputy prime minister agreed to "cooperate in undertaking security and military operations, and to undertake coordinated pre-emptive action and the pursuit of any armed elements that continue to threaten and attack both countries." The text of the communiqué is available at http://graphics8.nytimes.com/packages/pdf/world/joint-communique-kenya-somalia.pdf.
73. "Somali President Opposes Kenyan Military Intervention," AFP, 24 October 2011.
74. See David W. Throup, "Kenya's Intervention in Somalia," CSIS, 16 February 2012, at http://csis.org/publication/kenyas-intervention-somalia.
75. After a protracted argument about the details of re-hatting, the related financial arrangements, and the number of slots available to Kenyans in the new AMISOM headquarters in Mogadishu, in early June 2012, Kenya signed a memorandum of understanding integrating its forces into AMISOM.
76. *A Strategic Framework for the Horn of Africa* (Brussels: Council of European Union, 16858/11, 14 November 2011).
77. The panel chaired by Romano Prodi gave a good indication of where the debate on the UN–AU relationship on peacekeeping issues stood in late 2008. See *Report of the African Union-United Nations Panel on Modalities for Support to African Union Peacekeeping Operations* (UN doc. A/63/666-S/2008/813, 31 December 2008).

Chapter 12

Sudan: Darfur

Alex de Waal

Introduction

The little-known Sudanese region of Darfur achieved sudden notoriety in 2003–2004 as the locus of an intense civil war, massacres of civilians, a severe humanitarian crisis, and a strong campaign led by young Americans to intervene to halt what they identified as genocide. Almost from the outset, the Sudanese conflict in Darfur was internationalized in multiple ways, involving neighboring countries (Chad and Libya), the African Union (AU), the United Nations (UN), and the United States in a remarkably comprehensive manner, in part because of international engagement with Sudan's Comprehensive Peace Agreement (CPA), and in part because of an activist campaign led by the Save Darfur Coalition. The Darfur crisis set a number of significant precedents for international conflict resolution, including AU leadership in mediating peace talks and dispatching a peacekeeping force; an official US determination that genocide had been committed; a UN Security Council resolution calling for a peace support operation under Chapter VII, mandated to protect civilians; a hybrid AU–UN peacekeeping operation (the largest in the world); an arrest warrant issued by the International Criminal Court (ICC) against a sitting head of state; and diverse approaches to mediating a resolution of the conflict.

This chapter outlines the main events of the international engagement in Darfur between 2003 and 2011, and some of the issues arising from those events. It begins with the context in which the Darfur crisis erupted in 2003; specifically, with the maturing negotiations to bring about a peaceful resolution of the long-running war between the Government of Sudan (GoS) and the Sudan People's Liberation Movement/Army (SPLM/A), which entailed bringing a UN peacekeeping mission to Sudan, and with the relations between Sudan and Chad. This configuration brought the AU to Darfur as a major player. During 2004–2006, the AU was responsible for both a peace support

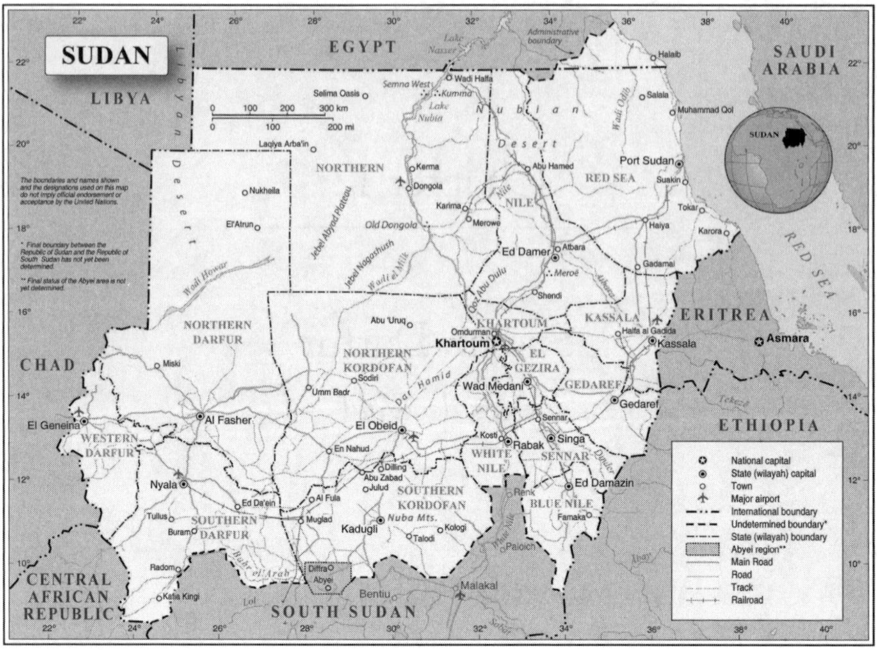

Source: Map No 4458 Rev 2, United Nations, Department of Field Support, Cartographic Section, March 2012

operation—the African Mission in Sudan (AMIS)—and for peace talks, in a situation in which the UN and the United States both took keen interest. By the end of 2006, no peace had been achieved and AMIS was regarded as unsustainable, but the GoS had also rejected a UN Security Council resolution that would have imposed a UN peacekeeping force. The compromise was a hybrid African Union/United Nations Hybrid Operation in Darfur (UNAMID) and a joint UN–AU mediation effort. Meanwhile, new dimensions to the conflict were added by reciprocal attacks by Sudanese-backed Chadian rebels on N'Djaména and Chadian- and Libyan-backed Sudanese rebels on Khartoum in 2008; by the ICC Prosecutor requesting an arrest warrant for Sudanese President Omar Hassan al Bashir in July that year; and by the AU's decision to establish a High-Level Panel on Darfur (AUPD) headed by the former South African President Thabo Mbeki, which began its activities in March 2009. The various efforts by the AUPD and the Joint Chief Mediator (JCM), Djibrill Yipènè Bassolé, illuminate divergent approaches to peacemaking in Darfur, including a traditional focus on the belligerents and their patrons, an all-inclusive "round table" approach aiming at achieving a democratic consensus, and efforts to achieve an internationally validated "document for peace" backed by donor funds.

As the crisis and the responses to the crisis have unfolded over eight years, the relationship between the UN and AU has varied between meticulous collaboration and rivalry for leadership. The two organizations have differed in their objectives, modes of operation, analyses of the situation in Darfur, and conceptions of peacemaking. Both have important lessons to learn.

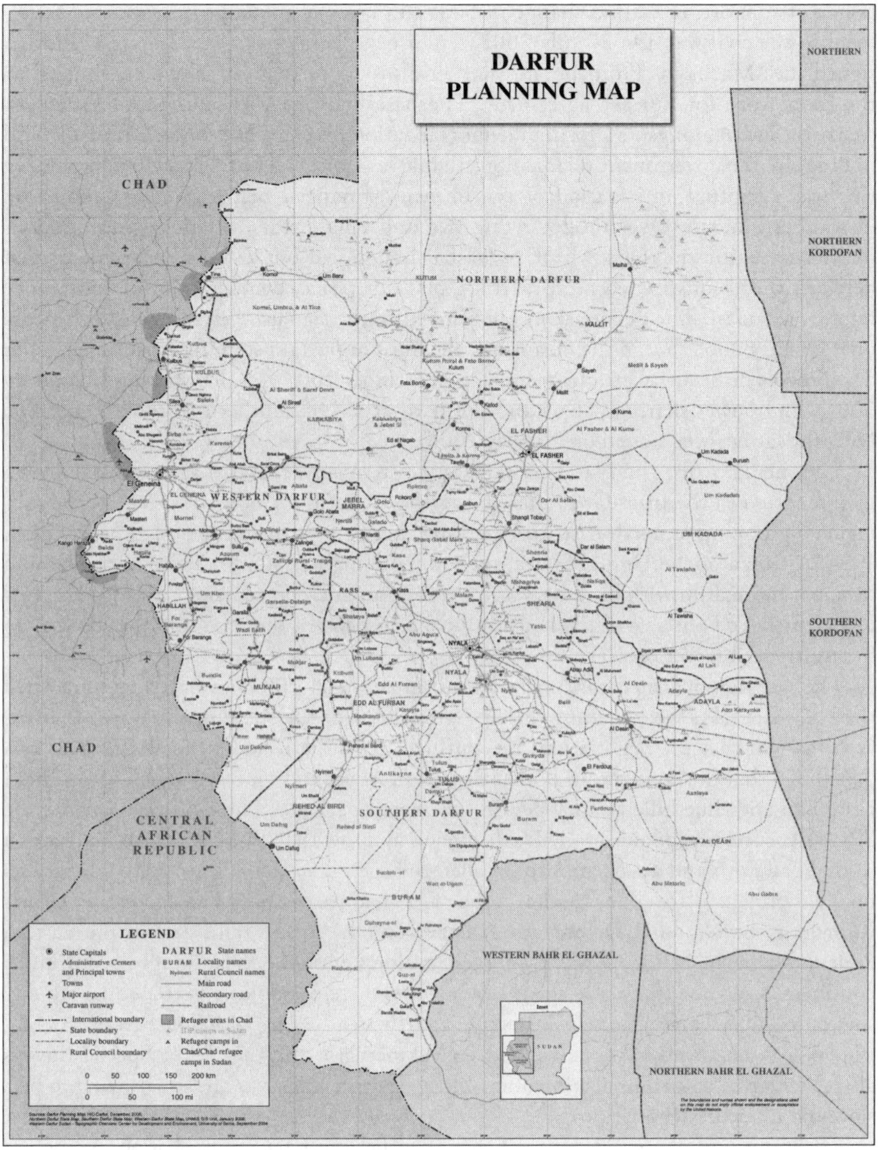

Source: Map No 4262 Rev 1, United Nations, Department of Peacekeeping Operations, Cartographic Section, December 2007

The Outbreak of the Darfur Conflict in Context

The Darfur war erupted in early 2003, just as the protracted negotiations for ending the north–south civil war in Sudan were bearing fruit. Eighteen months earlier, the incoming George W. Bush administration in Washington, DC, had reversed its predecessor's policy of supporting regime change in Sudan in favor of pursuing a negotiated settlement to the civil war. On 20 July 2002, senior negotiators from the GoS and SPLM/A signed the "Machakos Protocol" in the Kenyan town of that name, which established the framework for a peace agreement. The basic bargain was self-determination for southern Sudan alongside a form of democratization for the whole of Sudan that would not require the government to abandon Islamic law for northern Sudan. Underpinning this was a mutual anticipation of the immense financial benefits of oil production in southern Sudan. Over the following two and a half years, a series of negotiations in Kenya, mainly in the town of Naivasha, hammered out a series of protocols that between them constructed a far-reaching plan for peace, democracy, and governance reform in Sudan. The negotiations culminated in the signature of the CPA in Nairobi on 9 January 2005, but in the meantime, the most important steps forward were a series of protocols on security arrangements (25 September 2003), wealth-sharing (7 January 2004), and power-sharing, Abyei and the "two areas" of Southern Kordofan and Blue Nile (the latter three signed on 26 May 2004).

The mediator for the Naivasha talks was a Kenyan general, Lazarus Sumbeiywo, who reported to the Inter-Governmental Authority on Development (IGAD), the subregional grouping of north-east African states that had assumed the Sudan peace file in 1994. A troika of the United States, the United Kingdom, and Norway stood behind him, providing him with both heavyweight support and considerable latitude. The UN Department of Political Affairs had a full-time observer at the talks and the AU had an intermittent observer presence.

The eruption of armed conflict in Darfur in February 2003 occurred at a time when the Naivasha talks were making little progress. One of the sticking issues was that the GoS insisted that the negotiations be confined to southern Sudan, while the SPLM/A demanded that the contentious border district of Abyei and the "two areas" of Southern Kordofan and Blue Nile be included in the overall package. The GoS also accused the SPLM/A, correctly, of aiding the Darfur rebels and saw the SPLM/A role in Darfur as a sign of bad faith and an attempt to broaden the agenda of the talks so as to advance its political project of the "New Sudan."[1] The GoS had successfully blocked earlier efforts to include the National Democratic Alliance (NDA) in the talks and to put eastern Sudan, where the SPLM/A was a belligerent along with the Beja Congress and NDA contingents, on the Naivasha agenda. The GoS therefore objected strenuously to any suggestion that Darfur be included as the "fourth area" (along with Southern Kordofan, Blue Nile, and Abyei) in the talks. The IGAD mediator and the Troika Special Envoys also saw Darfur as a complication and a likely drag on what was already proving to be a slow and difficult negotiation.

The immediate alternative for the Darfur conflict was Chadian mediation. As soon as the conflict broke out, Chadian President Idriss Déby Itno correctly saw that it was a strategic threat to his position.[2] Déby, like his predecessor Hissène Habré, had seized power from a rear military base in Darfur. Since taking power in 1990, Déby had maintained a defense pact with Sudan whereby neither country tolerated the other's rebels. The fact that the most militarily capable of the Darfuri rebels from both the Sudan Liberation Movement/Army (SLM/A) and the Justice and Equality Movement (JEM) were ethnic Zaghawa, from the same group as Déby himself, complicated matters. Déby thus pursued a policy of collaborating with the GoS against some of the non-Zaghawa rebels,[3] while tacitly condoning his close relatives' support to the Zaghawa rebels in Darfur, and officially seeking a peace deal. Two rounds of talks in the Chadian town of Abeché in August–September and October–November 2003 resulted in cease-fires that did not hold.[4] As the war escalated, Déby convened a third round of talks in N'Djaména in March 2004, for which he brought in the AU as co-mediator and gladly accepted US support in bringing the rebels to the table. The GoS boycotted the opening on 31 March, objecting to the presence of international observers (apart from the AU), compelling the negotiations to be held as proximity talks. Only when the AU Commission Chairperson, President Alpha Konaré, intervened directly, meeting with President Bashir on 6 April,[5] did the talks accelerate to a conclusion. Two days later, the N'Djaména Humanitarian Ceasefire was concluded, which included the dispatch of AU military observers to monitor the cease-fire and a small contingent of African troops to protect the monitors—the initial deployment of the AMIS.

The Chadian–AU initiative, albeit with US backing, appears very modest when measured against the scale of the conflict and the associated human rights violations and humanitarian disaster. However, it must be seen in the context of Sudanese peace politics at the time. After his appointment in September 2001, the US Special Envoy, Senator John Danforth, stressed that the north–south negotiations were a Sudanese affair and that the parties should not expect a major peacekeeping force. In 2002, as part of the preliminary steps toward the CPA, Danforth helped to mediate a cease-fire in the Nuba Mountains (Southern Kordofan), which involved a small military observer mission (Joint Military Commission, JMC) of approximately twenty-five international personnel,[6] and a similarly small Civilian Protection Monitoring Team in southern Sudan. The Machakos Protocol included mention of an internationally chaired Assessment and Evaluation Commission but made no reference to peacekeepers. Diplomats at the Naivasha talks stressed that the Sudanese should not expect much more, partly with the aim of downplaying southern Sudanese expectations of a large-scale international protection force. The Protocol on Security Arrangements did not mention any international force, and the CPA annex on cease-fire implementation, signed just hours before the UN Security Council deadline of 31 December 2004 for concluding the negotiations, specified "a lean, effective, sustainable and affordable UN Peace Support Mission."[7] Meanwhile, in June 2004, in anticipation of the agreement, the UN dispatched the UN Advance Mission in Sudan (UNAMIS), a political mission to prepare the ground for the future peacekeeping force.

The GoS felt that its fears of foreign conspiracy were vindicated in 2005, when the UN Department of Peacekeeping Operations (DPKO) assessment mission recommended that the UN Mission in Sudan (UNMIS) consist of up to 10,000 troops, including full battalions in Southern Kordofan and Blue Nile, that is, within northern Sudan, plus 715 UN police and well-staffed civilian components for civil affairs and human rights. The GoS was taken aback by the size of the proposed mission and the breadth of its mandate, but accepted it on the understanding that CPA would lead to normalization of relations with Western countries, especially the United States.

The Security Council passed no fewer than five resolutions on Sudan in March 2005. The first two (1585 and 1588) merely extended the mandate of UNAMIS by one week each so that the Council could resolve the other Sudanese issues on its agenda—an indication of the difficulty of reaching consensus on how to handle those issues. Three substantive resolutions followed, dealing respectively with establishing UNMIS

(1590 of 24 March), establishing a committee to monitor violations of its resolutions on Darfur and sanction individuals accordingly (1591 of 29 March) and referring the crimes in Darfur to the ICC (1593 of 31 March). The Security Council was trying to do several distinct and potentially contradictory things at once: to commend Sudan for the CPA and support the implementation of that agreement, to restrict the capabilities of the belligerents in Darfur to conduct hostilities, and to bring the perpetrators of grave human rights violations in Darfur to justice.

The AMIS

The AMIS began as a small conventional cease-fire observer mission sent principally in support of the Ceasefire Commission (CFC) set up by the N'Djaména agreement. Initially, AMIS comprised ninety-six international observers—sixty from the AU, eighteen from Chad, and eighteen from the United States and European Union—and a force protection of 270, along with the members of the CFC (Sudanese army and rebels) and the parties' own military observers. It faced four major problems.

The first was that the N'Djaména ceasefire was not in fact an agreement. After the text had been approved and signed by the representatives of the Sudan Liberation Army (SLA) and JEM, the GoS delegation objected, arguing that they had agreed on the understanding that the text would include a provision that the rebels be encamped. (The chief military negotiator, Major General Ismat al Zain, had also wanted a cease-fire operations map, but he had been overruled by his civilian superiors.)[8] Consequently, at the insistence of the Chadian Minister of Foreign Affairs, the head of the AU mediation team wrote in this extra clause by hand, and the GoS signed. Thereafter, the GoS insisted that the free movement of the rebels around Darfur was a cease-fire violation warranting a military response by the Sudanese Armed Forces (SAF), and the rebels insisted that there was no such restriction. The CFC was continually hampered by disagreements over what actually constituted a violation of the agreement.

A second problem arose directly from this. The GoS signed the cease-fire at the point of its maximum military success. It had the rebels on the run. The SLA and JEM, had they abided by the cease-fire, would have been confined to the mountains and the desert. However, they regarded their setbacks during the just-concluded offensive as a tactical reverse only, and decided to take the war to parts of eastern and southern Darfur that had hitherto been relatively untouched. The new rebel counterattacks prompted in turn a new set of campaigns by the SAF and the militia, alongside aerial bombing, which were condemned by the rebels, international monitors, and human rights activists as cease-fire violations and human rights abuses. The period from June 2004 to January 2005 saw asymmetric violations by each side: The rebels attacked military and police outposts and convoys, overran new territories, and killed administrators and tribal chiefs. The army and militia burned villages, killed men and boys, and raped women and girls.[9]

The third and most evident problem with AMIS was that its size and mandate were wholly incommensurate with the scale of the conflict and the demand for civilian protection, which was voiced ever more stridently at the AU, UN, and by diplomats and activists. The concept of operation was reviewed in October to include "proactive monitoring" and "discourage[e] attacks on civilians,"[10] and the mandate revised accordingly, with the result that the number of troops was increased to 3,320.[11] This was the first of several increases that eventually brought AMIS up to 7,000 men. More important than the mandate, however, was the disposition and initiative of the Force Commander. The first AMIS commander, Brigadier-General Festus Okwonko, was proactive and interpreted his authority ambitiously. On one occasion, he publicly warned of an impending attack.

The greatest testament to AMIS's success is the evidence of declining lethal violence. The vast majority of killings took place between July 2003 and March 2004. The rebels' expansion of the war to southern and eastern Darfur in the second half of 2004 caused an upturn in violence, but on a smaller scale than before. From January 2005, the killings subsided further, with occasional spikes over the following years.[12]

It is difficult to definitively attribute the reasons for the reduction in lethal violence in Darfur to a particular source. One set of explanations focuses on the objectives of the leaders and the political, organizational, and logistical constraints on organizing offensives. According to this line of argument, the GoS had achieved its major political objectives by March 2004; namely, removing the immediate military threat of the insurgency and punishing the rebels for their earlier humiliations of the SAF. At this point, the army had exhausted its capabilities and the militia on which it had relied were also becoming reluctant proxies and potential dangers to the army and government itself. A second set of reasons offered for the reduction in violence focuses on international engagement, including media and diplomatic attention, the threat of ICC investigations, and efforts to find a negotiated solution. According to this argument, the AU monitors and the international humanitarian presence were instrumental in reducing the killings. A combination of both is also possible.

The decline in violence from April 2004 onward coincided with an increase in media coverage and a corresponding increase in reported violence, giving the plausible but incorrect impression that killings were increasing and the AU mission was wholly ineffective.[13] For several years, during 2005–2008, commentators routinely reported that "things were getting worse," while most indicators pointed in the opposite direction.[14] One of the challenges facing AMIS was that, because Darfur was heralded as a case of the responsibility to protect, media scrutiny was intense and expectations were unrealistically high.

The CFC and AMIS did not function well in terms of reporting cease-fire violations and acting on them. The Joint Commission—the political body to which the CFC reported—met just a handful of times. However, the very fact that the CFC existed and that there were troops and monitors spread across Darfur meant that information about what was happening in Darfur was widely disseminated. The poor functioning of formal mechanisms was less important than the deployment of observers, soldiers, and humanitarian staff, all of whom had their own means of telling their own governments and the world what was going on.

The fourth challenge to AMIS was that the AU was not well equipped to mount such an operation. The AU's peace and security architecture including the Peace and Security Council (PSC) had only just been established. There was no specialized department for peace support operations, and the Peace and Security Division was understaffed and overstretched, with virtually no experience in running such an operation.

The very first meeting of the AU PSC was held in February 2004, when it considered Darfur and Côte d'Ivoire. The United States hired private contractors for logistics. Funds were raised on an ad hoc basis. Although considerably cheaper than a UN mission of comparable size, because it was funded by discretionary contributions by donors rather than a mandatory assessment (as was the case for UN operations), AMIS continually suffered cash-flow problems. It repeatedly fell short of expectations in terms of operational efficiency, management, and financial reporting. Although initially AMIS enjoyed the benefit of the doubt from the international community, including the US administration, and from activists and journalists, after a few months, the international consensus was that it was out of its depth. Constant criticism in the media and condescension from international diplomats undermined the morale and effectiveness of the mission.[15]

There was no civilian component to AMIS. Alongside the AMIS troops, UNMIS had civil affairs offices in each of the three Darfuri states. They interpreted their tasks broadly and were active in a range of local-level political activities, notably conflict prevention and resolution. At the field level, they coordinated well with AMIS military officers, providing them with extensive local intelligence and advice. The UN also retained its humanitarian coordination role. Following his appointment in June 2004, the Special Representative of the UN Secretary General (SRSG), Jan Pronk, was also active, frequently visiting Darfur and including all aspects of the Darfuri crisis within his scope of activities. In the event, Pronk's activism on Darfur proved his undoing, as comments he made about the low morale of the army in October 2006 prompted the SAF command to demand, and obtain, his expulsion from the country.[16]

The Abuja Peace Talks

The Inter-Sudanese Peace Talks on the Conflict in Darfur began shortly after the N'Djaména cease-fire, initially in Addis Ababa and shortly afterward in Abuja.[17] The AU inherited the file from the Chadian mediation, which gradually recused itself because of its growing involvement in the Darfuri conflict. The Darfuri rebels continuously objected to the AU as mediator, demanding the UN or the United States, but eventually accepted under US pressure.[18]

The negotiations were entrusted to a small AU team headed by the former Secretary General of the Organization of African Unity (OAU), Salim Ahmed Salim, and the head of AU Peace and Security Department. The process of selecting the team was characteristically ad hoc, drawing upon available diplomatic retirees, mediation specialists, and Sudan experts personally known to the leaders of the team. The mediation continually faced budget constraints that meant that it was late in paying per diems to participants and mediation team members alike,[19] and it was under constant pressure to wind up the talks.

Although the UN was already deployed in Sudan, including with civil affairs officers in Darfur, the UN seconded just one staff member to the mediation team (Abdul Mohammed) and did not have its own observers at the talks. In fact, at the critical final session of the talks, the SRSG only arrived at 11.00 a.m. on 6 May, missing the previous week during which time the entirety of the final agreement was negotiated. Given that the UN was expected to be a major implementing partner for the agreement, most notably its security arrangements, the UN's absence from Abuja was a remarkable oversight.

The Abuja mediation was further hampered by the practice of "deadline diplomacy."[20] This criticism was made not only in response to the final deadline of 25 April (which slipped to 1 May and then to 3, 5, and 6 May), but more especially in reaction to the way in which the AU, the UN, and its most powerful member states imposed a set of rolling deadlines, month by month, on the talks. In October 2005, a deadline of the end of the year was imposed. When this was not met, a series of high-level political figures made declarations or came to Abuja to insist that the talks must conclude within a month or a few weeks. As Nathan notes, "[t]he posturing over deadlines was ignored by the Sudanese parties because it was not backed up by action," but the mediators were compelled to abide by their masters' decisions. As a result, it was impossible to develop a cogent mediation strategy, because staff were continually engaged in preparing for either the next high-level visit, or in preparing draft documents for a negotiating session that was supposed to result in a signature. Nathan concluded, "deadline diplomacy *was* the strategy and the plan, and it was far too simplistic, vacuous, and rigid for this purpose."[21] On one occasion, a visit by the then Chair of the AU, President Denis Sassou-Nguesso of the Congo Republic, entailed a seven-day disruption to the mediation schedule in order to prepare for his intervention, setting back the security talks at a delicate stage, with the sole outcome of the presidential intervention being an enjoinder to "hurry up."[22]

The reason for this relentless pressure was that President Bush had decided in December 2005 that UN peacekeepers should be deployed to Darfur. He made this decision as a compromise with the demand of the Save Darfur movement–and an indication he had made himself—that North Atlantic Treaty Organization (NATO) troops should go. He tasked Deputy Secretary of State Robert Zoellick with making it happen. The UN insisted that it would send troops only on the basis of an agreement with the host country and other belligerents. For the United States, therefore, the principal reason for the Darfur Peace Agreement (DPA) was that it was a requirement for getting UN peacekeepers into Darfur. The International Crisis Group (ICG) became a cheerleader for this approach, declaring in two of its critically timed reports that AMIS had lost credibility and that replacing it with a UN mission was indeed the number one priority.[23] The understanding between Zoellick and GoS Vice President Ali Osman Taha was that the GoS would accept UN troops after the signing of a Darfur agreement, and the United States would then start to normalize relations with Sudan in support of the implementation of the CPA.[24]

Given the central objective of replacing AMIS with a UN force, the DPA was remarkably silent about this transition. This was because the United States had clearly communicated to the mediators that this element of the deal was to be negotiated separately between Washington and Khartoum. Neither the United States nor the UN wanted the details of a UN deployment to be determined in the Abuja talks, in which neither the United States nor the UN would have a determining voice. The combination of keeping this central political purpose of the DPA taboo and pushing the parties to make an agreement—any agreement—to achieve this goal became deeply problematic when the

DPA failed to achieve its other objective of bringing the main rebel groups inside the political fold. The AU Mediator, meanwhile, was implicitly consigned to the secondary role of finalizing a text, while the real deal was cut elsewhere. Both GoS and rebels knew this, and the mediation's efforts were adversely affected as a result.

The primary reason why the DPA failed was that the SLM faction headed by Abdel Wahid al Nur did not sign; he refused to sign because he had no confidence in the GoS, the CPA, or the international guarantees around the agreement. He lacked confidence because the true leader of the Darfuri rebels was John Garang, whose role as first vice president and co-architect of the CPA had made real the vision of a "New Sudan" as democratic, secular, and multiethnic. When Garang died in July 2005, the project of the "New Sudan" was mortally wounded. Additionally, the Darfuri file was held by Majzoub al Khalifa, a political rival to Ali Osman Taha. Abdel Wahid looked instead for international guarantees to protect his position and a source of ready cash to build a political base. When the United States was tired of Abdel Wahid's vacillation and chose instead to back his bitter rival Minni Minawi as leader of the rebels, Abdel Wahid lost faith in international guarantees. When the DPA final draft contained only US$30 million in immediate funds for compensation under his personal discretion, rather than the US$100 million that Abdel Wahid had demanded, his motivation for signing faded away. The DPA's power-sharing arrangements had been deliberately designed for Abdel Wahid, with his active participation, but he did not have the political courage to seize the opportunity, preferring the comfort of joining his expatriate advisors and criticizing from abroad.[25]

A final reason for the talks' failure was that by December 2005, Chad and Sudan were in a state of proxy war and JEM had enrolled as the principal proxy for Chad. When the Darfur Declaration of Principles was discussed in June 2005, JEM had led the way in formulating an agreed text. Six months later, JEM was uninterested in a peace agreement. Peace in Darfur required peace between Sudan and Chad, and in turn that required an internal settlement in Chad, which President Déby was not, at that time, ready to countenance.

Security Council Resolution 1706 and the Transition to UNAMID

The failure of Abdel Wahid to sign the DPA quickly consigned the agreement to failure. In the months immediately following the non-signature, there was political confusion and an increase in violence. At the United States' bidding, the non-signatory groups (JEM and SLA-Abdel Wahid) were removed from the CFC, rendering that institution worthless. Meanwhile, the GoS, sensing that the United States was not about to meet its promises to normalize relations with Khartoum and to punish the non-signatory rebel groups, backed off from its private commitments to allow the UN into Darfur. This backtracking was related to a power struggle between Ali Osman Taha and the GoS chief negotiator, Majzoub al Khalifa, who argued that Ali Osman had conceded too much in the Naivasha talks with the SPLM. Majzoub won. In August 2006, Zoellick left the State Department for a job in the private sector.

In frustration, the UN abandoned negotiating a mission with Khartoum and, at US prompting, decided to try to impose one. Resolution 1706 of 31 August 2006 decided to expand UNMIS into Darfur, with an additional 17,300 troops and 3,300 police, plus up to sixteen formed police units, under Chapter VII authority. The resolution "invites the consent" of the GoS. President Bashir called the UN's bluff: He rejected the resolution outright. This put the UN in a quandary, as it was not prepared to escalate the confrontation and authorize an invasion. Instead, a compromise was hatched in November with the idea of a hybrid force, under UN command, reporting to both the UN and the AU, with a principally "African character." Thus was born UNAMID, with a transition from AMIS phased in over twelve months of a gradually upgraded support package from the UN.

In parallel, the UN and AU sought to conclude the deal that had evaded the AU in Abuja. Two special envoys, Jan Eliasson on behalf of the UN and Salim Ahmed Salim on behalf of the AU, spent eight months chasing the Darfuri rebels to try to make them constitute a joint negotiating team and come to the table. Modest progress was made with the rebels at a meeting in Arusha, Tanzania, in August 2007, but the heralded peace conference in Sirte, Libya, in October–November came to nothing, due to disagreements among the rebels. As a result, when AMIS formally handed over to UNAMID on 31 December 2007, there was no operative peace agreement in Darfur: UNAMID was deploying in an as-yet-unresolved war.

UNAMID

The UN–AU hybrid operation in Darfur (UNAMID) was mandated by UN Security Council Resolution 1769 of 31 July 2007, with a strength totaling more than 26,000 international troops, and police officers plus civilian staff. The support infrastructure necessary to sustain this enormous mission in a region of Africa a thousand miles from the nearest port added to the cost.

These huge numbers were derived from competing operational concepts for the mission. The AMIS numbers had been based on an operations map for the military observers, which was amended on an ad hoc basis as additional observers and protection forces became available. During the final round of the Abuja talks, the security track began with a conventional approach to a cease-fire based on three stages: disengagement of forces, withdrawal to identified areas, and limited disarmament.[26] This structure was painstakingly negotiated and agreed to, and remained the basic framework for the security chapter of the agreement. However, once the structure had been accepted, the talks stalled, and a new approach was adopted, based on recognizing the multiplicity of armed groups and the need to obtain the cooperation of each one if any security arrangements were to hold.[27] Rather than pursuing coercive disarmament, such an approach would have focused on addressing the reasons for the establishment of militia, and pursuing a gradual process of restricting the movement of militia and their use and ownership of heavy weapons, achieving the formation of regulated "home guards," and finally culminating with voluntary disarmament. One precondition for such an approach to succeed was political consensus and the active collaboration of traditional authorities. Over the final weeks in Abuja, the security element of the talks entered a problem-solving phase, identifying the range of specific issues that needed to be addressed, such as establishing law and order in camps for internally displaced persons (IDPs), protecting the perimeters of those camps, restricting the operations of paramilitaries and tribally based militia, ensuring open roads for humanitarian supplies and commercial trade, and drawing up workable models for controlling arms held by militias.

The new approach, however, could not be brought to fruition because of the deadline of 25 April imposed by the UN Security Council. As a result, the security arrangements chapter of the DPA is very long, a fusion of different concepts, with complicated and ambiguous detail, but nonetheless agreed in almost every detail by the GoS and each of the three rebel movements.[28] The ever-expanded text also resulted in an extremely long list of tasks that the peace support operation was expected to undertake. During the final month of the talks, the AMIS Force Commander, Gen. Collins Ihikere, tabulated these tasks and estimated a force size required, amounting to approximately 21,000 soldiers and police officers. Although Ihikere's figure was based upon the assumption that the force would be implementing the DPA, and the DPA was soon shown to be a dead letter, the number retained a life of its own and was faithfully reproduced in Resolution 1706.

Two other alternative concepts of operation existed. One was peace enforcement: physical protection of the at-risk populations and forcible disarmament of the Janjaweed. This was the preferred approach of ICG, which condemned the DPA for lacking immediate and verifiable mechanisms for disarming the Janjaweed. Noting that the GoS had promised and failed to disarm the Janjaweed on five occasions, ICG leveled the criticism that "the DPA requires the parties to disarm themselves, a task usually assigned to the peacekeeping mission."[29] ICG campaigned for NATO forces, including the French troops stationed in Chad, to move into Darfur, if necessary by force.[30] Like-minded US political leaders called for a no-fly zone over Darfur and, if necessary, ground forces.[31]

A second, contrasting approach was emerging within the Abuja security negotiations during their final weeks. This was based on the problem-solving approach, and proposed using an international force to facilitate the stabilization of Darfur by working with all of the armed groups within a consensual community-based security framework. This approach would have required a much smaller international force and a greater focus on civil affairs officers. However, the international political demand for a very large force would not have been met. In 2006, it was simply impossible to convince US or European diplomats that the 7,000-strong AMIS contingent should be replaced with a smaller force with a different concept of operations. The world was demanding a big force, and the UN was obliged to provide one.

Following the rejection of Resolution 1706 and its 21,000-strong UN force, the UN Security Council was obliged to increase the numbers for the proposed UNAMID. Resolution 1769 provides for 26,000 soldiers and police officers. This vast size of UNAMID meant that, for most of the first two years of its existence, the primary focus of UNAMID was on its own deployment levels. The first item on most of the Joint Special Representative's (JSR) reports to the Security Council was on the force level achieved.

Meanwhile, incident data indicated slowly declining levels of lethal violence.[32] As noted earlier with respect to AMIS in 2004–2005, it is difficult to attribute this decline to a single cause. It was, however, a point of some controversy. When the JSR, Rodolphe Adada, presented data to the Security Council on 27 April 2009 that indicated relatively low levels of lethal violence, and remarked that Darfur at that time represented a "low intensity conflict," he sparked a political storm.[33] Unfortunately, DPKO staff in headquarters had been preparing the SG's reports to the Council based on raw data from UNAMID incident reports, without knowing or without acknowledging that additional investigations had found that some of the figures contained therein were unreliable or inflated.[34] They therefore had before them one set of figures, including, for example, a report of a series of incidents in which 220 people were reported killed.[35] Then, JSR Adada authoritatively provided a different and lower set of figures, and called into question the position expressed by the US Permanent Representative to the UN, Susan Rice, that there was "ongoing genocide" in Darfur.[36] Shortly afterward, Adada's contract was renewed for just six months and, taking this as a vote of no confidence, he resigned. The AU Commission was not happy with this turn of events but, overwhelmed and distracted with other demands, did not rush to protect him.

In principle, both JSR Adada and his successor, Professor Ibrahim Gambari, could have used the dual reporting structure to carve out autonomy. Neither of them chose to play the AU and the UN against each other, preferring instead to seek consensus among their masters. However, DPKO found the experience of a hybrid operation unsatisfactory, as it involved novel administrative practices and interfered with established control procedures. The UN and AU frustrations over UNAMID were minor, however, compared with the problems they faced over the supposedly joint mediation process.

The Joint AU–UN Mediation and the Doha Process

When the joint UN–AU mediation efforts resumed in 2008, the context had changed again. In February, Chadian rebels extensively backed by Sudanese intelligence mounted an assault on N'Djaména that came extremely close to overrunning the Presidential Palace. France was ready to fly President Déby into exile, and it was only when he chose to stand and fight, using JEM forces as integral to his defense, while the rebels fatally dithered over delivering the knockout blow, that French troops intervened and helped to repel the attack. Three months later, a reciprocal strike across the desert from Chad by JEM forces reached the Nile bridges in Khartoum, where they were halted by Sudanese security forces. These battles signaled an interstate war between Sudan and Chad, with Libya allied with Chad, and JEM and the Chadian rebel coalition acting as proxies.

Another dimension to the Chadian crisis was the deployment of a European force in Chad and Central African Republic (EUFOR Chad/CAR), specifically in the regions bordering Sudan, that had the intention of transitioning to a UN Mission for CAR and Chad (MINURCAT). The stated aim was to prevent destabilization from Sudan, but Déby's hope that this would prove a defense pact with European forces was shattered. France, whose long-standing Operation Épervier was such a pact, which provided most of the forces for EUFOR but kept them under different commands from its own Épervier troops, took the view that Déby needed to broaden the base of his government and negotiate, rather than fight, his way out of trouble. Having fixed the elections and disposed of his most redoubtable internal opponents, Déby proceeded to make the necessary domestic deals.

The former foreign minister of Burkina Faso, Djibril Yipènè Bassolé, was appointed as JCM for Darfur in August 2008, reporting theoretically to both the UN Secretary General and the AU Commission Chairperson, with his main office in the UNAMID compound in al Fashir, Darfur. A month later, the Emir of Qatar offered to host peace talks. The prospect of a wealthy and generous host was attractive to the JCM, who was very rarely seen in Darfur. Qatar had leverage with the GoS, both because it was an occasional discreet financial donor, and also because it had played a role in trying to unite the Sudanese Islamic movement when that movement split in 1999–2000. Qatar also had links to JEM and its Islamist sponsors, reflected in the editorial line taken by Al Jazeera's Arabic service on Darfur. However, the choice of Doha set off a rivalry with the Libyan leader, Colonel Muammar Qaddafi, who felt that the Qataris were encroaching into his backyard and were promoting their own agenda, including their brand of Islamism, in North Africa.

Bassolé's first approach to making peace was to focus on JEM, as the principal fighting force and the one enjoying sponsorship from N'Djaména and Tripoli.[37] He supposed that, if he could cut a deal between the GoS and JEM, based on a hard calculus of power, then the rest of the rebel groups would have no option but to follow. It was a hard-headed and opportunistic approach that had not been tried since the very earliest days of the conflict. JEM insisted that it be the sole representative of the rebels in the peace talks, and signed a preliminary agreement on Good-Will and Confidence Building in February 2009, but then withdrew from the talks the following month, following the ICC confirmation of the arrest warrant against President Bashir and the GoS's subsequent expulsion of humanitarian agencies from Darfur.

One year later, the deal was made, though by Déby, not Bassolé. The Chadian leader knew that he was still vulnerable to being overthrown by rebels based in Sudan, and that the best option for both him and his estranged old friend, President Bashir, was a return to their erstwhile security pact. Déby had two alternatives for JEM: to expel them wholesale or to set in motion a peace process that could legitimize JEM's presence in Chad, though not any military activities across the border. Déby chose the latter. The Chadian foreign minister visited Khartoum in December 2009, and on 15 January 2010, the Sudanese Presidential Advisor Ghazi Salah el Din flew to N'Djaména to sign an accord on normalizing relations. Part of this deal was a framework agreement between GoS and JEM, which the Chadian leader presented to Ghazi Salah el Din and forced on JEM, before summoning JCM Bassolé to N'Djaména to witness it. The two countries and the mediator then took the agreement to Doha for a signing ceremony, allowing the Qataris to claim the glory for the deal hatched entirely in N'Djaména.

Déby followed this up by refusing entry to Chad to the JEM leader Khalil Ibrahim, who was compelled to fly to Tripoli instead. Libya was one weak link in the chain: Colonel Qaddafi decided not to cooperate. His reasons may have included annoyance at being excluded from the deal and a fear of being overshadowed by a growing Qatari role in the region. A second weak link was that the deal ignored all the other Darfuri rebel groups.

As would be expected with such a bargain, Article 2 of the framework agreement was a general amnesty for JEM. Bassolé signed as witness to this, contravening the UN policy of not endorsing such amnesties, and was reprimanded by the Secretary General for having failed to specify that the UN could not support this particular provision. Although in theory the AU upheld the same principle, the Commission was less attentive to the actions of its mediator, and only wrote in September 2010 to upbraid the JCM for his failure to report. Indeed, by 2010, Bassolé's reluctance to fully carry out the explicit instructions in his terms of reference to report equally to both the UN and the AU had become his modus operandi. He repeatedly ignored various instructions from Addis Ababa, including a request by the AU PSC to appear in person to provide a briefing. Nor was Bassolé forthcoming in his dealings with the AU High Level Implementation Panel (AUHIP), as he viewed the Panel's engagement in Darfur not as facilitating a resolution to the crisis but as an encroachment on his portfolio.

The most tangible outcome of the Sudan–Chad talks was a border security pact between the two countries, which involved joint operations along their common border. This involved no third party, only military officers from the two armies jointly monitoring and taking joint enforcement actions. As soon as this was implemented, Déby announced his intent to wind down MINURCAT. From March 2010 to the time of writing, the bilateral security arrangement has been operational.

During 2008 and 2009, in support of the Doha process, the United States tried to unite the fragments of the SLA and sundry other Darfuri rebels at a series of meetings in Tripoli. The location of the meetings was also designed to give an opportunity for Colonel Qaddafi to support the process. This had limited success due to the continual fragmentation and egotism of the various rebel leaders, notably Abdel Wahid. However, the financial and diplomatic inducements to joining the peace talks did have the effect of helping various groups coalesce around the Doha process. It became an exercise in constituting a sufficiently credible and cohesive rebel-negotiating partner to sit opposite the GoS in the talks, to create at least the semblance of formal negotiations. In early 2010, the Liberation and Justice Movement (LJM) was formed through this process, headed appropriately enough by a former senior UN staff member, Dr Tijani Sese Ateem.

The third approach adopted by JCM Bassolé and his team of UN advisors might be called the "blueprint for peace." The rationale for this was that the rebels were too fragmented and disorganized to be able to negotiate seriously, and that this provided the GoS with good pretext for doing nothing except sending a delegate to the talks, who could occupy his chair and repeat that he was there in good faith but that there was no one with whom he could negotiate. This was indeed the approach utilized to good effect by the GoS chief negotiator, Hassan Amin Omar. Additionally, it was questionable whether the rebels represented a significant constituency in Darfur; others, including civil society groups, tribal leaders, and representatives of IDPs, could claim to have greater clout among Darfurians. As a result, the mediation support team developed the plan of drawing up a text that enjoyed some credibility, based upon expert input and widespread consultation, including with civil society, which groups could sign on to as and when they decided to do so. According to this approach, the active engagement of civil society would stabilize the process. The key signature needed was that of the GoS: Once the GoS signed a credible blueprint for peace, it would be the basis for holding the GoS to the benchmarks contained therein, and cajoling the rebels to sign up one by one.

It is not clear if JCM Bassolé actually believed in this approach. He is reported to have privately dismissed the importance of civil society, and he never developed a strategy that would provide nonbelligerent actors anything other than walk-on parts. The cogent exponents of this approach were some senior UN staff members in private conversation with the author. Perhaps, because of the lack of internal consensus between the mediator and his support team, the process of achieving a document with sufficient credibility was neither straightforward nor transparent. The rebels were fractious and paid little attention to the content of the agreement. The GoS was obstreperous even when no obvious interest was served by obstruction. There were two exercises in bringing civil society representatives, IDP leaders, and tribal leaders to Doha to express their views, in November 2009 and July 2010, but on neither occasion were they able to examine or provide detailed input into the draft document itself. Many of the Sudanese negotiators who remained in Doha appeared to be motivated by the generous per diems and the lavish gifts provided by their Qatari hosts on each Muslim holiday. Most of the drafting was done behind closed doors by members of the Joint Mediation Support Team. The JCM complained that his position as sole mediator was undermined by the existence of the AUPD and by the efforts of the US Special Envoy General Scott Gration, but he made no efforts to convince these key actors that he had a viable mediation strategy, and still less to make them partners in his effort.

Much of the text of the Doha Document for Peace in Darfur (DDPD) is cut-and-paste from the Abuja DPA, redrafted to address some of the evident shortcomings of that agreement such as the compensation fund and the need for justice. The text itself is remarkable insofar as large parts of it bear little relation to the changed realities of Darfur. The power-sharing provisions of the DPA made sense only insofar as the DPA was a buttress to the CPA, with the key demands of the rebels for democratization already incorporated into the CPA. Returning to these same issues five years later, after the national elections and the secession of South Sudan, would require a major reconsideration, which was not attempted. This text descends to absurdity when it comes to the security arrangements chapter, which outlines the three-stage process of disengagement, withdrawal of forces, and limited disarmament. This was already recognized as inappropriate in 2006, and was still more so in 2011 when the sole signatory to the DDPD, the LJM, had just a few fighters on the ground and no territory under its control, and the GoS forces were widely spread throughout Darfur and actively involved in counterinsurgency against groups that had not signed the DDPD or any other deal.

The significance of the DDPD does not lie in the text. Much as the DPA was a supposed gateway for a UN mission, the DDPD is a mechanism for Qatari funds to be channeled to Darfur, partly through the Darfur Regional Administration and partly through a new development bank. These funds incentivize both government and rebels. Having taken the position of head of the Darfur Regional Authority, Tijani Sese sees his task as procuring funds, disbursing them, and pursuing rehabilitation and development activities with the aim of providing a degree of social and economic normality to Darfur, of a kind that Darfuris have not seen for decades. The Document also provides a framework against which the GoS performance can be judged, should the United States decide that it needs a mechanism to justify a decision to normalize relations with Sudan based on the GoS having behaved well in Darfur.

The Politics of Justice

The Darfur war marked an important change in international engagement in African conflict, insofar as the issue of justice for crimes committed rose quickly to the top of the international agenda. The AU recognized this early. In his speech at the inaugural meeting of the AU PSC in May 2004, President Konaré said, "We need to know the truth about what transpired and what is happening in this region of The Sudan."[38] The African Commission for Human and People's Rights sent a fact-finding mission to Darfur in July. It recommended urgent action to protect IDPs, even while it was completing its formal report. Meanwhile, in August, Chairperson Konaré sent an envoy to the Sudanese Minister of Foreign Affairs, Mustafa Ismail, with a message that the AU was considering a high-level investigation into the Darfur conflict, to deal with issues of peace and peacemaking, democratization, and (especially) justice. The envoy passed the verbal message that such an exercise would be modeled on the OAU's International Panel of Eminent Personalities for Rwanda, and this would allow the AU to retain control of the justice agenda, keeping it within a wider political framework that the GoS would understand. The offer was rebuffed: President Bashir instructed his foreign minister to reply that any issues of accountability for crimes committed would be dealt with domestically. Within weeks, the UN Security Council passed Resolution 1564 that set up the International Commission of Inquiry into Darfur (ICID).[39] Headed by Antonio Cassesse, the ICID reported in January 2005 and recommended that the crimes in Darfur be referred to the ICC. The UN Security Council acted on this recommendation and passed Resolution 1593 on 31 March 2005.

The matter of Darfur was under ICC investigation while the Abuja talks were ongoing. The rebels raised the question of justice and the chief mediator responded that, because it was being dealt with elsewhere, there was no need to raise the issue in the peace talks. This was understandable but shortsighted.[40] A careful exploration of the demand for justice within the peace negotiations could have forestalled some of the problems that were later to arise over the ICC arrest warrants.

The ICC's first two arrest warrants, issued on 27 April 2007, were for a serving minister, Ahmed Haroun, and a militia leader, Ali Kushayb. The cases were well documented and few disagreed that the two men had a case to answer. At this stage, the ICC Prosecutor Luis Moreno Ocampo was pursuing a cautious approach, eager to give the GoS any opportunity to cooperate, and conscious of the context of peace talks. Subsequently, Moreno Ocampo decided that he had been overcautious, and that he would be better served by being much more ambitious. He decided to demand an arrest warrant for President Bashir on charges including genocide, based on the argument that the head of state had hatched a genocidal plan long before the conflict erupted—that Stage one was the military offensives of 2003–2004 and Stage two was the gradual extermination of Fur, Masalit, and Zaghawa populations in IDP camps, through means including starvation and rape. The audacity of his charges and the shaky nature of the evidence and argument in support of them caused much discontent within the ICC. Nonetheless, Moreno Ocampo demanded the arrest warrant in July 2008, and the Court confirmed the warrant in March 2009.[41]

The arrest warrant was hugely controversial, both because of the substance of the charges and because of the feared impacts on peacemaking (in Darfur and between northern and southern Sudan) and on humanitarian operations in Darfur. The AU was also concerned about the implications of a head of state being designated a fugitive from international justice, and the sovereignty issues that this entailed. The AU promptly convened a meeting of the PSC that affirmed its opposition to impunity, expressed its concern that the pursuit of peace and reconciliation should not be jeopardized by an attempt to arrest and prosecute the Sudanese president, and called on the Security Council to use Article 16 of the Rome Statute to defer the arrest warrant for one year.[42] The PSC also resolved to establish "an independent High-Level Panel made up of distinguished Africans of high integrity, to examine the situation in depth and submit recommendations to Council on how best the issues of accountability and combating impunity, on the one hand, and reconciliation and healing, on the other, could be effectively and comprehensively addressed."[43]

The GoS explored the possibility of persuading a friendly country to bring a draft resolution based on Article 16 to the UN Security Council, but when it became clear that it would not pass—the United States, France, and Britain would lobby against it—it dropped the plan. However, one consequence of the arrest warrant, not immediately apparent, was that it made the AU into the indispensable facilitator of negotiations involving the GoS. The UN Secretary General, on advice from the legal office of the UN, deemed that it was inappropriate for any UN official to do business with an individual wanted by the ICC, except on essential business. Given that the SRSG for Sudan and head of UNMIS had essential business to transact with the president, further advice was given that he should not be photographed smiling with Omar al Bashir. Similar prohibitions or restrictions were applied to European and American diplomats, with the result that President Jimmy Carter became the only American to meet with or call President Bashir. Ironically, the greatest triumph of the Darfur advocacy movement in the United States—the criminalization of the president of Sudan—meant that the United States and UN were debarred from any practical engagement with the Sudanese leader, leaving the field open to the AU.

The AUPD

While the initial stimulus for establishing the AUPD was concern over how Africa should handle its principled commitment to accountability for grave crimes alongside its disquiet over the ICC arrest warrant, the Panel rapidly grew into something else. Although the PSC called for the AUPD in July 2008, the Panel did not become functional until the former South African President Thabo Mbeki was appointed as its chair in March 2009, and he brought on two former heads of state, Abdulsalami Abbubakar (Nigeria) and Pierre Buyoya (Burundi), as fellow members of the Panel.

Mbeki's fundamental reasoning was revealed in informal discussions with Darfuri leaders. He argued that the African National Congress (ANC) had faced a strategic dilemma when the UN General Assembly declared that Apartheid was a crime against humanity. Many ANC cadres concluded that the only place for the leaders of Apartheid South Africa was in the dock. However, members of the ANC leadership, including Mbeki, made the counterargument that the movement had a strategic objective—a democratic nonracial South Africa—that could not be compromised, and that all other goals, including justice for those responsible for crimes, should be negotiable within that ultimate goal. Consequently, the ANC decided to modulate its commitment to justice, creating a Truth and Reconciliation Commission as a compromise in order better to achieve its ultimate goal. Similarly, for Darfur, Mbeki did not see the dilemma as "peace versus justice" but rather, where peace and justice should fit within an overall democratic political project. His primary frustration with Darfur's political leaders was that they were poor at articulating an ultimate goal, and repeatedly confused tactical goals (a UN force, ICC prosecutions) with strategic ones.

The AUPD adopted an innovative method: It traveled to Darfur and, over a period of approximately forty days, held a series of public hearings in the major towns, in IDP camps, and in rebel-held areas. It consulted a wide range of Darfuris. What it heard from them was a plea for an integrated approach that combined peace, justice, and reconciliation, and a unanimous demand that each group represent themselves in the negotiations toward a final political settlement. The AUPD returned to Darfur a final time to present its recommendations to the same groups it had earlier consulted, and seek their opinions. It was a remarkable exercise in public consultation, the first of its kind in Darfur.

The AUPD report[44] echoed the findings of these consultations. It defined the conflict as "the Sudanese conflict in Darfur," making it clear that the source of the problem lay in the inequitable practices of governance in Khartoum, inherited from the colonial era and essentially unchanged during fifty years of independence. It recommended an inclusive negotiating process involving nonbelligerents as well as belligerents, leading to a putative Global Political Agreement that would integrate the issues of peace, justice, reconciliation, development, and Darfur's position within the Sudanese nation. It emphasized that this process should be expedited so that it could happen in advance of the 2010 general elections, in order to provide the best chance for democratizing the Sudanese state in advance of the end of the CPA Interim Period and the referendum on self-determination in southern Sudan.

The spirit of the AUPD report was to place the issue of justice within a wider context, both emphasizing that criminal justice was only part of a larger agenda of law and order and social justice, and also making specific decisions on justice subordinate to a democratic and consensual decision-making process. If the GoS expected the AUPD to recommend against the ICC, it was disappointed. Rather, the logic of the Report was that if the Sudanese people made a sovereign decision to invite the ICC to prosecute the crimes committed in Darfur, this was its right. However, imposing such a decision would make it impossible to be carried out in an effective manner. However, rather than leaving the justice issue to be dealt with by such a democratic process, not yet initiated, the AUPD report made an interim proposal for establishing hybrid courts, part national Sudanese and part African, to pursue cases in Darfur. This recommendation was mainly a tactical political move to signal a commitment to justice. In the event, the GoS did its best to block it and the AU did not pursue it energetically, and the issue of justice was later dealt with in a chapter within the DDPD.

The AUPD report was adopted by the AU PSC, meeting at the level of heads of state, in October 2009. It was a set of recommendations primarily to the JCM, with steps also that the GoS was expected to undertake unilaterally. Unsurprisingly, the GoS dragged its feet on even the simplest measures to promote justice, while the army and security forces ignored civilian policy directives. The JCM also studiously ignored the recommendations, preferring (at that time) to pursue his approach of focusing exclusively on JEM. Subsequently, he organized two civil society consultations in Doha, an idea that appeared to be drawn from the AUPD public meetings but which fell well short of the AUPD recommendation for all-stakeholder negotiations. At its October 2009 meeting, the PSC transformed the AUPD into the AUHIP, which was mandated both to implement its recommendations for Darfur and also to engage with a wide range of Sudanese issues including the national elections, the completion of the CPA, and preparation for the possibility that the January 2011 referendum in southern Sudan would lead to secession.

Outcomes

Deferring to the JCM's promise that his strategy for Darfur would yield quick results, the AUHIP decided not to push for the immediate implementation of its Darfur recommendations. However, the discord between the AUPD vision and the JCM's approach was such that the AU was obliged to institute the Sudan Consultative Forum (SCF), at which the UN and AU could meet at a high level to coordinate their approaches. The initial meeting of the SCF was held in Addis Ababa in April 2010, cochaired by the Under Secretary General for Peacekeeping Operations Alain Le Roy and the AU Commissioner for Peace and Security Ramtane Lamamra. President Mbeki of the AUHIP was present, as was JCM Bassolé, the SRSG for Sudan Haile Menkerios, the JSR for Darfur Ibrahim Gambari, and a host of special envoys and senior representatives. In this meeting, the AU introduced the concept of the "Darfur Political Process" to distinguish the all-stakeholder round table envisaged by the AUPD from the ceasefire-focused "Darfur Peace Process" pursued by the JCM, with the aim of making the two complementary. This distinction was agreed to and a plan of action was adopted by the UN and AU. The JCM pleaded for more time, and a similar routine was followed at subsequent meetings of the SCF, concluding in November 2010 when the JCM's timetable for winding down the Doha talks by December was adopted, with a proposed immediate transition to the Darfur Political Process.

The Doha talks did not, however, conclude according to the schedule, and the Darfur Political Process was postponed indefinitely. Senior officials in the UN and AU as well as the US Special Envoy expressed frustration that JCM Bassolé was neither consulting them nor reporting to them, and that the Doha process was being strung out without a clear end in sight. The JCM had practiced his own inverted version of "deadline diplomacy," holding others at bay with a rolling deadline for completion that was never met. By the time the Doha Document was finalized in May 2011, and the GoS and LJM signed a protocol on 14 July committing themselves to abide by it, the political dynamics had fundamentally changed both with the southern Sudanese vote for separation, and with South Sudan's emergence as the newest sponsor of the Darfuri rebels. There were also new political dynamics in northern Sudan, with the country needing to rediscover its identity and to reenergize its commitment to democracy after the loss of the South. Darfur now required a peace process recognizing these new realities.

While the Doha Document established a blueprint for rehabilitating Darfur with donor funds in a way that was probably accepted by most Darfuris as reasonable given the circumstances, the Doha process between 2008 and 2011 had the unfortunate consequence of marginalizing Darfuris in Sudanese national discourse at precisely the time when the most momentous national decisions were being taken. The 2010 elections were held when Darfur was not settled, giving the ruling National Congress Party almost a clean sweep of the seats. The possibility of Darfuris contributing to a national debate on the identity of Sudan, either before the southern referendum or afterward, was much reduced by Doha's focus on parochial Darfuri issues. And the first target of the JCM's attention, JEM, eluded any peace process, relocating first to Libya and then, after the collapse of the Qaddafi government, to South Sudan, from where it has continued its fight against Khartoum, in both Darfur and neighboring Kordofan.

Conclusions

The UN and AU engagement with the Darfur conflict illustrates how extreme complexity confounded a series of attempts to resolve the conflict, protect civilians, and promote the goals of democracy and justice. Under the pressure of the intrinsic difficulty of the conflict, the objections to international action repeatedly raised by the GoS, and the wreckage of earlier failed efforts that lay strewn across the obvious paths to take, the UN and AU crafted a number of ad hoc innovations that held out promise. Most of these, however, were designed and implemented in a rushed manner without a strategic plan. Moreover, the political relationships between the UN and AU, and between these and key governments such as the US and Qatar and other international institutions such as the ICC, themselves became an important factor in how the conflict was managed and in its ultimate outcome. A persuasive case can be made that the international response not only complicated but prolonged the conflict.

There was a virtue to the AU's low level of institutionalization. When visiting Darfur, the AU Commission Chairperson President Konaré, slipped away from his security detail and spent the night in a camp for displaced people, talking to the people who had congregated there. After his return from his visit to the camps, he requested an audience with President Bashir where he confronted him about the abominable situation he witnessed. Subsequently, he told the African leaders assembled to inaugurate the PSC that, with regard to Darfur: "We need urgent, exceptional activities, more than what we have done so far."[45] General Okwoko, the first AMIS Force Commander, was also ready to stretch his mandate, relying more on moral authority than on rules. The AUPD proposed an innovative political process, which was based on the recommendations of Darfuri people rather than any recognized models. Insofar as there is an "African" model of conflict resolution in Darfur, it is adapting to the specifics of circumstances. The UN response, by contrast, was highly constrained or even determined by political and institutional factors emanating from New York and Washington, DC. It brought far more resources, capacity, and operational experience to bear, as well as political weight.

The activities of the AU and UN were also strongly influenced by the active role played by the United States. During the early days of the crisis, the US Agency for International Development (USAID) was proactive in providing assistance and pushing the State Department to support peace talks, actions which undoubtedly saved many lives. Subsequently, the US role was unusual in that it was prominently influenced by a vocal domestic constituency. During the Abuja peace talks, the parallel negotiations between Khartoum and Washington helped set the pace and agenda of the negotiations, but ultimately did not help the mediator. During the Doha talks, the at best half-hearted endorsement of the US Special Envoy undermined the JCM. The United States was instrumental in making and unmaking AMIS and in the troubled transition to UNAMID. Throughout, the US role was both essential and problematic.

In dealing with Darfur, the UN and AU needed one another. Each institution has its strengths and its problems, some of them self-inflicted. Occasionally, the two have shown the utmost coordination, sometimes they have worked at cross purposes, and sometimes they have equally been unable to handle challenges, including managing some of their own senior officials. At several critical junctures, the AU was either sidelined or reduced to a supporting role. At some key moments, however, the UN and AU either worked out a division of responsibility or a joint approach. There is much to be learned from this experience, but as yet neither institution has shown an appetite for examining the record, analyzing what worked and did not work, and learning the lessons.

Notes

1. Julie Flint and Alex de Waal, *Darfur: A New History of a Long War* (London: Zed Books, 2008), pp. 88–91.
2. Roland Marchal, "The Unseen Regional Implications of the Crisis in Darfur," in *War in Darfur and the Search for Peace*, ed. Alex de Waal (Cambridge, MA: Harvard University Press, 2007).
3. In January 2004, the Chadian and Sudanese armies jointly pursued and killed an SLA leader of Chadian Masalit origin, Adam Bazooka. Flint and de Waal, *Darfur*, p. 129.
4. Dawit Toga, "The African Union Mediation and the Darfur Peace Talks," in *War in Darfur and the Search for Peace*, ed. Alex de Waal (Cambridge, MA: Harvard University Press, 2007).
5. Konaré stopped in Khartoum en route to Rwanda, where he was attending the tenth anniversary commemoration for the Rwanda genocide.
6. Paula Souverijn-Eisenberg, "Lessons Learned from the Joint Military Commission," UNDPKO Peacekeeping Best Practices Section, August 2005.
7. Comprehensive Peace Agreement, Annexure I: Permanent Ceasefire and Security Arrangements Implementation Modalities and Appendices, 31 December 2004, para. 15.1, CPA, 106.
8. Personal communication, Abuja, March 2006.

9. Brian Steidle, *The Devil Came on Horseback: Bearing Witness to the Genocide in Darfur* (New York: Public Affairs Publishers, 2008).
10. "Working Document on the Enhancement of the African Mission in Sudan," First Meeting of the Military Staff Committee of the Peace and Security Council, Addis Ababa, 18 October 2004, PSC/MSC(2)1.
11. African Union Peace and Security Council, 17th Meeting, 20 October 2004, Communiqué, PSC/PR/Comm. (XVII).
12. Flint and de Waal, *Darfur*, pp. 150–151.
13. This observation obliges us to be cautious in judging the efficacy of monitoring missions. For example, the UN's decision to withdraw its monitors from Syria in June 2012 may not have been based on a rigorous assessment of levels and patterns of lethal violence. See Bridget Conley-Zilkic, "Syria: What Would a Real Civilian Protection Agenda Include?" *Reinventing Peace*, 22 June 2012, http://sites.tufts.edu/reinventingpeace/2012/06/22/syria-what-would-a-real-civilian-protection-agenda-include/.
14. Alex de Waal and Sam Rosmarin, "Are Things Getting Worse in Darfur? There is No Simple Answer," *Making Sense of Darfur*, http://africanarguments.org/2007/06/20/are-things-getting-worse-in-darfur-there-is-no-simple-answer/.
15. Abdul Mohammed, "Don't Blame the AU," *The Guardian*, Comment is Free, 5 June 2007, http://www.guardian.co.uk/commentisfree/2007/jun/05/dontblametheau.
16. http://www.janpronk.nl/weblog/english/november-2006.html#b287.
17. Toga, *War in Darfur and the Search for Peace*.
18. The AU narrowly avoided a serious challenge to the legitimacy of its mediation role, which would have arisen had Sudan assumed the Chair of the organization as planned in July 2005. Sudan's turn had been scheduled a year earlier, in anticipation that the CPA would give President Bashir a new shine as the continent's newest peacemaker and democrat. The Darfur crisis intervened and in the run-up to that summit, African leaders decided discreetly to extend Nigeria's chairmanship for an extra six months, until the Khartoum summit of January 2006, hoping that the Darfur conflict would be settled by that time. During the Khartoum summit, the heads of state met in closed session for almost a whole day, pressing President Bashir to stand down his candidacy. He reluctantly did so in favor of the Congo Republic.
19. The AU consultancy rate for its specialists was a flat US$238 per day, to cover both fee and per diem, plus bed and breakfast and one return flight per session. Accommodation for the final round was in the desultory surroundings of the Chida International Hotel. In comparison to the natural beauty of Naivasha, the opulence of Doha and the attractions of Addis Ababa, there is no doubt that the final round of the Abuja talks, from November 2005 to May 2006 in the Chida Hotel, was the most unattractive and uncomfortable locus for a Sudanese peace effort. See also Thomas Kwasi Tieku, "How Perks for Delegates can Influence Peace Process Outcomes," Centre for International Governance Innovation Africa Initiative, Discussion paper no. 3, April 2012.
20. Laurie Nathan, "The Making and Unmaking of the Darfur Peace Agreement," in *War in Darfur and the Search for Peace*, ed. Alex de Waal (Cambridge, MA: Harvard University Press, 2007).
21. Nathan, ibid., p. 259.
22. *Sudan Tribune*, "Sudanese Parties Resume Direct Negotiations over Darfur Conflict," 11 April 2006.
23. International Crisis Group, "To Save Darfur," Africa Report No. 105, 17 March 2006, and "Getting the UN into Darfur," *Africa Briefing* No. 43 (12 October 2006).
24. Rebecca Hamilton, *Fighting for Darfur: Public Action and the Struggle to Stop Genocide* (New York: Palgrave Macmillan, 2011), pp. 77–82.

25. Alex de Waal, "Darfur's Deadline: The Final Days of the Abuja Peace Process," in *War in Darfur and the Search For Peace,* ed. Alex de Waal (Cambridge, MA: Harvard University Press, 2007), p. 283.
26. The question of disarming the Janjaweed in accordance with the requirements of Security Council Resolution 1556 was addressed simply by agreeing that it should be done, without attending to the problem of identifying who were the Janjaweed and how they might agree to be disarmed.
27. Mulugeta Gebrehiwot Berhe, "Analytical Study of Disarmament, Demobilization and Reintegration in Darfur, Sudan" (New York: Conflict Prevention and Peace Forum, March 2005).
28. de Waal, *War in Darfur and the Search For Peace.*
29. International Crisis Group, "Darfur's Fragile Peace Agreement," *Africa Briefing* No. 39 (20 June 2006): 5.
30. International Crisis Group, "To Save Darfur," op. cit.
31. Susan Rice, Antony Lake, and Donald Payne, "We Saved Europeans, Why Not Africans?" *Washington Post,* 2 October 2006.
32. Alex de Waal, Chad Hazlett, Christian Davenport, and Joshua Kennedy, "Evidence-Based Peacekeeping: Exploring the Epidemiology of Lethal Violence in Darfur," *Harvard Humanitarian Initiative,* March 2010.
33. Alex de Waal, "UNAMID and the Security Council: Evidence for Policy," *Making Sense of Darfur,* http://africanarguments.org/2009/04/29/unamid-and-the-security-council-evidence-for-policy/.
34. Report of the Secretary-General on the African Union-United Nations Hybrid Operation in Darfur, 14 April 2009, S/2009/201.
35. Ibid., para. 15.
36. United States Mission to the United Nations, "Statement by Ambassador Susan E. Rice, U.S. Permanent Representative, After Presentation of Credentials to the Secretary General, at the United Nations Stakeout," New York, 26 January 2009, http://paei.state.gov/usun.state.gov/usun/briefing/statements/2009/january/127019.htm.
37. There is little public documentation available for the Darfur peace process during 2009–2011. This account relies heavily on personal observation and internal memoranda.
38. Statement of the Chairperson of the Commission on the Occasion of the Solemn Launching of the African Union Peace and Security Council, Addis Ababa, 25 May 2004, p. 6.
39. UNSC Resolution 1564, 18 September 2004, para. 12.
40. Alex de Waal, "What Happened to Justice in the Darfur Peace Agreement?" *Making Sense of Darfur,* http://africanarguments.org/2008/06/25/what-happened-to-justice-in-the-darfur-peace-agreement/.
41. Initially the judges refused to confirm the charges of genocide, but reinstated them after an appeal by the Prosecutor.
42. African Union Peace and Security Council, 142nd meeting, 21 July 2008. http://www.sudantribune.com/AU-s-Peace-and-Security-Council,27982.
43. Ibid., para. 11(ii). In 2011, the PSC took the stand that it would not cooperate with an ICC arrest warrant against a head of state.
44. African Union High Level Panel on Darfur, *Darfur: The Quest for Peace, Justice and Reconciliation,* Addis Ababa, October 2009.
45. Statement of the Chairperson of the Commission on the Occasion of the Solemn Launching of the African Union Peace and Security Council, Addis Ababa, 25 May 2004, p. 6.

Chapter 13

South Sudan

Ann M. Fitz-Gerald

From Sudan's northern border with Libya and Eritrea to the southern border of the newly declared independent Republic of South Sudan, conflict has plagued the region since Sudan's independence in 1956. Since the end of the 1983 civil war between the north and south, a steady stream of third-party interventions and the acceptance of both countries that South Sudan should secede from its northern authority, led to the eventual signing of the 2005 Comprehensive Peace Agreement (CPA), which granted South Sudan the right to take the question of independence to the people. In a 2011 referendum, which was held exactly six years following the signing of the CPA, 98.3 percent of South Sudan's population voted for independence.

During the lead up to the signing of the CPA and thereafter, the United Nations (UN) has played a significant albeit less conventional role in Sudan, with its main role being support for the regional and continental-led interventions that have backed the peace process since 1993. However, unlike the experience of many of its former and existing missions, the UN's hope of bolstering its post–peace agreement role has been met with two key challenges. The first challenge was that, without having had a role in the peace process prior to the signing of the CPA, the UN lacked the same levels of credibility and ownership that continental actors had achieved between 1994 and 2005. The second challenge was the lack of acceptance of the organization by one of the parties to the conflict, both before and after the independence of the south. It therefore proved difficult for the UN to implement a peace process that it had not been instrumental to brokering.

This chapter provides an overview of the role of the UN and regional and continental actors in Sudan and South Sudan before and after the signing of the CPA. It argues that the lack of UN involvement in the earlier peace process, and Khartoum's unwillingness to accept the UN as a third-party intervener, precluded the organization from taking on a front-line leadership role consistent with a more traditional UN intervention. However, despite these challenges, the paper also argues that the UN Security Council (UNSC) played a critical role in propping up and "gap filling" in support of the continental leads

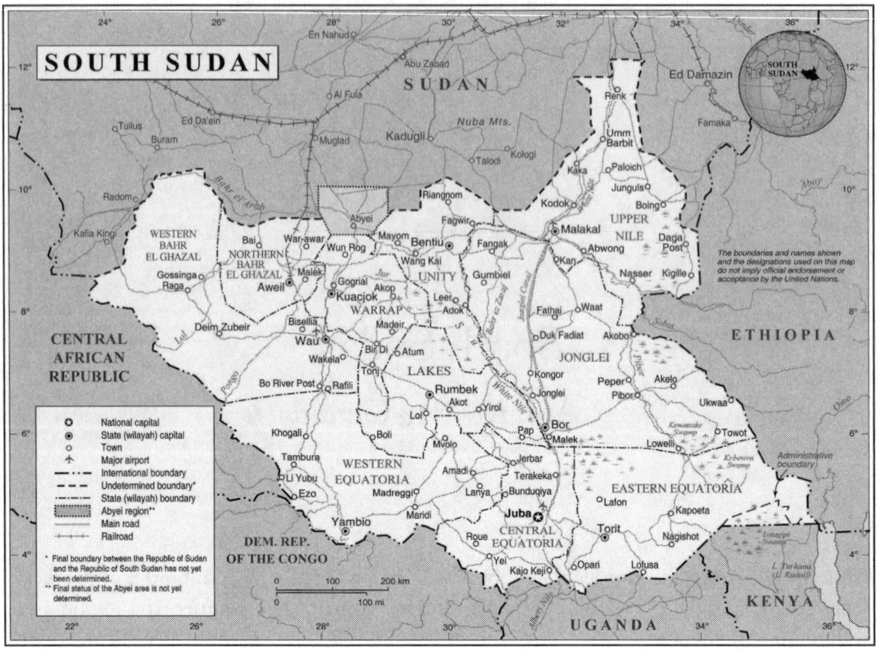

Source: Map No 4450 Rev 1, United Nations, Department of Field Support, Cartographic Section, October 2011

in both Sudan and the Darfur region. This support was felt mainly in terms of the ongoing provision of chronological and detailed records of a very fluid and fragmented peace process; the ability of the Security Council to keep the discussions on the table and provide international legal authority for some operational requirements; and appeals to both the parties to the conflict and the wider donor community, the latter of which was central for supporting financial and logistical requirements. Conclusions indicate that this type of ancillary support, which empowers regional and continental organizations, is a positive trend for future peace interventions.

Background: A Legacy of Distrust and Broken Promises

The troubles in present-day Sudan date back to the country's postindependence period. It was hoped that independence would bring the stability required to unify a country with a large northern population consisting predominantly of Arabic-speaking Muslims and sizeable Christian and Animist communities living in the southern region. However, following the rise and fall of many northern-led regimes between independence and the accession of Lieutenant-General Omar Hassan Ahmed Bashir's government in 1989, it became increasingly clear that the postindependence road would be long, difficult, and bloody. An appreciation of the historical legacies of distrust and broken promises is important for understanding the present-day impasses in the peace process.

Immediately following independence in 1956, the National Unionist Party (NUP) secured victory in the elections; it showed immediate signs of employing oppressive tactics against the southern region and developing economic policies.[1] Following a bloodless coup in 1958 by two senior Generals of the Sudan Armed Forces (SAF), the new leader, General Ibrahim Abbud, continued to prioritize the spread of Islamic law and the Arabic language in the south, with the north retaining control of all the key functions of the state.[2]

Unrest in Khartoum continued and violence between SAF and southern rebels groups further fueled this unrest. Between 1963 and 1964, the intelligentsia began to speak out against Khartoum's autocratic rule, which led to a large demonstration at the University of Khartoum in 1964 in which teachers, civil servants, and trade unionists all participated. This was followed by a general strike that spread throughout the country.[3] These wider levels of discontent also indicated that policies that extended beyond the treatment of the south were being used to judge Abbud's poor performance. With so many SAF forces in the south, the government could not impose order in the north and particularly around the capital city; this led to Abbud's resignation in favor of a transitional government.

Elections were held in 1965 in an effort to form a representative government but factional disputes continued to challenge the system and fighting continued between the SAF and the southern rebels. During this period, two political parties, the Sudan African National Union (SANU) and the Southern Front, also emerged, both of which represented the interests of the southern population. These parties came together and amalgamated into the SANU just before the 1968 elections, which resulted in no one political party winning a majority and increasing signs that the transitional leader, Muhammed Ahmed Mahjub, was strengthening his ties with the Arab world.[4] The resulting dissatisfaction gave rise to a coup in May 1969, led by Colonel Gafaad Nimeiri, whose regime dissolved parliament and outlawed all political parties.[5]

In response to Nimeri's oppressive rule, southern rebel groups united, combining the fighting units of the Anya Nya and developing a political wing of the resistance movement called the South Sudan Liberation Movement (SSLM) under the command of General Joseph Lagu, a former Captain in the SAF. By 1968, Lagu led the entire southern resistance movement.[6] The SSLM maintained a dialogue with the government on proposals for regional autonomy and an end to hostilities. Lagu also continued efforts to bring about a degree of autonomy for the southern region in the form of a South Sudan autonomous region with a separate legislature and executive body, with provisions for the military wing of the SSLM (the Anya Nya soldiers) to be integrated into both the SAF and the Police.[7] These efforts were underwritten by the 1972 Addis Ababa Agreement signed by Nimieri and Lagu, which, in addition to regional autonomy and the integration of the security forces, brought a halt to the increasingly bitter civil war and established terms for economic assistance from the north to the impoverished and undeveloped south.[8]

However, the Agreement only offered a temporary respite and the north continued to act derisively. By 1980, Muslim fundamentalism had grown and the Muslim Brotherhood had taken roots in the military, the civil service, and the schools.[9] Nimieri continued to act dictatorially, and repeatedly dissolved the parliament and the legislature of the southern region. In 1983, the country descended into civil war once again, with disenchanted southern soldiers taking up arms under the command of Colonel John Garang di Mabior[10] to form the Sudan Peoples' Liberation Army (SPLA). Nimeiri further violated the terms of the Addis Ababa Agreement by dividing the southern region into three provinces and changing the legal codes to Islamic law and the Shari'ah.[11] In response to the SPLA's resistance toward these efforts, Nimeiri deployed large numbers of the SAF to the south. The deployment of troops cut off food-distribution lines, which, during a period of intense drought across the arid lands, caused widespread famine. This only increased the marginalization of southern communities, aggravated existing grievances, and intensified the 1983 post–Addis Ababa Agreement conflict.

The Role of the Inter-Governmental Authority on Development

The 1984–1985 famine in the region prompted the creation of the Horn of Africa's first embryonic regional economic community, the Intergovernmental Authority on Disaster and Drought (IGADD), in 1986. IGADD's founding members were Kenya, Ethiopia, Uganda, Djbouti, Sudan, and Somalia. While IGADD's formation represented a significant development for the region, it came at a time of conflict in Somalia and Sudan, and tension between Ethiopia and what would later become Eritrea. IGADD was thus created in an atmosphere of difficult relations across its membership. These internal strains have remained a factor throughout its efforts to work toward a peaceful resolution to the Sudan conflict.

In 1985, Nimeiri was overthrown by a bloodless coup. The military oversaw multiparty elections in 1986, but Khartoum was left with a less-than-stable system of government. This led to a further coup in 1989, which left power in the hands of Lieutenant General Omar Bashir's Revolutionary Command Council for National Salvation. Fighting in the south continued to degrade the economy and the arable land. The impact of both would require years of recovery. The SPLA took control of the major towns in the south, to which Bashir responded by deploying the Arab militia (from northern Darfur) to target the Dinka-dominated SPLA groups. Large proportions of the population fled villages and towns, seeking sanctuary in both northern towns and neighboring Ethiopia.

In parallel to the fighting in Sudan, other developments were occurring in the wider region. The intermember tensions in IGADD, and the pressure of conflict developments in Sudan and Somalia, resulted in a growing interest in peacemaking for the organization. These developments prompted a 1995 IGADD decision to expand its mandate to include peace and security functions and change its name to the Inter-Governmental Authority on Development (IGAD).[12] Other strategic developments included the Tigrayan-dominated Ethiopia Peoples' Democratic Force overthrowing Mengistu Haile Mariam's oppressive Derg regime in 1991, an event that led to strengthened relations between Khartoum and Addis Ababa.[13] The rise of more proactive, engaged presidents in the region, such as Ugandan President Yoweri Mouseveni, Ethiopia's Prime Minister

Zenawi Meles and Kenya's President Moi—all of whom called for democratic and social change within their own countries[14]—also helped to provide IGAD with the highest level of political commitment to resolve issues in the region, including the deteriorating situation in Sudan.

1993 marked the transition in Khartoum from military to civilian rule. However, these changes proved more procedural than anything as, prior to its disbandment, the Revolutionary Command Council for National Salvation appointed Bashir as president of the new civilian-led government.[15] Bashir was reelected in 1996 and again in 2010. Soon after his 1993 appointment as head of the civilian government, Bashir appealed to IGADD[16] for support in containing the violence in Sudan. In response, IGADD launched a foreign minister–level regional peace initiative, led by Kenya, focusing on facilitating peace in Sudan. Notwithstanding the tense relations that remained across IGAD's membership, the organization held meetings in Kenya, which, in 1994, produced a series of protocols under a "Declaration of Principles" (DOP), which called for Sudan to develop as a secular state and provided an option for secession if desired.[17]

The civil war continued in Sudan and SPLA leader Colonel John Garang began to lose support from those SPLA groups who wanted complete independence from Khartoum. At that time, Garang was maintaining a more moderate position that called for a secular state and equal opportunities for development. Following a cease-fire, which ended the in-fighting across the SPLA, IGAD's regional initiative to support peace in Sudan was further strengthened by the 1996 change in its formal mandate to support mediation, dialogue, and conflict prevention.[18]

In 1997, due to the tension between Sudan and most of the other IGAD nations, the organization asked Kenya to continue to lead a facilitated dialogue with Khartoum, the result of which saw President Moi's success in persuading Bashir to return to negotiations. In this context, IGAD also proved resilient in managing discussions while dealing with both tensions and conflict across its membership. Due to the cross-border activities of pastoralist, nomadic, and non-state armed groups and networks, many conflicts in the Horn of Africa, including Somalia and Sudan, challenge the whole concept of statehood. The existence of Islamist groups operating in both Somalia and Ethiopia[19]; the alleged backing that Ethiopia was providing to certain warlords supporting their position against Eritrea[20]; and the connections among Khartoum, the Islamist groups in Chad, and the rebel forces in Darfur,[21] all underscore the extent to which domestic conflicts in the region had external implications.[22] Such regional security issues would arguably also pose difficulties for more conventional multilateral peace operations that depend on a clear mandate often derived from a centrally brokered peace agreement.

Keeping Discussions on Track

With Kenya in the lead role, and with further support emerging for the IGAD-led mediation efforts from what became known as the International Partners Forum (IPF),[23] the Sudanese Government signed the Khartoum Peace Agreement with non-SPLA southern factions in 1999. Although this Agreement failed, it left the door open to the central principles of the DOP, namely, a commitment to both secularism and the option for secession of the south. During 1997, further splits across the SPLA and in Bashir's National Congress Party, and a general "war weariness," all prompted calls for bolstered IPF support for IGAD to adopt a more institutionalized process for Sudan.

The IGAD-led talks progressed to the signing of the 2002 Machakos Protocol in Kenya, which broadly stated that Islamic law would continue in the north, and that a referendum would be held after six years to allow the southern population to vote on the issue of secession. The agreement also stipulated that a six-month "transition period" would be observed following the referendum in order to further discussions between the parties with regard to future governance arrangements. Other developments which took place during the same year, and which served to further strengthen external support for the process, included the visit of the UN Secretary-General to Sudan in 2002, the establishment of the Addis Ababa-based African Union (AU) (which looked to regional organizations to lead on crisis management) and the emergence of a European Union (EU) "troika" (including Norway, Italy, and the United Kingdom[24]) that was able to exert international pressure on both the north and south.

Bolstered US support came to Sudan following the events of 11 September 2001 (9/11). This support came as a result of both post-9/11 US foreign policy objectives (and the knowledge that Sudan had been one of a number of homes of Al-Qa'ida leader Osama bin Laden) and the strong Washington-based lobby groups supporting the plight of south Sudan.[25] Increased American resources and focus also led to President Bush's appointment of Senator John Danforth as US Special Envoy, and the passing of the *Sudan Peace Act* in the US House of Representatives in May 2002. The Act underlined the US Government's support for a comprehensive solution to the problems in South Sudan that built on the DOP and the Machakos Protocols.[26] It also condemned the human rights violations on both sides, and called for humanitarian relief and multilateral cooperation.

By the end of 2002, all significant fighting had stopped, with the exception of ongoing skirmishes in the Blue Nile region. The IGAD-led peace process had also given way to an agreement to form a Government of National Unity, which, although appearing as a positive development, left questions relating to the fair and equitable distribution of development support, oil wealth, key government positions, and political representation more generally. At the time, the western province of Darfur was facing a growing humanitarian crisis stemming from the tensions between the two main southern groups, the Sudan People's Liberation Movement/Army (SPLM/A) and the Justice for Equality Movement (JEM), and the Government of Sudan. Both southern groups accused the government of oppressing non-Arab Sudanese in favor of the Arab Sudanese population. Khartoum further exacerbated the violence in Darfur by despatching a Janjaweed rebel group, which primarily comprised the camel-herding nomadic tribes from the country's northern-most arid zones,[27] to push the non-Arab population out of the western region of Darfur and to ensure that the JEM and the SPLM/A lose their rebel bases. The Arab militia was further supported by other Arab immigrants from Chad, who had their own territorial ambitions in the region.[28]

Darfur proved to be an unfortunate and serious problem, with the potential to derail the sluggish progress being made on the implementation of the Machakos Protocols. Notwithstanding this additional threat to the peace process, and with the support of the IPF, IGAD maintained momentum in facilitating the signing of the January 2004 wealth and power sharing agreements between Juba and Khartoum.[29] This momentum was supported by a range of other regional and international initiatives, such as the European Commission's development of an African Peace Facility, which provided US$100 million for institutional capacity-building and US$600 million for peace support operations[30]; the Economic Community of Central African States–brokered "Non-Aggression Pact" between north and south Sudan; the AU-led Inter-Sudanese Peace Talks held in Abuja, and, in 2004, the Government of Chad and AU-brokered Ndjamena Ceasefire; and an agreement between the Government of Sudan and the two Darfuri rebel groups.[31]

The continued momentum culminated in the 9 January 2005 signing of the CPA in Nairobi, Kenya. The CPA was drawn up with the assistance of key IGAD mediators (Kenya, Uganda, Ethiopia, and Eritrea) and observer nations (Norway, the United States, the United Kingdom, and Italy). The CPA draws together the six agreements that had been signed by the north and south between 2002 and 2004.[32] These agreements included:

- The Protocol of Machakos, signed on 20 July 2002. The Protocol, a major step toward peace, established the framework for future discussions.
- The Protocol on Security Arrangements, signed on 23 September 2003, established a cease-fire and outlined procedures for the establishment of joint military forces during the six-year interim period.
- The Protocol on Wealth Sharing, signed on 7 January 2004, outlined the division of natural resources within the nation.
- The Protocol on Power Sharing, signed on 26 May 2004, outlined a new government structure.
- The Protocol on the Resolution of Conflict in Southern Kordofan/Nuba Mountains and Blue Nile States, signed on 26 May 2004, established representation arrangements for the two states and outlined options for self-government for these regions.
- The Protocol on the Resolution of Conflict in Abyei, signed on 26 May 2004, provided for special administrative status during the interim period and established provisions for oil revenue-sharing for the nation.[33]

The CPA represented an important step forward and a consolidated account of the key obligations and critical requirements for peace. The Agreement also included provision for a UN Mission in Sudan (as proposed by the UN Secretary General) and reiterated the commitment of all parties to holding a referendum for the south in 2011.

Notwithstanding the progress brought by the CPA, fighting continued in the region of Darfur—a parallel conflict that is given separate focus in Alex de Waal's chapter of this volume. While efforts were made to craft a more prominent role for the UN in support of the growing humanitarian crisis, in June 2006, and under the lead of UN Special Representative to Sudan Jan Pronk, the UNSC endorsed the deployment of a special political mission, the UN Advance Mission in Sudan (UNAMIS), to facilitate contacts with the parties concerned and to prepare for the introduction of a UN peace support operation.[34] It is at this stage in the planning for international interventions that Khartoum's opposition to a UN-led peacekeeping force became apparent. In this context, the role of China is important. Its "no strings," flexible approach and influence on ruling parties in Khartoum are reflected in the appointment of Ambassador Lui Guijin as China's Special Envoy for Darfur in May 2007. China continued to provide financial support for the deployment of both AU and UN peacekeepers, but operated on the principle that the Government of the Sudan (GoS) must be content with any Chinese support for peace operations before releasing any funding contributions.[35]

The conflict and humanitarian crisis in Darfur therefore introduced an interesting dimension to the conflict in Sudan as regards the UN. In May 2006, based on discussions among the AU, the UN, and the Government of Sudan, the Darfur Peace Agreement was signed. The Agreement endorsed the expansion of the UNMIS mandate (codified in the CPA) to include support to the implementation of the provisions of both the Darfur Peace Agreement and the N'Djamena Ceasefire Agreement[36] of 2004. However, the idea that the UN would lead on both humanitarian and peacekeeping efforts in the Darfur region was strongly resisted by Khartoum. This led to a "phased" strengthening of the existing AU Mission in Sudan (AMIS), which was deployed in 2004 together with the EU to monitor the N'Djamena Ceasefire Agreement. Due to ongoing clashes between parties who supported and who did not support the Darfur Peace Agreement, and the need for a more robust international military presence in the region, AMIS transitioned in July 2007 to become the UN–AU Hybrid Operation in Darfur (UNAMID) with a mandate to bring stability to the war-torn region while peace talks on a final settlement continued.[37] Notwithstanding this "joint role" of the UN and the AU, the government in Khartoum made it increasingly clear that very few international parties (including African countries themselves) had the leverage to play leading intervention roles or steer the future of the country. However, in the face of an expanding mandate, and with requirements for manpower and logistics that neither the AU nor any of its member states could provide, the UN remained poised in a significant support role—a presence that became more prominent the further away from the north–south border one traveled.

UN Involvement in the Sudan Peace Process

In a 2003 Presidential Statement, the Council established that the situation in Sudan touched on the collective security interests of all its members. It commended the signing of the Machakos Protocols, pledged its support to the continuation of the cease-fire and monitoring team, and confirmed its ongoing readiness to support financial and logistical requirements for ground-based operations.[38]

In 2004, the Security Council continued to support the efforts of all parties to reach a comprehensive agreement and reminded all parties of the far-reaching implications of the CPA, the implications for the international community at large, and that support for the AU's efforts in the region must continue. In addition to sending a Joint Assessment Mission to help plan for reconstruction and economic recovery, the Council approved the recommendation of UN Secretary-General Kofi Annan to establish a UNAMIS for an initial period of three months.[39] He appealed to member states to support the finances and logistics of the AU, and stated his hope that IGAD would continue to play an important role during this transition period.[40] At the same time, Annan also expressed concern about some elements on both sides that could undermine the peace in troubled areas and appealed to members for help in financing the southern army. He also committed to reporting back on the structure and the proposed size of mission to replace the advance mission.[41]

During this time, the UN called for continued peace and commended the outcome of the CPA and the efforts of both sides to establish a Government of National Unity.[42] It was at this stage that the UN began to refocus operationally on the wider Sudan peace process. In March 2005, the Council approved the creation of the United Nations Mission in Sudan (UNMIS). The Council tasked UNMIS with, inter alia, cease-fire monitoring; the formation of the Joint Integrated Units (JIUs), police reform and a rule of law program, reconciliation, and wider peace-building; and the protection of human rights.[43] Reminding all parties of the rigorous timetable for the CPA and what would need to be achieved in order for a referendum to occur, the Security Council also called for all elements of the UN system in Sudan to coordinate with all other actors.[44]

Until 2002, and in parallel with IGAD's ongoing efforts to mediate the Sudan peace process since 1994, the UN's involvement in Sudan was limited. Even following the brokering of the 2005 CPA, the UN's humanitarian interest in Darfur appeared to provide the driving impetus for its involvement in the broader Sudan peace process. This transition period was also significant from the perspective of IGAD, whose involvement had been primarily political and not operational. Irrespective of its success in brokering the 2005 peace agreement, IGAD required a range of partners with the capacity and will to support the implementation of the CPA. Considering the different perspectives of, and the various international and regional alliances with, the parties to the conflict, achieving agreement on the modalities of UN support would never be a straightforward exercise. However, while these difficulties were ongoing, the secretariat capacity in New York maintained a detailed and current account of the issues facing all parties in Sudan, and an appeal to all member states for continued dialogue, contingency planning, and assessment.

During 2006 and 2007, in addition to the further extension of the UNMIS mandate, the continued cooperation between the SPLM and the National Congress Party (NCP), and the encouragement given to parties to implement elements of the CPA (such as SSR, JIUs,[45] and the redeployment of troops), the UNSC also commented on Sudan in the context of wider regional issues. It condemned the violent activities of the Lord's Resistance Army (LRA), which operated from northern Uganda and Chad, and the activities of a number of other armed groups operating in the region.[46] In response to the outstanding issue of the border town of Abyei, and the growing tensions in that area, the UNSC called for all parties to agree to an UNMIS monitoring and verification force in Abyei, and urged the withdrawal of SPLA and SAF troops, the creation of an interim administration, and an agreement on boundaries.[47] It also noted the increasing number of restrictions being placed on UNMIS by Sudan and the implications that this might have on the UNMIS mandate.[48]

Problems in the Abyei region continued into 2008, in conjunction with increased tensions across the wider border line. The UN was forced to defend itself against accusations of "doing nothing" while Abyei "burned to the ground."[49] At the same time, the UN reported that there had been an increase in the number of armed tribesmen causing problems for herdsmen and farmers across migratory routes, as well as clashes between the SPLA and Misseriya tribes. Ashra Qazi, who in September 2007 succeeded Jan Pronk as the UN Secretary-General's Special Representative in Sudan, stressed that, without a Chapter VII peace operations mandate, there was little that the UN could do to address the tensions along the border.[50] However, Abyei remained the main stumbling block: On the one hand, the SPLM maintained that the recommendations of the Abyei Boundary Commission,[51] as set out in the CPA, were final.[52] On the other hand, the Government of Sudan was not prepared to recognize the recommendations as being final, and maintained a significant military presence in Abyei town. The UNSC continued to call for the deployment of UNMIS in and around the Abyei region accompanied by an Administrator, a JIU, and a Joint Integrated Police Unit—recommendations that continued to be resisted by Khartoum.[53] However, this idea was resisted by both SAF and SPLA units based in the area.[54]

In March 2009, the AU Peace and Security Commission on Darfur established an AU High Implementation Panel (AUHIP) to assist in all aspects of the recommendations of the African Union Panel on Darfur (AUPD) and to assist Sudanese parties with the implementation of the CPA. The panel was headed by three former African presidents, Thabo Mbeki (South Africa), Abdulsalami Abubaker (Nigeria), and Pierre Buyoya (Burundi).[55] This was a significant development, as it recreated some high-level continental capacity to take forward the IGAD-led peace process during a time when the UN mandate continued to be challenged. At the same time as the creation of the AUHIP, a new UN–AU cooperative mechanism was created in the form of a ten-year capacity-building program supported by a new UN Liaison Office (UNLO) in Addis Ababa.[56] This would support a more responsive role for UN support to AU and IGAD requirements on the African continent, and would also provide a support mechanism for both UNMIS and UNAMID.

Despite these progressive developments, the situation along the contested border worsened and continued to pose a great danger to the CPA. While a multi-donor trust fund (MDTF) had been created in 2008, donor funding in real terms had been slow to arrive.[57] Khartoum's refusal to allow the UN close to the border area, the situation in Abyei, the lack of agreement regarding the 1956 boundary line between the north and south agreed to at independence, and the absence of an agreed framework for disarmament, demobilization, and reintegration (DDR) were among the main issues that threatened the peace process. In addition to continued calls to the wider UN membership for donor support (the government's funding for DDR covered only a fraction of the overall cost), and reminders to the parties to the conflict of their obligations as set out in the CPA, the Council also recognized the number of outstanding issues that needed resolution in order to prevent the peace process from being derailed.

Due to the level of resources required to support the upcoming referendum on independence, scheduled for January 2011, the outstanding security-related issues concerning the common border, Abyei, and the rise in violent activity temporarily took a backseat to the referendum preparations. The focus on the referendum saw the UN continue to advocate for all parties to respect the outcome of the event and for UNMIS to maintain contingency planning in support. During this time, the UN Under-Secretary for Peacekeeping Operations expressed his ongoing concern about threats to southerners living in the north, and a lack of progress on difficulties in Abyei, Blue Nile, and South

Kordofan.[58] The truth was that the many challenges surrounding the common border area required an effort that went beyond the undersized resources of those organizations that had a mandate to operate in this large and sensitive area. Furthermore, based on the knowledge that a majority in the southern region would support the south's quest for independence, Khartoum continued to maintain a hard line on the border-related issues that impacted on them most, including security arrangements around the common border, Abyei, the division of oil wealth, and the management of outstanding debt.

Post-referendum Sudan

On 9 January 2011, 3 million people—or 98.83 percent of South Sudan's population—voted for independence. The referendum occurred peacefully, with the results recognized and accepted by Khartoum. During the months leading up to the referendum, the UN provided logistical and technical support through the UN Integrated Referenda and Electoral Division (UNIRED).[59] The overwhelming endorsement of independence carved the way for the Republic of South Sudan to be formally recognized as the world's newest nation. In keeping with the provisions of the CPA, both parties entered the six-month post-referendum transition period, which enabled discussions on the future governance and wealth-sharing structures and arrangements, all of which became formalized on 9 July 2011.

Notwithstanding the credible and relatively peaceful referendum (and the GoS's full acceptance of the election outcome), the lack of resolution on outstanding issues like Abyei continued to hamper progress. By March 2011, it was clear that the outstanding issues would need to be considered as part of the wider secession agenda. Since the referendum, these concerns had expanded to also include the repatriation of SPLA forces serving with the SAF,[60] violence between the SPLA and militia groups in the Upper Nile region and Unity State, and the increasing buildup of troops on both sides of the common border. The CPA's protocol on Abyei had called for a separate referendum on Abyei to be held at the same time as the referendum on secession. However, concern from both sides about who should be considered a citizen of Abyei, and therefore who should vote in the referendum, remained unresolved. As a result of these outstanding issues, the referendum was postponed. Renewed fighting around Abyei town broke out in March 2011, which drove an estimated 20,000 people from their homes.[61] Fighting also continued in the Blue Nile and South Kordofan states of Sudan.[62]

These and other issues prompted the AUHIP to bring parties from both sides together for further post-referendum peace negotiations. On 12 March 2011, the parties met in Addis Ababa for facilitated discussions regarding "outstanding issues" relating to the implementation of the CPA and the requirements for independence. Further talks were held at the end of March 2011 on how to defuse the recent military activity along the border. It became clear during the initial security-related discussions that third-party intervention to monitor what became known as the Common Border Zone (CBZ) would not be welcomed by Khartoum, and that a Joint Political and Security Mechanism (JPSM) should be established between the two parties to take forward and implement all security plans. The AUHIP-chaired meeting agreed that the CBZ would extend ten miles north and ten miles south of the 1 January 1956[63] borderline. This JPSM included many of the key security-related ministers and operational chiefs from both sides.

On 20 June, the parties regathered under the leadership of the former South African President Thabo Mbeki, and agreed on temporary administrative arrangements for the Abyei area and the redeployment of both SAF and SPLA forces, which would be replaced by the deployment of an interim security force for Abyei. An interim security force would be mandated by the UN, led by and comprised of Ethiopian troops. The agreement on provisions for Abyei recognized the inviolate nature of the 1956 borderline between the north and the south, which, unless informed differently by the outcome of a future referendum, would not change. The provisions for Abyei also included the establishment of an Abyei Police Force, a demilitarized area that would cater for the migration of pastoralist groups and the return of IDPs, and an administration with shared representation from both the north and the south.[64]

The agreement among the UN, the Government of Sudan, and the SPLM/A to deploy Ethiopian peacekeepers under a UN mandate represented an interesting development, both for the UN and for the regional mechanisms that had supported the Sudan peace process for the past decade. Until June 2011, Khartoum's reluctance to accept third-party intervention had caused a degree of disquiet with its southern counterparts, particularly due to the ongoing conflicts in the south and the presence of other armed groups. With the Government of Ethiopia representing the only party that both sides would accept as an intervention agent, this posed an additional challenge to the conventional model of UN peacekeeping deployments, particularly as Ethiopia's key condition was that it deployed to Abyei under its own command structure.[65] On 27 June 2011, acting under Chapter VII of the Charter, the Security Council authorized the creation of the United National Interim Security Force in Abyei (UNISFA).[66] UNISFA's mandate was to monitor and verify the redeployment of any SAF, SPLM/A, or its successor from the Abyei area. The resolution also charged the interim force with facilitating the delivery of humanitarian aid and the free movement of relief workers in and around Abyei.

On 9 July 2012, the Republic of South Sudan celebrated its independence. A new currency, flag, and constitution were all adopted to mark the occasion. The 9 July date also marked the end of the UNMIS mandate, which prompted calls from the UN Secretary-General for the mandate to be extended.[67] However, based on the view from Khartoum that third-party intervention would no longer be required postindependence, and that the provisions of the CPA and the planned termination date for the UN presence should be respected, an extension was not authorized—only an agreement to take twelve months to "drawdown" the UNMIS mandate under a new UN Mission in South Sudan (UNMISS).[68] By the end of the month, a brigade of Ethiopian peacekeepers was deployed to the region under a UN mandate as agreed by the UN, the Government of Sudan, the SPLM/A, and the Government of Ethiopia.[69]

Although the parties have since continued their discussions on "outstanding issues" under the auspices of the AUHIP and the chairmanship of former President Mbeki, sustained violence has continued to derail the process from the period following the deployment of UNISFA to the time of writing. Despite the authorization of a Joint Border Verification and Monitoring Mission, which would include personnel from Sudan, South Sudan, and UNIFSA, under a UN lead,[70] no further resolution has been reached on the status of Abyei town. Talks chaired by the AUHIP collapsed in late November 2011 after the GoS's rejection of the South's offer supporting the Panel's proposed payment of an annual percentage of oil exports.[71] Although the discussions were meant to continue in January 2012, they too broke down over issues concerning service fees that Sudan had asked South Sudan to pay for using oil infrastructure on its territories, and the arrears that have accumulated as a result of nonpayment by Juba.[72]

Despite the 13 February 2012 signing of a nonaggression pact[73] between the two countries, and a commitment by both parties to resume talks on all outstanding issues, fighting along the shared border, April 2012 witnessed an outbreak of violence around the border towns of both Bentui and Heglig, which broke down the talks, almost irreparably. These incidents featured the SPLA capture of Heglig, a disputed town with oil fields located north of the border in the South Kordofan state of Sudan. Just before and after this siege, GoS forces bombed the border town of Bentiu, which led to the death of a number of southern civilians. Even after talks under the AUHIP resumed on 20 July 2012, South Sudan again suspended its involvement in protest against a bombing raid by Sudan inside South Sudan, in the Northern Bahr el-Ghazal state.[74] Tensions continue to run high around Abyei, where the GoS forces maintain a significant presence, despite the ongoing return of the town's inhabitants.

Other issues continue to further complicate the situation. The lack of governance capacity in South Sudan is problematic, with senior ranks across the SPLA suffering from high rates of illiteracy. With the families of middle and senior security officers residing outside of South Sudan, the issue of ownership of the process and the commitment to transforming the country and responding to the most rural and impoverished areas remains questionable. The president has yet to introduce a decree in Parliament that would propose a new role for the SPLA. Such a decree would go some way toward changing the former culture of the SPLA from "fighting a war with the North" to something oriented to the external defence of South Sudan. South Sudan's position remains further weakened as a result of its lack of diplomatic capacity and its inability to match even a fraction of the strategic communications possessed by Khartoum.[75] The new nation maintains no representation in key strategic bases such as Washington, New York, London, or Brussels.

In March 2012, and as a result of a dispute over transit fees levied on South Sudan for the transport of oil across northern territory and the use of Sudan's export terminal, the Government of South Sudan decided to halt the flow of oil. This has affected what now accounts for one-third of the Government of South Sudan's oil revenues and its biggest source of hard currency. Failure to pay what the south regarded as excessive transit fees led to South Sudan shutting down the supply of crude oil and the south accusing the Government of Sudan of seizing US$815 million of crude oil as compensation.[76] Although in the past the south has proven its ability to survive the severing of food-distribution lines and the absence of oil wealth, the situation will have adverse effects on food prices, inflation, and a weakened currency in Sudan. With the majority of the oil reserves in South Sudan, and the majority of oil infrastructure in Sudan, continued tensions over resource and wealth management will continue to have a corrosive effect on the peace process. Indeed, Paul Collier and Lisa Chauvet have conservatively estimated that the domestic and regional cost of a new civil war between Sudan and South Sudan would amount to US$85 million.[77]

The Limits of UN Mediation and Operational Support

The chronological account of post-referendum developments outlined earlier offers some compelling insights into the UN's capacity to lead the world's peace and security agenda. By not having played a major role in the 1994–2005 IGAD-led Sudan peace process, the UN was not well placed in terms of carrying the credibility and respect of all parties to the peace process to lead a comprehensive and country-wide peace post-CPA peace mission. While IGAD members demonstrated resilience in driving forward the peace process between 1994 and 2005, at a time when the wider region remained unstable and some IGAD members were in conflict with one another, it remains questionable as to whether or not a larger international organization such as the UN could have taken on this role without facing resistance across its wider membership. This chapter also exposed ways in which the foreign policies of individual states, such as the United States and its Global War on Terror, could impact the way in which parties to the Sudan conflict viewed the UN, particularly as the agenda developed in parallel to the peace process. Even with a wide range of choice from within Africa, the UN, and IGAD, Ethiopia remained the only acceptable lead country for an operational role undertaken in a region close to the northern border. Generally speaking, a UN-led third-party intervention was a solution that remained strongly resisted by Khartoum.

Notwithstanding the limitations to UN leadership post-CPA, the organization, and the Security Council in particular, played an important role in areas other than operational leadership. Since the Machakos Protocols in 2002, and particularly following the signing of the CPA, the Security Council maintained an ongoing and detailed record of all political and security-related developments in Sudan. Supported by the work of Special Representatives and their assessment teams, these efforts informed continuous appeals to the international community for financial and logistical support in a number of priority areas. This effort also underpinned the UN's role in Darfur where one could argue that, although its presence was still challenged by Khartoum, a compelling humanitarian case more easily warranted its involvement. The situation in Darfur also prompted the UN to provide critical political and operational support to the AU, its monitoring mission, and its High-Level Panel. This effort was combined with the organization's wider endeavors across the southern region, which featured the deployment of UNMIS, support for the creation of an MDTF, UNIRED's technical support for the southern referendum, and the authorization for the deployment of UNISFA. Neither IGAD nor the AU would have had the secretariat capacity to manage such a wider portfolio of support functions, although their leadership was dependent on it.

Lastly, and as part of the secretariat role referred to earlier, the UN made an important contribution to keeping issues on the table, and to informing what became a "rolling" and continuously disrupted peace agenda. More specifically, without the Security Council's supporting statements, resolutions, and operational mandates (and the extension of these mandates), its appeals for wider assistance, its expressions of concern and applause, and the ongoing reports of the Secretary-General and Special Representatives, the many outstanding issues that emerged following the referendum risked diluting the impact of the CPA, which contained many commitments that required implementation in parallel to addressing the outstanding issues. The statements made by the Security Council during this time provided a vehicle for the rationalization and discussion of the dominant concerns of each party. Based on the different parallel and disjointed agendas, one could argue that the absence of a mechanism for tracking developments over ten years (and for keeping the key issues on the table) could have paved the way for destructive distractions to the peace process.

The difficulties now facing the AUHIP and prospects for peace in the region predominantly concern the long-standing disagreements over the distribution of oil wealth. As these issues continue to be addressed at the highest political level, the UN maintains its focus on the more practical governance, development, and security challenges of South Sudan. However, as this case study has demonstrated, the importance of maintaining a continental lead both for the peace process and for operations of a more sensitive nature has enabled the UN to continue with its critical supporting role. The UN's "gap-filling" experience in Sudan indicates just how much administrative, operational, and political capacity is required to prop up present-day integrated peace missions. Until such time as organizations like the AU, IGAD, and the wider regional economic communities are able to either separately or collectively manage all aspects of these missions, the UN—through the leadership of the Security Council—should focus on "integrated support" to regional-led interventions in the future.

Notes

1. Hamid Faki and Abdelmoneim Taha, "Distortions to Agricultural Incentives in Sudan," *Agricultural Distortions Working Paper 44* (Khartoum: Agricultural Economics and Policy Research Centre, Agricultural Research Corporation, World Bank's Development Research Group, 2007), p. 8.
2. International Crisis Group, *Understanding Islamism* (ICG Middle East/North Africa Report N°37, March 2005), as quoted in International Crisis Group, *Divisions in Sudan's Ruling Party and the Threat to the Country's Future Stability* (ICG African Report N°174, May 2011), p. 2.
3. Edward Hoagland, *African Calliope* (Guilford, CT: The Lyons Press,1995).
4. Justin Willis, Atta el-Battahani, and Peter Woordward, *Elections in Sudan: Learning from Experience*. UK Department for International Development, 2009.
5. Although a further coup that came as a result of in-fighting in Nimeiri's party was launched in 1971, the coup was only short-lived and Nimeiri was restored to power a few days later.
6. General Joseph Lagu's record of his experience leading the southern resistance movement, his efforts to bring political representation and regional autonomy to the South, and his efforts to sustain progressive dialogue with Khartoum are recorded in his book entitled *Sudan: Odyssey through a State: From Ruin to Hope* (London: MOB Centre for Sudanese Studies, 2007).
7. Paul Mitchell, "Conflict Resolution and Civil War: Reflections on the Sudanese Settlement of 1972," in *Working Paper No. 3, Centre for Conflict Analysis* (Washington, DC: George Mason University, 1989).
8. Ibid, p. 7.
9. Peter Woodward, "A Tale of Two Peace Processes," *The Round Table* 93:375 (2004): 471.
10. Garang had been a junior officer in Joseph Lagu's Anya Nya forces and had spent considerable time in the United States, where he completed his staff college studies at For Benning, Kansas, and his masters and doctoral studies at the University of Ohio.

11. John Howell, "Horn of Africa: Lessons from the Sudan Conflict," *International Affairs* 54:3 (1978): 421–436.
12. The decision was taken at an extraordinary summit meeting in Addis Ababa in April 1995. The revised mandate was formally adopted at a summit in Nairobi in 1996.
13. For the first time in over fifteen years, Ethiopia was received in Khartoum in 1991, following the overthrow of the Derg.
14. Sally Healy "Seeking Peace and Security in the Horn of Africa," *International Affairs* 87:1 (2011): 108.
15. P. M. Holt and M. W. Daly, *A History of the Sudan: From Islam to the Present Day* (Boulder, CO: Westview Press, 1979).
16. By this time, IGADD had expanded as a result of the accession of Eritrea following its secession from Ethiopia and subsequent independence in 1993.
17. IGAD's Peace Initiative, "Declaration of Principles," accessed at: http://www.gosscanada.org/pdf/igad_DOP.pdf.
18. Healy.
19. Stephen Burgess, "State Failure and a Sustainability and Stabilisation Assessment of the Horn of Africa," presented at the American Political Science Association Annual General Meeting, 2007.
20. Healy, 107.
21. Abdelkerim Ousman, "Meaning and Movement: The Spread of Radical Islam in Parts of the Sahel Region," *OECD Working Paper—International Conflict and Fragility Series* (Paris: OECD Publications, 2012).
22. Healy, 107.
23. The IPF was comprised of key national donors including Canada, the EU, Norway, the United Kingdom, and the United States. Norway played a critical leadership role in the IPF due to its good reputation for facilitating talks, the engagements of its NGOs in Sudan since the early 1990s, and its fewer and less-complicated foreign policy objectives. Ann Kelleher, "A Small State's Multiple-level Approach to Peace-making: Norway's Role in Achieving Sudan's Comprehensive Peace Agreement," *Civil Wars* 8:3–4 (2006): 285–311.
24. International Crisis Group, *Darfur Rising: Sudan's New Crisis* (ICG Africa Report N°76, March 2004), p. 27.
25. Woodward, 471.
26. See The Government of the United States of America, *Sudan Peace Act*, Congressional Record, Volume 148 (2002).
27. Sunday Edeko, "An Appraisal of the Darfur Crisis," *Sacha Journal of Policy and Strategic Studies* 1:2 (2011): 16.
28. Alex de Waal, "Darfur and the Failure of the Responsibility to Protect," *International Affairs* 83:6 (2007): 1041.
29. Among a number of issues concerning the management of the common wealth of the two parties, the wealth sharing agreement brokered under the IGAD-led Peace Process included the establishment of JIUs, comprising joint armed units that were deployed to major towns to help keep the peace. These units were intended to build confidence and national unity, and to ensure internal security was maintained during the period leading to the 2011 referendum on secession (see Sudan's Human Security Baseline Assessment, "Neither Joint nor Integrated," *Small Arms Survey*, No. 10 (2008), accessed at http://www.smallarmssurveysudan.org/pdfs/HSBA-SIB-10-JIUs.pdf).
30. African–European Partnership's *African Peace Facility* at http://www.africa-eu-partnership.org/successstories/african-peace-facility.
31. Humanitarian Cease Fire Agreement on the Conflict in Darfur, 2 April 2004.

32. Leslie Anne Schafer, "Negotiating the North-South Conflict: Sudan's Comprehensive Peace Agreement," *ISS Paper No 148* (South Africa: Institute for Security Studies, 2007), p. 3.
33. Ibid, p. 14.
34. UNSCR 1547, 11 June 2004.
35. Dan Large, "China's Role in the Mediation and Resolution of Conflict in Africa," Background paper, Oslo forum 2008, Centre for Humanitarian Dialogue, 2008.
36. The N'Djamena Ceasefire Agreement was brokered by a Chadian mediator in April 2004 and brought together the parties to the conflict (including the JEM, the SPLM/A, and the GoS) and the AU. The broad outcome of these discussions included the recognition that a meaningful and lasting peace in Darfur would only be achieved thought sincere and frank discussions. The agreement also called for the resolution of the conflict to exclude the use of force.
37. See UNSCR 1796 (2007).
38. PRST/2003/16, 10 October 2003.
39. UNSCR 1547, 11 June 2004. The mandate of UNAMIS was later expanded to include contingency planning for Darfur, and extended for a further 3 months. UNSCR 1556, 30 July 2004.
40. Press Release SC/8247 (18 November 2004).
41. S/PV.5094 (2004).
42. See Press Release SC/8249 (11 November 2004), S/PV.5050. Following the signing of the CPA, a Government of National Unity was installed in accordance with the interim Constitution that established two vice-president positions, one representing the south and one representing the north. Major-General Joseph Lagu became the vice-president representing South Sudan.
43. UNSCR 1590 (2005).
44. Ibid.
45. The JIUs were military units comprised of the SAF and SPLA. They were intended to meet internal security needs during the interim period prior to the 2011 southern succession referendum. They were also intended to demonstrate national unity, build confidence between parties, and lay a foundation for a future national army, if the referendum resulted in a vote for unity. More information regarding the origin of the JIU and an account of the JIU experience, please see Sudan's Human Security Baseline Assessment, "Neither Joint nor Integrated: The Joint Integrated Units and the Future of the CPA," *Small Arms Survey*, No. 10 (2008).
46. UNSCR 1663, 24 March 2006; S/PV.5396, 24 March 2006. The UNSC later welcomed the decision of the Government of Uganda and the LRA to extend the Cessation of Hostilities Agreement and resume peace talks in Juba. UNSCR 1755, 30 April 2007.
47. See UNSCR 1784 (2007).
48. Ibid.
49. Report of the Security Council's 5956th Meeting (2008).
50. Ibid.
51. The Abyei Boundary Commission was a mechanism agreed in the Abyei Protocol, which formed part of the six agreements embodied by the CPA. The Abyei Protocol supported the creation of the Abyei Boundaries Commission (ABC) that would define and demarcate the area of the nine Ngok Dinka Chiefdoms transferred to Kordofan in 1905, which was referred to as the "Abyei Area"; The Protocol also underwrote the composition and timeframe of the ABC, and confirmed that the Presidency would take necessary action to put the special administrative status of Abyei Area into immediate effect.

See "Abyei Mission Factsheet," *UNMIS,* 24/02/2009, found at http://unmis.unmissions.org/Portals/UNMIS/Fact%20Sheets/FS-abyeiprotocol.pdf.

52. These recommendations determined the boundary at approximately 10°22′30″N, 87 kilometres (54 miles) north of the town of Abyei (see "The Abyei Protocol Demystified," *Sudan Tribune*, 11 December 2007).
53. See the briefing given by Mr. Ashraf Jehangir Qazi, the head of UNMIS to the Security Council. S/PV.5956, 18 August 2008.
54. For more detailed accounts of both the SPLA and the SAF positions on the UN's role in the Abyei area, see Human Security Baseline Assessment, "The Drift Back to War: Insecurity and Militarisation in the Nuba Mountains," *Small Arms Survey*, No. 12 (2008): 8.
55. The mandate of the AUHIP was to investigate and recommend policies to achieve peace, reconciliation, and justice in Darfur. The Panel undertook wide consultations in Darfur and produced its report in October 2009. The AU Peace and Security Council then re-mandated the same three former presidents to oversee the implementation of the recommendations on Darfur, promote democratization, assist in the implementation of Sudan's Comprehensive Peace Agreement. (For more information on the AUHIP, see the World Peace Foundation's website at http://fletcher.tufts.edu/World-Peace-Foundation/Activities/AU-High-Level-Implementation-Panel-for-Sudan.)
56. Letter dated 11 December 2006 from the Secretary-General addressed to the President of the General Assembly, A/61/630.
57. OECD, *Aid Risks in Transitional Contexts: Improving Donor Behaviour* (Paris: OECD Publications, 2010), p. 4.
58. S/PV.6452, 16 December 2010. Also see S/PRST/2010, 28, 16 December 2010.
59. UNMIS website, www.un.org/UNMIS, accessed 26 June 2012.
60. Whereas the return of SAF troops serving with the SPLA had almost been completed, the repatriation of SPLA soldiers from the north to the south had only achieved 37 percent completion.
61. *Reuters*, "At Least 20,000 Flee Violence in Sudan's Abyei," May 24, 2011, accessed at http://www.reuters.com/article/2011/05/24/sudan-abyei-idUSLAE42890120110524.
62. The roots of the violence in these areas stemmed mainly from the presence of soldiers from what became known as the "SPLA-Northern sector" (SPLA-N). Provisions in the CPA did not directly address the plight of these soldiers, the SPLM supporters, and their communities. Since the official declaration of South Sudan's independence, ongoing conflict has continued in these two states. The conflict centers around the marginalization, and SAF's direct targeting, of these communities.
63. The 1.1.1956 borderline has become the reference used to describe the border agreed at the time of independence from British colonial rule.
64. Agreement between the Government of the Republic of Sudan and the Sudan People's Liberation Movement on Temporary Arrangements for the Administration and Security of the Abyei Area, Addis Ababa, Ethiopia, June 20, 2011.
65. Based on an interview with General Samora Yonus, Chief of the Ethiopian Defence Forces.
66. UNSCR 1990, 27 June 2011.
67. The UN Secretary-General, Remarks to the Media, Khartoum, 8 June 2011, found at http://unmis.unmissions.org/Portals/UNMIS/2011Docs/SGRemarks%20on%20south%20sudan%20independence-English.pdf.
68. See UNSCR 1996 (2011) and UN Presss Release SC/10298.
69. UNSCR 1990 (2011).
70. S/PV.6628, 6 October 2011.

71. *The Sudan Tribune*, "Sudan and South Sudan to Resume Talks in January," December 20, 2011.
72. The GoS had proposed that the arrears should be paid according to a fee of US$36 per barrel, which South Sudan claimed was excessive compared to international norms (see *Sudan Tribune*, "Talks between Khartoum and Juba on Oil Break Down Despite AUHIP's Efforts," January 18, 2012.) See also Jon Lunn and Gavin Thompson, "Sudan and South Sudan: All Out War?" *UK House of Commons Briefing Note* (27 April 2012): 3.
73. The Memorandum of Understanding on Non-Aggression and Cooperation was signed in the Ethiopian capital, Addis Ababa, which called for the respect for each other's sovereignty and territorial integrity, noninterference in the internal affairs, and rejected the use of force in relations between the two countries. "Secretary-General Welcomes Memorandum of Understanding on Non-Aggression and Co-operation between Sudan and South Sudan," SG/SM/14104 AFR/2335, 13 February 2012.
74. Federal Democratic Republic of Ethiopia, Ministry of Foreign Affairs, "Sudan-South Sudan Talks Resume under AUHIP Auspices," accessed at http://www.mfa.gov.et/news/more.php?newsid=937.
75. Erwin van Veen and Ann Fitz-Gerald, "Pride or Prejudice in Heglige," *Open Democracy*, 17 April 2012, accessed at http://www.opendemocracy.net/opensecurity/erwin-van-veen-ann-fitz-gerald/pride-and-prejudice-in-heglig.
76. See *Reuters*, "South Sudan Shuts Off Oil in Dispute with Sudan," in *New York Times*, 23 January 2012, accessed at http://www.nytimes.com/2012/01/24/world/africa/south-sudan-shuts-off-oil-in-dispute-with-sudan.html.
77. Lisa Chauvet and Paul Collier, "Policy Turnarounds in Failing States" (Centre for the Study of African Economies, April 2006), 28.

About the Authors

Jane Boulden holds a Canada Research Chair in International Relations and Security Studies at the Royal Military College of Canada. From August 2000 until December 2003, she was a MacArthur Research Fellow at the Centre for International Studies, University of Oxford. She is a coeditor of *The United Nations and Nuclear Orders* (with Ramesh Thakur and Thomas G. Weiss, 2009), and *Terrorism and the UN: Before and after September 11th* (with Thomas G. Weiss, 2004). She is the editor of *Dealing with Conflict in Africa: The United Nations and Regional Organizations* (2003), and the author of *Peace Enforcement* (2001).

Arthur Boutellis joined the International Peace Institute in January 2011 as a Senior Policy Analyst in the Coping with Crisis program, with a particular focus on peace-keeping. His recent IPI publications include *The Management Handbook for UN Field Missions* (coeditor, 2012); *What Army for Haiti?* (2011); *The Security Sector in Côte d'Ivoire: A Source of Conflict and a Key to Peace* (2011). He is also a regular contributor to theglobalobservatory.org. Before joining IPI, Arthur worked with the United Nations missions in Burundi, Chad, the Central African Republic and in Haiti. He holds a master's degree in public & international affairs from the Woodrow Wilson School at Princeton University and is a graduate of the Institut d'Etudes Politiques.

Tatiana Carayannis is the deputy director of the Social Science Research Council's (SSRC) Conflict Prevention and Peace Forum (CPPF) where she leads on CPPF's Africa programs, including exploring possible new SSRC programming around China–Africa issues. She also serves as the SSRC focal point and conflict research team leader for the London School of Economics-based Justice and Security Research Programme, an international research consortium, and is a visiting fellow at the Institute for Public Knowledge at New York University for 2011–2012.

Andrea Charron holds a PhD from the Royal Military College of Canada (Department of War Studies). She obtained a Masters in International Relations from Webster University, Leiden, The Netherlands, a Master's of Public Administration from Dalhousie University, and a Bachelor of Science (Honours) from Queen's University. Her book, *UN Sanctions and Conflict: Responding to Peace and Security Threats* (Routledge, 2011), explores the application of the United Nations (UN) Security Council's mandatory sanctions since 1946, and, in particular, the regimes adopted for specific types of conflict.

Katharina Coleman specializes in international relations, with a focus on international organizations; peacekeeping and peace enforcement; and international rules, norms, and law. Her regional area of expertise is sub-Saharan Africa. Her recent book highlights the importance of international organizations in generating legitimacy for contemporary peace enforcement operations. Her current research projects analyze the impact of venue on international norm negotiations and the significance of token forces in multinational military interventions. She was a visiting research fellow at the Centre for International Studies at Oxford University. Her home university is the University of British Columbia.

Alex de Waal is the executive director of the World Peace Foundation and a research professor at Tufts University. From 2009 to 2011, he served as a senior advisor to the African Union High Level Implementation Panel for Sudan. He was also the program director at the Social Science Research Council, with responsibilities for research programs on humanitarian issues, HIV/AIDS, and social transformation. His academic research has focused on issues of famine, conflict, and human rights in Africa. He was awarded an Officer of the Order of the British Empire (OBE) in the UK New Year's Honors List of 2009, was on the Prospect/Foreign Policy list of 100 public intellectuals in 2008 and the Atlantic Monthly list of 27 "brave thinkers" in 2009.

Ann M. Fitz-Gerald is currently the Cranfield University Course Director of the MSc Security Sector Management programme, which is run in both the United Kingdom and the Horn of Africa. She has managed a number of research programs that focus on national security and interdependencies between security and development, with a particular focus on Africa. She recently led the Organization for Economic Cooperation and Development (OECD) research project entitled "Global Factors Increasing the Risk of Conflict and Fragility" and the team commissioned by the UN Peacebuilding Support Office to undertake a thematic review of the Peacebuilding Fund and security sector reform. Ann is a Board member for a number of security-related research institutions including the Institute for Research on Public Policy and Saferworld. In 2011, she facilitated post-referendum security talks between parties from North and South Sudan.

Fabienne Hara joined Crisis Group in February 2008. As vice-president (Multilateral Affairs), she oversees Crisis Group's advocacy at the UN and the Security Council in New York, and directs the Crisis Group New York office. She has over eighteen years of experience in African conflict-management and resolution issues.

Gilbert M. Khadiagala is the Jan Smuts Professor of International Relations and Head of Department at the University of Witwatersrand in Johannesburg. His recent publications include *Eastern Africa: Security and the Legacy of Fragility.* New York: International Peace Institute, Africa Program Working Paper Series, October 2008, and *Conflict Management and African Politics: Ripeness, Bargaining, and Mediation* (coedited with Terrence Lyons). New York: Routledge, 2008.

Shawna Meister is a research analyst for the International Sanctions Research Consortium and volunteer Rapporteur at Canadian Council on Africa. She has an MA in Political Studies from Carleton University. Her research areas include: peace and security issues, project development, UN, UN Security Council, UN Peace-building Architecture, peace-building and conflict resolution, and development in Africa.

Thomas Kwasi Tieku, a native of Ghana, pursued his MA at Brock University in St. Catharines, Ontario, after completing his undergraduate degree at the University of Ghana. His experiences and the desire to contribute to society in both Africa and Canada motivated him to remain in Canada, where he earned his PhD in international relations at the University of Toronto. He has a cross-appointment at the Munk School of Global Affairs and New College at the University of Toronto. He directed the African Studies program at the university between 2006 and 2011. He has consulted for international organizations such as the World Bank Group and the African Union and also governments. Some of his recent works have been published in *Democratization, African Security Review* and *Canadian Foreign Policy Journal.* Thomas is an editor of the *African Journal of Political Science and International Relations.*

Anthoni van Nieuwkerk is an associate professor based at the Centre for Defence and Security Management, Graduate School of Public and Development Management (P&DM) at the University of the Witwatersrand in Johannesburg, South Africa. He has worked at various academic institutions, and between 1994 and 1999, managed the research program of the Institute for Global Dialogue. At Wits, he is a member of a team coordinating the research and training activities of the Southern African Defence and Security Management (SADSEM) network. He teaches on the graduate school's Masters programme and serves as the school's research director.

Paul D. Williams is an associate professor in the Elliott School of International Affairs at the George Washington University, USA. He also serves as a nonresident senior adviser at the International Peace Institute in New York and as a visiting professor at the Institute for Peace and Security Studies at Addis Ababa University in Ethiopia. Dr. Williams previously taught at the Universities of Aberystwyth, Birmingham, and Warwick in the United Kingdom and has been a visiting scholar at Georgetown University and the University of Queensland, Australia. His books include, *War and Conflict in Africa* (Polity, 2011); *British Foreign Policy under New Labour, 1997–2005* (Palgrave-Macmillan, 2005); *Understanding Peacekeeping* (Polity, 2nd ed., 2010); *Security and Development in Global Politics: A Critical Comparison* (Georgetown University Press, 2012); *Security Studies: An Introduction* (Routledge, 2nd ed., 2012); and *The International Politics of Mass Atrocities: The Case of Darfur* (Routledge, 2010). Professor Williams currently serves on the editorial boards of two scholarly journals, *African Affairs* and *Global Responsibility to Protect.*

Gilles Yabi—Before returning to Crisis Group as the West Africa Project Director in January 2011, Gilles Olakounlé Yabi was an independent researcher and consultant in the fields of conflict analysis, peacekeeping operations, and political governance in West Africa. His consultancy assignments included a research project on UN peacekeeping operations in Cote d'Ivoire and Sierra Leone with the Madrid-based think tank FRIDE, an assessment of the strategy of the Open Society Initiative in West Africa (OSIWA), and a study on the management of political crises in Guinea and Guinea-Bissau by the West African regional organization Economic Community of West African States (ECOWAS). He also published several articles on politics in West African countries.

Index

Index of UNSCR

Printed in the United States of America